The Development of Prosocial Behavior

This is a volume in the series entitled
DEVELOPMENTAL PSYCHOLOGY SERIES

Under the Editorship of Harry Beilin,
Developmental Psychology Program
City University of New York Graduate School
New York, New York

A complete list of titles in this series appears at the end of this volume.

The Development of Prosocial Behavior

Edited by

NANCY EISENBERG
DEPARTMENT OF PSYCHOLOGY
ARIZONA STATE UNIVERSITY
TEMPE, ARIZONA

ACADEMIC PRESS   **1982**

A Subsidiary of Harcourt Brace Jovanovich, Publishers

New York   London
Paris   San Diego   San Francisco   São Paulo   Sydney   Tokyo   Toronto

ACADEMIC PRESS, INC.
111 Fifth Avenue, New York, New York 10003

United Kingdom Edition published by
ACADEMIC PRESS, INC. (LONDON) LTD.
24/28 Oval Road, London NW1 7DX

Library of Congress Cataloging in Publication Data
Main entry under title:

The Development of prosocial behavior.

Includes bibliographies and index.
1. Altruism. 2. Helping behavior. 3. Child
psychology. I. Eisenberg, Nancy.
BF637.H4D38   155.2'32   82-1750
ISBN 0-12-234980-6   AACR2

PRINTED IN THE UNITED STATES OF AMERICA

82 83 84 85   9 8 7 6 5 4 3 2 1

Contents

1

Introduction   1
NANCY EISENBERG

I CONCEPTUAL ISSUES

2

The Generality of Altruism in Children   25
BILL UNDERWOOD and BERT S. MOORE

v

③

Altruism—A Rational Approach 53

DENNIS KREBS

④

Social Learning Theory and the Development of Prosocial Behavior 77

J. PHILIPPE RUSHTON

II EARLY DEVELOPMENT OF PROSOCIAL BEHAVIOR AND SOCIALIZATION MECHANISMS

⑤

The Development of Altruism: Alternative Research Strategies 109

CAROLYN ZAHN-WAXLER and MARIAN RADKE-YARROW

6

The Socialization of Altruism   139
JOAN E. GRUSEC

7

Response Consequences and Attributions:
Two Contributors to Prosocial Behavior   167
DONNA M. GELFAND and DONALD P. HARTMANN

III THE ROLE OF COGNITION

8

A Cognitive-Learning Model of
Helping Behavior Development:
Possible Implications and Applications   199
DANIEL BAR-TAL and AMIRAM RAVIV

⑨

The Development of Reasoning regarding Prosocial Behavior   219
NANCY EISENBERG

➉

Settings, Scripts, and Self-Schemata: A Cognitive Analysis of the Development of Prosocial Behavior   251
RACHEL KARNIOL

IV THE ROLE OF AFFECT

⑪

Development of Prosocial Motivation: Empathy and Guilt   281
MARTIN L. HOFFMAN

Contents

12

Sex Differences in Empathy
and Social Behavior in Children   315
NORMA DEITCH FESHBACH

13

Effects of Mood on Prosocial Behavior
in Children and Adults   339
ROBERT B. CIALDINI, DOUGLAS T. KENRICK, and DONALD J. BAUMANN

V PERSONALITY AND
PROSOCIAL DEVELOPMENT

14

Personality Development and
Liberal Sociopolitical Attitudes   363
PAUL MUSSEN

🄸🄢

Development of Prosocial Motivation:
A Dialectic Process   377
JANUSZ REYKOWSKI

Contributors

Numbers in parentheses indicate the pages on which the authors' contributions begin.

DANIEL BAR-TAL (199), School of Education, Tel-Aviv University, Tel Aviv, Israel

DONALD J. BAUMANN (339), Department of Psychology, Arizona State University, Tempe, Arizona 85287

ROBERT B. CIALDINI (339), Department of Psychology, Arizona State University, Tempe, Arizona 85287

NANCY EISENBERG (1, 219), Department of Psychology, Arizona State University, Tempe, Arizona 85287

NORMA DEITCH FESHBACH (315), Departments of Education and Psychology, University of California, Los Angeles, Los Angeles, California 90024

DONNA M. GELFAND (167), Department of Psychology, University of Utah, Salt Lake City, Utah 84112

JOAN E. GRUSEC (139), Department of Psychology, University of Toronto, Toronto, Ontario, Canada M5S 1A1

DONALD P. HARTMANN (167), Department of Psychology, University of Utah, Salt Lake City, Utah 84112

MARTIN L. HOFFMAN (281), Department of Psychology, University of Michigan, Ann Arbor, Michigan 48109

RACHEL KARNIOL (251), School of Education, Tel-Aviv University, Tel Aviv, Israel

DOUGLAS T. KENRICK (339), Department of Psychology, Arizona State University, Tempe, Arizona 85287

DENNIS KREBS (53), Department of Psychology, Simon Fraser University, Burnaby, British Columbia, Canada V5A 1S6

BERT S. MOORE (25), Department of Psychology, University of Texas at Dallas, Richardson, Texas 75080

PAUL MUSSEN (363), Department of Psychology and Institute of Human Development, University of California, Berkeley, Berkeley, California 94720

MARIAN RADKE-YARROW (109), Laboratory of Developmental Psychology, National Institute of Mental Health, Bethesda, Maryland 20205

AMIRAM RAVIV (199), Department of Psychology, Tel-Aviv University, Tel Aviv, 69978 Israel

JANUSZ REYKOWSKI (377), Department of Psychology, Polish Academy of Sciences, Plac Malachowskiego 1, Warsaw, Poland

J. PHILIPPE RUSHTON (77), Department of Psychology, University of Western Ontario, London, Ontario, Canada N6A 5C2

BILL UNDERWOOD[1] (25), Department of Psychology, University of Texas at Austin, Austin, Texas 78712

CAROLYN ZAHN-WAXLER (109), Laboratory of Developmental Psychology, National Institute of Mental Health, Bethesda, Maryland 20205

1. Present address: Southwestern Data Consultants, Austin, Texas 78753.

Preface

A few years ago, in the preface to our book *Roots of Caring, Sharing, and Helping: The Development of Prosocial Behavior in Children* (1977), Paul Mussen and I noted that the time was appropriate "to take stock of the present state of the field, to evaluate its accomplishments and deficiencies, and to delineate major gaps in our knowledge and theoretical understanding [p. viii]." Our book was an attempt to achieve these goals. Since then, several researchers have published other books reviewing the current literature, and through the efforts of numerous persons, some of the gaps in our knowledge and theoretical understanding have been filled. In the relatively brief period since 1977, methodologies have become increasingly sophisticated, more and frequently higher quality data have been collected, and important theoretical issues have been addressed by numerous researchers. Indeed, there has been a virtual explosion of interest and work in the field of prosocial behavior, and our understanding of this topic has advanced significantly.

To accommodate the increase in research and theorizing, several volumes of original papers written by major contributors to the literature on prosocial behavior have been published (for example, books by Rushton & Sorrento, and Wispé). In these volumes, the emphasis has been primarily on prosocial behavior among adults, not on the development of prosocial behavior during childhood. However, there is now a substantial amount of creative and fruitful research on prosocial behavior being conducted from a developmental perspective. The purpose of this book is to present some of the data and theory resulting from this exciting work.

To achieve this goal, a wide variety of issues is discussed by the chapter authors. Theoretical issues are addressed by many of the authors, with the current social-learning and cognitive-developmental models of prosocial behavior being outlined in detail by J. Philippe Rushton and Dennis Krebs, respectively. Furthermore, other issues and problems relating to the conceptualization of prosocial and altruistic behavior are addressed extensively in the introductory chapter by Bill Underwood and Bert Moore.

Current research and theory relating to a number of more specific topics also are presented by chapter authors. With regard to the very early socialization of prosocial behavior, Joan Grusec, Carolyn Zahn-Waxler, and Marian Radke-Yarrow discuss their innovative methods of examining the relationship between maternal child-rearing practices and children's prosocial responding in the earliest years of life. Their insightful discussion of methodological issues and of the data resulting from their research should be of great interest to researchers in the area of prosocial development and to students of early childhood development. Furthermore, in a jointly authored chapter, Donna Gelfand and Donald Hartmann present their empirical data and thinking regarding the role of reinforcement and children's attributional processes in the development of prosocial behavior. These data are relevant not only to researchers concerned with altruism, but also to those interested in the broader topic of social cognition.

Several chapter authors discuss controversial issues with regard to the role of affect and cognition in the development of positive behaviors. Martin Hoffman and Norma Feshbach, leading developmental researchers on topics relating to the development of empathy, present their most current research findings (Norma Feshbach) and theory (Martin Hoffman). Hoffman also addresses another topic at some length—the development of guilt. Robert Cialdini, Douglas Kenrick, and Donald Baumann, like Hoffman and Feshbach, focus on the topic of affect, but their emphasis is entirely different. They are concerned with the role of mood and mood enhancement in the elicitation of prosocial behavior. In a careful, thoughtful review of the research, they muster support for Cialdini's theory that altruism frequently is, in essence, hedonism.

In several other chapters, the authors explore somewhat more cognitive aspects of prosocial development. Daniel Bar-Tal and Amiram Raviv provide an overview of their theory concerning stages of altruistic motivation. They then use this framework to discuss potential avenues for the socialization of prosocial behavior. In another chapter, I review the research on children's attributions and moral reasoning relating to prosocial behavior, and implications of this research. In an extremely interesting chapter, Rachel Karniol, for the first time, presents in detail her argument regarding the crucial role of cognitive scripts in prosocial development.

The role of individual differences and personality in prosocial development is not neglected. In one of his few chapters in English, the eminent Polish psychologist, Janusz Reykowski, presents both his views and data from Poland on these issues. Furthermore, Paul Mussen discusses a neglected topic, the relationship of prosocial development to the development of political ideology, and similarities in socialization antecedents of these two aspects of development. Thus, Reykowski and Mussen relate the development of prosocial behavior to the broader realm of personality development.

The chapters in this book have been grouped under several titles, for example, "Conceptual Issues," "Early Development of Prosocial Behavior and Socialization Mechanisms," and "The Role of Affect." These groupings serve a primarily heuristic function; seldom does a chapter author address only the focal topic of one group. Rather, a variety of issues generally are intertwined in each chapter. However, to facilitate the readers' efforts to focus on a particular topic, the chapters have been organized to reflect what I view to be the major emphasis of each chapter.

This book is the product of the efforts of many people. The chapter contributors deserve a special note of gratitude. All were not only cooperative, but also exhibited scholarly dedication to producing a quality product. I also appreciate the efforts of the staff of Academic Press, who minimized the bureaucratic hangups and eased the completion of this project. Special thanks also go to Sally Carney, who greatly reduced the burden of organizing the volume by way of her always pleasant assistance in a variety of technical tasks; to Mark Barnett for his review of the Cialdini, Kenrick, and Baumann chapter; and to my colleagues and friends including Robert Berg, Robert Cialdini, and Susan Somerville, who provided much critical advice and/or emotional support. Similarly, I would like to express my gratitude to Paul Mussen for his suggestions and support with regard to this project, as well as many past projects. Finally, special appreciation goes to Jerry Harris for both his substantial critical advice regarding the introductory chapter, and for his valuable contribution to my mental health during the preparation of this volume.

The Development of
Prosocial Behavior

NANCY EISENBERG

Introduction

The nature of good and evil has been the topic of theorizing and philosophizing for thousands of years. For example, the ancient Greeks debated the nature of morality, virtue, and factors influencing the formation of positive moral development (e.g., Aristotle, 1952). Similarly, morality has been a basic issue in many passages of various religious documents (including both the Old and New Testaments) and is deeply embedded in Western religious philosophy and teaching (e.g., the Ten Commandments and moral directives such as "Love thy neighbor").

Whereas one can only speculate on the reasons for the human preoccupation with the topic of morality, it likely derives from the strong social component of human nature. Clearly, humans are highly social beings; people generally develop strong emotional relationships before 1 year of age (Ainsworth, 1973; Bowlby, 1969), and continue to be deeply involved with other people throughout their lives. Given that personal relationships are such a basic aspect of our functioning, the quality of human interactions is of vital importance to both society and the individual. Issues of moral development, although they need not always concern human social interactions (for example, acts in relation to supernatural beings, gods, and/or animals are sometimes within the domain of morality), generally revolve around the quality of human interactions.

It is probably true that the control of evil or harmful behaviors is more essential to the functioning of human social units than is the promotion of positive behaviors. The role of an individual's concern, support, and assistance in determining the quality of a relationship and the functioning of a

1

THE DEVELOPMENT OF
PROSOCIAL BEHAVIOR

society is relatively subtle in comparison to the role of the individual's aggressive, selfish, and hurtful behavior. In other words, negative behaviors seem to color the quality of an interaction more than do positive behaviors. Consider, for example, the prohibition-oriented emphasis of our code of law. Thus, it is not surprising that philosophers, theologians, and scientists alike have been more preoccupied with the roots of evil than with the sources of good, and that the control and elimination of negative behaviors have been, and continue to be, a major concern for human societies.

The emphasis in the psychological literature on aggression, dishonesty, and resistance to temptation in past years reflects the crucial importance of negative behaviors for human social interaction. In fact, until quite recently, the study of positive behaviors has been an area of considerable neglect. With some major exceptions (e.g., Hartshore, May, & Maller, 1929; Murphy, 1937), until the 1970s few researchers were seriously concerned with the development of positive behaviors such as sympathy, sharing, and helping. However, in the past decade, much attention has been focused on positive behaviors. Why might this be?

It has been suggested that humanitarian concerns in the social sciences reflect larger changes in human styles of interaction (Sears, 1975). Although there has been considerable fluctuation in patterns of societal and individual interaction over the centuries, in general, with the passage of time, humankind's inhumanity to itself has decreased as humanitarian concerns have increased. Attitudes toward the dignity of human life, and toward slavery, torture, and similar issues have, on the average, become more humanitarian over time. Furthermore, as humanitarian attitudes have increased, there seems to have been a corresponding increase in concern for the weak, helpless, poor, sick, and other needy or dependent groups, including children (Sears, 1975). Such a shift in perspective may well have laid the groundwork for—and, perhaps, stimulated an interest in—the development of positive behaviors and concern for others.

It is noteworthy that interest in the maintenance and development of positive behaviors increased dramatically in the 1960s and early 1970s. This was a time in which the sociopolitical atmosphere took a swing to the left—a time when civil rights, aid to the poor, and other humanitarian issues were at the forefront of the political scene. Indeed, according to some research, many of the leftist activists who caused campus unrest at that time or were engaged in civil rights activities were motivated by humanitarian concerns and values (Flacks, 1970; Kenniston, 1967; Soloman & Fishman, 1964). Thus, it may be no coincidence that the upsurge in interest in positive, humanitarian behaviors occurred at that time. Indeed, some researchers have linked the development and socialization of humanitarian political attitudes and behavior to the development of other types of positive social behaviors (see Mussen, Chapter 14).

Whatever the reasons, the recent explosion and interest in positive behaviors is obvious. Until the 1960s, there were only a few books concerned with empirical research on the topic (e.g., Hartshore et al., 1929; Murphy, 1937). In the 1960s and early 1970s, other research-oriented books began to appear (e.g., Latané & Darley, 1970; Macaulay & Berkowitz, 1970). By the mid-1970s, a few books reviewing the topic were published (Bar-Tal, 1976; Mussen & Eisenberg-Berg, 1977), as were a number of journal reviews (e.g., Krebs, 1970; Rushton, 1976) and even a special issue of a journal devoted to the topic (*Journal of Social Issues,* 1972). The research literature continued to expand so rapidly that several new books summarizing and interpreting the literature appeared in the late 1970s and early 1980s (Rushton, 1980; Staub, 1978, 1979). Furthermore, whereas 15 years ago the journals contained few papers on prosocial development, articles on altruism and prosocial behavior are in nearly every recent issue of developmental and social journals.

The outgrowth of this enormous interest in positive behaviors has been a rapid expansion of our knowledge concerning the topic, diversification and refinement of our methodologies for its study, and a concurrent proliferation of issues and questions to be addressed. In this book, data, methodologies, and issues relating to current developmental research on prosocial behavior will be presented. Specific topics will include conceptual issues relating to the definition and classification of various positive behaviors, theoretical approaches to conceptualizing altruism, the socialization of altruism, and the role of cognition and affect in the development of positive behaviors. Throughout, the focus is on the emergence of prosocial behaviors in childhood—the roots and determinants of prosocial thought and behavior.

DEFINITION OF TERMS

The authors of the chapters in this book do not always agree on the definition of terms such as *altruism* and *prosocial behavior.* This lack of concensus reflects a larger lack of agreement in the field. Part of the reason for this disagreement probably is the newness of the topic—the fact that the study of prosocial behavior is just emerging from its infancy. Another reason for differences of opinion with regard to definition is that definitional issues involve conceptual and theoretical components, and there is debate as to the essence and nature of prosocial and altruistic behaviors. A look at the following definitions and/or comments regarding altruism and prosocial behavior illustrates the point:

Bar-Tal and Raviv (Chapter 8):

> Altruism, as one type of helping act that is at the highest level of quality, is defined as voluntary and intentional behavior carried out for its own end to benefit a person, as a result of moral conviction in justice and without expectations for external rewards.

Gelfand and Hartmann (Chapter 7):

> Our social learning theory orientation caused us to doubt the utility of definitions of altruism that excluded the possibility of external reinforcement, and suggested instead that these definitions should be stripped of their nonobservable characteristics.

Cialdini, Kenrick, and Baumann (Chapter 13):

> By altruism, we refer to actions taken to benefit another for reasons other than extrinsic reward.

Hoffman (Chapter 11):

> ... which may be defined generally as behavior such as helping or sharing that promotes the welfare of others without conscious concern for one's own self-interest.

Krebs (Chapter 3):

> ... willingness to sacrifice one's own welfare for the sake of another.

Underwood and Moore (Chapter 2):

> ... behaviors done with the apparent intent of benefiting another more than oneself.

Zahn-Waxler and Radke-Yarrow (Chapter 5):

> Altruism is formally defined as regard for or devotion to the interests of others.

There is considerable variation among these definitions of altruism. For some researchers, altruism is defined as explicitly excluding behavior motivated by external reward (e.g., Bar-Tal & Raviv, Cialdini *et al.*, Hoffman); for others, this is not so (Gelfand & Hartmann). Whereas most definitions of altruism seem to imply that an altruistic act is intentional, not all require that altruistic behavior be motivated by the desire to benefit another. Furthermore, some researchers explicitly state that another's welfare must be the primary concern (Krebs, Hoffman, Underwood & Moore, Zahn-Waxler & Radke-Yarrow); others do not restrict the range of motivations other than to eliminate extrinsic rewards (Cialdini *et al.*); and still others explicitly include motives in addition to concern for another (Bar-Tal & Raviv). For example, according to Bar-Tal and Raviv's definition, an altruistic act must be motivated by moral convictions and justice; most other chapter authors do not define altruism so stringently. Furthermore, there is disagreement on the role of cost to the benefactor. Some researchers and theorists define an act as altruistic only if it costs the benefactor (e.g., Krebs); others do not.

It is clear that researchers' definitions differ, in part, because of varying spheres of interest among researchers. For example, the behaviors that Bar-Tal and Raviv are most concerned with are quite developmentally sophisticated, and require higher levels of cognition, moral judgment, and role-taking ability than does the domain of interest to Gelfand and Hartmann—the domain of behaviors that overtly benefit another regardless of the individual's reason for performing an act. This difference reflects the theoretical orientations of the authors. Bar-Tal and Raviv have based their theory and research on cognitive developmental conceptions emphasizing cognitive growth, whereas Gelfand and Hartmann focus primarily on overt behavior because they are strongly rooted in the social learning tradition.

In part, disagreements regarding definitions can be viewed as a game of semantics. Researchers seldom restrict their research to the circumscribed domain of behavior included in their definitions of *altruism* or *prosocial behavior*. For example, theorists interested in altruism that is not extrinsicly reinforced often study the effects of reinforcement on prosocial behavior (e.g., Bar-Tal & Raviv, Chapter 8). In fact, most researchers are concerned with the entire range of behaviors that benefit another regardless of the motivation behind the behavior—researchers merely differ in which behaviors they label as altruistic and which they consider to be developmental precursors of altruism or related behaviors. Furthermore, even if researchers wished to restrict the domain of behaviors examined to the specific group of behaviors consistent with a particular definition of altruism, it would be difficult to do so because an observer seldom knows for certain why one person assists another. More specifically, it is frequently difficult to discern if a particular positive behavior was performed intentionally or not, if it was carried out for extrinsic rewards (such as approval or concrete rewards), and if the actor was genuinely concerned with the potential recipient's welfare. Usually the best a researcher can do is to try to make inferences regarding an actor's motives from contextual variables or the actor's verbalizations.

Although it is difficult to differentiate positive behaviors performed for various motives from one another, it is still conceptually useful to make distinctions among different types of positive behaviors—that is, behaviors that benefit another regardless of their motivation (Staub, 1978). Two important distinctions concern intentionality of an act (is it performed accidently or intentionally?) and motivation (for example, is a behavior performed to achieve extrinsic reinforcement or for one of a number of internal reasons?).

Although researchers generally study many types of positive behaviors, the majority of researchers concerned with sharing, helping, comforting, and other positive behaviors are primarily interested in behaviors that benefit another, are voluntary and intentional, and are not performed to obtain extrinsic reinforcement. Usually researchers presume that the purpose of such behaviors is to benefit another, although the actor's motive may be more abstract—for example, to support internalized principles of justice. These behaviors generally are defined as *altruistic*, although, as we have seen, some definitions of altruism differ a bit from this one. Thus, altruistic behaviors can be conceptualized as a select subtype of positive behaviors. However, not all positive behaviors that are intentional are motivated by internal factors such as concern for others and, moreover, it is often difficult to determine the motive for seemingly intentional positive behavior. Consequently, many intentional positive behaviors cannot be classified as altruistic, but should be differentiated from behaviors that accidently benefit another. Although the terms *prosocial behavior* and *altruism* frequently have been used interchangeably (e.g., Mussen & Eisenberg-Berg, 1977), researchers increasingly have used the term *prosocial behavior* to designate helping, sharing, and other seemingly intentional and voluntary positive behaviors for which the motive is unspecified, unknown, or not altruistic. The need to distinguish altruism conceptually, as well as empirically, from the larger domain of intentional positive behaviors (prosocial behaviors) may encourage the use of a more differentiated vocabulary.

GENERAL CONCEPTUAL AND THEORETICAL ISSUES IN THE STUDY OF PROSOCIAL AND ALTRUISTIC BEHAVIOR

As has been discussed previously, differences in definitions of altruism and prosocial behavior reflect, in part, differences in researchers' theoretical perspectives. One of the major approaches to the study of the development of prosocial behavior has its roots in learning and social learning theory, and has been described as "empirical" (Krebs, Chapter 3). Theorists and researchers who adhere to a social learning perspective tend to emphasize overt observable behaviors, and frequently do not define altruism on the basis of internal motives or cognitive processes. Accordingly, these theorists and researchers frequently define a broad range of positive behaviors as being altruistic, and/or they do not clearly differentiate among various positive behaviors. In contrast, researchers guided by a cognitive–developmental or "rational" approach (see Krebs, Chapter 3) attend carefully to cognitive–motivational elements of an individual's behavior, and define altruism with stringent criteria related to the structure of the actor's cognitive motives. This difference in perspective results in a smaller range and number of behaviors which are defined as "altruistic" by cognitive–developmental theorists than those so defined by behavioral theorists.

In recent research, several investigators have noticed relatively systematic changes in both the development of prosocial behavior (Bar-Tal & Raviv, Chapter 8; Hoffman, Chapter 11; Zahn-Waxler & Radke-Yarrow, Chapter 5) and reasoning regarding prosocial behavior (Bar-Tal & Raviv, Chapter 8; Eisenberg, Chapter 9; Krebs, Chapter 3). These changes seem to reflect developmental advances in role taking and/or the child's reasoning processes, and, perhaps, the early development of the capacity to understand and implement needed interventions. At the very least, it appears that there frequently is a qualitative difference in an individual's prosocial behavior at different ages, and that it is important to consider these distinctions if one is to understand the development of prosocial behavior. Certainly, if one considers the chapters in this book as representing the range of theoretical perspectives in the field, it is clear that issues relating to the sequence, consistency, universality, and significance of qualitative changes or "stages" in prosocial behavior are likely to be major topics in the future.

One current, thorny conceptual issue has its roots in both the empirical data related to prosocial behavior and the ongoing theoretical debate in psychology concerning specificity versus generality in personality (Bem & Allen, 1974; Bem & Funder, 1978; Kenrick & Stringfield, 1980; Mischel, 1968). Stated simply, the issue is as follows: Is there consistency in an individual's prosocial (or altruistic) responding, or do situational factors determine when and if an individual acts prosocially? Or, phrased differently, is there an altruistic personality (Rushton, 1980)? Interestingly (but consistent with analyses of the same question with regard to other domains of functioning), given the same data base, people draw rather different conclusions (for examples, see Chapters 15, 4, and 2 by Reykowski, Rushton, and Underwood & Moore, respectively). Some researchers see consistencies in individuals' prosocial responding, whereas others focus more on situational variation.

Related to the issue of consistency, a current topic of debate is whether or not different modes of prosocial behavior (e.g., comforting, rescuing, donating, sharing, and helping) are conceptually distinct—that is, if they represent different classes of behavior resulting from different internal and/or environmental factors (Radke-Yarrow, Zahn-Waxler, & Chapman, in press; Reykowski, Chapter 15; Underwood & Moore, Chapter 2). In more concrete terms, one can ask if there is greater consistency in prosocial responding within a given domain of behavior—for example, with regard to sharing— than across domains of prosocial behavior. Underwood and Moore (Chapter 2) address this question by considering similarities and differences in the developmental course of various types of prosocial behavior, and by examining the relationship of different modes of prosocial responding to factors of conceptual import including moral judgment, sex, and personality characteristics of the actor. Theirs is a somewhat more sophisticated approach to the question than the common tactic of examining intercorrelations among instances of prosocial behavior from different domains. The results of Underwood and Moore's analyses, and of other researchers' analyses (Radke-Yarrow, Zahn-Waxler, & Chapman, in press), suggest that various modes of prosocial behavior may have different developmental roots and may represent somewhat different behavioral responses. At the very least, it seems clear that researchers should be alert to possible differences in various modes of prosocial behavior—differences that could account for discrepant patterns of findings in the literature.

It is likely that other, more subtle differentiations within the realm of prosocial behavior are also of conceptual importance. For example, prosocial behavior in response to a request may represent a very different behavior from prosocial behavior that is spontaneously emitted (Eisenberg, Cameron, Tryon, & Dodez, 1981; Eisenberg-Berg & Hand, 1979). According to recent data, it is likely that the former type of prosocial behavior frequently represents a compliant response, whereas spontaneous behaviors reflect other types of motivation including empathic responding (Eisenberg-Berg, Cameron, & Tryon, 1980). Similarly, in the future, researchers may wish to differentiate between prosocial behaviors that are responses to obvious distress cues and prosocial behaviors that occur when there are no signs of need. In some cases the latter type of prosocial behavior may represent a bid for attention, the desire to initiate social contact, or other self-centered motives rather than a response to another's needs. In other words, inappropriate and/or unneeded prosocial behaviors may derive from different motives and serve different purposes than appropriate, beneficial prosocial behaviors.

To summarize, the study of the development of prosocial behaviors is in its fledgling stage. Thus, there are many theoretical and conceptual issues to be addressed. Some of these issues are relatively general; for example, they concern the definition, classification, and generality of positive behaviors. Often such conceptual issues directly reflect current controversies concerning personality development in general. Other issues concern the role of

specific processes in the development of prosocial behavior, such as socialization and the effect of developmental advances in affect and cognition.
According to all appearances, the conceptual issues of the future will be
largely interactional in nature, that is, they will concern models for delineating the interplay of various inputs and processes in the development of
prosocial behavior. Given the diversity of factors that may influence the
development of prosocial behavior, it is likely that no simple model can fully
account for the phenomenon.

THE EARLY DEVELOPMENT AND SOCIALIZATION OF PROSOCIAL BEHAVIOR

One of the most fascinating and important findings in recent research
on prosocial behavior is that prosocial behaviors are evident in the repertoires of very young children (see Grusec, Chapter 6; Zahn-Waxler &
Radke-Yarrow, Chapter 5). This finding has enormous implications for
theory and conceptual models of prosocial behavior.

According to traditional psychoanalytic and cognitive developmental
theories, young children should not display altruistic behavior until around
age 5-7 years, after the resolution of the Oedipal or Electra conflict and after
the onset of concrete operations (and the role-taking abilities characteristic
of this cognitive stage). However, it is relatively clear that children can act
altruistically—intentionally assist others in situations in which there are no
clear external reinforcers—at the age of 1½-2 years. Furthermore, it appears
that early individual differences in style of prosocial responding are somewhat stable at ages 2-7 (Radke-Yarrow & Zahn-Waxler, 1980). These data
have relevance for conceptualizations of altruism, and of the role of sophisticated role-taking and moral reasoning abilities in its development. Either
one does not consider early displays of helping, sharing, comforting, and
such behaviors as altruistic, or one has to concede that the sophisticated
skills discussed by many researchers are not necessary for early altruistic
responding. These skills include advanced levels of role-taking ability or
moral judgment (Bar-Tal & Raviv, Chapter 8), a learned association between
prosocial responding and rewards as a result of socialization during the
school year (Cialdini *et al.,* Chapter 13), and elaborate cognitive scripts
(Karniol, Chapter 10). Rather, seemingly altruistic responding apparently can
be based on relatively rudimentary role-taking skills, empathic responding
(vicarious emotional responding, Hoffman, Chapter 11), and/or other processes. What this means is that most explanations for the genesis of altruism
in childhood are, in themselves, inadequate because they involve
mechanisms that develop in the school years or even later. A major task for

future research and theory is to identify the bases of early prosocial behavior, and to learn how later developmental changes resulting from social and cognitive development and experience reinforce and modify initial patterns of prosocial responding.

Socialization, broadly defined, is obviously a potentially important process in shaping children's prosocial tendencies. Clearly, one can influence the *frequency* of prosocial responding, at least in the short run, via reinforcement, punishment, and techniques such as direct instruction (Gelfand & Hartmann, Chapter 7; Rushton, Chapter 4), although lack of variation in parental behaviors relating to prosocial behavior may limit the explanatory powers of some disciplinary mechanisms (Grusec, Chapter 6). More interesting, however, is the accumulation of data consistent with the conclusion that various types of child-rearing techniques may influence the *quality* as well as the quantity of positive behaviors—that is, the internal processes that accompany and serve as the motivation for a prosocial behavior (Reykowski, Chapter 15). For example, different verbalizations and/or reinforcement techniques seem to induce children to make different attributions regarding the motivational basis for their own behaviors, and these attributions sometimes influence a subsequent prosocial behavior (possibly via their effect on self-perceptions and/or the encoding and processing of information embedded in the attributions [see Gelfand & Hartmann, Chapter 7; Grusec, Chapter 6; Rushton, Chapter 4]). Specifically, it appears that social reinforcement (rather than solely concrete rewards) and attributional statements that induce children to attribute their own behavior to prosocial motives alter children's thinking about why they themselves assist others. These data clearly illustrate the subtle effects that various modes of child rearing may have—effects that hitherto have been ignored or minimized because the importance of the child's own reasoning and attributional processes has not been fully recognized. Once proper significance is granted the child's role in the socialization process, the entire issue of socialization is rendered much more complex because factors such as reactance to disciplinary techniques (see Staub, 1979), the development of cognitions about the self, and individual differences and developmental changes in the child's interpersonal understanding (for example, Damon, 1977; Selman, 1980; Youniss, 1980) must be considered along with situational variables.

Moreover, once one acknowledges that there are different qualities of prosocial behavior—that some prosocial acts are altruistic whereas others are done for "baser" reasons—one must carefully examine the conclusions drawn from the research on socialization. For example, although it is true that material reinforcements sometimes increase the frequency of prosocial reasoning, it is likely that it is primarily nonaltruistic prosocial responding that is enhanced—that is, prosocial actions motivated by factors other than the desire to benefit another regardless of the extrinsic reinforcers. In brief, whereas the effects (especially the short-term effects) of a particular socialization practice may seem desirable, if the socializer is concerned with the *quality* of the child's prosocial behavior, the result, in reality, may be undesirable. Clearly, one must be cautious about accepting or recommending any simple formula for rearing a prosocial child.

THE ROLE OF COGNITION

If it is assumed that positive behaviors differ in quality (for example, altruistic behaviors differ from prosocial behaviors performed for self-oriented rather than other-oriented reasons), then it is clear that cognitive capacities and processes must play a major role in the development of prosocial behavior. Furthermore, the fact that the quality of children's prosocial behavior changes in systematic ways with age (Bar-Tal & Raviv, Chapter 8; Eisenberg, Chapter 9; Hoffman, Chapter 11; Zahn-Waxler & Radke-Yarrow, Chapter 5) strongly suggests that the young child's rapidly changing cognitive abilities influence the development of prosocial behavior.

The influence of cognitive growth and change on the development of prosocial behaviors is evident throughout youth from early childhood into adolescence. Even in the first 2–3 years of life, one can see dramatic changes in the child's prosocial responding—changes that seem to be related to cognitive development. For example, children in the first year to approximately 20 months of age respond to another's distress primarily by merely orienting to the other and/or displaying generalized affective agitation (such as crying, whimpering, seeking out one's caretaker). However, by 2 years of age, the child is much more likely to exhibit focused efforts to interact positively with the victim of distress, and to intervene in a positive way (Zahn-Waxler & Radke-Yarrow, Chapter 5). It is likely that this change in behavior is linked to the child's greater understanding of the difference between self and other, of cause and effect in the behavioral realm, and of the meaning of affective cues.

The qualitative changes in prosocial behavior noted in school-aged children can also be tied to cognitive development. Younger school-aged children are more likely than older children to assist others for the purpose of obtaining concrete or material rewards, or as an act of compliance to adults' dictates, whereas adolescents are somewhat more likely than younger children to assist others for highly internalized, abstract reasons, such as those due to conceptions of right and wrong and the desire to adhere to beliefs relating to moral principles (Bar-Tal & Raviv, Chapter 8; Eisenberg, Chapter 9). Clearly, the abstract reasoning that sometimes characterizes the older child's thinking regarding prosocial action is more developmentally advanced than the concrete reasoning that usually underlies the young child's prosocial behavior. Again, the role of cognition in its development seems to be central.

Theorists and researchers frequently have discussed the importance of role-taking abilities in the development of prosocial behavior (Hoffman, Chapter 11). In brief, it is assumed that children who can imaginatively take the perspective of another, and thus have some understanding of the other's internal affective state and cognitive processing, would be more likely to comprehend and respond to another's needs. Although it is likely that the child must have some understanding of the other's internal processes before he or she can act altruistically, the centrality of the development of role-taking ability in the development of prosocial behavior must be questioned. Certainly, if, as was already discussed, 2-year-olds display behavior that frequently appears to be altruistic, sophisticated role-taking abilities are not necessary for prosocial responding. Furthermore, as was suggested by Karniol (Chapter 10), it is possible that children frequently acquire information concerning others' internal states by accessing stored information, not by vicariously taking the role of another.

In brief, it is logical to assume that certain rudimentary role-taking skills (such as the ability to differentiate between self and other, and one's own versus others' needs) are essential for the performance of prosocial behavior (Hoffman, Chapter 11). However, whereas sophisticated role-taking abilities may sometimes underlie older children's prosocial behavior (Eisenberg, Chapter 9), such role-taking skills do not appear to be sufficient or necessary for all types of prosocial behaviors.

Just because an individual understands another's perspective does not mean that he or she will act in a manner consistent with the other's needs. The individual must be *motivated* to act in ways consistent with one's understanding of the situation. Often the core of this motivation is affective. Thus, it is important to consider affective motives as well as cognitive motives in the development of prosocial behavior.

THE ROLE OF AFFECT

At the present time we know relatively little about the role of affect in the development of prosocial behavior. This is not surprising if one considers the paucity of research concerning the development of affect and affective motives in general, including the interaction of affective and cognitive motivation in guiding perception, thought, and action.

Affective motivations probably influence the performance of prosocial behavior at several levels. First, affect will influence what an individual processes and how an event is processed. Events that have a strong affective significance to a given individual will probably be noticed more often and/or more quickly than events with little affective significance. For example, if an individual has been the victim of hunger, he or she may be more likely to notice and process cues denoting malnourishment or hunger in another. Second, affective motives will influence how cognitive inputs are interpreted, and whether an individual invokes role-taking skills and uses other types of social cognition with another. For example, it is likely that Nazi guards in World War II concentration camps interpreted cues of distress from family members and prisoners quite differently, in part because of the nature of the affective bond with the two groups of individuals. Furthermore, Nazi guards were probably less motivated to try to understand the prisoners' internal processes, including thoughts and feelings, than they were those of family members. Finally, affective factors will play a role in determining if an individual responds to another's need in a particular situation. The affective meaning of a situation (for example, if the components of the situation resonate with an affectively charged value or meaning), the emotional relationship between the potential benefactor and the recipient of aid, and the degree to which the individual vicariously feels another's plight may all influence the likelihood of a prosocial response. Clearly, affect and its development merit greater attention in the study of prosocial behavior.

The importance of affective inputs in prosocial action should vary across situations and individuals. For example, when the flow of events is rapid, people may engage in relatively little cognitive processing; rather, their responses are probably affected more by a variety of affective and personality factors. Thus, individuals may be much less likely to process the meaning of interpersonal events when there is a situational press; rather, they should be more likely to act on the basis of emotions and affective motives elicited by the specific situation (Staub & Eisenberg, in press). Furthermore, there may be individual differences in the tendency to weight and respond to cognitive versus affective considerations when involved in interpersonal interactions. For example, some young children typically respond to others' distresses in a cognitive, nonemotional manner, whereas other children generally react quite emotionally (Radke-Yarrow & Zahn-Waxler, 1980).

Theorists and researchers usually have addressed the role of affect in the development of prosocial behavior through examination of the mechanism of empathy. In general, empathy is hypothesized to be *the* major or, at least, a major cause of prosocial behavior (Feshbach, Chapter 12; Hoffman, Chapter 11). Once a child has reached the stage of development when he or she can cognitively differentiate between self and other and between one's own and other's emotional states, the child's vicarious emotional responding to another's distress is believed to function as a motivator for prosocial behavior. Although the data do suggest some relationship between empathy and prosocial behavior (Feshbach, Chapter 12; Hoffman, Chapter 11; Krebs, 1975; Peraino & Sawin, 1981; Sawin, 1979), it is not clear why such a relationship exists. Do people assist another when they are empathically aroused to reduce their own empathic distress? Or, do people experience a feeling of compassion, along with a conscious desire to help, because they feel sorry for the needy other, and not solely to relieve their own empathic distress? Alternatively, does empathic arousal facilitate recall and processing of norms and self-perceptions related to helping? Empathy may be an affective motivator of prosocial behavior for more than one reason, and the process mediating this association may change with age. Furthermore, a complex age-related association may exist between empathy and guilt, another potential motivator of prosocial behavior (Hoffman, Chapter 11). One of the major challenges facing researchers in the area of prosocial behavior is determining the frequency with which empathy motivates prosocial behavior, the mechanisms involved, and how the process changes with age.

Until recently, research on empathy has been relatively simplistic and unidimensional. However, refinements in recent research on empathy have produced data consistent with the conclusion that our approach to the study of empathy needs to be more differentiated and multifaceted. For example, it has become increasingly clear that the development of empathy and its relationship to prosocial behavior may vary somewhat depending on the sex of the child (Eisenberg-Berg & Mussen, 1978; Feshbach, Chapter 12; Hoffman, 1977). Furthermore, the relationship between prosocial behavior and empathic arousal varies depending on one's operationalization of empathy—for example, if intensity of arousal is considered or just presence versus absence of empathic response. Moreover, general valence (positive or negative) and type of affect (for example, sadness, happiness, fear, anger) may be important both in the assessment of empathy and in the strength of association between empathic responding and prosocial behavior. For example, Feshbach (Chapter 12), found that boys' (but not girls') tendency to empathize intensely with another's emotional state was positively related to prosocial behavior if the emotion in question was negative—that is, if the boy empathized with another's sadness, fear, or anger. In contrast the intensity of empathizing with another's positive affect (pride and happiness) was negatively related to prosocial behavior, and positively related to antisocial behavior. These relationships are logical if one considers that prosocial behavior is much more likely to result from empathizing with another's distress than with positive states. Furthermore, people who empathize strongly (rather than moderately) with individuals who are happy (and, in general, who would not need assistance) frequently may be doing so to elevate their own mood (see Cialdini et al., Chapter 13). At least for boys, individual differences in the tendency to use empathy to elevate one's own moods may reflect general differences in modes of coping and/or social interaction.

Although empathy is a major affective response that may contribute to the development of prosocial behavior, it is not the only one. It appears that positive and negative affect resulting from a variety of experiences (e.g., success or failure, receipt of material goods, embarrassment, negative feedback about the self) can influence moods, and that individuals' temporary mood states are related to the probability that they will behave in a prosocial manner (Cialdini et al., Chapter 13). Again, as for the research on empathy, it appears that valence of the induced affect is a variable of major import Furthermore, as for empathy, it is possible that differences in socialization practices based on sex of the child influence the nature of the relationship between empathy and prosocial behavior. The relationship between mood and prosocial behaviors is complex, but potentially understandable, if one considers relevant variables such as sex and age of the individual, and cost of prosocial action (see Chapter 13 for more details).

THE RELATIONSHIP BETWEEN PROSOCIAL BEHAVIOR AND MORAL REASONING

In this book, both the development of prosocial behavior and moral judgment are discussed. The perennial question that arises when one considers both types of data concerns the relationship between these two domains of moral development. Does level of moral judgment influence prosocial behavior, and is there consistency across the two domains of moral development?

Researchers who have reviewed the literature on the association between moral judgment and prosocial behavior have concluded that there is a relationship between the two, but of only moderate strength (Blasi, 1980; Eisenberg, Chapter 9). The current literature on prosocial behavior suggests a variety of factors that may diminish the magnitude of this relationship. Indeed, when one considers the number of factors that could intervene between cognitive evaluation of a situation and actual behavior, it is surprising that the association between moral judgment and prosocial behavior is as strong as is indicated by the literature.

Moral judgments entail a complex process involving a variety of cognitive and affective components. In making a moral judgment about a particular situation, many factors must be considered, such as who is involved, the costs and benefits to self and others, and the cognitive and affective relationship of the specifics in that situation to a variety of broader moral and social issues. Since different situations involve different configurations of personal, social, and moral issues, each situation may elicit somewhat different reasoning (Eisenberg-Berg & Neal, 1981). Thus, it is not surprising that, when researchers have examined moral judgment about prohibition-oriented issues (issues related to obedience to authorities, laws, rules, and punishment), they sometimes have not found an association between prohibition reasoning and prosocial (rather than prohibition) behavior in an entirely different situation. In such research, both the actual event or incident being considered and the domain of morality involved (prosocial or prohibition) differ. Similarly, it is to be expected that children's reasoning regarding conflicts about solely prosocial issues is not always related to the occurrence of prosocial behavior in a situation entirely different from that about which moral reasoning had been elicited. Different moral issues are frequently inherent to different situations. Thus, reasoning about a particular moral conflict in a specific situation (Situation 1) may differ from reasoning about a second situation (Situation 2) in which behavior, not reasoning, is assessed, and any lack of association between reasoning in Situation 1 and behavior in Situation 2 may be due to differences in the reasoning elicited by the two situations, rather than to lack of a relationship between reasoning and behavior. Only when reasoning and behavior are assessed in the same situation can a researcher really determine if an individual's reasoning is predictably related to a specific mode of behavior.

Another factor that could weaken the empirical relationship between reasoning and behavior is that more than cognitive processing of relevant moral, social, and personal issues is involved in engendering behavior, prosocial or otherwise. Competing concerns can lessen the effect of a moral judgment on subsequent behavior. For example, an individual may feel that he or she should assist another for specific highly internalized reasons, but may not do so in a particular situation owing to the feeling that another, even more important situation demands attention. Similarly, people may not help in a particular situation because they feel that assisting in that situation will have negative side effects on the recipient's sense of autonomy, or that the recipient will not benefit in the long run due to the influence of the third party. For example, if a teacher protects a child from being teased by peers, the child may be seen as "teacher's pet" or a "baby," and subsequently may be teased even more. Moreover, people may not assist another, even if they feel that prosocial behavior is morally justified, because they lack skills, knowledge, or resources. Finally, affective factors must be considered. A person may be inhibited from helping regardless of the individual's moral reasoning because of his or her emotional response in that situation. For example, fear or embarrassment evoked by the events at hand could preclude prosocial behavior.

Of course, one reason moral judgment does not always relate to prosocial behavior is that people do not always do what they know they should do. Factors such as laziness, selfishness, and competing affective responses, including dislike for the potential recipient of aid, sometimes determine the presence or absence of prosocial behavior, even when one's moral reasoning about the situation is based on loftier considerations. Because a difference exists between "should" and "would" in human behavior, moral judgment will never be entirely consistent with moral behavior. People sometimes verbalize "should" reasoning (reasoning relating to what they feel should be done and why) rather than "would" reasoning (reasoning that includes consideration of factors that would influence an individual's actual behavior). Whereas young children seem relatively uninhibited in verbalizing "would" reasoning, older children and adults frequently do not openly discuss their "would" reasoning because of potential social sanctions.

In considering the relationship between moral judgment and behavior, it is worth emphasizing that prosocial behavior may not always be the best or most "moral" action in a particular situation. For example, it would not be particularly moral to assist someone who wanted to complete a task alone, to aid someone who subsequently would use that assistance to injure another, or to help someone who asked for assistance that was not needed and who manipulates others to provide assistance so that he or she need not shoulder appropriate responsibilities. Thus, correlations between level of moral reasoning and presence of prosocial behavior may be poor indicators of the actual association between moral judgment and behavior in some situations. The significance of a prosocial behavior in a particular context must be considered.

METHODOLOGICAL ISSUES

There are a number of current methodological issues in the area of prosocial development worth noting, some of which are addressed either directly or indirectly by the authors of chapters in this volume. One important issue—the need to utilize multiple measures of prosocial development—is discussed by Zahn-Waxler and Radke-Yarrow (Chapter 5). As is true for any other social behavior, it is difficult to obtain accurate measures of prosocial behavior as it naturally occurs. In contrived settings, such as the laboratory, measurements may not be ecologically valid. However, it is difficult to obtain observations of prosocial behavior as it naturally occurs because of subjects' responses to being observed—that is, the tendency for people to act in other than a natural manner when they know they are being observed. Furthermore, data on prosocial development obtained by verbal report may be inaccurate owing to purposeful distortions, lapses of memory, or misrepresentation stemming from unconscious psychological needs. In brief, there are potential pitfalls with all the commonly used measures of prosocial development. Consequently, it is desirable, if possible, to assess prosocial behavior via several different techniques. Furthermore, because there may be important differences between various modes of prosocial responding—for example, sharing and helping—if one wants to make broad generalizations about the development of prosocial behavior, it would be useful to obtain data regarding a variety of prosocial behaviors.

These conclusions concerning measures apply to the study of moral judgments, as well as to the study of overt behavior. Moral reasoning can be assessed by eliciting responses about hypothetical situations, about the individual's own behavior in a contrived setting, or concerning naturally occurring, real-life prosocial behavior. Each method has its advantages and disadvantages (Eisenberg, Chapter 9); more reliable conclusions can be drawn from data collected by a variety of techniques, especially if there is a consistency in results across methodologies.

A particularly promising technique that has only recently been adapted for the study of prosocial behavior is maternal report of naturally occurring prosocial behavior in a child's home (Grusec, Chapter 6; Zahn-Waxler & Radke-Yarrow, Chapter 5). With this method, it is possible to obtain data relatively unobtrusively regarding real-life prosocial behavior for extensive periods of time. By means of this assessment procedure, researchers have obtained exciting data concerning the emergence and socialization of prosocial behavior in the earliest years of life. Innovative methods such as this are needed in future research.

The assessment of empathy, its development, and its relationship to behavior is an especially thorny methodological problem. How does one accurately measure an internal affective reaction that the individual may or may not be able to label and report? Physiological measures are very difficult to obtain and interpret with children, and the usual problems with verbal reports hold for the assessment of empathy. Furthermore, it is not clear that empathic reactions are always expressed with nonverbal behaviors that can be observed and measured. Thus, a multifaceted methodological approach is especially important with regard to the assessment of empathy. Various techniques for the measurement of empathy are currently being tested and refined by Feshbach (Chapter 12) and Zahn-Waxler and Radke-Yarrow (Chapter 5). Their research may take us a few steps closer to the goal of accurately assessing this elusive response and of understanding its relationship to prosocial behavior.

In much of the research in which the relationship between prosocial behavior and a potential determinant (for example, empathy or level of moral judgment) is examined, measures of prosocial behavior have been obtained in a different setting from that in which measures of the potential determinant were obtained. Thus, the data can be interpreted as indicating the strength of association between prosocial behavior and the tendency to exhibit the other variable—for example, the disposition to react empathically or to use high levels of moral judgment. Such data do not really indicate whether or not the variable in question causes prosocial behavior. Research in which the sequencing of events and behaviors is observed (for example, Zahn-Waxler & Radke-Yarrow, Chapter 5) is needed to differentiate the determinants of prosocial behavior from behaviors that merely develop or are exhibited concurrently with prosocial responding.

One final comment concerning methodology is appropriate. At the present time most of the research on prosocial development has been conducted with "normal," middle-class Caucasian children. It is possible, however, that prosocial development differs in various socioeconomic and ethnic groups. Furthermore, the examination of prosocial development in "abnormal" populations (such as in homes with depressed parents, see Zahn-Waxler & Radke-Yarrow, Chapter 5) and in various cultures and subcultures may provide new insights into the dynamics underlying the development of prosocial tendencies.

REFERENCES

Ainsworth, M. D. S. The development of infant-mother attachment. In B. M. Caldwell & H. N. Riciuti (Eds.), *Review of child development research* (Vol. 3). Chicago: University of Chicago Press, 1973.

Aristotle. *Nicomachean ethics*. In R. M. Hutchins (Ed.), *Great books of the Western world* (Vol. 9). Chicago: Encyclopedia Britannica, 1952.

Bar-Tal, D. *Prosocial behavior: Theory and research*. New York: Wiley, 1976.

Bem, D. J., & Allen, A. On predicting some of the people some of the time. *Psychological Review*, 1974, *81*, 506–520.

Bem, D. J., & Funder, D. C. Predicting more of the people more of the time: Assessing the personality of situations. *Psychological Review*, 1978, *85*, 485–501.

Blasi, A. Bridging moral cognition and moral action: A critical review of the literature. *Psychological Bulletin*, 1980, *88*, 1–45.

Bowlby, J. *Attachment and loss* (Vol. 1). London: Hogarth, 1969.

Damon, W. *The social world of the child*. San Francisco: Jossey-Bass, 1977.

Eisenberg, N., Cameron, E., Tryon, K., & Dodez, R. Socialization of prosocial behavior in the preschool classroom. *Developmental Psychology*, 1981, *17*, 773–782.

Eisenberg-Berg, N., Cameron, E., & Tryon, K. *Prosocial behavior in the preschool years: Methodological and conceptual issues*. Paper presented at the International Conference on the Development and Maintenance of Prosocial Behavior, Warsaw, Poland, June–July 1980.

Eisenberg-Berg, N., & Hand, M. The relationship of preschoolers' reasoning about prosocial moral conflicts to prosocial behavior. *Child Development,* 1979, *50,* 356-363.

Eisenberg-Berg, N., & Mussen, P. Empathy and moral development in adolescence. *Developmental Psychology,* 1978, *14,* 185-186.

Eisenberg-Berg, N., & Neal, C. The effects of person of the protagonist and costs of helping on children's moral judgment. *Personality and Social Psychology Bulletin,* 1981, *7,* 17-23.

Flacks, R. The revolt of the advantaged. In R. Sigel (Ed.), *Learning about politics.* New York: Random House, 1970.

Hartshorne, H., May, M. A., & Maller, J. B. *Studies in the nature of character* (Vol. 2). *Studies in self-control.* New York: Macmillan, 1929.

Hoffman, M. L. Sex-differences in empathy and related behaviors. *Psychological Bulletin,* 1977, *54,* 712-722.

Journal of Social Issues. 1972, *28*(3).

Kenniston, K. The sources of student discontent. *Journal of Social Issues,* 1967, *23,* 108-135.

Kenrick, D. T., & Stringfield, D. O. Personality traits and the eye of the beholder: Crossing some traditional philosophical boundaries in the search for consistency in all of the people. *Psychological Review,* 1980, *87,* 88-104.

Krebs, D. L. Altruism: An examination of the concept and a review of the literature. *Psychological Bulletin,* 1970, *73,* 258-302.

Krebs, D. L. Empathy and altruism. *Journal of Personality and Social Psychology,* 1975, *32,* 1134-1146.

Latané, B., & Darley, J. *The unresponsive bystander: Why doesn't he help?* New York: Appleton, 1970.

Macaulay, J., & Berkowitz, L. (Eds.), *Altruism and helping behavior.* New York: Academic Press, 1970.

Mischel, W. *Personality and assessment.* New York: Wiley, 1968.

Murphy, L. B. *Social behavior and child personality.* New York: Columbia University Press, 1937.

Mussen, P., & Eisenberg-Berg, N. *Roots of caring, sharing, and helping: The development of prosocial behavior in children.* San Francisco: Freeman, 1977.

Peraino, M. M., & Sawin, D. B. *Empathic distress: Measurement and relation to prosocial behavior.* Paper presented at the Biennial Meeting of the Society for Research in Child Development, Boston, April 1981.

Radke-Yarrow, M., & Zahn-Waxler, C. *Roots, motives, and patterning in children's prosocial behavior.* Paper presented at the International Conference on the Development and Maintenance of Prosocial Behavior, Warsaw, Poland, June-July 1980.

Radke-Yarrow, M., Zahn-Waxler, C., & Chapman, M. Prosocial dispositions and behavior. In P. Mussen (Ed.), *Manual of child psychology* (E. M. Hetherington, Vol. Ed.). New York: Wiley, in press.

Rushton, J. P. Socialization and the altruistic behavior of children. *Psychological Bulletin,* 1976, *83,* 898-913.

Rushton, J. P. *Altruism, socialization, and society.* Englewood Cliffs, N.J.: Prentice-Hall, 1980.

Sawin, D. B. *Assessing empathy in children: A search for an elusive construct.* Paper presented at the Biennial Meeting of the Society for Research in Child Development, San Francisco, 1979.

Sears, R. R. Your ancients revisited: A history of child development. In E. M. Heatherington (Ed.), *Review of child development research* (Vol. 5). Chicago: University of Chicago Press, 1975.

Selman, R. L. *The growth of interpersonal understanding: Developmental and clinical analyses.* New York: Academic Press, 1980.

Solomon, F., & Fishman, J. R. Youth and peace: A psychosocial study and student peace demonstrators in Washington, D.C. *Journal of Social Issues*, 1964, *20*, 54-73.

Staub, E. *Positive social behavior and morality: Social and personal influences* (Vol. 1). New York: Academic Press, 1978.

Staub, E. *Positive social behavior and morality: Socialization and development* (Vol. 2). New York: Academic Press, 1979.

Staub, E., & Eisenberg, N. Social cognition, affect, and behavior: An essay and review of Robert Selman's *The growth of interpersonal understanding: Developmental and clinical analyses. Developmental Review*, in press.

Youniss, J. *Parents and peers in social development: A Sullivan-Piaget perspective.* Chicago: University of Chicago Press, 1980.

CONCEPTUAL ISSUES

BILL UNDERWOOD
BERT S. MOORE[1]

The Generality of Altruism
in Children

Ever since Mischel published his classic critique of trait psychology, *Personality and Assessment* (1968), there has been a continuing debate as to whether or not social behaviors show cross-situational and cross-temporal stability (Block, 1975; Wiggins, 1973) and, if they do, what the boundary conditions might be for such stability (Bem & Allen, 1974; Epstein, 1979). One consequence of this extensive debate has been the formal emergence of what has been termed the *interactionist perspective* (Magnusson & Endler, 1977). Whereas there is nothing terribly revolutionary about this formulation, it has made explicit the value in conceiving behavior as being the joint product of personal characteristics of the behaver and characteristics of the situation in which the behavior occurs. The contention is that whereas in some situations an individual's dispositions may be the most potent determiner of his or her behavior and that in other contexts the aspects of the situation will outweigh differences among individuals, in general the interaction term will account for a greater proportion of the variance than will either dispositional or situational factors. These concerns become relevant for us for two related reasons. First, the focus of this book is on prosocial behavior, and by designating it thus there is an implication that the behaviors falling under that rubric are somehow related and are representative of a common underlying process. This brings us to the second basis for our interest, the processes that might be implicated in the development of altruistic behavior. Of course, delineation of those processes is what this entire

1. Each author contributed equally to the writing of the chapter.

25

THE DEVELOPMENT OF
PROSOCIAL BEHAVIOR

Copyright © 1982 by Academic Press, Inc.
All rights of reproduction in any form reserved.
ISBN 0-12-234980-6

book is about, but, to the extent that diverse types of prosocial behavior are organized by common mechanisms, we should find some degree of consistency among measures of altruistic behavior. We shall be looking for evidence that particular processes have a similar influence on all types of altruistic behavior, which would increase our confidence in the belief that there is considerable generality in prosocial behavior. If, on the other hand, different types of prosocial behavior are found to be influenced by different processes (or in different ways by the same process), this would call into question the generality of prosocial behavior and perhaps incline us to the belief that prosocial behavior is a collection of distinct behavioral patterns rather than a unified whole.

The questions of consistency and generality is a complex one from a developmental perspective, for developmental theories do not in general rest on the traditional trait assumptions of cross-behavioral consistency. Rather the assumption is that different behaviors may show somewhat different courses of development, and that there may be behavioral "regressions" as the child consolidates elements in the progression from one stage to the next. It is felt also that the same patterns of behavior may be undergirded by different mechanisms at different stages (Bar-Tal, Raviv, & Leiser, 1980; Kohlberg, 1976). Bar-Tal contends that if we look solely at presence or absence of a particular type of prosocial behavior, we may miss the fact that the behavior may occur for very different reasons at different times. For this reason, we should not necessarily expect that because a behavior is present at one age it will continue to be present at later ages. It is also important to note that one's beliefs and actions may be under the control of different mechanisms. Complex relationships between moral judgment and moral behavior illustrate this point, for whereas theorists such as Kohlberg imply that judgment forms the basis of moral behavior, the data suggest that there is not an easy correspondence between the two.

However, it is still the case that developmental theorists of prosocial behavior (Hoffman, 1975; Staub, 1979) believe that, in general, we should see increasing convergence among measures of prosocial action across time. For the remainder of the chapter we shall examine the data bearing on this issue, and address the questions of whether speaking of the development of prosocial behaviors as a class of behaviors is justified and what mechanisms might serve to organize the development.

DEFINITIONS AND OPERATIONALIZATION OF PROSOCIAL BEHAVIOR

As has been seen elsewhere in this volume, defining prosocial behavior (see Chapter 1) entails some difficulties. Mussen and Eisenberg-Berg (1977) define prosocial behavior as "actions that are intended to aid or benefit another person or groups of people without the actor's anticipation of external rewards. Such actions often entail some cost, self-sacrifice or risk on the part of the actor [pp. 3-4]." Staub (1978) wishes to distinguish between prosocial behavior and altruism. He refers to prosocial behavior as any behavior benefiting others which might include behaviors such as cooperation that could entail benefit for the actor as well as the recipient of the action. He employs the term *altruism* for the more restrictive case in which the action appears to have been intended to benefit others rather than to gain material or social rewards. We shall restrict our attention in this chapter to behaviors fitting Staub's definition of altruism, behaviors done with the apparent intent of benefiting another more than oneself. Although this eliminates cooperation from our consideration, there remains the question of whether the wide variety of behaviors that has been investigated under the rubric of altruism—helping, sharing, going to the aid of a victim, comforting—does show generality and does show similar developmental courses. Because the behaviors that have been described as prosocial are so diverse, it may be that they are regulated by different mechanisms. We hope that our evaluation of the data will allow us to come to conclusions regarding these issues. First, we need to examine studies that have investigated changes in prosocial behavior over time, and see what age trends emerge.

AGE TRENDS

If the many different measures that have been used in studies of altruism are to be considered equivalent measurements of a common underlying dimension of altruistic concern, then they must follow similar courses of change across different ages. The vast majority of studies relating age to altruism have focused exclusively on generosity as an instance of prosocial behavior. A few studies (Buckley, Siegel, & Ness, 1979; Eisenberg-Berg & Hand, 1979; Green & Schneider, 1974; Yarrow & Waxler, 1976) have included measures of helping and/or comforting in addition to generosity, and fewer still (Staub, 1970, 1971a) have documented age trends in bystander intervention. The data on generosity are reasonably consistent, generally revealing a significant—and usually linear—relationship between age and sharing, with older children sharing more often and more generously than younger ones. This relationship, of course, is more evident in studies employing a broad range of ages than in those with only a limited age range (see Table 2.1).

Although there is an extensive literature on age trends in generosity, there is very little work on age trends in other measures of altruism. There are four studies relating age to helpfulness in nonemergency situations. Of these

Table 2.1
Studies of Age Trends in Generosity

Age range	Studies finding no significant age effect	Studies finding significant age effect
Adjacent or near-adjacent ages or grades in school	Israel & Brown (1979) Midlarsky & Bryan (1972) Zinser, Perry, & Edgar (1975)	Elliott & Vasta (1970) Gelfaud, Hartman, Cromer, Smith, & Page (1975) White & Burnham (1975)
Two nonadjacent ages or grades	Grusec (1972)	Barnett & Bryan (1974) Harris (1971) Rushton & Wiener (1975)
Broad age range	Buckley, Siegel, & Ness (1979) Yarrow & Waxler (1976)	Barnett, King, & Howard (1979) Coke & Bradshaw (1980) Emler & Rushton (1974) Froming & Underwood (1980) Grant, Wiener, & Rushton (1976) Green & Schneider (1974) Grusec, Kuczynski, Rushton, & Simutis (1978) Handlon & Gross (1959) Hull & Reuter (1977) Midlarsky & Bryan (1972) Rushton (1975) Skarin & Moely (1976) Ugurel-Semin (1952) Underwood, Froming, & Moore (1977)

four, two (Buckley et al., 1979; Yarrow & Waxler, 1976) have found no significant variation of helpfulness with age; one (Eisenberg-Berg & Hand, 1979) has found a positive but nonsignificant ($p < .12$) correlation between age and altruism; and the fourth (Green & Schneider, 1974) found a significant positive relationship with age for one measure of helpfulness but not for another. Although this rather dismal record would not encourage one to believe that there was a real age trend in helpfulness, there cannot be a definite conclusion as yet, owing to the small number of studies examining helpfulness.

In bystander intervention, at least, we do not find the conflicting results in age trends that we noted for research on nonemergency helpfulness. Unfortunately, this is because there are not enough studies of nonadult bystander intervention for them to come into conflict with each other. There are two studies that document an age trend in bystander intervention, both by Ervin Staub (1970, 1971b). Staub's (1970) initial study in this area found bystander intervention to vary significantly with age during the elementary school years, according to an inverted-U-shaped function. That is, the tendency to intervene began at a fairly low rate among kindergarteners, rose to a peak during the middle elementary school years, and fell to a low rate once more (in fact, to its lowest rate) for sixth graders. This inverted-U shape held both for helping when alone and for helping when another child was present.

Staub (1971b) later reported a series of studies on bystander intervention among seventh graders and young adult females. This report indicated that there was, in general, a higher rate of intervention for young adults than there was for seventh graders. While it is certainly risky to base conclusions on a single set of results, these studies do allow us to draw at least a tentative picture of the development of bystander intervention from early childhood to young adulthood. Intervention initially occurs at a low rate in the early elementary school years, first increasing with age, but decreasing during the late elementary school period. From this low level during late childhood and early adolescence, intervention increases to its highest level (among the ages studied in these reports) during early adulthood.

The data concerning age trends point to at least one definite conclusion about the generality of altruistic behvior. Bystander intervention seems to develop in a quite different fashion from generosity. Given the rather inconsistent nature of the data, it is difficult to know whether the developmental pattern for helpfulness is similar to that for generosity, or if it represents a third distinct pattern of change over time. In any event, there seem to be at least two distinct subtypes of altruism indicated by data on age changes, one represented by intervention in an emergency and the other by generosity (and perhaps also by helpfulness in nonemergencies).

THE GENERALITY OF PROSOCIAL BEHAVIOR

Now it is time to turn to the data on the generality of prosocial behavior. The nature of that generality can take two forms: (a) consistency across behaviors; and (b) consistency across time. From a developmental perspective, of course, we are interested in the convergence of these two types of consistency with the expectation that changes in behavioral consistency will form a coherent picture over time in terms of the hypothesized underlying mechanisms. Unfortunately, although there are a fairly large number of studies that have examined multiple measures of prosocial actions, there are only a couple of reports that focus on cross-time stability. We shall first examine studies using multiple measures of prosocial behavior, and, after evaluating the evidence on behavioral consistency, try to extrapolate from those studies using children of different ages to see if age trends in consistency emerge. Then we shall look at the available evidence on consistency from longitudinal research on prosocial behavior.

Studies Using Multiple Measures of Prosocial Behavior

In this section, we shall review a representative sample of research using several measures of prosocial behavior in an attempt to gain some estimate of the degree to which children who behave prosocially in one domain are likely to do so in another. Because of the limitations of space, the review of the relevant literature is selective. However, the authors have made every effort to ensure that their selectivity has not produced a biased sample. The reader interested in additional relevant research, however, should refer to works by Elliot and Vasta (1970); Midlarsky and Bryan (1972); and Mussen, Rutherford, Harris, and Keasey (1970). We will start with research conducted using younger children, and then examine the data with older children and adults.

Studies Using Limited Age Range

Rheingold, Hay, and West (1976) investigated the social interactions of very young children (15–24-month-olds). Although these interactions were not strictly prosocial by our definitions, Rheingold et al. sampled behaviors that they felt might be precursors of prosocial behavior, in that they represent examples of taking the perspective of the other and of reciprocal play. They assessed the children's showing of objects or toys to parents or unfamiliar people, giving of the objects, and partner play. The authors found examples of those behaviors at all ages, and increases in them with age. They also found positive relationships between showing and giving ($r = .24$, $p < .05$) and giving and partner play ($r = .50$, $p < .001$). The relationship between showing and partner play was nonsignificantly positive ($r = .18$). They interpreted these findings as possible organization among precursors of prosocial action.

Several studies have been conducted using nursery school-aged children. Rutherford and Mussen (1968) used middle-class 4-year-old boys. The boys were given an initial "altruism assessment" in terms of how many candies they gave to a friend. From the initial sample of 63 children, two groups were taken. One group of 14 had given no candies away at all, whereas 17 were selected for their high levels of generosity. These two groups were then compared on several measures: (a) teacher's ratings of generosity; (b) a measure of competitiveness based on a car racing game; and (c) a doll play situation designed to elicit information about the socialization practices in the child's family and the child's identification with his parents.

In general, the teachers' ratings of the high generous subjects reflected a generalized prosocial tendency. The high generous subjects were rated significantly higher on dimensions of kindness. They were rated as less competitive, less quarrelsome, and less aggressive than children low in generosity. In addition, the high generous children were found to be less competitive in the car racing game. The authors of this study concluded that generosity does appear to be a part of a pattern of interrelated altruistic characteristics that may develop together as a result of internalization of moral standards through identification processes.

Although these results may indicate a generalized prosocial orientation, they are inconclusive on this count, because there was actually only one index of altruistic action since we do not consider low competitiveness in a car racing game as altruistic. Also, the teacher ratings may represent global perceptions of the children rather than an accurate index of behavior.

Rubin and Schneider (1973) took two measures of altruism from 55 5-year-olds. The first measure was an opportunity to share candy with a charity. The other measure consisted of the amount of work done for a peer. These two measures of generosity and helping showed a positive relationship ($r = .40$, $p < .01$). There thus appeared to be a fair measure of concordance for two fairly disparate indexes of prosocial intervention. This finding is partially supported by a study employing naturalistic observations in a nursery school by Friedrich and Stein (1973). They found that there was a fairly strong positive correlation between nurturance and cooperative behaviors for boys, but that the correlations for girls were nonsignificant.

Strayer, Wareing, and Rushton (1979) report a naturalistic study using nursery school children that found impressive relations among several measures of prosocial behavior. Strayer et al. had raters code acts for 11 categories of child-directed behaviors and five categories of adult-directed behaviors. These categories were combined to form four measures for child-directed actions and three for adult-directed acts. They found a correlation of .62 between peer object activity (sharing, etc.) and peer helping, a relation of .52 between peer cooperation and peer object activity, and a correlation of .42 between peer cooperation and peer helping. All of these were significant. They also found appreciable temporal stability over the 6-week observation period. The relationship between child-directed behaviors and adult-directed behaviors were all nonsignificant, as were most correlations among measures of adult-directed behaviors. This study shows that children do seem to show considerable consistency in prosocial acts among themselves, whereas when significant situational aspects are altered (change from child recipients to adults) there is far less consistency.

Using preschool children, Eisenberg-Berg and Hand (1979) examined children's moral reasoning and prosocial behavior. These authors used naturalistic observations to obtain ratings of the frequency of the children's sharing of toys in games, and ratings of the frequency with which children helped another child. When correlations were run between these two different forms of prosocial behavior, no significant relationship was found. For these younger children there seemed to be no tendency for those who engaged in sharing to be more likely to help or comfort their classmates.

We were able to find only one study that included measures of emergency intervention and sharing in the same study (Weissbrod, 1976). This appears to be a curious dearth because of the speculation (Mussen & Eisenberg-Berg, 1977; Staub, 1979) that emergency intervention may follow a different developmental course from other types of prosocial behavior, and be regulated by different mechanisms. The study by Weissbrod investigated how adult warmth affected imitative donation and rescue behavior in first graders. After the "warmth" induction, children had a chance to witness the experimenter donate some of her winnings from a bowling game to a fund for crippled children. They then played the game and had an opportunity to donate winnings. The same children were subsequently exposed to an emergency intervention situation in which they overheard the apparent crash of a cabinet and crying and pleas of help of a little boy in the next room. The children could intervene by either pressing a button to summon the experimenter or by going to the door that connected the two rooms.

When Weissbrod examined the relationship between the two measures of prosocial behavior, she found a nonsignificant negative relationship between sharing and intervening ($r = -.194$). Although the order of opportunity to perform these behaviors was not counterbalanced and Weissbrod apparently did not compute correlations within experimental conditions, these results certainly suggest that situational factors or different individual characteristics may control these two forms of prosocial intervention.

For these younger children, then, the data are inconclusive. Some studies find moderate correlations between different measures of prosocial action, and others do not. Let us now turn to studies using older children.

A study by Krebs and Sturrup (1974) was conducted with 23 7- and 8-year-old children. Three categories of altruistic response were observed in a naturalistic setting: offering help, offering support, and suggesting responsibly. Offering help was found to correlate .21 with offering support and .09 with suggesting responsibly, which showed a .24 correlation with offering support. These correlations do not suggest a highly generalized prosocial syndrome. However, when Krebs and Sturrup derived a composite altruism score based on the three measures, the composite score showed a .47 relationship with an independently derived teacher rating of the child's overall altruism. This finding, of course, is subject to the potential problems mentioned above when overall impressionistic ratings are made by teachers, parents, or peers.

Grusec, Kuczynski, Rushton, and Simutis (1978) also provide data relevant to our question of stability. In a study examining the effects of models and attributions on prosocial behavior they took two different measures of sharing and also took measures at two different times, from 7–10-year-olds. The measures were highly similar, sharing marbles that could be exchanged for a prize with poor children and sharing pencils. They also had a chance 2 weeks later to share marbles again. The relationship between the two opportunities to share marbles was quite high ($r = .71$, $p < .01$), showing an appreciable degree of stability across the 2-week time span. However, the correlations between the two different sharing measures were quite low, showing an $r = .09$ between sharing marbles and sharing pencils at the initial test and a correlation of only $r = .04$ between pencil sharing and the delayed test of marble sharing. These results seem strikingly low when we consider that the behaviors sampled were highly similar. However, it may be that the relationship between the two measures may have been attenuated by the fact that children who had shared marbles may have felt that they had done "their part" already and thus showed a reduced tendency to share pencils.

Hampson (1980) reports a study using eighth grade children. These children were rated on their performance of six different prosocial actions: (a) rate of return of permission slips to participate in the study (social responsibility); (b) degree of verbal response to an audiotape of a peer in distress (nurturance); (c) degree of assistance in helping a secretary pick up papers (helping); (d) volunteering to meet and help the audiotaped peer (helping); (e) classroom volunteering to participate in a peer tutoring project (helping); and (f) response to a telephone request to be a big brother or sister to a handicapped child (helping). Across all subjects there were low relationships among these different measures, with correlations generally nonsignificant. When subjects were divided into outgoing and less outgoing groups, significant relationships are obtained, but not across all measures. The popular children tend to show more of (and higher correlations for) those measures involving public or verbal responsiveness. Less popular children showed higher rates of prosocial behavior on such acts as rate of return of permission slips or response to a specific nonpublic request such as agreeing to be a big brother or sister. So it appears that for these subjects very different processes may be producing the different forms of prosocial action and that, in general, consistency across all measures is low no matter how the subjects are divided.

Although there have been large numbers of studies done on prosocial behavior with adult subjects, most of them have not focused on the issue of consistency. An experiment by Ervin Staub (1974) has addressed the complex question of whether we can predict a person's tendency to behave prosocially from knowing his or her personality. Staub's study is important because it is one of the few that attempts actually to access individuals' prosocial orientation and relate it to specific prosocial behaviors. Male undergraduate subjects took several personality tests chosen to measure their concern about the welfare of others, their feeling of responsibility for others' welfare, and their belief in moral and prosocial values. Later, while working on a task, these subjects heard sounds of distress coming from an adjoining room. The sounds were made by a male confederate and were supposed to indicate that the victim had severe stomach cramps. The subjects had several opportunities to help the so-called victim. The subject was given 135 seconds to enter the adjoining room and see about the confederate; if the subject did not act within this time, the confederate then entered the subject's room and asked if he could lie down on a sofa; after a few minutes the confederate offered to go to another room where he would not bother the subject; finally the confederate asked the subject for a favor, either to call his roommate or to get a prescription filled for him.

The general findings of this study support both the idea that personality is related to prosocial behavior and the idea that personality factors alone are insufficient to predict whether a person will behave prosocially across all situations. For example, subjects with a high prosocial orientation were more likely to intervene during the first 135 seconds to help the confederate. They also showed a higher tendency to perform each of the other helping acts allowed for in this experiment. However, Staub also emphasized the importance of looking at how personality variables interact with aspects of the situation. This point is nicely illustrated by the previously mentioned study by Hampson (1980), in which a quality such as sociability moderated which forms of prosocial action were engaged in. In a follow-up report Staub (1979) states, "Our findings clearly show that a general personality characteristic which I referred to as prosocial orientation . . . tends to lead people to behave prosocially. It is also true that this personality orientation tended to exert influence jointly with other characteristics of the person or with characteristics of the situation [p. 14]." Staub's work represents a promising direction in assessing individual characteristics that may predict people's tendency to engage in prosocial actions. He attempts to assess both prosocial motivation and influence of specific situational factors in altruistic behavior.

Studies Examining Several Different Ages

Several studies have examined the consistency of prosocial behavior at different ages using a cross-sectional approach. Green and Schneider (1974) used four age groups: 5–6, 7–8, 9–10, 13–14. They offered children opportunities to perform three different prosocial acts: (a) sharing candy bars that they were given with other children in the school; (b) helping the experimenter pick up spilled pencils; and (c) volunteering to help make books for poor children. Whereas age changes were found for sharing, showing increasing sharing with age, and similar age changes were found for helping, there were no age changes for volunteering. But more centrally for us, there were no significant relationships among the three measures of prosocial behavior at any of the ages. These results, then, do, not support the findings by Rubin and Schneider (1973), Rutherford and Mussen (1968), or Friedrich and Stein (1973), in which significant relationships among measures of prosocial behavior were found. This inconsistency is not easily explainable, since the measures employed were highly similar to those employed in the other research. It is also interesting to note that whereas the Green and Schneider results, in general, supported the frequently observed positive relationship between age and prosocial behavior, they did not find increased consistency with age. This raises some questions as to whether similar mechanisms underlie these separate behaviors. Let us examine several additional cross-sectional studies to see if clarifications of these issues can be found.

In a study reported by Dlugokinski and Firestone (1973) four measures of "other-centeredness" were used. These authors were interested in using convergent methods to try to assess the generality of prosocial concern in 10–13-year-old children. They employed a paper and pencil measure of the child's understanding of kindness; Rokeach's value scale designed to tap the child's advocacy of other-centered as opposed to self-centered or neutral values; sociometric peer ratings of considerateness and selfishness; and a behavioral test of sharing based on the amount of money that they donated to UNICEF from 50¢ they received. The six possible correlations were all positive and ranged from .19 to .38. Girls tended to be more other-centered than boys on several measures. Girls also showed a nonsignificant tendency toward greater consistency among measures, and fifth graders showed a nonsignificant tendency toward greater consistency than eighth grade students.

In a second study by Dlugokinski and Firestone (1974) we find essentially a replication of the previous research. This study varied from the previous work in that in the donation situation two different induction techniques were employed; one emphasized consideration for others, and the other was power-oriented and mentioned that the school principal and the teachers thought that the children should give to UNICEF. Interrelations between the measures of other-centeredness were again generally significant, ranging from .16 to .55. However, Dlugokinski and Firestone (1974) state, "Few of these correlations are impressive, but five sixths of them are reliable at the .05 level of confidence. Whether relationships of this magnitude are strong enough to merit consideration as 'facets of a construct' is debatable. Demonstration of common ties to the socialization process would strengthen such an argument [p. 25]." In the remainder of their paper, Dlugokinski and Firestone provide evidence relating their measures to parental socialization styles, evidence which they feel supports "the existence of an other-centered trait." The extent to which this other-centered trait serves to govern behavior is still called into question, however, by the generally low order relationships found among the measures of other-centeredness.

A study by Rushton and Wiener (1975) also looked at the pattern of generality at different ages. Using 30 7-year-olds and 30 11-year-olds, three behavioral measures of prosocial behavior were obtained: donating tokens to a charity, sharing candy with a friend, and a competitiveness score from a car racing game. Note that these last two measures are borrowed from the previously described study by Rutherford and Mussen (1968). When data were combined across age, generosity to a friend related positively ($r = .24$, $p < .05$) with generosity to a charity, and negatively ($r = -.55$, $p < .001$) with competitiveness. Age differences were also found. There was an increase in the positive relationship between generosity measures from the 7- to the 11-year-old groups ($r = .19$, n.s. to $r = .40$, $p < .01$). (There was also a decrease in the negative relationship between competitiveness and generosity to a friend with a decline between ages 7 and 11 of $r = -.63$, $p < .001$ to $r = -.34$, $p < .05$.) For neither age group was competitiveness related to generosity to a charity. These data support the moderate relationships that seem to be emerging from our review of these studies among measures of prosocial behavior. This study differed from the Green and Schneider (1974) report in that Rushton and Wiener (1975) did obtain greater consistency with age between their two measures of generosity. It is difficult to know exactly how much to make of this increase, since it represents a change from a nonsignificant positive relationship to a moderately strong significant relationship at age 11.

Yarrow and Waxler (1976) report an extensive study of prosocial behavior in children ranging in age between 3 and 7½ with groups spaced at 6-month intervals. This study involved both experimental and naturalistic measures of prosocial behavior. Six experimental measures were taken from two separate adult–child play periods, and three naturalistic measures were taken from observations of the children during free play. Yarrow and Waxler (1976) set up six situations calling for prosocial responding, which they blended as naturally as possible into a stream of events involving play, tests of perspective taking skills, and interactions with an adult. The experimental tasks were two situations each of (a) a sharing task in which the child has an opportunity to share some resources with an adult experimenter (e.g., subject and experimenter are served unequal portions of a snack); (b) a test of helping in which the experimenter spills objects such as a box of tennis balls and the child has an opportunity to aid in picking them up; and (c) a test of comforting in which an experimenter gives evidence of distress (e.g., pinches her finger or appears saddened over reading a sad story). These situations were presented during two 4-minute experimental sessions with one each of the sharing, helping, and comforting tasks presented during each session. The child's responses were recorded on a 1–6 scale by observers who witnessed the interactions through a one-way glass.

The nursery school-aged children (77 out of the total 108 subjects) were also observed in four 10-minute samples of indoor and outdoor free play. Categories of responses included acts of comforting, sharing, and helping someone attain a goal.

In general, no relationship was found between the prosocial measures and age, a result which, although not unique, is inconsistent with the bulk of the studies of prosocial development. Unfortunately, Yarrow and Waxler do not report interrelationships among their individual measures, but we do have some information relevant to the issue of consistency. Scores on sharing (presumably the combined scores from the two sharing tasks) correlated with scores of comforting ($r = .32$, $p < .001$). However, neither sharing nor comforting was related to helping (r's $= -.13$ and .10, respectively). The correlation in the naturalistic data between helping and sharing–comforting was not significant. If the data were combined for sharing and comforting in the experimental situations and correlated with the combined sharing–comforting measure in the naturalistic setting a significant correlation, $r = .29$, $p < .02$, was obtained. Helping scores across settings were not related.

Because of the incomplete reporting of the data, interpretation of the Yarrow and Waxler (1976) findings is difficult. There are also some issues inherent in their design that cloud our conclusions. Since all of the experimental measures involved rendering aid to an adult, Yarrow and Waxler may have been tapping somewhat different processes than is traditionally meant by prosocial intervention. We could reasonably suppose that this factor could increase prosocial intervention because of demand characteristics or decrease it because of children's perceptions of adults as aid givers rather than aid needers. Also since the measures were taken in the same context by the same experimenter, there may have been some reactive effects of the assessment situation that acted to confound the results. However, with these possible limitations in mind we note that, in general, the relationships among different measures of prosocial behavior are not strong, and that there is no evidence of increasing consistency across these ages.

The data from the naturalistic settings are not subject to the potential confounds mentioned above, and they also show very little consistency across measures.

Studies Using Longitudinal Data

There have been very few studies designed to answer the question of this chapter. These would be studies using multiple measures of prosocial behavior and examining children across time to try to ascertain whether coherence increases over time and whether that coherence can be traced to specific underlying processes.

We have found only three studies that have focused on consistency in children's prosocial behavior over time. In the first phase of a longitudinal study (Baumrind, 1971), measures of nurturance toward other children, expressions of sympathy toward them, and understanding of others' perspectives were found to be significantly related to each other. In elementary school, 5-6 years later, ratings were taken again on indexes of social responsibility and altruism. Baumrind found significant relationships among measures at both ages, but more impressively found substantial correlations between measures of a child's prosocial behavior in nursery school and their prosocial behavior 5 or 6 years later ($r = .60$ for boys, $r = .37$ for girls).

In another longitudinal study (Block & Block, 1973), teachers' ratings of prosocial behavior (generosity, helpfulness, empathy) were found to be significantly related to the child's tendency a year later to share earned rewards with a child who was not going to participate in the study.

Finally, Bar-Tal and Raviv (1979) examined sociometric measures of prosocial behavior and behavioral intentions at 2-year intervals. Children were 280 sixth graders. These children were rated by their peers in terms of classroom helping and overall prosocial behavior. They were also rated by their teachers. The children were also assessed on their willingness to volunteer to tutor first and second grade children, willingness to volunteer to spend time reading stories to disadvantaged children, and willingness to volunteer to help poor children in an enrichment program.

The results of the study showed a considerable degree of consistency among the various measures. Two of the volunteering measures showed a correlation of $r = .70$. There also was high agreement in terms of peer and teachers' ratings of altruism ($r = .64$, $p < .01$). In general, the other measures showed positive relationships of a lesser magnitude.

Not all of the measures were administered 2 years later. In general there was a moderate degree of consistency ($r = .19$, $r = .36$) in terms of peer and teacher ratings. This same cross-temporal consistency did not appear for the measures of behavioral intention. None of those correlations were significant.

It should be noted then that impressionistic ratings appear relatively stable across time, but that in terms of behavior there appears to be very little stability. The impressive correlation found within ages should be interpreted in light of the fact that they tapped a rather narrow domain of prosocial behavior which, in fact, only involved volunteering to help, not actual performance of a prosocial action. Volunteering may be under control of very different processes from actual helping.

We now have examined a large number of studies that have employed multiple measures of prosocial behavior. Although we have noted that some consistency does exist, that consistency is far from complete. Thus, the question remains as to what points distinguish among these behaviors. We now will briefly examine some suggestions as to factors that influence prosocial behavior, and which may serve to produce discrepancies among measures of prosocial behavior.

INFLUENCES ON PROSOCIAL BEHAVIOR

Although much of the remainder of this book is devoted to detailing factors that influence prosocial tendencies, we wish to consider some of these processes here in order to see what implications they may have for the question of generality (see also Moore & Underwood, 1981). We shall focus on factors whose effects on different types of altruistic behavior have been noted, which have had differential effects on different types of altruistic behavior, and whose effects lend themselves to speculation about the essential nature of certain types of altruistic behavior.

There has been continuing attention to the possibility of sex differences in children's altruism. Although there have been a number of studies that found no significant sex differences in generosity, there have also been a number that did find significant differences in generosity between male and female children (see Table 2.2). Interestingly, all of these reports of significant sex differences have found females to be more generous than males. Given the number of findings of sex differences and the fact that all these differences are in the same direction, the most reasonable interpretation of this pattern of results would seem to be that there is a sex difference in the population that manifests itself only occasionally because it is a very small difference. The data on helpfulness and comforting show a pattern similar to that for generosity (see Table 2.2), and would seem to justify a similar conclusion. For children's bystander intervention, there has been no report of significant sex differences, and the nonsignificant differences that exist have generally favored males. In fact, there have been reports of adult males scoring significantly higher than adult females on measures of bystander intervention (e.g., Darley & Latané, 1968; West, Whitney, & Schneidler,

Table 2.2
Studies of Sex Differences in Altruism

Type of behavior	Studies finding no significant difference	Studies finding a significant difference
Generosity	Bryan, Redfield, & Mader (1971)	Doland & Adelberg (1967)[a]
	Dreman & Greenbaum (1973)	Harris & Siebel (1975)
	Eisenberg-Berg & Geisheker (1979)	McGuire & Thomas (1975)
	Eisenberg-Berg & Hand (1979)	Midlarsky & Bryan (1972)[b]
	Elliott & Vasta (1970)	Moore, Underwood, & Rosenhan (1973)
	Emler & Rushton (1974)	Rice & Grusec (1975)
	Grusec (1972)	Sawin, Underwood, Weaver, & Mostyn (1980)*
	Grusec, Kuczynski, Rushton, & Simutis (1978)	Skarin & Moely (1976)
	Handlon & Gross (1959)	White (1972)
	Harris (1971)	
	Hull & Reuter (1977)	
	Isen, Horn, & Rosenhan (1973)	
	Israel & Brown (1979)	
	O'Bryant & Brophy (1976)	
	Rosenhan, Underwood, & Moore (1974)	
	Rushton (1975)	
	Ugurel-Semin (1952)	
	Underwood, Froming, & Moore (1977)	
	Yarrow & Waxler (1976)	
Helpfulness–comforting	Eisenberg-Berg & Hand (1979)	Friedrich & Stein (1975)*
	Yarrow & Waxler (1976)	O'Bryant & Brophy (1976)
		Whiting & Whiting (1975)
Bystander intervention	Staub (1970)	
	Staub (1971a)	
	Staub (1971b)	

[a] Significant difference on Trial 1
[b] Significant difference on one of two measures.
*$p < .10$.

1975). It seems that the study of sex differences reveals a pattern for bystander intervention.

A cognitive–developmental variable that has been related to altruism is moral judgment. Several studies have reported higher altruism scores among children with more advanced levels of moral judgment, as measured both by Piagetian strategies (e.g., Emler & Rushton, 1974; Olejnik, 1976) and by Kohlberg's procedures (e.g., Harris, Mussen, & Rutherford, 1976; Rubin & Schneider, 1973). As with perspective taking, one of these studies (Rubin &

Schneider, 1973) found a measure of moral judgment to be significantly related to both generosity and helpfulness. This would seem to be evidence for the equivalence of these two types of prosocial behavior. There is, however, evidence for nonequivalence from a more recent study. Eisenberg-Berg and Hand (1979) used measures of moral reasoning that had been derived empirically (Eisenberg-Berg, 1979) from children's responses to stories about prosocial moral dilemmas. Eisenberg-Berg and Hand found that a measure of spontaneous sharing based on naturalistic observation in a nursery school was significantly related to two of the measures of prosocial moral reasoning, whereas none of the components of prosocial moral reasoning were significantly related to asked-for sharing, spontaneous helping, or asked-for helping. This is an initial indication that generosity and helpfulness may not be equivalent forms of prosocial behavior in children. Indeed, it suggests that there may be important differences among indexes of generosity that could render them nonequivalent. As a final note on moral maturity and altruism, we should point out that the results of Eisenberg-Berg and Hand (1979) cannot truly be said to conflict with results from earlier studies (e.g., Rubin & Schneider, 1973). The Eisenberg-Berg and Hand findings derive from the use of a more differentiated measure of moral reasoning, one constructed specifically for prosocial behavior. Although it may well be true that generosity and helpfulness show similar relationships to a generalized measure of moral reasoning (Rubin & Schneider, 1973), they nonetheless show different relationships to the more differentiated and specific measures of Eisenberg-Berg and Hand.

We shall now turn to individual-difference measures more traditionally associated with the field of personality. Unfortunately, there are so few studies relating personality characteristics to children's altruism that there is relatively little useful information for us in this area. Indeed, the types of personality characteristics measured in different studies vary so dramatically that it is difficult to find a dimension to compare across different measures of altruism. One dimension that has seen recurrent use in studies of children's altruism is the sociability dimension. Rutherford and Mussen (1968) divided nursery school boys into high generous and low generous groups on the basis of the number of candies the boys shared, and compared the two groups on a number of measures, including teacher ratings of the boys. The boys in the high generous group were rated as more sociable than those in the low generous group. Eisenberg-Berg and Hand (1979) examined the relationship between nursery school children's naturally occurring prosocial behaviors and other measures, including a measure of sociability derived from naturalistic observation. They found sociability to be positively and significantly related to both spontaneous helping and asked-for helping, but it was not significantly related to their measures of sharing. This would seem to conflict with Rutherford and Mussen's (1968) finding of a relationship between sharing and sociability in their sample of nursery school boys. Yet another study (Underwood, Froming, & Guarijuata, 1980) has resulted in nonsignificant relationships between sharing and sociability, in this case with elementary school children. It is not entirely clear what to conclude from these studies. If sociability is positively related to helpfulness, as was the case in the only study which investigated that possibility (Eisenberg-Berg & Hand, 1979), and is unrelated to generosity, as was the case in two of the relevant studies (Eisenberg-Berg & Hand, 1979; Underwood et al., 1980) but not the third (Rutherford & Mussen, 1968), then this is further evidence for a psychological distinction between generosity and helpfulness. If sociability is positively related to both generosity and helpfulness, this provides a point of psychological comparability between the two.

A situational variable that has been of great interest to child psychologists is nurturance by adults. Staub (1971a) found that a brief nurturant interaction with the experimenter increased kindergarten children's tendency to intervene in an emergency, and Weissbrod (1976) replicated this promotive effect of experimenter nurturance on children's bystander intervention with first grade boys. Research into the effects of experimenter nurturance on generosity has produced a very different set of findings, most dramatically illustrated by the fact that the same study that found a significant promotive effect of experimenter nurturance on bystander intervention found a significant inhibitory effect on generosity (Weissbrod, 1976). The finding that experimenter nurturance reduces children's generosity has been reported elsewhere (Grusec, 1971), whereas other studies have found no effect of nurturance on generosity (Grusec & Skubiski, 1970; Rosenhan & White, 1967).

Another situational factor that seems to have a differential influence on different types of altruistic action is permission to engage in the action. Staub (1971b) has demonstrated that permission to enter an adjoining room, in which an accident is subsequently heard to occur, significantly increases the bystander intervention scores of both adults and children. The only study that has used instructions giving permission to donate found no facilitative effect of such permission on children's generosity (White & Burnham, 1975). In fact, even mild exhortations to donate have failed to increase children's generosity by significant amounts (Bryan & Walbek, 1970; Grusec & Skubiski, 1970).

Implications of Differential Effects

Whereas the existence of differential influences on different forms of prosocial behavior can often be concluded definitely, the implications of such effects must remain—for the moment at least—speculation. We would certainly be remiss, however, if we did not consider some of the potential implications. The sex differences seem to be consistent with ideas about sex-role orientations. The appearance of a sex difference favoring females in generosity and helpfulness is consistent with an orientation toward nurturance and concern about people, which is often considered part of the traditional feminine role. The absence of a sex difference in bystander intervention (perhaps even, in adulthood, a sex difference favoring males) points to factors unique to bystander intervention as a form of altruism—namely, a necessity for decisive action in a crisis and the possibility of danger to the actor—factors that seem to favor the traditional masculine role. Since several authors have pointed to the importance of concern about the judgments of others—considered more a part of the traditional feminine role—in inhibiting bystander intervention, this factor might also prove to be critical in explaining the distinct pattern of gender differences for this form of altruism.

Maturity of general moral reasoning seems likely to exert its influence through the potential benefactor's perception of his or her own moral obligation to assist others who are in need. This rather general factor in prosocial behavior may even prove to influence children's bystander intervention, although that possibility has not yet been investigated. The finding that spontaneous sharing is negatively related to hedonistic reasoning whereas other forms of prosocial behavior (asked-for sharing, spontaneous and asked-for helping) are not (Eisenberg-Berg & Hand, 1979) may also shed some light on the nature of different forms of prosocial action. It seems understandable that hedonistic reasoning should be related to generosity rather than helpfulness, since one's material resources—presumably a major focus for the hedonist—are diminished through generosity but not through helpfulness. It also seems reasonable that it should be spontaneous rather than asked-for sharing that shows this relationship, since performing asked-for assistance may have more in common with social conformity or compliance than with the voluntary altruistic actions usually thought to be related to moral development.

It is somewhat more difficult to explain why only spontaneous sharing would show a significant positive relationship to needs-oriented reasoning (Eisenberg-Berg & Hand, 1979). It may be that needs-oriented reasoning is related to spontaneous sharing only because of its very substantial negative relationship to hedonistic reasoning. The instrument and scoring system that produced this result are quite recent innovations (Eisenberg-Berg, 1979), and it may be that the natural course of further research involving the instrument will clarify the reasons for this rather puzzling result. The finding that sociability is positively related to helpfulness but not to generosity (Eisenberg-Berg & Hand, 1979) seems to make a great deal of sense because of the nature of those types of behavior. Generosity typically involves an act of sharing that is of limited duration and provides little opportunity for interaction. Helpfulness, however, often involves working with the other person for some period of time. Given the nature of the types of altruistic behavior, it seems likely that the highly sociable person—who, by definition, is attracted to interactions with others—would show a preference for helpfulness.

The different age trends in altruism may also allow us to make useful inferences about the nature of different kinds of prosocial needs. The trend for helpfulness is difficult to ascertain from current data, whereas generosity typically increases with increasing age except for the possibility of a slight decrease in middle childhood. For bystander intervention, however, the initial increase is followed by a dramatic decrease during late childhood or early adolescence, followed by subsequent increase into the adult years. Staub (1971b) speculates that the reason for this decrease is an increasing sensitivity to social censure during late childhood and early adolescence, accompanied by the possibility that children's intervening in such a situation will somehow involve acting when they were not supposed to. If this analysis is correct, it should suggest some variations in the bystander intervention paradigm that would increase the tendency to intervene. For example, simple permission to enter the room in which the emergency occurs should remove the possibility of social censure and increase intervention. Staub (1971b) not only confirmed this prediction, but found that the increase in his sample of early adolescents was sufficient to make their level of intervention roughly comparable to that of his sample of young adults.

The additional finding that short-term experimenter nurturance promotes bystander intervention but may actually inhibit generosity provides additional support for this view. Presumably, interaction with a nurturant experimenter would decrease the likelihood that he or she would express disapproval over the child's attempt to intervene. The very different effect on generosity may clarify some of the differences between generosity and bystander intervention. It is presumed that there is inhibition of intervening in some novel situation due to a fear of social censure. For generosity, there is a very real loss of material resources that may inhibit action, so removing the possibility of censure may remove an obstacle to action for bystander intervention, but serve only to remove an obstacle to inaction in the case of generosity.

SUGGESTIONS FOR FUTURE RESEARCH

Perhaps the most important contribution altruism researchers could make toward establishing the general or differentiated nature of altruistic behaviors would be to broaden their operationalizations of altruism beyond the donation-to-charity paradigm that dominates current research. One of the biggest stumbling blocks to answering the central questions in this area is the dearth of information about children's bystander intervention and, to a somewhat lesser extent, helpfulness. The most useful, although admittedly most tedious, studies would involve multiple measures of altruism so that some judgments about generality could be made on the basis of the results from that individual piece of research even before those results are compared to other work in the field. There have been a few such studies (e.g., Eisenberg-Berg & Hand, 1979; Weisbrod, 1976; Yarrow, Scott, & Waxler, 1973), but many more are needed.

The other major contribution that could be made would be to focus research efforts on what seem to be critical points of differentiation of different forms of prosocial behavior. These points could be derived from the implications of previous work (e.g., the link between hedonistic reasoning and sharing, sociability and helpfulness, or social sensitivity and bystander intervention). Alternatively, they might be derived from a conceptual analysis of altruism, which points to some factors' being important only for certain types of behavior (e.g., rapid processing of information and making decisions in the case of some forms of bystander intervention).

CONCLUSIONS

So what is to be made of these data? We have reviewed a large number of studies that have employed a variety of different methodologies, and we have come up with sometimes contradictory results. Our task of making sense of these data is made more difficult by the fact that, in general, the research has not been developmental in nature, and it has not been very diverse in tapping the domain of prosocial action. For instance, there is only one study that we encountered in which emergency interventions were related to other measures of prosocial action.

Whereas some research finds impressive correlations between measures of prosocial behavior (Block & Block, 1973; Dlugokinski & Firestone, 1973, 1974; Strayer et al., 1979), other studies do not (Green & Schneider, 1974; Yarrow & Waxler, 1976). In general, the relationships that are obtained are of the moderate size (average r about .30) that are frequently observed in studies of interrelationships between measures of behavior sampled in diverse settings. There also does not appear to be much evidence of consistency increasing with age. Whereas Rushton and Wiener (1975) do report a change between 7 and 11 in the amount of consistency observed, Yarrow and Waxler (1976) do not, and Dlugokinski and Firestone (1973) showed a nonsignificant tendency for high consistency among fifth as compared to eighth grade students. If we extrapolate from our research using single-age subjects, we also do not note any greater consistency among measures in studies done with older subjects.

More impressive findings are found by Block and Block (1973) and Baumrind (as reported in Mussen and Eisenberg-Berg, 1977) for consistency within subjects across time. These results are encouraging, and we hope that more research of this nature will be conducted and reported. As we examine the research, it appears that when relationships are obtained that exceed .30 by any great degree they usually involve measures such as impressionistic ratings by teachers or peers or highly similar measures of prosocial behavior (e.g., two measures of volunteering in Bar-Tal & Raviv, 1979).

We are struck by the fact that the meaning that is made of the data on the consistency of prosocial behavior varies to a great degree among individuals. Our conclusions from these data are that there is evidence of a consistency among measures that is of a low to moderate magnitude and is easily disrupted by changes in method of measuring the behavior. Mussen and Eisenberg-Berg (1977) on reviewing essentially the same literature conclude that, "according to the bulk of the evidence, children's prosocial dispositions show appreciable degree of consistency across situations and stability over time [p. 23]." So when we examine the data we note inconsistencies and low-order relationships, whereas Mussen and Eisenberg-Berg examine the same data and see overall coherence and order. These different perspectives doubtless derive from both theoretical predilection and the inconclusive nature of the data.

Mussen and Eisenberg-Berg (1977) feel that "the reported correlations probably underestimate the 'true' relationships between measures [p. 23]." Although we cannot determine with any degree of certainty whether the true magnitudes have been underestimated or overestimated, we feel that we should examine some of the potential sources of misestimation. It has been suggested (Block, 1975) that relationships may be underestimated because some measures are unreliable. If only reliable measures are used, according to this argument, the true magnitude of interrelationships will emerge from the research data, so that research with less reliable measures can—indeed, should—be ignored. This suggestion is completely proper and reasonable given one assumption: namely, that the underlying quantity we are attempting to measure is (at least to a great extent) static and invariant. This is the traditional view from measurement-based psychology that an obtained score consists of a true score that is fixed and an error score that may vary.

Whereas this is certainly one plausible assumption, it is far from being the only plausible viewpoint. We might assume, for example, that obtained scores are (at least to a great extent) perfect measures of the underlying qualities. Adopting this viewpoint, we would conclude that the measures that are most reliable are those that are least affected by the environment, whereas relatively unreliable measures are simply measures that are subject to extreme variation due to environmental presses. We would then expect to find weaker relationships using less reliable measures, simply because elapsed time and a changing situation allow for the person to change what he or she is like. We do not maintain that this viewpoint is correct or that the true-score viewpoint is incorrect. We merely note that they are alternative views of human behavior, and that neither can be safely asserted to be true or false because we cannot directly observe true scores as we would have to do in order to determine the truth of these viewpoints. Since we cannot be certain that the true-score model is correct, we cannot be certain that obtained correlations underestimate the true values.

Another related contention is that strong relationships can only be expected to emerge from the use of composite measures (Epstein, 1979; Mussen & Eisenberg-Berg, 1977). Individual measures, it is argued, are so subject to variation (i.e., unreliable) that they cannot reveal the true strength of the relationship. It is only by summing across individual measures to form a composite score that one can obtain a sufficiently reliable estimate of prosocial tendency to estimate accurately its relationship to other measures. Indeed, it is sometimes the case that composite altruism scores show stronger relationships to other measures (e.g., Krebs & Sturrup, 1974).

Although some differences among people may be revealed by such a strategy, however, others may be obscured rather than revealed. For example, people who score as moderately altruistic on a composite measure may show very different patterns of altruistic action. One person may have such a ranking solely because of great generosity in donations to charity, another because of extensive volunteer work in hospitals and schools, a third because of extreme considerateness and helpfulness in day-to-day contacts with people, and still others because they score as moderately altruistic on all the component dimensions. Such potentially important, and certainly interesting, differences among people are lost when only a composite measure is considered. Empirically, we have noted some cases in which a variable that was significantly related to one measure of altruism was not significantly related to others (e.g., Eisenberg-Berg & Hand, 1979) or was significantly related to another measure but in the opposite direction (e.g., Weissbrod, 1976). In such cases the use of a composite measure would certainly dilute the strength of the relationship, perhaps even to the point of nonsignificance.

Of course, composite measures need not combine across different components of altruism (e.g., combining measures of generosity and bystander intervention into a single composite). It could be argued that combining several instances of the same type of altruistic action should produce a superior measure of altruism, with few attendant weaknesses. This may be true, but there are reasons to believe that even combining within the same modality of prosocial behavior may obscure some important differences. For example, Hampson (1980) pointed to important and predictable differences among adolescent boys in pattern of helpful actions, even among a subsample that had scored quite high on a composite measure of helpfulness.

Even having considered the question of reliability and the use of composite measures, then, we remain convinced that there is evidence for substantial specificity in children's prosocial behavior, as well as evidence for a degree of generality. We should note, however, that the absence of extremely high generality in prosocial behavior does not imply a lack of predictability, or even a high degree of situational influence. There have been several elaborations of interactional models for behavior in general (e.g., Magnusson & Endler, 1977), and of prosocial behavior in particular (e.g., Staub, 1978), which might account for the less than substantial generality in the research data. The model Staub (1978) proposed involves interaction among personality characteristics and elements of the situation to activate what Staub refers to as "personal goals" of helping. Once these prosocial personal goals—a somewhat idiosyncratic set of motives—have been activated, behavior to satisfy those prosocial motives follows. Staub (1978) presents some empirical evidence in support of this model, which would suggest limited generality of prosocial behavior because of differential activation of prosocial personal goals by different situations.

Hampson (1980), in providing evidence for an interactionist model for prosocial behavior, has also demonstrated a possible reason for limitations on generality. Hampson selected the half of his sample of adolescents who had scored as most helpful on six helping tasks. The subjects whom peers had named as more popular were more likely to help on tasks involving interaction with peers, whereas less popular helpers were more likely to help on noninteractional tasks. This is somewhat similar to Eisenberg-Berg and Hand's (1979) finding that sociability is related to a more interactional type of prosocial (helpfulness) but not to a less interactional type (generosity). It is also an excellent example of how a composite measure of helpfulness may obscure predictable differences among people, and perhaps lead to an overestimate of the generality of prosocial behavior. People who are about equally altruistic may express this altruistic tendency in somewhat different ways, producing interbehavior correlations of limited magnitude (as was the case for the correlations among different behaviors in Hampson's study).

These interactionist models seem to be increasing in popularity and, although we recognize that popularity may not be an index of validity, such models seem to be consistent with the data currently available on generality of prosocial behavior. These models certainly would predict some degree of generality, while nonetheless maintaining that the people most likely to exhibit one particular form of altruism are not always the same people who are most likely to display some different form. Both these expectations seem to be met by the data on generality reviewed in this chapter.

REFERENCES

Barnett, M. A., & Bryan, J. H. The effects of competition with outcome feedback on children's helping behavior. *Developmental Psychology,* 1974, *10,* 838–842.

Barnett, M. A., King, L. M., & Howard, J. A. Inducing affect about self or other: Effects on generosity in children. *Developmental Psychology,* 1979, *15,* 164–167.

Bar-Tal, D., & Raviv, A. Consistency of helping-behavior measures. *Child Development,* 1979, *50,* 1235–1238.

Bar-Tal, D., Raviv, A., & Leiser, T. The development of altruistic behavior: Empirical evidence. *Developmental Psychology,* 1980, *16,* 516–524.

Baumrind, D. Current patterns of parental authority. *Developmental Psychology Monographs,* 1971, *1,* 1–103.

Bem, D. J., & Allen, A. On predicting some of the people some of the time. The search for cross-situational consistencies in behavior. *Psychological Review,* 1974, *81,* 506–520.

Block, J. *Recognizing the coherence of personality.* Paper presented at the International Conference on Interactional Psychology, Sweden, 1975.

Block, J., & Block, J. H. *Ego development and the provenance of thought: A longitudinal study of ego and cognitive development in young children.* Progress report for National Institute of Mental Health, Grant no. MH 16080, January 1973.

Bryan, J. H., Redfield, J., & Mader, S. Words and deeds about altruism and the subsequent reinforcement power of the model. *Child Development,* 1971, *42,* 1501–1508.

Bryan, J. H., & Walbeck, N. Preaching and practicing generosity: Children's actions and reaction. *Child Development,* 1970, *41,* 329–354.

Buckley, N., Siegel, L., & Ness, S. Egocentrism, empathy, and altruistic behavior in young children. *Developmental Psychology,* 1979, *15,* 329–330.

Coke, J. S., & Bradshaw, J. C. *Effect of perspective-taking on children's helping.* Unpublished manuscript, University of Kansas, 1980.

Darley, J. M., & Latané, B. Bystander-intervention in emergencies: Diffusion of responsibility. *Journal of Personality and Social Psychology,* 1968, *10,* 202–214.

Dlugokinski, E. L., & Firestone, I. J. Congruence among four methods of measuring other-centeredness. *Child Development,* 1973, *44,* 304–308.

Dlugokinski, E. L., & Firestone, I. J. Other-centeredness and susceptibility to charitable appeals: Effects of perceived discipline. *Developmental Psychology,* 1974, *10,* 21–28.

Doland, D. J., & Adelberg, K. The learning of sharing behavior. *Child Development,* 1967, *38,* 695–700.

Dreman, S. B., & Greenbaum, C. W. Altruism or reciprocity: Sharing behavior in Israeli kindergarten children. *Child Development,* 1973, *44,* 61–68.

Eisenberg-Berg, N. Relationship of prosocial moral reasoning to altruism, political liberalism, and intelligence. *Developmental Psychology,* 1979, *15,* 87–89.

Eisenberg-Berg, N., & Geisheker, E. Content of preachings and power of the model/preacher: The effect on children's generosity. *Developmental Psychology,* 1979, *15,* 168–175.

Eisenberg-Berg, N., & Hand, M. The relationship of preschoolers' reasoning about prosocial moral conflicts to prosocial behavior. *Child Development,* 1979, *50,* 356–363.

Elliott, R., & Vasta, R. The modeling of sharing: Effects associated with vicarious reinforcement, symbolization, age, and generalization. *Journal of Experimental Child Psychology,* 1970, *70,* 8–15.

Emler, N. P., & Rushton, J. P. Cognitive-developmental factors in children's generosity. *British Journal of Social and Clinical Psychology,* 1974, *13,* 277–281.

Epstein, S. The stability of behavior: I. On predicting most of the people much of the time. *Journal of Personality and Social Psychology,* 1979, *37,* 1097–1126.

Friedrich, L. K., & Stein, A. H. Aggressive and prosocial television programs and the natural behavior of preschool children. *Monographs of the Society for Research in Child Development,* 1973, *38* (4, Serial No. 151).

Friedrich, L. K., & Stein, A. H. Prosocial television and young children: The effects of verbal labeling and role playing on learning and behavior. *Child Development,* 1975, *46,* 27–38.

Froming, W. F., & Underwood, B. *Age and generosity.* Unpublished manuscript, University of Florida, 1980.

Gelfand, D., Hartmann, D. P., Cromer, C. C., Smith, C. L., & Page, B. C. The effects of institutional prompts and praise on children's donation rates. *Child Development,* 1975, *46,* 980–983.

Grant, J. E., Weiner, A., & Rushton, J. P. Moral judgment and generosity in children. *Psychological Reports,* 1976, *39,* 451–454.

Green, F. P., & Schneider, F. W. Age differences in the behavior of boys on 3 measures of altruism. *Child Development,* 1974, *45,* 248–251.

Gruseç, J. E. Power and the internalization of self-denial. *Child Development,* 1971, *42,* 93–105.

Grusec, J. E. Demand characteristics of the modeling experiment: Altruism as a function of age and aggression. *Journal of Personality and Social Psychology,* 1972, *22,* 139–148.

Grusec, J. E., Kuczynski, J., Rushton, J. P., & Simutis, Z. M. Modeling, direct instruction, and attributions: Effects on altruism. *Developmental Psychology,* 1978, *14,* 51–57.

Grusec, J. E., & Skubiski, L. Model nurturance, demand characteristics of the modeling experiment and altruism. *Journal of Personality and Social Psychology,* 1970, *14,* 352–359.

Hampson, R. B. Helping behavior in children: A person-situation model. *Developmental Review,* 1981, *1,* 93–112.

Handlon, B. J., & Gross, P. The development of sharing behavior. *Journal of Abnormal and Social Psychology,* 1959, *59,* 425–428.

Harris, M. B. Models, norms and sharing. *Psychological Reports,* 1971, *29,* 147–153.

Harris, M. B., & Siebel, C. E. Affect, aggression, and altruism. *Developmental Psychology,* 1975, *11,* 623–627.

Harris, S., Mussen, P., & Rutherford, E. Some cognitive behavioral, and personality correlates of maturity of moral judgment. *Journal of Genetic Psychology,* 1976, *128,* 123–135.

Hoffman, M. L. Moral internalization, parental power, and the nature of parent-child interaction. *Developmental Psychology,* 1975, *11,* 228–239.

Hull, D., & Reuter, J. The development of charitable behavior in elementary school children. *Journal of Genetic Psychology,* 1977, *131,* 147–153.

Isen, A. M., Horn, N., & Rosenhan, D. L. Effects of success and failure on children's generosity. *Journal of Personality and Social Psychology,* 1973, *27,* 239–247.

Israel, A. C., & Brown, M. S. Effects of directiveness of instructions and surveillance on the production and persistence of children's donations. *Journal of Experimental Child Psychology,* 1979, *27,* 250–261.

Kohlberg, L. Moral stages and moralization: The cognitive-developmental approach. In T. Lickona (Ed.), *Moral development and behavior: Theory, research, and social issues.* New York: Holt, Rinehart and Winston, 1976.

Krebs, D. L., & Sturrup, B. *Role taking ability and altruistic behavior in elementary school children.* Paper presented at the annual meeting of the American Psychological Association, New Orleans, August 1974.

McGuire, J. M., & Thomas, M. H. Effects of sex, competence, and competition on sharing behavior in children. *Journal of Personality and Social Psychology,* 1975, *32,* 490-494.

Magnusson, D., & Endler, N. S. *Personality at the crossroads: Current issues in interactional psychology.* Hillsdale, N.J.: Lawrence Erlbaum Associates, 1977.

Midlarsky, E., & Bryan, J. H. Affect expressions and children's imitative altruism. *Journal of Experimental Research in Personality,* 1972, *6,* 195-203.

Mischel, W. *Personality and assessment.* New York: Wiley, 1968.

Moore, B., & Underwood, B. The development of prosocial behavior. In S. Brehm, S. Kassin, & F. Gibbons (Eds.), *Developmental social psychology: Theory and research.* New York: Oxford University Press, 1981.

Moore, B. S., Underwood, B., & Rosenhan, D. L. Affect and altruism. *Developmental Psychology,* 1973, *8,* 99-104.

Mussen, P. H., & Eisenberg-Berg, N. *Roots of caring, sharing and helping.* San Francisco: Freeman, 1977.

Mussen, P., Rutherford, E., Harris, S., & Keasey, C. B. Honesty and altruism among preadolescents. *Developmental Psychology,* 1970, *3,* 169-194.

O'Bryant, S. L., & Brophy, J. E. Sex differences in altruistic behavior. *Developmental Psychology,* 1976, *12,* 554.

Olejnik, A. B. The effects of reward-deservingness on children's sharing. *Child Development,* 1976, *47,* 380-385.

Rheingold, H. L., Hay, D. F., & West, M. J. Sharing in the second year of life. *Child Development,* 1976, *47,* 1148-1158.

Rice, M. E., & Grusec, J. E. Saying and doing: Effects on observer performance. *Journal of Personality and Social Psychology,* 1975, *32,* 584-593.

Rosenhan, D. L., Underwood, B., & Moore, B. S. Affect moderates self-gratification and altruism. *Journal of Personality and Social Psychology,* 1974, *30,* 546-552.

Rosenhan, D., & White, G. Observation and rehearsal as determinants of prosocial behavior. *Journal of Personality and Social Psychology,* 1967, *5,* 424-431.

Rubin, K. H., & Schneider, F. W. The relationship between moral judgment, egocentrism, and altruistic behavior. *Child Development,* 1973, *44,* 661-665.

Rushton, J. P. Generosity in children: Immediate and long-term effects of modeling, preaching, and moral judgment. *Journal of Personality and Social Psychology,* 1975, *31,* 459-466.

Rushton, J. P., & Wiener, J. Altruism and cognitive development in children. *British Journal of Social and Clinical Psychology,* 1975, *14,* 341-349.

Rutherford, E., & Mussen, P. Generosity in nursery school boys. *Child Development,* 1968, *39,* 755-765.

Sawin, D. B., Underwood, B., Weaver, J., & Mostyn, M. *Empathy and altruism.* Unpublished manuscript, University of Texas at Austin, 1980.

Skarin, K., & Moely, B. E. Altruistic behavior: An analysis of age and sex differences. *Child Development,* 1976, *47,* 1159-1165.

Staub, E. A child in distress: The influence of age and number of witnesses on children's attempts to help. *Journal of Personality and Social Psychology,* 1970, *14,* 130-140.

Staub, E. A child in distress: The influence of nurturance and modeling on children's attempts to help. *Developmental Psychology,* 1971, *5,* 124-132. (a)

Staub, E. Helping a person in distress: The influence of implicit and explicit "rules" of conduct on children and adults. *Journal of Personality and Social Psychology,* 1971, *17,* 137-145. (b)

Staub, E. Helping a distressed person: Social, personality, and stimulus determinants. In L.

Berkowitz (Ed.), *Advances in experimental social psychology* (Vol. 7). New York: Academic Press, 1974.

Staub, E. *Positive social behavior and morality,* Vol. 1: Social and personal influences. New York: Academic Press, 1978.

Staub, E. *Positive social behavior and morality,* Vol. 2: Socialization and development. New York: Academic Press, 1979.

Strayer, F. F., Wareing, S., & Rushton, J. P. Social constraints on naturally occurring preschool altruism. *Ethology and Sociobiology,* 1979, *1,* 3-11.

Ugurel-Semin, R. Moral behavior and moral judgment in children. *Journal of Abnormal and Social Psychology,* 1952, *47,* 463-474.

Underwood, B., Froming, W. J., & Guarijuata, K. *Perspective-taking temperaments, and generosity in children.* Unpublished manuscript, University of Texas at Austin, 1980.

Underwood, B., Froming, W. J., & Moore, B. S. Mood, attention, and altruism: A search for mediating variables. *Developmental Psychology,* 1977, *13,* 541-542.

Weissbrod, C. S. Noncontingent warmth induction, cognitive style, and children's imitative donation and rescue effort behaviors. *Journal of Personality and Social Psychology,* 1976, *34,* 274-281.

West, S. G., Whitney, G., & Schnedler, R. Helping a motorist in distress: The effects of sex, race, and neighborhood. *Journal of Personality and Social Psychology,* 1975, *31,* 691-698.

White, G. M. Immediate and deferred effects of model observation and guided and unguided rehearsal on donating and stealing. *Journal of Personality and Social Psychology,* 1972, *21,* 139-148.

White, G. M., & Burnam, M. A. Socially cued altruism: Effects of modeling, instructions, and age on public and private donation. *Child Development,* 1975, *46,* 559-563.

Whiting, B., & Whiting, J. W. M. *Children of six cultures.* Cambridge, Mass.: Harvard University Press, 1975.

Wiggins, J. S. *Personality and prediction.* Reading, Mass.: Addison-Wesley, 1973.

Yarrow, M. R., Scott, P. M., & Waxler, C. Z. Learning concern for others. *Developmental Psychology,* 1973, *8,* 240-260.

Yarrow, M. R., & Waxler, C. Z. Dimensions and correlates of prosocial behavior in young children. *Child Development,* 1976, *47,* 118-125.

Zinser, O., Perry, J. S., & Edgar, R. M. Affluence of the recipient, value of donations, and sharing behavior in preschool children. *Journal of Psychology,* 1975, *89,* 301-305.

DENNIS KREBS

Altruism—
A Rational Approach

"As one surveys the psychological literature of the last ten years concerned with altruism and helping behavior, one finds that the theoretical clarification of basic concepts which has characterized [the work of] many of the philosophers has not yet been undertaken. On the whole, psychologists have been content with the common sense meaning of the basic terms [Katz, 1972, p. 65]." So wrote Joseph Katz in 1972. In spite of the fact that Katz went on to employ one of my early definitions of altruism as a bad example, I must agree with his general point.

I have given considerable thought over the past few years to the disquieting possibility that when psychologists discuss altruism they do not know what they are talking about, and have come to decide that there is an important sense in which it is true. However, my interpretation of the cause and my prescription for a cure differ quite drastically from those of Katz. Katz recommends two means by which psychology can "move beyond common sense terms": The first is "by causing a wider empirical net. . . . We need . . . to investigate helping in many different social contexts, . . . different rules of conduct, different concepts of 'justice' (altruism) need to be developed for different situations [p. 67]." The second is "by linking investigations to a developing theory of personality and social functioning [p. 67]."

I believe that current research on altruism *is* linked to a general theory of social functioning, and one that is guided by the goal that Katz recommends—investigating helping behaviors in different social contexts. However, I have some questions about the extent to which the theory, or more exactly the epistemology that guides contemporary research on al-

53

THE DEVELOPMENT OF
PROSOCIAL BEHAVIOR

truism, is equipped to supply "theoretical clarification" of the concept. Such conceptual tasks are inconsistent with the general aim of this approach, and may well extend beyond its realm of competence.

THE INFLUENCE OF EMPIRICISM IN
THE STUDY OF ALTRUISM

Let me attempt to explicate some of the defining characteristics of the approach to the investigation of altruism that is most popular in contemporary psychology. Even though the overriding epistemological framework is largely implicit and undefined, it is of some heuristic value to label it. For this purpose I will characterize it as *empiricism*. Historically, empiricism has been contrasted with rationalism. It contains the schools of thought that emphasize the impact of specific, external, tangible, measurable aspects of the environment on learning and knowledge. Locke's tabula rasa concept captures and symbolizes this orientation. The goals of empiricist research are largely practical—to predict and to control behavior. Behaviorism is its most popular form. Social learning theory also stems from this perspective. Rationalism, as portrayed in the philosophical works of Kant and Descartes, emphasizes the impact of the internal organization of the mind on learning and knowledge. It proposes that the mind contains natural organizing and structuring properties that determine what we know.

The original goal of psychology was to understand the mind; but, according to most historians, the field soon came to abandon that aim. In the words of Alexander (1976), "The concept of mind involves a host of intangibles and nonobservables, including thought, emotions, imagination, and will." Thus, in order to "get a grip upon what was at best a slippery discipline anyway, most American psychologists subscribed to the 'behavioural' view that since the mind could not be studied scientifically [i.e., by the methods of empiricism], psychology should ignore it [p. 295]." As pointed out by Pittel and Mendelsohn (1966), this orientation has steered the field away from the investigation of mentalistic phenomena like values: "In attempting to divorce themselves from the methods and conceptualizations of philosophy and religion, psychologists have not only avoided making explicit value judgements but have also slighted moral values as objects of investigation. . . . The behavioristic orientation of modern psychology has fostered a reluctance to study a problem that by its very nature involves subjective processes [p. 22]."

The influence of empiricism on contemporary research on altruism is apparent in the opening sentences of a recent review of the literature on children's helping (Bryan, 1972): "It has been practical concerns which have served as the major impetus for studies of children's helping behavior. There is much interest in developing a technology through which helping behaviors might be generated [p. 87]." From the point of view of empiricism, one behavior is much the same as another behavior—it is determined by the same types of forces. For example, Weiss, Boyer, Lombardo, and Stick (1973) have shown that "altruistic" behavior is controlled by the same principles of reinforcement—delay of reward and punishment, for example—that determine other learned behaviors. Studies on modeling (Bryan, 1972; Rosenhan, 1972) have shown that the same parameters that apply to the modeling of aggressive behavior apply to the modeling of helping (see also Harris, Liquori, & Joniak, 1973). From a strict empiricist perspective, all that is needed is a manipulatable antecedent and a helping behavior to control. Operational definitions are sufficient. Terms like *altruism* or *prosocial behavior* serve to orient the reader and put him or her in a behavioral ballpark. To the empiricist, the enterprise of clarifying concepts is a task for philosophy; the goal of psychology is to predict and control behavior.

If all researchers of prosocial behavior were clear about the explanatory realm in which they operated, they could dismiss the criticisms of scholars such as Katz (1972) as a failure to understand their goals. Unfortunately, however, many of them appear to be taken in by their own labels. They depart from their operations when they characterize their dependent variables—they assume that they are studying "altruism" (which I will define as the willingness to sacrifice one's own welfare for the sake of another) rather than externally defined helping behavior. And they endow their independent variables with a conceptual status that extends far beyond the variables they manipulate. For example, subjects who win at games or find dimes in telephone coin returns (the operationally defined independent variable) are said to help others because of the "warm glow of success" (Isen, 1970). Subjects who are induced to harm others are said to increase their helping behavior because they feel "guilty" (Darlington & Macker, 1966; Freedman, Wallington, & Bless, 1967). Subjects who are led to believe that another is dependent on them for the money he or she makes are said to help because they are reminded of the "norm" of social responsibility (Berkowitz & Daniels, 1963). Some studies take a small conceptual step from their operations; others take an overnight trip. Even if the studies were able to validate the inference that the external operations affected internal processes such as guilt, they would still lack an adequate basis on which to characterize the behaviors they affect as altruistic. Is helping that arises from a "warm glow" more altruistic than helping that arises from feelings of "guilt"? The empiricist approach is poorly equipped to supply answers to questions such as this.

One consequence of the external orientation of empiricism is that almost all studies that purport to elucidate altruism are open to alternate interpretations. Katz (1972) supplies some examples. He questions Fellner and Marshall's (1970) conclusion that kidney donors experience an increase in self-esteem as a consequence of their act because "their life had served a major purpose by greatly helping another person," and wonders whether "some of their sense of well-being arose from a feeling of expiation [p. 66]." Similarly, Katz questions Perry London's interpretation of the factors that influenced Christians who rescued Jews in Nazi Germany (a "zest for adventure, strong identification with a moralistic parental model, and social marginality"): "The suggestion I derive from this study is that these are somewhat alienated people with perhaps a strong dose of reaction formation [p. 66]."

Although I do not feel particularly comfortable with the explanations Katz offers, there is nothing in the studies he cites to establish that his alternate explanations are incorrect. Katz could equally easily reinterpret almost every study on helping behavior in the literature, because the assumption that the helping behaviors that were investigated were mediated by internal *altruistic* dispositions is almost always gratuitous—only one of the many possible interpretations of the results.

I have been evaluating the ability of contemporary research to clarify the concept of altruism. Many psychologists may not share that goal. Indeed, some might dismiss it as uninteresting, untestable, or unscientific, and insist that we should focus our energy on the practical goal of discovering quantifiable causes of helping behavior. However, I cannot help but wonder how many investigators have entered the area with a desire to understand altruism, and have had this complex and significant concern transformed into more simple questions that are amenable to the methods of empiricism. There is reason to wonder whether questions like "Do people help more when they are stationary or moving [Morgan, 1973]?"; "Do people donate more after they see other people donate [Bryan & Test, 1967]?"; and "Do females, males, blacks, or whites help other females, males, blacks, or whites more than other people [Wispé & Freshley, 1971]?" are methodologically simplified substitutes for more significant "philosophical" questions about the meaning and motivation of altruism.

TOWARD THEORETICAL CLARIFICATION OF THE PHENOMENON OF ALTRUISM

When investigating a social phenomenon like altruism, it is worthwhile taking a couple of steps back from the psychological literature and asking what altruism means to the average person. We may not be able to answer the questions that lay people bring to the area. We may have to refer them to a philosopher, minister, or poet. However, I hope to show that there is an approach in psychology that is equipped to answer many of the questions that average people ask about altruism, and thereby to supply the type of theoretical clarification of the concept that Katz found lacking in the contemporary literature.

Let us consider a simple incidence of helping—say one in which an old man carries a young lady's groceries to her car for her. What question does this raise for the impartial observer? Well, the first thing he or she would want to know is *why* the old man helped the young lady. At first glance it appears that the observer is asking the same question as an empirically oriented psychologist. The observer *is* asking the same question, but the types of answers that he or she is searching for are different. The person on the street does not want to predict and control the old man's behavior; the average person wants to *define* the behavior and *evaluate* it (and through the behavior in most cases, to define and evaluate the old man). He or she wants to know something about the old man's motives, his intentions, his reasons for helping. The average person interprets behavior in terms of the contents of people's minds—the "host of intangibles and nonobservables, including thought, emotions, imagination, and will"—the excess baggage that empiricism jettisoned decades ago.

Let us consider some reasons why old men help young ladies. For subsequent convenience, let us consider six:

1. To avoid a punishment or obtain a reward—the old man's wife may have told him to help the young girl, or else
2. To initiate an exchange with the young girl, who, he has been led to believe, likes old men
3. To fulfill the expectations of his social role—he may believe that men should help women
4. To conform to a social norm—he may believe that everyone in his society is obliged to help those who need help
5. To behave in a way that is consistent with maximizing the benefits of the greatest number of people
6. Out of moral principle—because it is consistent with his conception of justice

From a behavioral perspective, the reasons underlying helping behaviors such as these do not affect the conceptual status of the dependent variable—carrying a bag of groceries. Studies that have investigated each of the six determinants of helping typically are classified together as studies on "altruism" or "prosocial behavior." However, from the perspective of the average person, the externally similar behaviors take on different meanings in terms of the value attached to the underlying causes. The average person might characterize the first act as fearful, cowardly, or obedient; the second as expedient or opportunistic; the third as stereotyped or conforming; the fourth as socially responsible; the fifth as humanitarian; and the sixth as moral or principled. The person on the street makes little distinction between philosophical and empirical concerns. When he or she observes an act of helping, the scientist in him or her wants to know what caused it so the ethical philosopher in him or her can evaluate it. The main reason why empirical psychology falls short of answering the questions that the average person has about altruism is that it is primarily equipped to take only the first step—determining the antecedents of helping behaviors—in a two-step process that gives the behaviors meaning.

Even the most ardent empiricists acknowledge that people evaluate the behavior of others. Skinner acknowledges that inasmuch as an impartial observer infers that the latter examples of helping we have been considering are more internally determined than the earlier ones, he or she would believe that they are of higher value: "Any evidence that a peron's behavior may be attributed to external circumstances seems to threaten his dignity or worth. We are not inclined to give a person credit for achievements over which he has no control [Skinner, 1972, p. 44]." Skinner, of course, argues that the idea that we control our own behavior, and the accompanying ideas of autonomy, responsibility, freedom, and dignity are popular illusions. I do not know for sure how exclusively our behavior is controlled by the external environment; however, I would like to argue that dismissing the types of inferences that the average person makes, including his or her evaluations, because they do not correspond to the scientist's theory of behavior may cause one to overlook a centrally significant determinant of behavior. The ideas that people have about altruism—their values and evaluative processes—help determine how they behave. One way of extending the analysis of altruism, of studying issues that are relevant to the average person, and, I believe, of obtaining greater clarification of the concept, is to investigate the ways in which people form values such as altruism. Even if such values are inaccurate representations of the external world, they are real to the people who make them.

TRADITIONAL APPROACHES TO THE
INVESTIGATION OF EVALUATIVE IDEAS

The research of Milton Rokeach (1971a, b; 1973) is representative of psychological research on values. It is useful, therefore, to examine it in search of a basis from which to clarify the construct of altruism.

Rokeach (1971a) opens the description of a recent series of studies on values by saying, "Suppose you could take a group of people, give them a

20-minute pencil-and-paper task, talk to them for 10-20 minutes afterward, and thereby produce long-range changes in core values and personal behavior in a significant portion of this group [p. 68]." The purpose of such an exercise? "For openers, it would of course have major implications for education, government, propaganda and therapy [p. 69]." The author defines values as "either a desirable end-state of existence (a terminal value) or a desirable mode of behavior (an instrumental value). . . . A person can have thousands of attitudes, but only a few values that transcend and dynamically determine these thousands of attitudes [p. 70]." Rokeach suggests that there are about 18 "terminal" values, and a slightly larger number of "instrumental" values. Some terminal values are "a comfortable life," "family security," "happiness," "wisdom," "love," "friendship," "freedom," and "equality." Some instrumental values are "ambitious," "clean," "obedient," "responsible," and "helpful" ("working for the welfare of others"). Rokeach employed terminal values in the study I will now describe, but he just as easily could have employed the instrumental value of altruism.

Subjects were required to rank the 18 terminal values in order and indicate their attitude toward the civil rights movement. Rokeach (1971b) found that about 40% of his subjects either: (a) ranked the value freedom above the value equality; or (b) ranked the value equality low on their value hierarchy, yet indicated sympathy for the civil rights movement. The experimenter made subjects aware of the apparent inconsistency between their attitudes and values and/or the inconsistency among their attitudes. He suggested by implication that the subjects were "much more interested in their own freedom than other people's," or he led students to discover "that they had been doing their liberal thing because it was fashionable rather than because of principle." The author found that these simple manipulations had far reaching effects: "Fifteen to 17 months after the experimental session . . . the experimental group had increased its ranking of equality an average of 2.68 units (on an 18-point ranking scale) while the control group had increased its ranking of equality only .32 units [Rokeach, 1971a, p. 456]." Freedom increased by 1.59 units and .22 units. The author also found that experimental subjects manifested more positive attitudes about civil rights than control subjects, and, most dramatically, that they were significantly more prone to respond favorably to a request to join the NAACP.

I have described Rokeach's research in considerable detail in order to exemplify the following point: Although we might expect research on subjective events such as values to depart significantly from the empiricist tradition, and therefore to supply a basis from which to clarify the construct of altruism, it typically does not. Note the similarities between Rokeach's approach and the approach that characterizes the typical study on helping behavior. The overriding goal of both types of research is practical—to "understand causation" and "master nature." Research on "altruism" seeks to predict and control helping behavior, and research on values seeks to change hierarchies of values in order to manipulate social behavior. The fruits of both types of research are most relevant to the socializing agents and institutions of society—parents, teachers, politicians, therapists. Common-sense definitions serve to orient the reader. Operational definitions are employed for the purpose of experimentation. Specific external stimuli are maniuplated, and their effect on specific measurable responses is assessed. The average responses of groups of subjects are employed as dependent measures of change. Subjective events like values obtain significance inasmuch as they relate systematically to externally manipulated variables and externally measured behavior.

In addition to methodological empiricism, Rokeach endorses a theoretically empiricist framework to explain the origin and development of values. According to Rokeach (1973), people acquire values from the social environment: "Every human value is a 'social product' that has been transmitted and preserved in successive generations through one or more of society's institutions [p. 24]." Theoretical assumptions about the nature and number of values follow from assumptions about their determinants. Rokeach (1973) acknowledges that all the possible permutations of values far exceed the combinations that people possess. He explains the reduction as follows:

> We may expect that similarities in cultures will sharply reduce the total number of possible variations to a much smaller number, shaping the value systems of large numbers of people in more or less similar ways. Further reductions in possible variations can moreover be expected within a given culture as a result of socialization by similar social institutions; similarities of sex, age, class . . . race, . . . religious upbringing, . . . ; political identification . . . ; and the like [p. 23; This quotation and subsequent quotations from Rokeach: *The Nature of Human Values* are reprinted with permission from The Free Press, a division of Macmillan Publishing Co., Inc., copyright © 1973.].

Having attempted to show how research on values such as that of Rokeach is shaped by the methods and theory of the empiricist epistemology, I would now like to identify what I believe to be some shortcomings of this approach. Permit me to make explicit reference to the research I have been describing. Although undoubtedly uncharitable, such argument by example is, at least, heuristic.

My major point is this: In rendering complex subjective events like values amenable to manipulation and measurement, empiricist approaches typically remove them from their natural context and render them superficial. Consider, for example, some of the assumptions that follow from the operationalization and quantification of values in the Rokeach study: (a) "Values" like happiness, friendship, and, indeed, pleasure are qualitatively the same as values like freedom and equality; (b) values like freedom and equality mean the same thing to different people; (c) when one person ranks equality lower than freedom, it is comparable to the same rank ordering in another person; (d) changes in rank order are quantitative rather than qualitative—2.68 versus .32 units on a scale; (e) a person who receives a gain score of 2.00 because he or she changes equality from eighteenth to sixteenth is indicating the same value orientation as a person who changes equality from third to first; and so on. Values are treated as canned products with labels like freedom and equality, to be arranged and rearranged on the shelves of the mind. In operationalizing phenomena such as values and in treating them as specific stimuli and specific responses, empiricist research robs them of their richness and renders them artificial. Indeed, in cases where subjects protest that the list of values that the experimenter supplies is not representative of their own or in cases where subjects ask for clarification, they may well be instructed to do the task in the best way they can in order not to confound the experimental manipulations; or they may be thrown out of the experiment.

Considered behaviorally, Rokeach found that some people changed the rank order of the "value" equality on paper after they were implicitly told that they would seem inconsistent or hypocritical if they did not. I believe that there is good reason to doubt whether this finding reflects a "significant change in bedrock standards [p. 68]." It is worth taking the role of a subject in the experiment and trying to understand from the subject's point of view why he or she might change the rank order of the value equality and change his or her behavior. It seems plausible to assume that most subjects inferred that the experimenter was trying to determine what kinds of things they desired for *themselves*. The average subject may have thought: "It is important to me that *I* am free, but it is less important to me that *I* am equal." Then, along comes an experimenter who says, in effect, "Ranking freedom higher than equality means that you don't value freedom for *other* people." "But," thinks the subject, "that's not what I believe at all." He or she feels falsely accused, and thinks, "I *do* value freedom for all, and if the way to communicate it is by ranking equality higher, that's what I will do." Thus, the behavior of the subjects in this experiment may not have revealed a change in bedrock values at all; rather, it may have signified only the clarification of an ambiguous situation, some social influence, and perhaps a little conformity. Most people are willing to make concessions to avoid the appearance of hypocrisy.

VALUES AND VALUE JUDGMENTS

I have been arguing that the task of supplying conceptual clarification of concepts like freedom, equality, or altruism generally falls outside of the range of concern of empiricist approaches to psychological research. One implication of the inability of the popular empiricist approach to teach us what altruism and other values are is that they are also unable to teach us what values are better than others, that is, to evaluate values. It is only when we understand the nature of evaluative ideas that we have a basis for deciding among them.

Many psyhologists believe that the institution of science (by which they typically mean empiricism) is value-free, and that as psychologists they cannot (and should not?) make value judgments. Consider for example the following typical statement by Harold Kelley (1971):

> I am attempting to analyse the processes by which people make judgments of what is morally good or bad; the processes by which moral judgment are rendered of persons and their behavior, the processes by which persons make statements about what ought to be done. I find no basis in this analysis for saying what is morally good or bad, or what people should regard as morally good or bad. And I give no independent definition of moral judgments. For my purposes, they are judgments the people who render them would say are "moral" [p. 293].

If you assume that ideas exist "out there" in the environment as isolated events that are waiting to be internalized, one idea is much the same as another. The belief that certain phenomena (say freedom and equality) are better than other phenomena (say a comfortable life or pleasure) is arbitrary and relative. The only basis on which the value of values can be judged is empirical—if a society or group or person believes that the uncontrolled pursuit of pleasure is more lofty than the pursuit of justice, the empiricist must simply report this fact as the way their world is arranged. Similarly, if one society, group, or person believes that altruism means helping others in order to maximize personal gain, and another society, group, or person believes that altruism means helping others in order to fulfill a social contract, there is no way an empiricist can determine the validity of these ideas. Definitions of phenomena like altruism are as arbitrary as hierarchies of values. Any group or person can create a definition of altruism in the same way that any group or person can create a hierarchy of values.

On the face of it, the empiricist point of view seems quite reasonable. It makes sense to assume that different people could possess concepts like altruism that have a unique meaning to them. The same goes for values. Empiricists are quick to argue that, although we consider it terribly wrong to kill old people in our culture (but, perhaps, permissible to allow them to wither away), other groups, such as Eskimos, consider it proper to do away with their elders. We might feel quite strongly that the Eskimos' values are wrong, but an objective scientist would insist that our reactions are ethnocentric. Although *we* believe in freedom and equality, and although *we* believe it is right to help people who need help, these are *our* arbitrary values. Other people in other places may not share them. Similarly, if I believe that it is right to help people and you believe it is wrong, there is no way scientifically to resolve the conflict.

As popular as the empiricist's characterization is, I believe that it is essentially incorrect. At least I am willing to argue with conviction that it is limited. It succeeds quite well in the task for which it is equipped—to supply a refined reflection of the environment; however, it fails to supply meaning to the environment, because it looks in the wrong place. In my view, meaning does not exist out in the external world; rather, it is manufactured by people. The *contents* of the mind might roughly match the contents of the environment—*what* people believe, *what* problems they encounter, *what* symbols they employ—but the relationship among the units, the organization of thought, is not simply internalized from outside; it is created as an interaction between our ability to know and the subject matter on which this ability operates. It is possible that the order and organization of ideas can supply a basis for defining altruism, and, indeed, it may even supply a basis for evaluating the adequacy of hierarchies of values.

SOME DEPARTURES FROM EMPIRICISM

I have used the research of Rokeach as a typical example of research on values, and I have argued that it is limited by the empiricist epistemology in which it is rooted. I would now like to discuss two important senses in which the research of Rokeach departs from the dominant epistemology. Although statements like "Suppose you could take a group of people, give them a 20-minute pencil-and-paper test, talk to them for 10 to 20 minutes afterward, and thereby produce long-range changes in core values and personal behavior . . ." lead us to believe that the locus of change is the environment, Rokeach identifies a more proximal locus of change that bears a less direct relationship to the external world—cognitive inconsistency. It is important to note that this force, which is treated as an intervening variable in Rokeach's study, is not an aspect of the external world like the influence of the experimenter; it is a cognitive structural variable that relates to the internal organization of thought. It is interesting to ask what caused the reported change in values—the fact that the experimenter thought that there was an inconsistency or that the subjects believed their values were inconsistent. It is my guess that the "long-range" changes that were reported in the experiment were a function of the social influence of the experimenter and, as such, superficial and tentative (to be changed again by the next person in authority). I suspect that truly deep and permanent changes in thought are caused by structural forces like cognitive inconsistency, and that it takes a lot more than a disparity in the rank order of values in a psychological experiment to produce them.

If an investigator were to accept the idea that there is a logic to hierarchies of values and the inconsistency is intrinsically inadequate, he or she would have a platform from which to evaluate systems of values. The investigator could, as a scientist, follow the natural example of his or her subjects rather than imposing his or her own point of view on them. Rokeach (1973) actually does accept the idea that certain values are better than others, but, perhaps sensing that this assumption is inconsistent with the overriding methodological perspective that guides his research, he steps out of this perspective and appeals to a qualitatively different theoretical approach:

> Thus far in this discussion we have deliberately avoided labeling certain values as better or of a higher order than others. We have done so in the hope of demonstrating that it is possible to describe the values that people hold in a value-free manner. But it is now perhaps appropriate to suggest that values serving adjustive, ego-defensive, knowledge, and self-actualization functions may well be ordered along a continuum ranging from lower- to higher-order, as is suggested by Maslow's well-known hierarchical theory of motivation [p. 16].

I believe that, in the final analysis, purely empirical explanations of values will prove internally inconsistent. If values are internalized from outside, what is the basis on which they can be judged as higher or lower than one another? Do systems of values reflect the order of the environment, or are there structural characteristics like internal consistency that affect their order and determine their change? Are people passive recipients of environmentally supplied values, or do they contribute to their formation? The obvious answer might seem to be that ideas are affected from both the inside and the outside, and this answer seems certainly correct; but the explanations supplied by most investigators do not address the interaction between the internal and external forces; and they do not synthesize them in a coherent way. Most studies in the literature—I have used those of Rokeach as one of many possible examples—are entrenched in the perspective of empiricism, but occasionally and inconsistently break free. They take short jaunts out of the parent point of view in order to supply obvious explanations of isolated events, and they adopt other perspectives to explain phenomena that are inexplicable within the dominant framework. However, they fail to follow the logic of their departures to its full significance, which, I believe, would eventually entail major modifications in the perspective from which they began.

A RATIONAL APPROACH TO THE INVESTIGATION
OF EVALUATIVE IDEAS

At this point I would like to introduce another approach to the study of altruism, one that I believe is equipped to help solve the problems associated with the empiricist approaches that I have reviewed. What is needed is a perspective that can (a) account for the fact that people evaluate phenomena like helping behavior; (b) explain the fact that people have different values—that they evaluate helping behavior differently; (c) respond to and explain people's conceptions of phenomena such as altruism in all their complexity; (d) explain the nature and origin of values; and (e) most ambitiously, supply a basis for making value judgments—indicating which conceptions of values are most adequate, and why. To respond to these demands, I will turn away from the epistemological tradition of empiricism and follow a quite different trend of thought—one that springs from the ideas of early rationalist philosophers. It is called by several names in its modern forms: "genetic epistemology," "cognitive development theory," and "structuralism."

Howard Gardner's (1973a,b) introduction to the methods and goals of structuralism supplies an engaging introduction to the epistemology of rationalism:

> Suppose you, as the proverbial visitor from a distant planet, were to land in Yankee Stadium. A baseball game is in progress and, curious about the folkways of earthlings, you follow the action with great attention. At first the proceedings seem senseless. You do not understand the reasons for uniforms, the crowd of people in the stands, the numbers on the scoreboard, the loud-speaking system, the peculiar behavior of the players. Ignorant of the language, you must rely exclusively on your perception of the activities to unravel the game.
>
> Soon you begin to recognize certain regularities. You notice that the men in dark blue remain stationary throughout the game; that the players fall into two discrete groups; that the groups alternatively remain in the field, then take their turns at bat. It would take you longer to discern the subtleties of play: the rules that determine balls and strikes, innings, runs, hits and errors. And you probably would have to watch for months before sorting out the gyrations of the first- and third-base coaches, and the key to ground-rule doubles.
>
> Eventually, given sufficient ingenuity and patience, you should be able to ferret out the rules of the game, teasing the incidental features (color of uniforms, peanut vendors, size of the ball park) from essential ones (number of men on a team, rules for pinch hitting, procedure for a double play).
>
> In its broadest outlines, the task of structural analysts like Jean Piaget and Claude Levi-Strauss is akin to the task confronting the alien at Yankee Stadium. Structuralism is a method or approach that attempts to get below the flow of day-to-day events and discover the arrangements of elements that govern our behavior [pp. 166–167].

The "complex phenomenon" that is in question here is the rules that govern the evaluation of helping behavior. Gardner suggests that if we observe people in helping situations long enough, "given sufficient ingenuity and patience," we should be able to "ferret out the rules of the game." According to Gardner this task will involve separating out arbitrary, culturally relative styles or twists from deeper universal laws. The reason why structuralists believe that they will find a universal order to behavior is because they believe there is a universal order to the mind—that what people do is governed by how they view their world:

> The primary vision underpinning this approach is the faith that human beliefs, human development and human institutions reflect the fundamental nature of human thought and the biological structures of the mind. The idea that the mind is central to human behavior is controversial, but it is an idea deeply ingrained in Piaget, Levi-Strauss and their colleagues. It serves as a point of departure for their theories [Gardner, 1973b, p. 58].

Let us pause here for a moment and acknowledge the most frequent and powerful question that is (and should be) raised about the methods of structuralism. Walter Mischel (1969) puts the point well:

> Clinically, it seems remarkable how each of us generally manages to reconcile his seemingly diverse behaviors into one self-consistent whole. A man may steal on one occasion, lie on another, donate generously to charity on a third, cheat on a fourth, and still construe himself readily as "basically honest and moral." Just like the personality theorist who studies them, our subjects also are skilled at transforming their seemingly discrepant behavior into a constructed continuity, making unified wholes out of almost anything [p. 1012].

What can structural theory do when two different scientists or people on the street present two equally coherent or internally consistent "unified wholes," or systems of explanation for the same phenomenon? I must admit that reading some structural analyses feels a little like intruding on someone's private delusions. One answer is that it is impossible for two structural analyses of the same phenomena to be equally well differentiated, integrated, organized, and veridical. I think most structuralists would adopt the point of view that there is only one set of laws that govern the mind, and their job is to find it. Whether this is true or not, I believe we need more than an end point analysis of the structure of events. I believe the reason why early rational philosophers never convincingly proved their point was because they had no way to evaluate their analysis from the outside, and no objective way to decide between the systems of ideas proposed by different philosophers.

It was part of the extraordinary genius of Jean Piaget to supply a criterion of evaluation for structural analyses that lies outside their systems (see Krebs, 1978b). Like so many great ideas, Piaget's method of solving the rationalist's problem is deceptively simple. Piaget proposed that instead of attempting to decipher the finished product (the laws of behavior and the laws of the mind), we should observe the *development* of cognitive structures. The developmental strategy allows an investigator to begin at the beginning—to observe the simpler, more concrete, and manageable conceptions and evaluations of infants. It alerts him or her to one of the most basic differences among people—the differences that come with age and maturity. Observing the growth of ideas allows an investigator to map the laws of their organization and change. It allows him or her to discover regularities among the systems of thought that characterize children of various ages and to attend to the organizational principles within each system.

The central empirical claim of cognitive-developmental theories like that of Piaget is that children's ideas about their world change with maturity. The central conceptual claim is that there is an inherent logic to the change—ideas *grow* in systematic ways. When a cognitive-developmental theorist speaks of stages of reasoning, he or she does not mean arbitrary or environment-induced changes in what people think. He or she means qualitative transformations that encompass and improve upon previous ways of thinking. Piaget (1960) clarified his conception of stage by listing four essential characteristics:

1. Stages imply distinct or qualitative differences in structures (modes of thinking) which still serve the same basic function (e.g., intelligence) at various points in development.
2. These different structures form an invariant sequence, order ot succession in individual development. While cultural factors may speed up, slow down, or stop development, they do not change its sequence.
3. Each of these different and sequential modes of thought forms a "structured whole." A given stage-response on a task does not just represent a specific response determined by knowledge and familiarity with that task or tasks similar to it; rather, it represents an underlying thought-organization.
4. Stages are hierarchical integrations. Accordingly, higher stages displace (or, rather, reintegrate) the structures found at lower stages [Kohlberg, 1973, p. 498].

It is not that older children are at a different stage (i.e., have a different point of view) from younger children that matters most; it is that they have a point of view that "contains" the points of view that they had when they were younger. The systems of thought that define mature stages of reasoning are "better" than immature systems of thought, because they account for everything that the earlier systems accounted for, and more—more logically, and in a more differentiated and integrated manner. From this perspective, the essential difference among adults is that some possess more mature values (or conceptions of phenomena like altruism) than others; they have conceptions that are more fully developed, mature, and, therefore, better.

Cognitive-developmental theorists have one foot in the domain of the empiricist—they examine the way people actually think; and they have one foot in the domain of the rational philosophy—they look at the structure and organization of systems of thought. It is this dual orientation that permits the cognitive-developmental theorist to bridge the gap from the empirical world to the world of values. He or she has two bases from which to argue that one system of ideas is better than another—because it entails a more advanced step in the developmental sequence (i.e., everyone who thinks that way has already thought the previous way), and because it contains more elaborate and sophisticated transformations of previous systems of thought. In the same way that each system or "stage" in the developmental sequence can be examined within itself, all the systems of thought can be examined as a whole, and the laws of change can be plotted.

It is easy to see how a structural analysis of a phenomenon like altruism would require different methods from the methods of an empiricist analysis. The structuralist is concerned with the rules of overriding systems of thought and behavior, not with the relationship between specific causes and effects. The structuralist observes a multitude of behaviors in their natural form and searches for regularities. This much is empirical. However, the primary task is conceptual. In order to interpret the behavior, the structuralist must engage in the creative exercise of discovering the systems of rules that explain it. Structural theory assumes a kind of faith or trust in the human mind that empiricist theory does not. The empiricist seeks to understand how the environment controls behavior. The structuralist assumes that the behavior of humans is primarily controlled, or at least regulated, by their minds. One of the greatest aids to structural analysis is what people say about what they do. In assuming that the behavior of "subjects" is governed by the organization of their thought, the structuralist can appeal to them to help explicate the implicit rules. The task of structuralism is similar in many ways to the traditional task of the anthropologist. Both structuralists and anthropologists attend to what people do and to what they think about what they do; but, ultimately, these investigators must develop an overriding system of explanation (an ethnology) that accounts for both types of observation.

STRUCTURAL ANALYSIS: AN EXAMPLE

This is not the place to undertake a structural analysis of altruism. However, some sense of the nature of the approach can be conveyed by returning to the six examples of helping behavior that I presented previously, and interpreting them from a structural point of view.

I argued that average people evaluate acts of helping in a relatively predictable way. To take one example, they evaluate acts of helping that are predicated on fear of punishment less favorably than acts of helping that stem from a sense of duty, a value, or moral principle. These claims are empirically verifiable. We could go out into the streets and observe people's reactions to various acts of helping; we could rely on their memories and ask them to report how they reacted to incidents such as these; or we could present people with samples of helping behavior and ask them to evaluate them. Our goal would be to "ferret out the rules of the game"—to discover the principles they employ in making their evaluations, and to search for the types of relationships that define the overriding evaluative system.

Inevitably, people who possess the same evaluative structures will evaluate the same acts of helping in somewhat different ways. The task of the investigator is to discover the core characteristics of superficially different evaluations—to tease out the "accidental features" from the "essential ones." Consider for example the responses of two children I once interviewed to one of Piaget's (1932/1965) classic questions—is it worse to break 15 cups accidentally or one cup with bad intentions? One child said it was worse to break 15 cups. Another of the same age said, "one cup." Clearly, their answers were different. When I asked the first child why he believed it was worse to break 15 cups he said, "Because 15 cups are worth more money than 1 cup." When I asked the second child why it was worse to break 1 cup, he said, "Because 1 cup is rare, and rare things are expensive." The children's initial answers (like most isolated behavior acts) were ambiguous. Although they appeared different on the surface, they were similar in underlying structure. Both children based their judgments of naughtiness on tangible concerns of material loss—a characteristic that has been found by a number of investigators to characterize the (moral) thought of young children (see Damon, 1977; Kohlberg, 1976; Piaget, 1932/1965).

A structural-developmental strategy helps us separate the superficial from the significant because it permits us to identify the ways in which people's conceptions of phenomena such as altruism and morality change as they develop, and to trace the form of their transformation. In Chapter 9 of this volume, Nancy Eisenberg reviews research on the development of children's conceptions of kindness, altruism, and prohibitive morality. Eisenberg and her colleagues have found that the typical reasons given by children concerning why people should help others undergo a number of qualitative changes as the children grow older (see Eisenberg-Berg, 1979; Eisenberg-Berg & Hand, 1979; Eisenberg-Berg & Roth, 1980). These researchers have isolated five "stages" of prosocial reasoning, roughly defined in terms of children's orientation to (a) their own needs; (b) directly and simply, the needs of others; (c) conventional role expectations and social approval; (d) empathy, social norms, and social responsibility; and (e) ethical responsibility.

Research such as this supplies a basis for explaining why, in the examples I gave earlier, most adults would evaluate the first act of helping (where the old man helped to avoid his wife's wrath) less favorably than the second act (where the old man sought to initiate a reciprocal exchange of sorts with the young lady). It also supplies a basis for understanding the sense in which the second act is "better" or of higher value than the first act. It is predicated on a more mature and sophisticated evaluative system (available only to relatively mature people), which, if the assumption of structural theorists such as Piaget and Kohlberg is correct, subsumes the first system (i.e., organizes conceptions of rewards, punishments, and duty into a better equilibrated and more complex system).

This is not the place to give an exhaustive characterization of the stages of evaluative thought that have been outlined by various investigators. Structural researchers of various persuasions (those studying cognitive development, moral development, the development of prosocial reasoning, ego development, development of idea self) have found that there are a number of characteristics that tend to differentiate early orientations from later modes of thought. The observable surface characteristics of early social and moral thinking (i.e., the *content* of the young child's thought) typically include an orientation to physical, material, tangible consequences, to rewards and punishments, to the power of authorities, and to the child's own needs and point of view (see, for example, Eisenberg's scheme, Chapter 9). Structural analyses such as those of Damon (1977), Kohlberg (1976), and Piaget (1932/1965) attribute this pattern of observable ideas and attitudes to underlying structural characteristics such as the tendency to think in either-or, black and white terms (i.e., the inability to make fine differentiations and broad integrations); the inability to understand abstract, subjective phenomena such as intentions; and the young child's egocentricity.

It is helpful to note that an empiricist analysis of such patterns of thought would focus exclusively on the content—the correlated system of ideas, attitudes, and values. In this type of analysis the association of ideas would not be attributed to the internal structure of thought, but, rather, to the external environment: the fact that different people have different sets of attitudes and values occurs because they grow up in different subcultures. Structural-developmental theory, of course, explains the correlation of attitudes in a much different way. It proposes that it is a "natural" product of the structure of thought. The reason why children analyze altruism in terms of rewards, punishments, and their own needs is not because their worlds contain only rewards, punishments, and their own needs, but rather because they understand their worlds in these terms (i.e., the form of their thought is concrete [versus abstract], physicalistic [versus attentive to internal subjective events], egocentric, etc.).

How can the validity of the structural versus empiricistic interpretation of the correlation of attitudes about events like helping be determined? We might examine people in different families, subcultures, and societies and check for differences in thought. This is a notoriously difficult enterprise, and it may be unnecessary. If children's ideas about issues like helping change in the predictable, systematic ways outlined by structural theorists, and if there is intergenerational change in a culture's attitudes and values, it is difficult to see how the ideas could simply have been internalized from the environment. The central claim of a structural approach to altruism would be that all people develop ideas about altruism in an orderly manner—that, for example, all people first believe that people help in order to obtain rewards and avoid punishments, then they believe that people also help in order to maintain expedient exchanges, then also to conform to social expectations, and so on. This claim is empirically verifiable. If the evidence supports the claim, and if no corresponding systematic change in the environment can be invoked plausibly to explain it, there must be a strong presumption that the systems of ideas reflect the ordering properties of the mind as it is formed by and gives meaning to the social world.

In an important sense, the empirical task of verifying the existence of certain ideas about helping, determining the correlation among them, and assessing the order of their development is the easy part of a structural analysis. The difficult part is determining which characteristics of the ideas stem from aspects of underlying structures of knowing, and which do not—much like the hypothetical alien analyzing Gardner's baseball game. This task involves determining the organizing principles and logic of the system, and, I believe, it supplies the only way of obtaining theoretical clarification of ideas like altruism. Returning to the example, we would ask why people evaluate the behavior of the old man increasingly favorably (I am assuming for the sake of the discussion that we have found through observation that they do), and why the six types of evaluation define developmental trends. We might note that each incident is determined by events that are more internal, general, abstract, inclusive, rational, and less directly dependent on environmental events or other people. We might note that each system of interpretation is more differentiated, integrated, and well organized. The model that emerges is one of increasing power to the O (organism; in this case the structure of prosocial reasoning) in the S-O-R (stimulus-organism-response) sequence. The incidents appear to stem more and more from the forces of higher cognitive processes and to become increasingly well adapted to the purposes they are put.

If thought does develop through structural transformations, and if the later structures contain earlier structures, we would expect people at later stages of development to be able to resolve conflicts between competing alternatives that people with less mature conceptions could not. For example, two Stage 1 children might believe that it is right for them to take another child's toy, but wrong for another child to take theirs. At Stage 2, the children would be able to resolve conflicts such as this with the aid of conceptions of reciprocity. The Stage 2 system of concrete reciprocity, even though it is essentially expedient, organizes the rewards and punishments, gains and losses of interpersonal exchanges into a balanced system that guides social life in a more adaptive manner than the unmitigated control of power and pleasure. Further up the hierarchy, we might devalue a person who reciprocates in a concrete way when this course of action comes into conflict with a still higher principle intrinsic to a still more balanced, more adaptive system of social exchanges (if, of course, we can comprehend it). Stage 2 concrete reciprocity is a better system than the unhindered pursuit of pleasure; but as feuds and revenge show, it is quite imperfect. It is not efficient to return every favor in kind, tit for tat. There are times when we need more help than other times; there are people, for example children and individuals with various handicaps, who need more help than other people, etc. We would devalue a mother who kept track of all she had done for her children, and demanded it back. We would devalue a policeman who asked the owner of the goods he recovered to repay him in kind. The system (or, at least one system) that extends the system of concrete reciprocity is the system of social roles (a defining characteristic of the Stage 3 orientation). From the Stage 3 point of view, we expect certain types of people to help other types of people in the ways prescribed by their social roles, and, frequently, not in other ways. We may not resent it when our boss asks us to type a letter, but we may feel quite put out when the same request comes from a fellow secretary or a stranger. We may accept with gratitude a grocery boy's offer to help us pack our bags, but feel disconcerted by the same offer when it comes from a little old lady. The reason why some "liberated" women refuse to allow males to open doors for them is because they believe it reinforces a system of sex roles in which the role of women is subordinated to the role of men.

What I am doing, of course, is attempting to explain why each of the first three systems of evaluation is better than its predecessor—to explicate the logic of the natural progression. I will not continue with my analysis because it is not original, and it has, for all intents and purposes, been done better elsewhere (see Kohlberg, 1976).

Before closing this description of structural analysis of helping behavior, I should address one final concern. I have asserted that a number of different investigators have conducted structural analyses of social and moral thought, and I have implied that these analyses have produced essentially the same results. I must acknowledge, however, that the products of different analyses are not identical. To consider one comparison, for example, Eisenberg (Chapter 9) concludes that "reasoning regarding different types of moral dilemmas may vary in structure and developmental course [p. 245]." This conclusion raises an important question. To what extent does the thought of the child (or adult) stem from one overriding cognitive structure, and to what extent does it stem from a number of different structures that govern, if you will, different domains of experience (prohibitive morality vs. prosocial morality, physical phenomena versus social phenomena, etc.)? At present this question is unanswered. Piaget (1932/1965) appears to endorse the assumption of a single overriding structure; Kohlberg (1976) suggests that certain structures are necessary for the development of others; and Turiel (1977) and Damon (1977) assume that different structures develop in different domains (see Krebs & Gillmore, in press, for an elaboration and empirical investigation of this issue).

MORAL DEVELOPMENT AND ALTRUISM

I opened this discussion with a quote by Joseph Katz, and have spent considerable time attempting to respond to his main point—that psychologists have failed to clarify the concept of altruism because they have not produced an adequate theory to explain it. I would like to close this paper with a brief discussion of what I believe to be a confusion in Katz's conception of altruism—one that is quite common in the literature. Katz (1972) wrote "different rules of conduct, different concepts of justice (altruism) need to be developed for different situations [p. 67]." I have already taken exception to the focus on situations. I now want to take exception to the equation of justice and altruism. In my view, altruistic behavior is not necessarily moral or just behavior. In fact, inasmuch as the idea of altruism means giving more than one's share, or giving more than one "should," it entails a violation of the balance of reciprocity that defines justice (which we can visualize as two equal scales) (see Krebs, in press). It is doubtless true that one of the most common ways to behave unjustly is to behave selfishly (i.e., take more than one's share); and that is probably why we tend to equate selfishness with injustice. However, behaving justly involves much more than living by a simple rule of generosity. It is not enough to err on the side of others even if it does tend to make them happy. In order to behave justly a person must understand what is owed to whom by whom, and what he or she has a right to expect in return. Any violation of the equilibrium, be it positive or negative, disrupts the balance that defines justice.

One of the implications of this point is that relatively well-documented stages of moral development outlined by Kohlberg and his colleagues do not define stages of altruism. Similarly, the "stages" of prosocial moral reasoning outlined by Eisenberg (Chapter 9, this volume) are not based on increasingly "altruistic" motives (by which I mean the willingness to sacrifice one's own welfare for the sake of another). In fact, concerns about altruism and the belief that the way to behave morally is to behave altruistically probably peak at Kohlberg's Stage 3 (which is usually reached in early adolescence and is characteristic of a sizable portion of the adult population). I have attempted elsewhere (Krebs, 1978a) to explain why this peak occurs at Kohlberg's Stage 3. Briefly, I attributed it to the change from the concretely reciprocal role-taking perspective that helps define Stage 2 moral reasoning ("Do unto others as they do unto you") to the ideally reciprocal role-taking perspective characteristic of Stage 3 ("Do unto others as you would have them do unto you"). When a person is capable of viewing a decision from only one perspective at a time (his or her own, then another person's, etc.), the reasoning provides little basis for the decision to sacrifice his or her own interest. When a person becomes able to adopt the perspective of the "generalized other" (the abstract expectations of all relevant others that are sometimes embodied in social roles), he or she sees many more reasons to behave altruistically (i.e., for the good of others).

Although we tend to like people who are guided by a Stage 3 moral orientation because they tend to be concerned with empathy, generosity, and self-sacrifice, the Stage 3 moral orientation contains serious deficiencies. Inasmuch as moral conceptions become motivating forces, Stage 3 altruism seeks to meet the expectations of significant others, fulfill the demands of stereotyped social roles (for example, to be a good husband or wife, father or mother), and to gain social approval. The deficiencies of the Stage 3 moral orientation become apparent when conflicts occur between the expectations of two or more groups of significant others. It fails to contain higher order principles that can be employed to resolve the conflicts. For example, when asked whether it would be as right to steal a drug to save the life of a stranger as to steal a drug to save the life of a friend, people who employ Stage 3 reasoning typically believe that it is more morally correct to save their friend. This type of thinking is susceptible to disequilibrium because it implies asserting that one act is moral for one person and that the opposite act is moral for another person. If Person A is my friend and Person B is your friend (but a stranger to me), there is no way from a Stage 3 perspective we can agree on the morally correct course of action. It is intuitively obvious to most of us that behaving in a way that shows favoritism to friends, making decisions that please the members of our reference group, and seeking to maximize approval from others fall short of our moral ideals.

It is appropriate to conclude this discussion with some reference to the relationship between morality and altruism, because it supplies, in my view, an unfinished example of the type of conceptual clarification of ideas like altruism that can be obtained through structural analysis. As I pointed out in an early review of the literature on altruism (Krebs, 1970), altruism is an idea in the minds of people. It can be whatever people think it is. What I have been discovering in the years since I wrote the review is that considerable "theoretical clarification" of ideas about phenomena such as altruism can be obtained by studying them in a developmental context (see Krebs & Russell, 1981).

REFERENCES

Alexander, T. Psychologists are rediscovering the mind. In D. Krebs (Ed.), *Readings in social psychology: Contemporary perspectives.* New York: Harper & Row, 1976.

Berkowitz, L., & Daniels, L. R. Responsibility and dependency. *Journal of Abnormal & Social Psychology,* 1963, *66,* 429-436.

Bryan, J. H. Why children help. *The Journal of Social Issues,* 1972, *28,* 87-104.

Bryan, J. H., & Test, M. A. Models and helping: Naturalistic studies in aiding behavior. *Journal of Personality and Social Psychology,* 1967, *6,* 400-407.

Damon, W. *The social world of the child.* San Francisco: Jossey-Bass, 1977.

Darlington, R. B., & Macker, C. E. Displacement of guilt-produced altruistic behavior. *Journal of Personality & Social Psychology,* 1966, *4,* 442-443.

Eisenberg-Berg, N. The development of children's prosocial moral judgment. *Developmental Psychology,* 1979, *15,* 128-137.

Eisenberg-Berg, N., & Hand, M. The relationship of preschoolers' reasoning about prosocial moral conflicts to prosocial behavior. *Child Development,* 1979, *50,* 356-363.

Eisenberg-Berg, N., & Roth, K. The development of children's prosocial moral judgment: A longitudinal follow-up. *Developmental Psychology,* 1980, *16,* 375-376.

Fellner, C. H., & Marshall, J. R. Kidney donors. In J. Macaulay & L. Berkowitz (Eds.), *Altruism and helping behavior.* New York: Academic Press, 1970.

Freedman, J. L., Wallington, S. A., & Bless, E. Compliance without pressure: The effect of guilt. *Journal of Personality & Social Psychology,* 1967, *7,* 117-124.

Gardner, H. France and the modern mind. *Psychology Today,* 1973, *7,* 58. (a)

Gardner, H. *The quest for mind.* New York: Alfred A. Knopf, 1973. (b)

Harris, M. B., Liguori, R., & Joniak, A. Aggression, altruism, and models. *The Journal of Social Psychology,* 1973, *91,* 343-344.

Isen, A. M. Success, failure, attention and reaction to others: The warm glow of success. *Journal of Personality & Social Psychology,* 1970, *15,* 294-301.

Katz, J. Altruism and sympathy: Their history in philosophy and some implications for psychology. *The Journal of Social Issues,* 1972, *28,* 59-70.

Kelley, H. H. Moral evaluation. *American Psychologist,* 1971, *26,* 293-300.

Kohlberg, L. Stages and aging in moral development—Some speculations. *The Gerontologist,* 1973, Winter, 497-502.

Kohlberg, L. Moral stages and moralization: The cognitive-developmental approach. In T. Lickona (Ed.), *Moral development and behavior.* New York: Holt, 1976.

Krebs, D. Altruism—An examination of the concept and a review of the literature. *Psychological Bulletin,* 1970, *73,* 258-302.

Krebs, D. A cognitive-developmental approach to altruism. In L. Wispé (Ed.), *Altruism, sympathy, and helping.* New York: Academic Press, 1978, 141-164. (a)

Krebs, D. The moral judgment of the child: Reconsidered. *Human Nature,* January 1978, 93-95. (b)

Krebs, D. Prosocial behavior, equity, and justice. In J. Greenberg & R. L. Cohen (Eds.), *Equity and justice in social behavior.* New York: Academic Press, in press.

Krebs, D., & Gillmore, J. The relationship among the first stages of cognitive development, role-taking, and moral development. *Child Development,* in press.

Krebs, D., & Russell, C. Role-taking and altruism. In P. Rushton & R. Sorrentino (Eds.), *Altruism and helping behavior.* Hillsdale, N.J.: Lawrence Erlbaum, 1981.

Mischel, W. Contituity and change in personality. *American Psychologist,* 1969, *24,* 1012-1018.

Morgan, W. G. Situational specificity in altruistic behavior. *Representative Research in Social Psychology,* 1973, *4,* 56-66.

Piaget, J. *The moral judgment of the child.* New York: Free Press, 1965. (Originally published, 1932.)

Piaget, J. The general problem of the psychobiological development of the child. In J. M. Tanner & B. Inhelder (Eds.), *Discussion on child development* (Vol. 4). New York: International Universities Press, 1960.

Pittel, S. M., & Mendelsohn, G. A. Measurement of moral values: A review and critique. *Psychological Bulletin,* 1966, *66,* 22-35.

Rokeach, M. Long-range experimental modification of values, attitudes, and behavior. *American Psychologist,* 1971, *26,* 453-459. (a)

Rokeach, M. Persuasion that persists. *Psychology Today,* September 1971, *92,* 68-71. (b)

Rokeach, M. *The nature of human values.* New York: Free Press, 1973.

Rosenhan, D. L. Learning theory and prosocial behavior. *The Journal of Social Issues,* 1972, *28,* 151-164.

Skinner, B. F. *Beyond freedom and dignity.* New York: Alfred A. Knopf, 1972.

Turiel, E. The development of concepts of social structure. In J. Glick & A. Clark-Stewart (Eds.), *Personality and social development* (Vol. 1). New York: Gardner Press, 1977.

Weiss, R. F., Boyer, J. L., Lombardo, J. P., & Stick, M. H. Altruistic drive and altruistic reinforcement. *Journal of Personality & Social Psychology,* 1973, *25,* 390-400.

Wispé, L., & Freshley, H. Race, sex, and sympathetic helping behavior: The broken bag caper. *Journal of Personality & Social Psychology,* 1971, *17,* 59-65.

Social Learning Theory and the Development of Prosocial Behavior

INTRODUCTION

This chapter is divided into three major sections. The first of these describes four phenomena in the development of prosocial behavior that require explanation. These are (a) the increase of prosocial behavior with age; (b) the development of moral judgment toward increasing ethical altruism with age; (c) the positive relationship between moral judgment and prosocial behavior; and (d) the trait of altruism or consistency across situations. The second major section describes the social learning theory explanation of prosocial behavior and moral judgment. Here emphasis is on experimental rather than correlational and observational studies. Considered will be Pavlovian and instrumental learning and learning through the observation of others and through verbal procedures. The final section discusses the degree to which social learning theory accounts for the phenomena described in the first section and illuminates some challenging issues that remain.

THE PHENOMENA TO BE EXPLAINED

The Increase of Prosocial Behavior with Age

Piaget (1932) charted the emergence of "true" cooperation around the age of 7 and suggested that this occurred because children could at that age see the world from the perspectives of other people. Wright (1942) provided

77

early evidence that sharing increased with age. For example, 8-year-olds were more generous than 5-year-olds when asked to let a friend play with the more attractive of two toys. In yet another early study on sharing, Ugurel-Semin (1952) gave Turkish children nine nuts to share with a friend. In terms of behaving generously and giving the extra nut to their friend, Ugurel-Semin (1952) found a dramatic increase as the children became older. Whereas only 33% of 4-6-year-olds gave away the extra nut, 77% of 7-10-year-olds did, and 100% of 11-16-year-olds did so.

Other researchers also have found that children's sharing increases with age. The procedure used in many of these studies was as follows: Children aged 6-13 played a bowling game (see Figure 4.1) from which they could win tokens. These tokens could be exchanged for prizes at the end of the game on the basis of the more tokens won, the better the prize given. The tokens were therefore of some value to the children. Before playing the game, the children were shown a picture of an unhappy-looking child depicted on a "Save the Children Fund" charity poster. This child was de-

Figure 4.1. **The author and experimenter (ca., 1973) and a miniature bowling alley of the type often used in studies of children's generosity. Players reward themselves with tokens for "winning" scores (e.g., 20). These tokens are later exchangeable for various prizes on the basis of the more tokens, the better the prize. Before taking the tokens to the experimenter, however, children have the opportunity to donate some of them to "poor little Bobby," the child depicted on the charity poster.**

scribed as "poor little Bobby," who has "no mummy or daddy or anybody to look after him." Below the poster was a charity box. The children were told that if they wanted to they could share some of their winnings with Bobby by putting some of their tokens into the donation box. The children then were left entirely alone in the room to play the game and give to Bobby if they wanted to. Unknown to each child, the bowling game was programmed in such a manner that each child won exactly the same number of tokens, that is, 16. In this way it was possible to quantify exactly how generous each child was. As a single test of children's generosity, this procedure appears to be both reliable, as measured by test–retest correlations, and construct-valid, as indexed by teacher ratings and correlations with other measures of children's altruism (Rushton & Wheelwright, 1980).

The percentage of the child's winnings donated to Bobby in three studies is shown in Table 4.1 as a function of age. In each study the 11-year-olds gave away a greater percentage of their winnings than did the 7-year-olds. The column on the right gives the Pearson-product-moment correlation between age in months and number of tokens shared, and also indicates the sample size.

In one of the studies, the children were brought back 2 months later to play the bowling game a second time to see if their behavior would remain consistent (Rushton, 1975). Once again, they were given the opportunity of donating. There was considerable consistency in the two testing occasions, and, as can be seen, the differences between older and younger children became even clearer.

In another of the studies, a second measure of generosity was also taken (Rushton & Wiener, 1975). After the children had played the bowling game and given to Bobby, they were given 24 candies as a prize. They were also given two paper bags. On one was written the child's name, and on the other the name of his or her best friend. They were told that if they wished to give any of the candies to their friend they could do so in the bag provided. The experimenter then left the children alone to divide their candies. As the children left the room, the experimenter suggested they leave the two bags on a nearby shelf until the end of the day. This allowed the experimenter to count the candies. Table 4.1, shows that this measure also yielded the expected age difference. Eleven-year-olds shared 42% of their candies, but 7-year-olds shared only 21%.

It is not only generosity that increases with age. Green and Schneider (1974) found evidence that children's helping also increases. In one situation, the experimenter "accidentally" dropped a number of pencils on the floor. The results of the study showed that helping to pick up the pencils increased over the age range of 5–10 years, at which time virtually all the children helped. Friedrich and Stein (1973) coded the free play behavior of

Table 4.1

Generosity in Children: Percentage Shared as a Function of Age

Study	Measure of generosity	Age/years							Correlation
		7	8	9	10	11	12	13	
Emler & Rushton (1974)	Valued tokens donated to a charity on immediate test	14%	37%	24%	31%	29%	34%	36%	$r = .22^*$ (N = 60)
Rushton (1975)	1. Valued tokens donated to a charity on immediate test	19%	26%	28%	25%	33%			$r = .18^*$ (N = 134)
	2. Valued tokens donated to a charity on 2-month retest	17%	14%	26%	23%	41%			$r = .41^{**}$ (N = 134)
Rushton & Wiener (1975)	1. Valued tokens donated to a charity	19%				38%			$r = .47^{**}$ (N = 60)
	2. Candies shared with best friend	21%				42%			$r = .68^{**}$ (N = 60)

Source: J. Philippe Rushton, Altruism, Socialization, & Society, © 1980, p. 68. Reprinted by permission of Prentice-Hall, Inc., Englewood Cliffs, N.J.
$^*p < .05.$
$^{**}p < .001.$

3-5-year-old children into several categories of prosocial behavior. They found that both cooperation and nurturance increased with age.

It might be noted that some studies have found no relationship between age and prosocial behavior (e.g., Hartshorne, May, & Maller, 1929). Nonetheless, enough studies have found this relationship for us tentatively to assume its existence, a conclusion also reached by other reviewers of this same literature (e.g., Mussen & Eisenberg-Berg, 1977; Staub, 1979).

Before leaving this section, we might note in passing that, in addition to age, there are many other "person characteristics" associated with prosocial behavior that there is not space to explore. Among the most interesting, perhaps, are the studies that find that girls are, on average, more prosocial than boys (see Rushton, 1980, for a review). These other person characteristics also need explanation.

The Development of Moral Judgment toward Increasing Ethical Altruism with Age

Piaget (1932) is the beginning reference here. His research methodology involved telling children a variety of stories and then asking them what they thought. For example, these two are concerned with sharing:

> One afternoon, on a holiday, a mother had taken her children for a walk along the Rhone. At four o'clock she gave each of them a roll. They all began to eat their rolls except the youngest, who was careless and let his fall into the water. What will the mother do? Will she give him another one? What will the older ones say [Piaget, 1932, p. 267]?

and

> Two boys, a little one and a big one, once went for a long walk in the mountains. When lunch time came they were very hungry and took their food out of their bags. But they found that there was not enough for both of them. What should be done? Give all the food to the big boy or to the little one, or the same to both [Piaget, 1932, p. 309]?

On the basis of responses to stories such as these, Piaget (1932) described three broad "stages" of development in conceptions of justice. The first was the *authority* stage, at which there is no idea of justice as distinct from the arbitrary demands of elders. Children at this stage of development would be likely to respond to the first story in terms of the mother punishing the child, and to the second in terms of the elder child having more, simply because he is the bigger. Next comes the stage of *equality*, in which authority is subordinate to the requirements of strict equality of treatment. Thus in the first story, the child would argue that the mother ought to give her child another roll so that "everybody would have the same amount." Likewise, in the second story, "both children should have equally." Finally, the *equity* stage sees a shift from rigid equality toward recognition of the relativity of individual needs and circumstances. Thus in the first story, the child might be excused and given another roll because he or she was "the youngest and it was an accident," and in the second either the older "because he would have a bigger appetite" *or* the younger "because he couldn't manage as well as the other."

This tripartite-stage theory of the development of justice overlaps with Piaget's (1932) views on wider aspects of morality in which essentially the child is viewed as progressing from a stage of egocentric morality based on authority and punishment to one based on cooperation, mutual respect, and the awareness of others' needs. According to Piaget, the morality of cooperation begins to emerge around the age of 7 and increases until around the age of 12, when mutual respect and consideration for others are firmly established.

Kohlberg (1969) extended Piaget's work to include six stages (grouped into three "levels") of development into adulthood. More recently, Kohlberg (1978) suggested that Stage 6 may not exist, and that Stage 5 is the highest level. Regardless of the number of stages, many individuals never reach the higher levels. Kohlberg (1969), like Piaget, presented moral dilemmas in the form of stories to listeners, and asked them what they thought. An example of such a dilemma is

> In Europe, a woman was near death from cancer. One drug might save her, a form of radium that a druggist was charging $2,000, ten times what the drug cost him to make. The sick woman's husband, Heinz, went to everyone he knew to borrow the money, but he could only get together about half of what it cost. He told the druggist that his wife was dying and asked him to sell it cheaper or let him pay later. But the druggist said, "No." The husband got desperate and broke into the man's store to steal the drug for his wife. Should the husband have done that? Why [Kohlberg, 1969, p. 379]?

The classification of possible responses to this moral dilemma involves six stages beginning with punishment-based obedience, and developing through instrumental hedonism, approval-seeking conformity, respect for authority, contractual legalistic observance, and finishing with internalized universal ethical principles.

It might be interesting for the reader to attempt to provide rationales *against* Heinz stealing the drug from the perspective of each of the stages and compare these with those of Kohlberg (1969, pp. 379–380). Examples of arguing *in favor,* from each of the stages, are the following (based on Kohlberg, 1969, pp. 379–380):

Stage 1. It is okay to steal because the drug is worth only $200. It is not as though he were stealing a $2000 drug.

Stage 2. It is all right to steal because she needs it and he wants her to live.

Stage 3. He should steal the drug. He was doing only what was natural for a good husband to do.

Stage 4. If you did nothing you would be letting your wife die, and it is your responsibility if she dies.

Stage 5. The law was not set up for these circumstances. Taking the drug in this situation is not really right, but he is justified in doing it.

Stage 6. In choosing between the two evils of stealing and letting your wife die, it becomes morally right to steal because preserving life is more important.

Responses to these stories show a developmental trend with age to increasing ethical altruism. Furthermore, within age, higher moral development is found with higher IQ, higher level of education, and higher socioeconomic status. (For research even more explicitly concerned with *prosocial* reasoning, see Eisenberg's Chapter 9, this volume.)

The Positive Relationship between Moral Judgment and Prosocial Behavior

Numerous studies have found that individuals with "high" levels of moral judgment as assessed on a variety of moral reasoning tasks are also those who are most prosocial in their behavior (Eisenberg-Berg, 1979; Emler & Rushton, 1974; Harris, Mussen, & Rutherford, 1976; Krebs & Rosenwald, 1977; Rubin & Schneider, 1973; Rushton, 1975; Rushton, Chrisjohn, & Fekken, 1981; and Staub, 1974). These studies differed considerably from each other in the age range tested, the measure of moral judgment used, and the indexes of prosocial behavior assessed. For example, Rubin and Schneider (1973) gave 55 7-year-olds six moral judgment dilemmas as adapted from Kohlberg, and two opportunities to behave generously. The first measure of generosity was donating candy to poor children, and the second was helping a younger child complete a task. They found a significant positive relationship between level of moral judgment and the degree of altruism shown on both tasks.

Emler and Rushton (1974) used the two moral judgment stories from Piaget (1932) described above, and found that prediction of 60 7–13-year-olds' donations to charity could be made from knowledge of their level of moral judgment. Rushton (1975) replicated the Emler and Rushton

(1974) findings with 140 7-11-year-olds, and showed that the relationship between moral judgment and altruism held up over a 2-month retest.

The findings are not limited to laboratory measures. For example, Harris et al. (1976) used *peer ratings* of how prosocial the children were, and found these correlated positively with moral judgment.

Finally, there are studies with adults. Perhaps the most extensive of these was by Staub (1974). He found that adults at higher "stages" on Kohlberg's test engaged more frequently in helping and rescue behavior in laboratory situations than those at lower levels. Krebs and Rosenwald (1977) demonstrated that "scores" that adults received on Kohlberg's tests predicted whether they would mail a questionnaire back to the experimenter at some inconvenience to themselves. Whereas over 90% of those at Stages 4 and 5 helped in this way, only 40% of those at Stages 2 and 3 did so. Finally, Rushton et al. (1981) found that level of moral judgment, as assessed by Rest's (1979) objectively scored *Defining Issues Test*, correlated positively with whether respondents report, on a self-report altruism scale, having engaged in such behaviors as making change for a stranger, donating blood, and allowing someone to go first at a supermarket checkout counter.

In summary, there is now increasing evidence that knowing the "stage" of moral reasoning at which a person is allows prediction as to how considerate of others he or she will be. A recent review by Blasi (1980) demonstrates that this statement holds for a variety of moral behaviors.

The Trait of Altruism: Consistency across Situations

For several decades there have been two opposing viewpoints on the question of whether human behavior is generally consistent in different situations. Known as the "specificity versus generality" controversy, the question has loomed particularly large in the area of personality and moral behavior. The classic study of this problem was the enormous "Character Education Enquiry" carried out by Hartshorne, Maller, May, and Shuttleworth in the 1920s and published from 1928 to 1930 in three books: *Studies in Deceit, Studies in Service and Self-Control,* and *Studies in the Organization of Character.* These investigators gave 11,000 elementary and high school students some 33 different behavioral tests of their altruism, self-control, and honesty in home, classroom, church, play, and athletic contexts. At the same time, extensive ratings of the children's reputations with their teachers and their classmates were taken in all these areas. By intercorrelating the children's scores on all these tests, it was possible to discover whether the children's behavior was specific to situations or generalizable across them. If the children's behavior is generalizable across situations, then the correlations should be substantial. We thus have a crucial test of the generality hypothesis.

What were the results from this extremely large and intensive study? First, let us consider the measures of altruism. The behavioral measures intercorrelated a low average of +.23 with each other, thus suggesting support for the specificity viewpoint. However, if the five measures were combined into a battery, they correlated a much higher +.61 with the measures of the child's altruistic reputation among his teachers and classmates. Furthermore, the teacher's perceptions of the students' altruism agreed extremely highly ($r = +.80$) with that of the students' peers. These latter results indicate a considerable degree of generality and consistency to altruistic behavior. Virtually identical results as the above were found for the measures of "honesty" and "self-control." Any one behavioral test correlated, on average, only a lowly +.20 with any one other behavioral tests. If, however, the measures were combined into batteries, then much higher relationships were found with either teacher ratings of the children or with any single measure taken alone. Typically, these correlations were of the fairly high order of +.50 and +.60. Correlations of this magnitude are really quite high, and allow for prediction of what a person will do in a new situation from knowledge of how he or she has behaved in similar situations in the past.

Since the pioneering work of Hartshorne et al. (1928, 1929, 1930), many other studies have provided data that speak directly to the "specificity versus generality" of altruism. As has been reviewed elsewhere (Rushton, 1976, 1980, 1981b), the typical correlation between any two behavioral indices is about +.30. Combining measures, however, again led to a substantially greater degree of predictability. For example, Dlugokinski and Firestone (1973) took four measures from 164 children aged 10-13; a pencil-and-paper measure of how they understood the meaning of kindness; a pencil-and-paper measure of the relative importance of altruistic as opposed to selfish values; judgments from their classmates of how generally considerate they were viewed to be; and a behavioral measure of donating money to a charity. The six possible correlations were all positive and ranged from +.19 to +.38. Further multiple correlations of any three variables as predictors of the fourth ranged from +.42 to +.51. In a later paper, Dlugokinski and Firestone (1974) replicated these relationships. Other studies have examined the relations among children's naturally occurring altruism. For example, in an extensive study of children's free-play behavior in a natural setting, Strayer, Wareing, and Rushton (1979) observed 26 children over a 3-hour period. These authors found relationships of +.50 and +.60 among such coded altruism as donating and sharing objects, cooperation, and helping.

On the basis of a great deal of evidence, it would seem that there is a "trait" of altruism (Rushton, 1980, 1981b). Some people *are* consistently more generous, helping, and kind than others. Furthermore, such people are readily *perceived* as more altruistic, as is demonstrated by the several studies showing positive relationships among behavioral altruism and peers' and teachers' ratings of how altruistic a person seems (Dlugokinski & Firestone, 1973, 1974; Hartshorne *et al.*, 1929; Krebs & Sturrup, 1974; Rushton & Wheelwright, 1980). The stability of individual differences in behavior traits is not, of course, limited to altruism (see Rushton, Jackson, & Paunover, 1981, for a more extended discussion).

THE SOCIAL LEARNING OF PROSOCIAL BEHAVIOR AND MORAL JUDGMENT

Overview

From the social learning point of view, the degree to which a person engages in prosocial behavior, as well as the frequency and patterning of that behavior, is largely the result of the person's previous learning history. In other words, a person is honest, generous, helpful, and compassionate to the degree to which he or she has learned to be so. Thus, if we wish to understand how children develop prosocial consideration for others, it is necessary first to understand the "laws of learning."

It must be stated at the outset, however, that there are many, rather different theories of social learning that differ among themselves on such issues as (a) what the most important processes of learning are; (b) what they conceptualize the hypothetical products of learning to be; and (c) how important they believe genetic factors are.

The theory put forward by Eysenck (1977), for example, emphasizes the role of Pavlovian conditioning, that the product of learning is conditioned affect (usually anxiety), and that large individual differences exist in the nervous systems people inherit that predispose them to being "conditionable." The theory put forward by Aronfreed (1976) also stresses the importance of Pavlovian conditioning. This theory, however, emphasizes the attachment of affect to cognitive representations of reality known as "schemata" or "templates," which are then said to guide behavior. The theory does not speak to the issue of the genetics of behavior. Bandura's (1977) social learning theory, however, emphasizes the role of learning from the observation of others (referred to as "models"). This theory views the products of learning as consisting of a variety of cognitive constructs that together make up the "self-system." Generally speaking, the theory de-emphasizes and/or even opposes an explanation of behavior in terms of genetic predispositions. One theory perhaps even more cognitive is the approach of Mischel and Mischel (1976). This approach views all forms of learning as mediated through cognitive representation, and appears to place less emphasis on the role of affect. Finally, at the other extreme is Skinner's (1971) radical behaviorism, which states that operant conditioning is the primary method of human learning, and that a scientific explanation of human behavior does not require recourse to *any* hypothetical mediators, including those of affect and cognition.

Although it is necessary to point out the differences that exist among learning theorists, it must be said that the similarities among them are even more striking. The essential similarities appear to be (a) the focus on observable behavior as the phenomena to be explained; and (b) the focus on the laws governing the acquisition, maintenance, and modification of observable behavior, that is, the laws of learning.

In the remainder of this section, a brief overview of some of the ways in which children, and adults, have learned to be prosocial will be considered. Four procedures of learning will be outlined: classical conditioning, observational learning, reinforcement learning, and learning from such verbal procedures as instructions and preachings. Although different views exist as to which of these are primary, we will not concern ourselves with this here.

Classical Conditioning: The Learning of Emotional Responses

Initially, most stimulus events in a child's environment are emotionally "neutral" to him or her. By the time the child is an adult, however, the range of significant emotional stimuli has increased considerably. The simplest procedure by which this might come about is through classical or Pavlovian conditioning. In this analysis, positive or negative associations are formed between stimuli presented together. For example, an initially neutral stimulus comes to acquire a positive or negative valence as a result of having been associated in time with one already valenced. For example, the aroma of cooking can result in either the digestive juices flowing or in feelings of nausea, depending on the previous associations of the smell with delicious or nauseous food.

Researchers have used the procedures of positive and aversive classical conditioning to demonstrate the acquisition, elimination, and change of a variety of emotional reactions including those of fear and anxiety, attitudes and other evaluative responses, and interpersonal attraction and sexual behavior. More important for present purposes, Pavlovian procedures have also been used to develop *empathy*, a widely postulated motive underlying prosocial behavior.

Aronfreed and Paskal carried out two relevant experiments. One of these was based on positive affective empathy, and the other on empathic distress. Their first experiment, with 6- and 8-year-old girls, attached positive affect to the verbalizations of an adult (Aronfreed & Paskal, 1965). In the critical experimental condition, whenever an adult said "There's the light," she joyously hugged the child. Later, under testing conditions, the child preferred to press a lever that resulted in the adult's joyously saying, "There's the light," than to press a lever that resulted in candy for the child. By contrast, in control conditions in which the verbalization of "There's the light" had not been associated with hugs, the child pressed the lever for candy. This study was subsequently replicated and extended by Midlarsky and Bryan (1967).

Aronfreed and Paskal (1966) also carried out a study on empathic distress. Seven- and eight-year-old girls heard expressions of distress by an adult who clutched her ears and grimaced while listening to noise. In one condition the child also heard the aversive noise, and in another she did not. In a series of test trials, the child was faced with a confederate of the experimenter who emitted the distress cues that the experimenter had done previously. When this happened, children who had gone through the appropriate conditioning trials helped the child confederate more than children who had not had the empathy conditioning.

Observational Learning of Prosocial Behavior

From a social learning perspective, the overwhelming majority of human social behavior is learned from observing others. This has been well documented in numerous studies covering a wide range of behaviors from aggression to language acquisition to psychopathology (Bandura, 1977; Rosenthal & Zimmerman, 1978). Learning from the observation of others has also been shown to be a powerful influence on prosocial behavior. An extensive review of these studies can be found in Rushton (1980). Only a few of these will be discussed here.

One procedure for investigating the observational learning of altruism involves the bowling game shown in Figure 4.1. In my own studies, a procedure was used such that, on average, children give about 25% of their winnings to "Bobby," the child on the charity poster. Within this setting the child is introduced to a model who "would like to play the game too." The model then plays the game and, while the child watches, either generously donates or selfishly refuses to donate to the charity.

One question often raised is what happens if a model preaches one thing but *acts* in the opposite way? Which of these conflicting cues will a child follow? One series of studies carried out by Bryan and summarized by him in 1975 showed that children attended to what a model did, not what he or she said. Subsequent studies, however, showed that a model's verbal preachings *can* be effective in influencing observer's behavior. In one of these, either the children saw the model being generous and giving half of his or her winnings away, or the children saw the model being selfish and giving none of his or her tokens away. At the same time, one-half of the models preached that one should be generous, and the other half preached that one should be selfish. These preachings involved the model looking

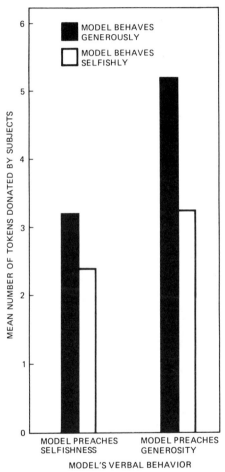

Figure 4.2. **The effects of a model's words and deeds on children's delayed willingness to donate to charity. Subjects contributed more of their winnings when the model preached generosity than when she preached selfishness, and also donated more when she acted generously than when she acted selfishly. Note that these effects of the model's verbal statements became visible only several weeks after subjects were exposed to her behavior; no immediate impact of the model's preachings was observed. (Source: Based on data from Rushton, 1975.)**

directly at the child and saying with emphasis, either "We *should* share our tokens with Bobby" or "We *should not* share our tokens with Bobby" (Rushton, 1975).

The results? Whereas what the model *did* had clear effects on both an immediate and 2-month retest, what the model said, surprisingly, made little impact on the *immediate* test of the child's generosity. However, when the children were retested in the same setting 2 months later, an effect of the model's preaching did emerge (see Figure 4.2). Children exposed to a model who preached generosity donated more of their winnings to charity than children exposed to a model who recommended selfishness. There is little doubt that parents and teachers and other socializing agents spend a fair amount of time exhorting their charges to be generous. It would appear that in the long run this will have some effect. Modeling, though—learning from others—is demonstrably powerful both immediately and over a period of time. This has also been shown in other research (e.g., Rice & Grusec, 1975).

If modeling is having an effect on children's generosity, as these studies seem to show, then another variable of interest might be the *amount* of modeling the child is exposed to. Rushton and Littlefield (1979) examined this hypothesis in a study that provided children with an opportunity to observe a model donate either 0, 2, or 8 of her won tokens to "Bobby." The observing children then were tested to see how generously they behaved, both immediately and again 2 weeks later. As seen in Figure 4.3, there was a

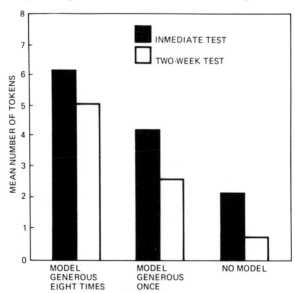

Figure 4.3. **Tokens donated on immediate and 2-week retest as a function of number of times generous behavior was modeled. (Source: Based on data from Rushton & Littlefield, 1979.)**

clear effect to the "amount of modeling." Furthermore, the results were still there 2 weeks later.

The studies discussed so far have been concerned with children's behavior. Similar powerful effects for models have been found with adults. In an experiment by Rushton and Campbell (1977), carried out in a quasi-natural setting, modeling significantly increased the number of female observers who (a) volunteered to donate blood (67% versus 25%); and (b) in turn actually gave their blood (33% versus 0%). In this study the opportunity to donate the blood in fact was not assessed until, on average, 6 *weeks after* the commitment, and in a setting quite different from the original modeling.

The Implications of Observational Learning for Television as a Socializer

If one of the main ways in which children learn is by observing others, then it follows that children should learn a great deal from viewing others on television. Television provides access to a very wide range of observational learning experiences. By simply sitting in front of their television sets in their own living rooms, children can observe a vast array of people behaving in response to a whole variety of situations. In this way television can have quite diverse effects. On the one hand, it is capable of promoting valued cognitive and social development. On the other, because of the prevalence of aggressive modeling, it also serves as an important disinhibitor and teacher of antisocial styles of behavior.

Altogether, over 30 different studies have now demonstrated the ability of prosocial television to modify children's behavior in a prosocial direction. These include such categories of prosocial behavior as altruism, friendliness, self-control, and courage. These have been reviewed extensively elsewhere (e.g., Rushton, 1979, 1980, 1981a). Unfortunately, space permits discussion of only two of these studies here.

Friedrich and Stein (1973) studied 97 children aged 3–5 years attending a 9-week summer program. For 3 weeks the children's free-play behavior was coded into categories such as "aggressive," "prosocial," and "self-control," and baseline rates were established. Children were randomly assigned to one of three groups and shown 4 weeks of selected television. One group watched aggressive television films such as *Batman* and *Superman* cartoons. A second watched neutral films such as children working on a farm, and a third watched *Mister Rogers' Neighborhood,* a prosocial educational television program stressing cooperation, sharing, sympathy, affection, and learning to accept rules. The results demonstrated that the programs affected both the children's aggressive and prosocial behavior. Aggressive television content led to increased aggression, whereas exposure to prosocial television led to increased prosocial behavior. Both the aggressive and prosocial films had effects on the measures of self-control; the aggressive films decreased these behaviors, whereas prosocial films increased it. Furthermore, these latter effects lasted over a 2-week retest.

Coates, Pusser, and Goodman (1976) carried out a similar experiment on preschoolers. First, the frequency with which the children behaved in one of three categories was recorded. The categories were (a) *Positive reinforcement*, consisting of giving positive attention such as praise and approval; (b) *Punishment*, consisting of giving verbal criticism and rejection; and (c) *Social contact*, consisting of any physical or verbal contact between a child and another child or adult. Following these baseline measures, children watched either 15 minutes of *Sesame Street* or 15 minutes of *Mister Rogers' Neighborhood* on each of 4 days. The results showed that the programs significantly affected the children's social behavior. For all children, *Mister Rogers' Neighborhood* significantly increased giving positive reinforcement to, and having social contacts with, both other children and adults. For *Sesame Street*, the effects were found only for children who had low baseline scores.

The Effects of Reinforcement on Prosocial Behavior

Modeling is a particularly useful way of getting children to learn. Once children try out what they see others doing, the question becomes whether they will continue to perform it. To a large extent this rests on the consequences that the children's actions bring for them, that is, whether it results in positive reinforcement or punishment. Rushton and Teachman (1978) carried out an experiment within the bowling game situation to examine this idea in the context of generosity. Seven- to eleven-year-old children, of both sexes, were first induced to behave altruistically by having generosity modeled to them as in the previous studies described earlier. This time, however, the model stayed in the room to observe whether the child was also generous. Not surprisingly, this resulted in a high level of donating by the children. The model, then seeing the child behaving generously, either rewarded the child for his or her imitative generosity by saying "Good for you, that's really nice of you," or punished the child by saying "That's kind of silly for *you* to give to Bobby. Now you will have fewer tokens for yourself." To a third group of children, a control group, the model turned away and gave neither positive reinforcement nor punishment. The child was then left alone to play and to donate or not as he or she wished. Two weeks later the child was given yet another opportunity to play on the game and to donate or not. As can be seen from Figure 4.4, the reinforcement conditions had strong effects, not only on the immediate test, but also on a 2-week retest. This study therefore demonstrates that the verbal praise or

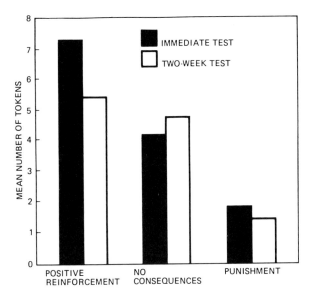

Figure 4.4. **Tokens donated on immediate and 2-week retest as a function of reinforcement. (Source: Based on data from Rushton & Teachman, 1978.)**

rebukes that a socializing agent delivers to a child following that child's imitation of her subsequently modifies that child's behavior. Results such as these have direct implications for modifying children's generosity, as in applications to teaching sharing in the classroom (e.g., Barton & Osborne, 1978).

Prior to leaving the section on reinforcement, it will be useful to consider briefly the role of *punishment* in bringing about internalization of standards. The effects of punishment have not been studied as extensively as the effects of other variables, but the study by Rushton and Teachman (Figure 4.4) shows that punishing generosity decreases it. Usually, however, punishment is delivered for antisocial behavior in an attempt to decrease the frequency of cheating, stealing, and being selfish. Whereas it seems that punishment is effective in suppressing such behavior, the conditions that maximize its effectiveness (e.g., type of punishment) are not completely clear (see Walters & Grusec, 1977, for a review). Some theorists, such as Eysenck (1977), have suggested that punishment is so effective that "conscience" can be conceptualized as a "conditioned reflex." According to this view, if a person is punished for engaging in such antisocial behavior as cheating, stealing, and being selfish, he or she will subsequently act in a prosocial manner in order to avoid the anxiety experienced as a result of the earlier punishment. Other theorists have taken the opposite view and suggested that punishment should not be used because it is ineffective, inhumane, or both. This seems extreme, however. From the punishments delivered, people undoubtedly construct appropriate rules of social conduct that then serve to guide their behavior in the future. Punishment can surely be effective in aiding children to generate their own self-regulatory controls. Personal standards require judgment of what is wrong as well as what is right.

Verbal Procedures Such as Instructions and Preachings

Socializing agents spend much of their time preaching the virtues of various actions, and instructing and reasoning with their children about how to behave. Although correlational data on the importance of reasoning have implicated it for the development of prosocial behavior (e.g., Hoffman, 1975), the effects of verbal socialization procedures have not been studied as extensively in the experimental laboratory as has, say, modeling. Nonetheless, several experimental studies have now demonstrated its impor-tance. For example, in a study already mentioned, Rushton (1975) found that preachings to children about what they ought to do affected their generosity 8 weeks later in a somewhat different situation. Rice and Grusec (1975) found that preaching about what was expected produced just as much generosity from children as modeling did. These effects lasted over a 4-month retest period. Grusec, Saas-Kortsaak, and Simutis (1978) gave chil-dren both modeling and different kinds of moral exhortation, including *specific* preaching ("It's good to donate marbles to poor children to make them happy") and a *general* exhortation ("It's good to help them in any way one can"). Grusec *et al.* (1978) also provided a range of behavioral tasks for the children in order to assess their effects. These included (a) an immediate and a 3-week retest of donating to charity; (b) an immediate test of helping the experimenter pick up paper clips; (c) an immediate test of sharing pen-cils with children in the school who had not been able to take part in the study; and (d) a test 5 weeks later, which was making drawings and collect-ing craft articles for the Hospital for Sick Children. Although the exhortations did not have much effect on the immediate donation test or on the helping test, it appeared to be more successful in other tests. Boys in the specific preaching conditions shared more than those in the other conditions (al-though there were no effects for girls). Girls and boys collected more craft items for the Hospital for Sick Children in the general preaching condition. This study therefore provided evidence that preaching can have generaliz-able effects, even weeks later.

It is still uncertain under what circumstances preaching is likely to affect behavior. One possibility is that children took them to be weak forms of *instructions.* Certainly when direct instructions are given, as in a study by Grusec, Kuczynski, Rushton, and Simutis (1978), then just as much donating on immediate, delayed, and generalization tests is found as with modeling. Probably, as with modeling, children abstract out appropriate rules of behavior (see section on "Internalization," later in this chapter).

The Social Learning of Moral Judgments

Bandura and McDonald (1963) showed the influence of modeling (and reinforcement) on 5- and 11-year-old children's moral judgments. First the children's baseline moral judgments were assessed by giving them pairs of stories such as the following to respond to:

Story 1: *A girl who is named Susan is in her room. She is called to dinner. She starts to go into the dining room, but behind the door there is a chair. On the chair is a tray with 15 cups on it. Susan doesn't know that all of this is behind the door. She pushes on the door, the door knocks against the tray, and bang go the 15 cups! They are all broken.*

Story 2: *A girl named Mary wants to get some biscuits. But her mother tells her she can't have any more biscuits, and she leaves. But Mary wants a biscuit, so she climbs up on a chair and reaches up to the shelf. But she knocks over one cup and it falls to the floor and breaks!*

Question: *Which of the two children is naughtier? Why?*

Children with "low" levels of moral judgment think Susan is naughtier because she broke 15 cups rather than only 1. Such children are basing their judgments on the *consequences* of the act. Children with "high" levels of moral judgment, however, think Mary is naughtier because her *intentions* were wrong, regardless of the consequences. According to Piaget (1932), these represent two distinct stages of development, which he referred to as "objective" and "subjective" morality, respectively.

Having assigned children to one or the other of these two categories based on their major way of responding to such stories, Bandura and McDonald (1963) then exposed the children to highly salient models who made judgments in a direction *opposite* to the orientation of the child. Thus, children who had previously made judgments based on a rule about the "consequences" of behavior heard a model make judgments on the basis of the "intentions" of the actor, and children who had based their judgments on the actor's intentions now heard a model make judgments based on the consequences of the behavior. After this training session, generalization was tested. The results showed that children's moral judgments shifted in the direction modeled. These results were extended by Crowley (1968), LeFurgy and Woloshin (1969), Prentice (1972), and Schliefer and Douglas (1973) to show durability over time and generalizability across situation and sample (e.g., to delinquents and adolescents). As Rosenthal and Zimmerman (1978) conclude on reviewing all of this data: "No violence is done by treating all of the preceding studies as cases of rule learning. The essential change was always a shift from an initial rule (e.g., 'judge material damage') to the modeled rule (e.g., 'judge subjective intentions') [p. 158]."

Thus, moral judgments, according to social learning theory, are cognitive rules abstracted as a result of modeling and reinforcement contingencies. According to this perspective, people vary in what they teach, model, and reinforce with children of different ages. For example, very young children are more likely to be punished as a result of the amount of consequential damage they do. As they grow older, however, their intentions will be taken into account and, indeed, they will be increasingly expected to provide acceptable reasons for their behavior.

Some efforts have also been made to test the modifiability of moral judgments within the Kohlberg framework by exposing children to divergent levels of reasoning (Keasey, 1973; Turiel, 1966). These demonstrate that children *can be moved up a stage as a result of social influence procedures.* Although the interpretations of such results are in dispute, they are certainly compatible with, and indeed expected from, a social learning perspective (Bandura, 1977; Rosenthal & Zimmerman, 1978; Rushton, 1980). In short, from a social learning perspective, moral evaluations and judgments are based on generalizable cognitive rules that can be modified by exposure to appropriate models.

ACCOUNTING FOR PHENOMENA AND THE CHALLENGING ISSUES THAT REMAIN

Age, Sex, and Group Correlates of Prosocial Behavior

How does social learning theory account for the fact that both prosocial behavior and moral judgment increase in the direction of more consideration for others with age, as was discussed in the first section of this chapter? And how does it account for the consistent patterns of individual differences that also were discussed in that section? How also would it account for other possible differences among people as in any ethnic, national, regional, religious, sex, or socioeconomic groups that might be found (e.g., Korte, 1981)? Any complete theory of the development of prosocial behavior must be able to explain such individual and cultural differences.

The social learning view is that such differences arise as a result of differential social learning. In regard to age differences, for example, the most parsimonious account is to suggest that as children grow older they *learn* to be more empathic, to adhere to moral principles, and to be more altruistic. Similarly, if it turns out that females, on the average, are more prosocial than males, then social learning theory would view this difference as most parsimoniously explained in terms of differences in early socialization. The social learning view would hold that any other individual or group differences also arose from differential learning experiences.

One possible objection to this analysis is that it is circular; that is, an example of individual or group difference in prosocial behavior arises and is immediately "explained" by invoking the previous learning histories of the individual or group under discussion. The advantage of the social learning explanation, however, is that it is possible, at any point in time, to break the circularity and reverse or change the behavior. Procedures such as modeling and reinforcement can be used in ways that directly promote prosocial behavior within a family. Indeed, the implications of these procedures for understanding the family, educational, and television systems allow for the possibility of altering these systems in ways that promote altruism within a whole society (see Rushton, 1980, for an extended discussion).

To summarize so far, whenever a correlational relationship occurs between a "person variable" (e.g., age, sex, personality, IQ, level of moral reasoning or other measure of cognitive maturity, socioeconomic status, or ethnic background), the immediate prediction from social learning theory is that, in the absence of further information, the relationship is mediated by social learning. Let us consider this from the perspective of the increasingly well established positive relationship between moral reasoning and moral behavior.

The Positive Relationship between Moral Judgment and Prosocial Behavior

As discussed in the first section, many studies have found that individuals with "high" levels of moral judgment, as assessed on Piagetian and Kohlbergian moral reasoning tasks, are also those who are most prosocial in their behavior (e.g., Eisenberg-Berg, 1979; Emler & Rushton, 1974; Harris *et al.*, 1976; Krebs & Rosenwald, 1977; Rubin & Schneider, 1973; Rushton, 1975; Rushton *et al.* 1981; and Staub, 1974). The social learning perspective is that both moral evaluations, judgments *and* behavior, are based on internalized personal standards. One would expect, therefore, a positive relationship between moral rules and moral behavior to the degree to which a person had been socialized to behave in accord with his or her principles.

Some people have learned to act with "integrity" (i.e., to behave in accord with previously endorsed rules), and others have learned to act opposite to the rules they espouse. Still others have learned to be adept at justifying immoral acts after they have occurred. It is incumbent on theories of moral development to explain all the varieties of the relationship between moral reasoning and moral behavior.

There is another reason for conceptualizing moral judgments as reflecting internalized rules. This is the evidence that altruistic behavior can also be predicted from conventional indexes of personal norms, attitudes, and values, as well as from responses to Kohlbergian and Piagetian stories. Numerous studies reviewed elsewhere (Rushton, 1980) have shown that paper-and-pencil measures of social responsibility, empathy, nurturance, and having equality and helpfulness as personal values predict individual differences in altruistic behavior. For example, Berkowitz and Daniels (1964) found that among university students, high scorers on a questionnaire measuring social responsibility behaved more altruistically than low scorers did. The questionnaire measuring social responsibility was composed of such items as "I am the kind of person people can count on." The measure of altruism consisted of the number of cardboard boxes made for another person who was allegedly dependent on the subject for his or her help. Midlarsky and Bryan (1972) used a similar scale with children and found that it predicted both donating money to a charity on an immediate test and donating candies on a subsequent test. In another study, Willis and Goethals (1973) measured individuals' social responsibility with the Values Scale of Allport, Vernon, and Lindzey (1960), and found that although 80% of the subjects high on social responsibility made an altruistic donation, only 43% of the subjects low on social responsibility did so. Finally, Rushton et al. (1981) found that social responsibility scores allowed a greater than chance prediction of whether respondents report having engaged in a number of self-report prosocial behaviors. In the Rushton et al. (1981) study, the measures of social responsibility also correlated with scores on tests of moral judgment (in this case Rest's Defining Issues Test). This positive relationship between traditional questionnaires of social responsibility and more recently devised tests of moral judgment has also been found by Staub (1974).

In short, there appears to be a "trait" of altruism—indeed, one sufficiently broad to warrant the concept of "the altruistic personality." This personality trait can be assessed by the manner in which a person endorses or responds to items on a number of pencil-and-paper measures of moral judgment, social responsibility, and moral knowledge, all of which, in turn, are predictive of actual helping. The most parsimonious way to order these diverse data is to invoke the hypothetical construct of an internalized personal rule or standard mediating them all. According to this account, a response to a moral judgment dilemma is similar to an item on a personality test or questionnaire. It is a sample of behavior, and a manifestation of an underlying rule governing that behavior. On a rule to "be altruistic," altruists will score higher than nonaltruists on numerous indexes. Thus, from the social learning perspective being presented here, moral judgments reflect cognitive rules that have been learned via the same processes as other behaviors, that is, through the laws of learning. The question of how internalized rules come to guide behavior remains a challenging issue for all theories.

Producing Internalization of Moral Standards

In the preceding sections it was suggested that different forms of prosocial behavior can be readily modified from observing the behavior of salient others. These studies partially had the strong effects that they did because they capitalized on contexts that were sensitive to demonstrating the effects. In one sense they can be seen as "situational" in their nature, that is, change the type of model or situation, and you change the observer's behavior. However, social learning theorists do not believe that people change quite as easily as that—particularly not in their moral behavior. In this sense the studies are not analogues of real life; rather, they are experiments designed to elucidate the basic processes and characteristics of learning phenomena. It is presumed that years of accumulated social learning in the family, the peer group, the school system, and so on result in fairly substantial internalization of standards of behavior. Furthermore, these standards often have powerful affective components to them such that violation of them can result in self-condemnation (guilt), whereas living in accord with them results in self-approval. Thus, a different level of analysis of the development of prosocial behavior can be at the level of internal mediation and the "products" of the moral learning.

How do these effects work? As already suggested, the social learning theory view is that people abstract standards of appropriate conduct from the environmental contingencies to which they are exposed. In this sense, reinforcement and modeling, in addition to their undoubted affective tone, also function in terms of informational and incentive value. From information about what is likely to be valued, people construct standards of appropriate social behavior. According to this formulation, if people see others rewarding prosocial consideration for others, then this will become internalized as an appropriate standard of behavior. If the reinforcement contingencies change and altruism becomes socially devalued, then the internal standards might be expected to alter. This, of course, does not always happen. Indeed, often individuals attempt to convince their society that the society's values are wrong.

Personal standards are internalized to varying degrees. Those that are held strongly enough to be considered "oughts" are often referred to as "moral principles." Those held in a more abstract way may be referred to as "values," and those held tentatively, and felt to be arbitrary, are called "conventions" or "social rules." What leads us to internalize a rule so strongly that it prescribes an "ought" as to how we should behave? Putting it another way, how can social learning theoriests account for the development of *integrity,* that is, when a person's behavior could be predicted both from his or her past behavior and from knowledge of his or her moral standards?

One view that has been put forward is to stress "conditioned affect," usually the anxiety that results from punishment (e.g., Aronfreed, 1976; Eysenck, 1977). Here, if the punishments have been provided across a wide enough range of transgressions and with sufficient intensity, the internal standards that are constructed will contain a sufficient aversive component to them that transgression from them will be avoided. Evidence also suggests that providing cognitive rules will help "anchor" this negative affect, and make the internal standards easier to construct. For example, Walters and Grusec (1977) examined how *reasoning* can socialize children. As with preaching, moral exhortation, and direct instruction, reasoning relies on a form of rule provision. This is what Walters and Grusec (1977) concluded about reasoning in the context of punishment.

> Children respond to reasoning either to reduce anxiety or not to be punished. A parent who relied solely on reasoning as a disciplinary technique would not be very successful in obtaining response suppression. *Reasoning becomes effective only when it is supported by a history of punishment* [Walters & Grusec, 1977, p. 207, italics added].

Perhaps all methods of rule provision are effective to the degree to which they are anchored by positive and negative affect and supported by predictable consequences. Certainly, if parents preached but paid little attention to how their children behaved, it is doubtful that their verbalizations would have much impact.

One conceptualization of the internalization of moral norms that some researchers have recently tested derives from attribution theory. Dienstbier, Hillman, Lehnoff, Hillman, and Valkenaar (1975) proposed that although the negative emotional states associated with punishment remain much the same over an individual's life span, the causal attributions made to these states can change; so they feel that it is these attributions that determine subsequent behavior. Thus, if children attribute anxiety after deviation to fear of being found out and punished, they should be less likely to suppress deviation when there is no chance of detection than if the anxiety is attributed to the knowledge that personal standards of behavior have been violated. Thus, to the extent that children can be persuaded to attribute behavioral standards to themselves, attribution theory might prove useful. Two studies found support for this idea by altering attributions experimentally.

Grusec et al. (1978) first induced children to donate winnings from the bowling game to charity, either by having seen a model donate, by being instructed to donate, or by a combination of the two. It was then suggested to them that they had donated either because they were the type who must enjoy helping others (internal attribution) or because they thought they were expected to (external attribution). A third group was not given any reason for its behavior (control group). The effects of these attributions were then tested on the usual immediate and delayed tests but, in addition, on quite a different test to see whether the results generalized. (Generalization has to be expected if the children had internalized the rule into their self-concept.) The hypotheses were confirmed. There was more donation both immediately and 2 weeks later in the modeling group given an internally oriented attribution. Furthermore, on a generalization test, children in the self-attribution group shared more than either those in the no-attribution or those in the external-attribution group. Grusec and Redler (1980) subsequently replicated and extended these findings.

Challenging Issues That Remain

Related to the issue of internalization is the challenging issue of the stability of altruistic behavior, both across situations and across time. Indeed, as has been discussed, this stability is pervasive enough to warrant the concept of "the altruistic personality". Furthermore, the onset of this stability apparently occurs relatively early in the child's development. Radke-Yarrow and Zahn-Waxler (1980) showed that 15-month-old toddlers could be reliably classified into types of prosocialness and that, 6 years later, when the children were 7 years old, they were still classifiable into the same categories. It is interesting that Murphy (1937), in her studies of toddlers, also felt that she could reliably classify those children who would share from those who would not. Such consistency of behavior, and its early onset, poses a potential problem for all theories of socialization. Let us consider the social learning theory position in this regard.

The social learning perspective really involves a set of logical deductions that goes something like this:

1. Experimental studies in laboratories show that altruism can be promoted through social learning procedures.
2. Behavioral modification procedures based on principles of social learning show success where they have been implemented in, for example, educational, familial, and therapeutic settings.

3. Therefore, the naturally occurring altruism one sees, and also its patterning, is due to the same processes.

Clearly this last statement, although it may well be very reasonable, is not yet "proved." Indeed, an extensive review of the literature pertaining to natural socialization of altruism has failed to demonstrate conclusively that any approach to the socialization of altruism is definitively effective (Rushton, 1980). Socialization research, when it is not of the experimental laboratory type described in this chapter, is overwhelmingly correlational and observational. The trouble with this latter research, as almost everybody knows, is that you cannot infer causality from a correlation. There might always be some third factor operating as the real "active ingredient." Thus, if a researcher maintains a positive correlation between maternal reasoning and child altruism, the mediator might actually be maternal modeling (mothers who generally *act* prosocially just happen to reason with their children). Similarly, perhaps heredity underlies much more of personality development and social behavior than has previously been thought (Rushton, 1982). These are all possibilities worthy of future research. The problems posed here apply to all theories of development, not just social learning theory.

From the present vantage point, the procedures of social learning theory outlined in this chapter go a long way to order the extensive, and growing, literature on the development of prosocial behavior, and to suggest direct ways of helping to create a more altruistic society.

REFERENCES

Allport, G. W., Vernon, P. E., & Lindzey, G. *A study of values.* Boston: Houghton Mifflin, 1960.

Aronfreed, J. Moral development from the standpoint of a general psychological theory. In T. Lickona (Ed.), *Moral development and behavior: Theory, research, and social issues.* New York: Holt, Rinehart & Winston, 1976.

Aronfreed, J., & Paskal, V. *Altruism, empathy, and the conditioning of positive affect.* Unpublished manuscript, University of Pennsylvania, 1965. Cited by J. Aronfreed in "The socialization of altruistic and sympathetic behavior: Some theoretical and experimental analyses." In J. Macaulay & L. Berkowitz (Eds.), *Altruism and helping behavior.* New York: Academic Press, 1970.

Aronfreed, J., & Paskal, V. *The development of sympathetic behavior in children: An experimental test of a two-phase hypothesis.* Unpublished manuscript, University of Pennsylvania, 1966. Cited by J. Aronfreed in "The socialization of altruistic and sympathetic behavior: Some theoretical and experimental analyses." In J. Macaulay & L. Berkowtiz (Eds.), *Altruism and helping behavior.* New York: Academic Press, 1970.

Bandura, A. *Social learning theory.* Englewood Cliffs, N.J.: Prentice-Hall, 1977.

Bandura, A., & MacDonald, F. J. Influence of social reinforcement and the behavior of models in shaping children's moral judgments. *Journal of Abnormal and Social Psychology,* 1963, *67,* 274–281.

Barton, E. J., & Osborne, J. G. The development of classroom sharing by a teacher using positive practice. *Behavior Modification*, 1978, *2*, 231-251.

Berkowitz, L., & Daniels, L. R. Responsibility and dependency. *Journal of Abnormal and Social Psychology*, 1963, *66*, 429-436.

Blasi, A. Bridging moral cognition and moral action: A critical review of the literature. *Psychological Bulletin*, 1980, *88*, 1-45.

Bryan, J. H. Children's cooperation and helping behaviors. In E. M. Hetherington (Ed.), *Review of child development research* (Vol. 5). Chicago: University of Chicago Press, 1975.

Coates, B., Pusser, H. E., & Goldman, I. The influence of *Sesame Street* and *Mister Rogers' Neighborhood* on children's social behavior in the pre-school. *Child Development*, 1976, *47*, 138-144.

Crowley, P. M. Effect of training upon objectivity of moral judgment in grade school children. *Journal of Personality and Social Psychology*, 1968, *8*, 228-232.

Dienstbier, R. A., Hillman, D., Lehnhoff, J., Hillman, J., & Valkenaar, M. C. An emotion-attribution approach to moral behavior: Interfacing cognitive and avoidance theories of moral development. *Psychological Review*, 1975, *82*, 299-315.

Dlugokinski, E. L., & Firestone, I. J. Congruence among four methods of measuring other-centeredness. *Child Development*, 1973, *44*, 304-308.

Dlugokinski, E. L., & Firestone, I. J. Other centeredness and susceptibility to charitable appeals: Effects of perceived discipline. *Developmental Psychology*, 1974, *10*, 21-28.

Eisenberg-Berg, N. Relationship of prosocial moral reasoning to altruism, political liberalism, and intelligence. *Developmental Psychology*, 1979, *15*, 87-89.

Emler, N. P., & Rushton, J. P. Cognitive-developmental factors in children's generosity. *British Journal of Social and Clinical Psychology*, 1974, *13*, 277-281.

Eysenck, H. J. *Crime and personality* (3rd ed.). St. Albans, Herts. U.K.: Paladin, 1977.

Friedrich, L. K., & Stein, A. H. Aggressive and pro-social television programs and the natural behavior of preschool children. *Monographs of the Society for Research in Child Development*, 1973, *38*(4, Serial No. 151).

Green, F. P., & Schneider, F. W. Age differences in the behavior of boys on three measures of altruism. *Child Development*, 1974, *45*, 248-251.

Grusec, J. E., Kuczynski, L., Rushton, J. P., & Simutis, Z. M. Modeling, direct instruction, and attributions: Effects on altruism. *Developmental Psychology*, 1978, *14*, 51-57.

Grusec, J. E., & Redler, E. Attribution, reinforcement, and altruism: A developmental analysis. *Developmental Psychology*, 1980, *16*, 525-534.

Grusec, J. E., Saas-Kortsaak, P., & Simutis, Z. M. The role of example and moral exhortation in the training of altruism. *Child Development*, 1978, *49*, 920-923.

Harris, S., Mussen, P., & Rutherford, E. Some cognitive, behavioral and personality correlates of maturity of moral judgment. *Journal of Genetic Psychology*, 1976, *128*, 123-135.

Hartshorne, H., & May, M. A. *Studies in the nature of character* (Vol. 1): *Studies in deceit*. New York: Macmillan, 1928.

Hartshorne, H., May, M. A., & Maller, J. B. *Studies in the nature of character* (Vol. II): *Studies in service and self-control*. New York: Macmillan, 1929.

Hartshorne, H., May, M. A., & Shuttleworth, F. K. *Studies in the nature of character*. (Vol. III): *Studies in the organization of character*. New York: Macmillan, 1930.

Hoffman, M. L. Moral internalization, parental power, and the nature of parent-child interaction. *Developmental Psychology*, 1975, *11*, 228-239.

Keasey, C. B. Experimentally induced changes in moral opinions and reasoning. *Journal of Personality and Social Psychology*, 1973, *26*, 30-38.

Kohlberg, L. Stage and sequence: The cognitive-developmental approach to socialization. In D. Goslin (Ed.), *Handbook of socialization theory and research*. New York: Rand McNally, 1969, pp. 347-480.

Kohlberg, L. Revisions in the theory and practice of moral development. In W. Damon (Ed.), *Moral development: New directions for child development.* No. 2. San Francisco: Jossey-Bass, 1978.

Korte, C. Constraints on helping behavior in an urban environment. In J. P. Rushton & R. M. Sorrentino (Eds.), *Altruism and helping behavior: Social, personality and developmental perspectives.* Hillsdale, N.J.: Lawrence Erlbaum Associates, 1981.

Krebs, D. L., & Rosenwald, A. Moral reasoning and moral behavior in conventional adults. *Merrill-Palmer Quarterly,* 1977, *23,* 77–87.

Krebs, D. L., & Sturrup, B. Role-taking ability and altruistic behavior in elementary school children. *Personality and Social Psychology Bulletin,* 1974, *1,* 407–409.

LeFurgy, W. G., & Woloshin, G. W. Immediate and long-term effects of experimentally-induced social influence in the modification of adolescents' moral judgments. *Journal of Personality and Social Psychology,* 1969, *12,* 104–110.

Midlarsky, E., & Bryan, J. H. Training charity in children. *Journal of Personality and Social Psychology,* 1967, *5,* 408–415.

Midlarsky, E., & Bryan, J. H. Affect expressions and children's imitative altruism. *Journal of Experimental Research in Personality,* 1972, *6,* 195–203.

Mischel, W., & Mischel, H. N. A cognitive social-learning approach to morality and self-regulation. In T. Lickona (Ed.), *Moral development and behavior: Theory, research and social issues.* New York: Holt, Rinehart & Winston, 1976.

Murphy, L. *Social behavior and child personality: An exploratory study of some roots of sympathy.* New York: Columbia University Press, 1937.

Mussen, P., & Eisenberg-Berg, N. *Roots of caring, sharing, and helping: The development of prosocial behavior in children.* San Francisco: W. H. Freeman, 1977.

Piaget, J. *The moral judgment of the child.* London: Routledge & Kegan Paul, 1932.

Prentice, N. M. The influence of live and symbolic modeling on prompting moral judgments of adolescent delinquents. *Journal of Abnormal Psychology,* 1972, *80,* 157–161.

Radke-Yarrow, M., & Zahn-Waxler, C. *Roots, motives and patterning in children's prosocial behavior.* Paper presented at the International Conference on the Development and Maintenance of Prosocial Behavior, Warsaw, Poland, June 1980.

Rest, J. R. *Development in judging moral issues.* Minneapolis, Minn.: University of Minnesota Press, 1979.

Rice, M. E., & Grusec, J. E. Saying and doing: Effects on observer performance. *Journal of Personality and Social Psychology,* 1975, *32,* 584–593.

Rosenthal, T. L., & Zimmerman, B. J. *Social learning and cognition.* New York: Academic Press, 1978.

Rubin, K. H.., & Schneider, R. W. The relationship between moral judgments, egocentrism, and altruistic behavior. *Child Development,* 1973, *44,* 661–665.

Rushton, J. P. Generosity in children: Immediate and long term effects of modeling, preaching, and moral judgment. *Journal of Personality and Social Psychology,* 1975, *31,* 459–466.

Rushton, J. P. Socialization and the altruistic behavior of children. *Psychological Bulletin,* 1976, *83,* 898–913.

Rushton, J. P. Effects of prosocial television and film material on the behavior of viewers. In L. Berkowitz (Ed.), *Advances in experimental social psychology* (Vol. 12). New York: Academic Press, 1979.

Rushton, J. P. *Altruism, socialization, and society.* Englewood Cliffs, N.J.: Prentice-Hall, 1980.

Rushton, J. P. Television as a socializer. In J. P. Rushton & R. M. Sorrentino (Eds.), *Altruism and helping behavior: Social, personality and developmental perspectives.* Hillsdale, N.J.: Lawrence Erlbaum Associates, 1981. (a)

Rushton, J. P. The altruistic personality. In J. P. Rushton & R. M. Sorrentino (Eds.), *Altruism and* helping behavior: Social, personality and developmental perspectives. Hillsdale, N.J.: Lawrence Erlbaum Associates, 1981. (b)

Rushton, J. P. Sociobiology: Toward a theory of individual and group differences in personality and social behavior. Unpublished manuscript, The University of Western Ontario, 1982.

Rushton, J. P., & Campbell, A. C. Modeling, vicarious reinforcement and extraversion on blood donating in adults. Immediate and long term effects. *European Journal of Social Psychology*, 1977, *7*, 297-306.

Rushton, J. P., Chrisjohn, R. D., & Fekken, G. C. The altruistic personality and the self-report altruism scale. *Personality and Individual Differences*, 1981, *2*, 293-302.

Rushton, J. P., Jackson, D. N., & Paunonen, S. V. Personality: Nomothetic or idiographic? A response to Kenrick and Stringfield. *Psychological Review*, 1981, *88*, 582-589.

Rushton, J. P., & Littlefield, C. The effects of age, amount of modeling, and a success experience on seven- to eleven-year-old children's generosity. *Journal of Moral Education*, 1979, *9*, 55-56.

Rushton, J. P., & Teachman, G. The effects of positive reinforcement, attributions, and punishment on model induced altruism in children. *Personality and Social Psychology Bulletin*, 1978, *4*, 322-325.

Rushton, J. P., & Wheelwright, M. Validation of donating tokens to charity as a measure of children's altruism. *Psychological Reports*, 1980, *47*, 803-806.

Rushton, J. P., & Wiener, J. Altruism and cognitive development in children. *British Journal of Social and Clinical Psychology*, 1975, *14*, 341-349.

Schliefer, M., & Douglas, V. I. Effects of training on the moral judgment of young children. *Journal of Personality and Social Psychology*, 1973, *28*, 62-67.

Skinner, B. F. *Beyond freedom and dignity*. New York: Alfred A. Knopf, 1971.

Staub, E. Helping a distressed person: Social, personality, and stimulus determinants. In L. Berkowitz (Ed.), *Advances in experimental social psychology* (Vol. 7). New York: Academic Press, 1974.

Staub, E. *Positive social behavior and morality* (Vol. 2). *Socialization and development*. New York: Academic Press, 1979.

Strayer, F. F., Wareing, S., & Rushton, J. P. Social constraints on naturally occurring preschool altruism. *Ethology and Sociobiology*, 1979, *1*, 3-11.

Turiel, E. An experimental test of the sequentiality of development stages in a child's moral judgments. *Journal of Personality and Social Psychology*, 1966, *3*, 611-618.

Ugurel-Semin, R. Moral behavior and moral judgment of children. *Journal of Abnormal and Social Psychology*, 1952, *47*, 463-474.

Walters, G. C., & Grusec, J. E. *Punishment*. San Francisco: W. H. Freeman, 1977.

Willis, J. A., & Goethals, G. R. Social responsibility and threat to behavioral freedom as determinants of altruistic behavior. *Journal of Personality*, 1973, *41*, 376-384.

Wright, B. Altruism in children and the perceived conduct of others. *Journal of Abnormal and Social Psychology*, 1942, *37*, 218-233.

II

EARLY DEVELOPMENT OF PROSOCIAL BEHAVIOR AND SOCIALIZATION MECHANISMS

CAROLYN ZAHN-WAXLER
MARIAN RADKE-YARROW

The Development of Altruism: Alternative Research Strategies

THE DEVELOPMENT OF PROSOCIAL BEHAVIORS: ALTERNATIVE RESEARCH STRATEGIES

The capacity to care for persons in need is an important aspect of social development. Adaptive, mature interpersonal interactions depend upon abilities of individuals to recognize needs of others, to feel concern for their fellow humans, and to behave in ways that are congruent with this concerned understanding. The very process of civilization is intricately linked with the abilities of societies caregivers to nurture and protect their offspring, and furthermore, to devote a considerable portion of their interest to the welfare of the young. An important related issue concerns the normal development of these same altruistic or prosocial behaviors in the offspring. The developmental origins of many conditions of psychopathology might also be effectively explored within a conceptual framework that emphasizes the determinants of prosocial as well as antisocial behaviors. Certain affective disorders and pathological aggression often are characterized, in part, by egocentrism, self-preoccupation, or by a dearth of caring reciprocal interactions with others. Excesses in expression of empathic feelings or prosocial behaviors, sometimes referred to as pathological altruism, also can interfere with adaptive social interactions. For both pragmatic and scientific reasons, it is important to explore the normal and deviant development of human potentials for prosocial interactions.

Questions about the origins of altruistic and moral acts have been explored within a number of disciplines. Philosophy, psychiatry, sociobiology,

THE DEVELOPMENT OF
PROSOCIAL BEHAVIOR

ISBN 0-12-234980-6

the behavioral and social sciences—each has used different procedures to provide data and theories about the evolution of moral humanitarian behaviors and codes of social interaction. Philosophies about human nature are characteristically based on belief systems reflecting the life experiences, education, and values of the individual philosopher. Sociobiology has relied for data about the evolution of altruism on mathematical, hypothetical models and on evidences of collaborative behaviors of subhumans, especially insects and birds. Psychoanalytic insights about early moral development have been based on hypothetical reconstructions of childhood and other retrospections about the behavior of children.

The research procedures used in social and behavioral sciences can provide a special perspective on questions about the origins of altruism. The research methods make it potentially possible to achieve the following: (a) to gain more direct access to the subject populations of interest for developmental questions, namely children; (b) to use standardized observational and experimental procedures for nonretrospective assessments of the emotions, behaviors, and cognitions that constitute altruism; (c) to examine the reliability of observers' judgments of altruism—that is, to achieve consensus among different individuals as to what defines a given prosocial act; and (d) to explore the validity of different measures of prosocial behavior. Many research methods have been used to study prosocial behaviors— experiments, observations in structured and natural settings, interviews, questionnaires, ratings, projective tests, sociometric techniques, and so forth. The purpose of this chapter is to describe a combination and adaptation of some of these research methods (namely of experimental, observational, and interview methods) in order to study the development of altruism. Mothers are trained as observers of their young children's responses to others' emotions, especially others' expressions of distress, as these may serve as potential elicitors of compassionate behaviors.

Altruism is formally defined as regard for or devotion to the interests of others (e.g., Webster, 1965). Often implicit in definitions of altruism are concepts of self-sacrifice, empathy, noble actions, and lack of expectation of external gain for the actor. Irrespective of theoretical persuasion, the task of defining and operationalizing altruism for research purposes poses considerable difficulty. There are many categories of prosocial intervention, each of which may or may not contain elements of altruism—help, statements of sympathy, rescue, protection, physical comfort, sharing, cooperation, and so forth. Each of these forms of prosocial behavior could occur for different reasons. Sharing might result from true generosity, a reciprocity norm, or an expectation of reinforcement; helping might be genuine, or manipulative, or intrusive, or instructed. Multiple motives for a given act are also possible. The label "prosocial behavior" has provided a useful, convenient summary label for these diverse behaviors and motives. At the same time, it has submerged some of the problems of definition. Because of the very real difficulties of distinguishing between altruistic and altruistic-like behaviors, it has been common to ignore the underlying developmental questions and to deal with relatively neutral prosocial behaviors in research operations. Yet the intriguing questions that have tantalized students of human behavior for centuries remain and will continue to remain: Why do acts of altruism occur and what are the developmental transitions? Under what circumstances and determining conditions do human beings first begin to show concern for others in ways that primarily benefit the other person? How are these behaviors channeled, patterned, consolidated, submerged, and fostered in the course of socialization and development?

In our earlier laboratory research on altruism in preschool-aged children (Yarrow, Scott, & Waxler, 1973), the focus was on how children learned concern for others as a function of different socialization experiences. Many of these children, ranging in age from 3 to 5, showed compassionate behavior to victims in distress in ways suggesting that children were not performing these responses for the very first time in laboratory sessions. Thus we inferred that performance rather than learning often was being measured when "older" children were studied, and that the origins of altruism actually might well be assessed in children in the first years of life. There are widely divergent estimates in the literature about when altruism begins (see review by Radke-Yarrow, Zahn-Waxler, and Chapman, in press). Whereas some investigators find interpretable prosocial behaviors occurring in preschool-aged children (e.g., Murphy, 1937; Rheingold, Hay, & West, 1976), other investigators (e.g., Chandler, Note 1) and most existing developmental theories propose a much later age of occurrence of real, mature prosocial behaviors. The age of reason and the beginning of operational thought (about 7 years) and the age of resolution of Oedipal conflicts (about 6 years) are thought to mark the approximate time of emergence of altruism in cognitive and psychoanalytic theories. Research designs based on social learning principles have been concentrated principally on school-aged children, and hence the early elementary school years have emerged as a significant developmental period. The choice of method and the age of the children selected for study may play a major role in "determining" the age of emergence of altruism in children, the relative frequencies of occurrence, and the qualitative differnces in the form and function of prosocial responding.

In spite of all our theories about altruism, there are virtually no *developmental* studies of the ontogeny of altruism. Perhaps one reason is that research strategies have not been appropriately adapted to ask the necessary questions. The method would need to provide ready access to elicitors of altruism and to the altruistic acts, both of which have been relatively inaccessible to researchers. The methods would ideally yield raw data in a form that would permit analysis of the content (and ultimately of the motives as well) of various forms of prosocial responding. The new research strategies would also need to be appropriately adapted to use with very young children, a population underinvestigated in research on altruism. Furthermore, multiple assessments of each child's behavior over an extended period would be needed for a longitudinal, developmental study of altruism.

It would be important to try to explore environments that permit the study of altruistic behaviors or close approximations (e.g., possible precursors) to altruism, namely, actions that indicate significant regard or concern for the interests of others. In retaining for research purposes the ambiguity and complexity of the phenomenon, we recognized that not all of the behaviors studied would qualify as altruistic, and similarly, that it would not always be possible to distinguish altruistic behaviors from some other forms of prosocial behaviors. We tried, however, to narrow the focus by careful specification of the eliciting stimuli that would be most similar to those that ordinarily elicit altruism when adults or older children are studied. An attempt was then made to duplicate these kinds of eliciting conditions in studying the young child. Altruism often (although not always) occurs in response to a real or perceived distress stimulus (e.g., someone is injured, helpless, sad). The misfortune is real and compelling; it is not necessarily brief in duration, and is usually not neutral or innocuous in expression. Often empathy, that is, feeling the concern of the other person, is part of the definition of altruism. Affective distress situations might be especially likely to elicit similar affect (empathy) in the bystander to the distress. How ethically and realistically to provide the young child with many distresses to witness was a major methodological challenge.

Parke (1979) has pointed out that in order to address the complexities of social interactions effectively, research paradigms should make use of both laboratory and field approaches, each of which, in turn, incorporates naturalistic and experimental research procedures. This chapter represents an attempt to illustrate the application of this approach to the study of prosocial interactions. Any given research strategy can provide only a partial view of altruism. Experiments permit only relatively benign simulations of distress. They cannot easily recreate the natural environment of the child, and hence generalizations are sometimes limited (Baumrind, 1980). Interviews or questionnaires rely on children's and caretaker's verbal reports, which are usually retrospective. Furthermore, one cannot sample specific sequences of interaction adequately, especially over time with interview procedures. Naturalistic observation often requires long periods of time, because neither distress nor altruism is ordinarily frequent or predictable in appearance. Often, serious distresses are not likely to occur at all in the presence of outside observers. At the same time, each of these methods also has useful features that might be effectively incorporated into alternative research strategies that would begin to address some of the existing problems. This includes, for example, (a) the control and rigor afforded by experimental procedures; (b) the ecological validity of naturalistic observations; and (c) the richness and depth of coverage of an interview procedure. The research strategy adopted was to train mothers to make systematic observations of their children's reactions to others' emotions of distress. In addition to providing narrative reports of children's reactions to naturally occurring emotional incidents, mothers were trained to observe and report children's responses to simulations of emotions.

The early baby biographies were often the products of skilled parent-observers. Piaget's theory of sensorimotor development was based largely on astute, detailed parental observations (Flavell, 1963). In the clinical research and in the behavior modificaion studies, parents are used to report children's adaptive and maladaptive behaviors (e.g., Achenbach & Edelbrock, 1981; Reid, 1978). Studies of temperament and affective development sometimes have included parent reports (e.g., Birch, Thomas, Chess, & Hertzig, 1962; Wenar, 1963; Goldsmith, Campos, Benson, Henderson, & East, Note 2; Weston & Main, Note 3). The research of Goodenough (1931) on children's anger and that of Clifford (1959) on parental discipline have made use of parental observations as the primary data source. For certain research questions, there are many reasons to expect the parent to be a good reporter of his or her own child's behavior. The parent has a built-in history of information about the research subject, comprehensive and unique knowledge of that child, and a context within which to view the child's specific behaviors. The parent also may have special motivation and investment that can lead either to biased observations or to careful, objective reporting. What the parent usually lacks is systematic training and experience in techniques of observation that would permit objective, detailed reporting.

Parents, especially mothers, do not have good reputations in research circles as observers or interpreters of their own children's behaviors. There is a commonly held belief, an axiom learned early in the course of the researcher's training, that mothers are not competent or qualified to observe their young. Although the belief is not based on data, it continues: Mothers are likely to be forgetful, biased, and selective, and to distort reality to fit what is socially desirable and acceptable. Thus, they are likely to "read in" what they wish to see, or deny what they do not wish to see, and so on.

The premature rejection of parental reports as useful and valid indices of behavior undoubtedly stemmed from disenchantment with early interview studies in which mothers provided data on child-rearing practices and child behaviors. Often the parent–child interactions about which mothers were interviewed were focused on past experiences, sometimes experiences that had occurred several years earlier (see review by Yarrow, Campbell, & Burton, 1970). Trained psychologist–observers also might be expected to show little accuracy under such circumstances. For research purposes, it should be possible to reduce greatly the problems of observer bias, distortion, memory loss, and social desirability (a) by training mothers to make observations; (b) by providing mothers with an observation scheme that imposes specificity and focus on the reporting before it begins; (c) by requiring the mothers' reporting to be close in time to the occurrence of the critical incidents; (d) by focusing in observation and analysis on specific behaviors that are relatively easy to see (if one is sensitized) and that require relatively low levels of inference for categorization; (e) by using procedural controls that provide conditions of equivalent sampling of incidents across mothers; and (f) by attempting to obtain construct validity through some independent behavioral assessments. The parent–observer would need to be trained in the same way that a research assistant would be trained to make the same observations.

What follows is a description of how these procedures were developed and used with a sample of 24 mothers and their children who were in the first years of life. Substantive findings on the origins of altruism are presented, with special emphasis on the methods used to generate the findings and on the further questions the data raise for theory and research. Finally, we focus on recent extensions of the research strategies.

RESEARCH METHODS

Since the purpose of the research was to study the origins and development of altruism, a longitudinal design was used. Twenty-four white, middle-class children and their mothers comprised the sample. Three additional mothers had earlier dropped out of the study; one had moved to another city, and the other two found the procedures too time-consuming. Mothers had high school or college educations. They received financial remuneration for their data collection. Children were in one of three age cohorts. Children in Cohort A (four boys and four girls), began the study at 10 months of age; children in Cohort B (four boys and five girls) at 15 months of age, and children in Cohort C (three boys and four girls) at 20 months of age. Each child was studied for 9 months. These age ranges were selected because the upper limit constituted a time at which children were hypothesized to be capable of sympathy (Hoffman, 1975; Murphy, 1937;

Yarrow et al., 1973), and the lower limit represented a time at which children were unlikely yet to show sympathy. Hence developmental transitions in children's prosocial responses to others' distress might be expected to occur within this time frame.

Mothers were trained to function both as observers (reporting on children's responses to others' emotions) and as experimenters (performing simulations of emotions in the children's presence). These procedures were carried out on a regular basis over the 9-month period of time. Mothers were instructed to report on children's responses to events in which anger, fear, sorrow, pain, or fatigue (or any other negative emotion) was expressed. To provide a comparative base, mothers also were asked to observe children's responses to others' emotions of affection and pleasure.

Mothers were taught a prescribed format for observing and reporting. Mothers were to dictate their observations into tape recorders, providing a narrative account of (a) the emotion expressed and what preceded it; (b) what the person(s) did and said in expressing the emotions; (c) the circumstances of the event; (d) the child's affective, verbal, and behavioral responses to the emotion; and (e) the responses of mother (and others) to the child. Two classes of events were to be observed: those in which the child was a bystander to someone else's emotions (e.g., child sees father choke), and those events in which the child caused emotion (e.g., child bites sibling). Accurate, sequential reporting was emphasized: Mothers were asked to adopt the style of a news reporter by giving a literal, concise but complete blow-by-blow account of the emotion incident. They were asked to report every relevant incident and to record immediately after the event. If they wished to make interpretations this was to be done after the behavioral account. Anything unusual or atypical at the time of reporting was also to be noted. Excerpts of the content of two incident reports follow.

Julie, at 80 weeks: A neighbor asked me to watch her child. Julie had just awakened. When the neighbor brought the baby in Julie danced around, smiling and very excited. After the mother left, the baby began to really shriek and pound his fists on the floor, and he was very upset by my efforts to comfort him, so I finally put him in a high chair and gave him some cookies. Julie, as soon as he began to cry, looked very worried, startled, and anxious. Her body stiffened; she leaned toward him and cocked her head. She kept reaching toward him but didn't actually touch him. She followed me over to the high chair. He began to throw the cookies and cry; she tried to return them to him, which surprised me because usually she tries to eat everybody's cookies. She would put the pieces back up on the tray and she was very worried; her eyebrows were up and her lips were pursed. Then I put him back on the floor. She hovered over him, whimpering herself, and looking at me very questioningly. I put him in the playpen, he continued to cry, and Julie continued to look very anxious and cry once in a while. She began to try to stroke his hair, and she reached into the playpen and patted his shoulder as well. He continued to cry and pulled away from her. I tried to ignore him; I could hear her cooing and making very concerned sounds to him. Then she came to me in the kitchen, took my hand and led me to the living room. She kept looking up at me, with a very concerned, worried look. I didn't do anything for him. Julie looked at him, and looked up at me again. Then she took my hand and tried to put my hand on top of Brian's head. I didn't know what to do for him but I didn't want Julie to be so upset, so I picked him up and took him upstairs.

Bobby, at 82 weeks: As I [mother] was vacuuming I began to feel a little faint and sick to my stomach. I turned off the vacuum and went into the bathroom kind of coughing and gagging a little. Bobby followed me to the bathroom door, and the whole time that I was in there he was pounding on the bathroom door saying, "OK Mommie, OK Mommie?" And I finally came out and picked him up and he looked at me with a very concerned, worried look in his eyes, and I said, "Mommie OK." Then he put his head on my shoulder and began to love me.

The observation procedures yield descriptive accounts of children's responses to naturally occurring variations in affect expressed in different family environments by the different family members and by others who enter into family interactions. Mothers were also asked to simulate emotions in order to obtain data based on more equivalent event sampling across families. Each week, the mother portrayed a different emotion according to a script and schedule, and then recorded the child's responses to the event. This provided assessments of different children's responses to the same emotions, at the same ages. There were seven different emotions: sorrow (crying), physical pain, respiratory discomfort (coughing), anger over the telephone, fatigue, laughter, and affection. As one example, the script for the simulation of pain required the mother to bump her foot (or head) against some object, verbalize "Ouch, my foot, (or head)," "Ooooh," rub the injured part gingerly, repeat "ow" softly a couple of times, and grimace. Mothers were to practice, but not in the children's presence, until they felt comfortable and natural performing each simulation.

Training for data collection consisted of one 2-hour individual session and two 3-hour sessions with small groups of mothers prior to formal data collection. All sessions included at least one senior staff member and one research assistant experienced in techniques of observation. The reporting procedures were described in detail during the first session with each individual mother. The project was described as a study of children's reactions and interactions in relation to others' emotions. Mothers were asked to try out the observation procedures following this session, and then to discuss their observations and observing problems in the small group setting. During the group session, observing and reporting procedures were discussed in detail, examples of incidents were presented, practice observations were reviewed, and questions were answered. The necessity for obtaining detailed, narrative accounts of specific sequences of behaviors was emphasized. The importance of on-the-spot reporting and the hazards of delayed reporting also were stressed. At the group meetings, mothers were also given directions as to the circumstances of the simulations. (In some of the subsequent studies, group training sessions have been replaced by individual training sessions, and a training manual has been provided for the mother.)

Every third week an investigator spent 2 hours in the home. One purpose was to review and supervise the mother's data collection. Mothers mailed their tapes to the laboratory at the midpoint between home visits, and they were then typed. During the home visit, the transcript of the mother's previous observations was reviewed for accuracy, clarity of content and sequence, range of incidents sampled, and quality of reporting. On each visit the investigator carried out a simulated emotional incident (pain, anger on the phone, coughing, or laughter) according to a schedule. On one occasion, a second investigator visited each home in order to observe the child's response to the simulation. On another occasion the mother simulated an incident of emotion (pain). The purpose of the simulations during the home visits was (a) to provide behavior samples for estimates of observer reliabilities between mothers and investigators; and (b) to compare the child's responses to distress expressed by mother and by a relatively unfamiliar adult. The home visit was also used as an opportunity to make observation ratings of some affective and social dimensions of mother–child interactions.

All of the reported observation incidents were categorized (a) by the type of affect; (b) by the identity of distress victims; (c) whether the child was a bystander or the cause of the emotion; and (d) whether the incident was natural or simulated. Eight categories of child reactions were coded. Estimates of observer agreement between mother and investigator, based on children's response to simulations of distress, are shown as percentages of agreement in the parentheses. The child behaviors were (a) no reaction to others' distress (94%); (b) orientation to distress stimulus, but no further response (82%); (c) self-distress, expressed in cries, frets, whimpers (100%); (d) imitation of others' emotion (91%); (e) positive emotion, expressed as laughter or smiling (53%); (f) verbal or physical seeking of caregiver (67%); (g) physical or verbal aggression, such as hitting or scolding (100%); and (h) prosocial interventions, such as attempts to alleviate distress by helping, sharing, or comforting (86%). With the exception of categories of no reaction and orientation to distress, child behaviors were not mutually exclusive. An additional category of behavior, verbal labeling or inquiries about distress, was also observed to occur but was not analyzed here. Coder reliabilities based on two coders' independent assessments of each mother's reports of children's responses to affect incidents were also calculated. Percentages of agreement ranged from 79% to 96%. Scores based on adjudications of the two coders were used in data analyses.

The sequencing of age cohorts was planned such that the ages of children in Cohort B, during the first 4½ months of their participation in the study, were the same as those of children in Cohort A, during the second 4½ months of their participation (i.e., 62–85 weeks); a parallel age overlap for Cohorts B and C was achieved (i.e., 86–109 weeks). The cross-sequential design (Schaie, 1973), which represents a combination of longitudinal and cross-sectional designs with specified age overlaps, makes possible several forms of analyses: (a) examination of developmental transitions *within* each cohort; (b) examination of age differences *across* age cohorts; (c) group comparisons of different cohorts at the same ages (as a control for effects of reporting based on length of time in study); and (d) assessments of patterns of individual differences in children at the same ages (e.g., the combination of Cohort A [second 4½ months] and Cohort B [first 4½ months] constitutes a sample for correlational analyses). Analyses of variance and t tests were used to assess patterns of age changes and group differences, and correlations were used to assess patterns of individual differences. A total of approximately 2000 incidents was reported by the 24 mothers. To analyze children's responses to others' expressions of distress, ratio scores were used: The frequency of occurrences of a given child reaction within a given time period was weighted in relation to the total number of relevant distress episodes.

EARLY FORMS OF ALTRUISM: RESEARCH FINDINGS AND INTERPRETATIONS

Children's Responses to Distress as a Function of Age

A rudimentary but important question concerns the basic content of the behavior repertoires that result from children's early exposure to others in need. Then we may, in turn, ask how these patterns of reactions change as children begin to show signs of helping, sharing, caring, and comforting, if indeed they do show prosocial behavior. The distress of another person is a remarkably compelling stimulus for children in the first years of life: Distress elicits some form of response on between 80–90% of all occasions in which it occurs. Sometimes the child's reaction is no more than a sustained orientation to the stimulus, but often there is further evidence of affective involvement, cognitive exploration, or behavioral intervention in circumstances of others' distress. Children sometimes laugh or cry or seek their caregiver for reassurance. They can be seen to imitate components of the other's distress expressions or circumstances (e.g., copying father's cough or baby's cry). Children also make prosocial interventions in behalf of the victim, and sometimes they will behave aggressively toward the injured party. The relative frequencies of some of these response tendencies change with age.

A developmental perspective on children's reactions as bystanders to distress emotions in others is presented in Table 5.1A and B. Here and elsewhere, sexes are combined because there were virtually no sex differences. The categories of child behaviors are summarized in terms of average ratio scores, separately for the first and second 4½-month time periods and for each age cohort. Analysis of variance on each of these categories include cohort, sex, and distress type (natural [N]/simulation [S])

Table 5.1
Children's Reactions to Distress Emotion in Others:
Average Percentage of Distress Incidents to Which the Child Responded

	Ages (in weeks)					
	38–61	62–85	62–85	86–109	86–109	110–134
	Cohort A T-1, %	Cohort A T-2, %	Cohort B T-1, %	Cohort B T-2, %	Cohort C T-1, %	Cohort C T-2, %
A. Natural distresses observed by child						
No response	10	11	7	7	11	10
Orients to emotion	26	33	21	16	8	5
Distress cries	28	14	16	12	5	10
Seeks care giver	2	10	26	25	11	18
Positive affect	7	5	9	5	5	4
Aggression	4	10	12	11	8	13
Imitation	4	14	16	19	14	12
Prosocial intervention[a]	11	11	16	30	39	32
B. Simulated distresses observed by child						
No response	15	10	11	14	21	23
Orients to emotion	19	33	9	11	6	4
Distress cries	5	4	9	3	4	2
Seeking care giver	19	30	48	29	22	26
Positive affect	29	24	19	9	7	6
Aggression	4	6	6	10	9	2
Imitation	12	13	22	22	26	12
Prosocial intervention[a]	4	5	19	30	33	33

[a] In comparisons of prosocial behaviors of children of the same age but of different lengths of participation in the study (i.e., Cohort $A_{Time 2}$ with $B_{Time 1}$ and $B_{Time 2}$ and $C_{Time 1}$) there were no significant differences between groups.

as factors. Analyses were done separately for Time 1 and Time 2. Main effects of age cohort and interactive effects of age cohort by distress type (N/S) are reported here, whereas distress type main effects are deferred to a later section on methods in which children's responses to natural and simulated distresses are discussed. In the analyses of age changes here, the focus is on statistical changes *across* age cohorts; the reader can then usually readily infer, on the basis of these analyses and visual inspection of the tables, where the within-cohort changes occur. Because statistical analyses were unvariate rather than multivariate, some caution in the interpretation may be warranted. Developmental patterns regarding children's reactions to witnessed distresses can be summarized as follows: Children's early responses to naturally occurring expressions of distress emotions tended to consist of affective arousal and lack of interactive engagement with victims. Sustained orientation, general affective agitation (such as crying, whimpering, seeking out the caregiver), and positive arousal constituted the majority of initial reactions to others' distresses. With increasing age, there were significant changes in this pattern. Self-distress as a response to the naturally occurring distress of others decreased in relative frequency across age cohorts at Time 1. This was seen in the analysis of variance main effect of age, $F (2, 18) = 5.27$, $p < .05$ and the age x distress type (N/S) interaction, $F (2, 18) = 11.64$, $p < .001$. Children's expressions of laughter or smiling in response to simulations of distress also showed a significant decrease in relative frequency across age cohorts at Time 2. The analysis of variance yielded a main effect of age, $F (2, 18) = 6.21$, $p < .01$, and an age by distress type (N/S) interaction, $F (2, 18) = 3.76$, $p < .05$. Seeking the caregiver in circumstances of distress yielded a significant main effect of age at Time 1, $F (2, 18) = 7.88$, $p < .005$. Visual inspection of Table 5.1A and B indicates a curvilinear trend, with seeking behavior most predominant in the Cohort B children.

The early affective reactions by children to others' emotions of distress were replaced developmentally by more focused efforts to interact positively with victims in distress. Comparisons of Cohorts A, B, and C indicated significant increases across age cohorts in prosocial interventions at Time 1, $F (2, 18) = 6.69$, $p < .01$, and again at Time 2, $F (2, 18) = 6.25$, $p < .01$. The rates of increase were similar for prosocial responses to natural and simulated distresses. Examination of Table 5.1A and B indicates that within Cohort B there was a substantial shift in frequency of prosocial interventions, beginning when children are about 1 ½ years of age. Imitative and aggressive reactions to distress occurred with relatively low frequencies in these early years of life, with one developmental trend: Imitation showed a significant increase with age at Time 1, $F (2, 18) = 3.76$, $p < .05$.

There are possible theoretical links between children's early sympathetic responses to victims they have caused to be distressed and to victims of distress they have witnessed as bystanders. If interventions on behalf of the victim occur when circumstances of distress are child-caused (i.e., as a response to one's own aggressive behaviors), the prosocial acts are likely to be conceptualized as reparations for wrongdoing or as indicators of conscience or guilt. If, however, the child is an innocent bystander to distress, the same positive behaviors are more likely to be interpreted as prosocial actions or as altruism. If the young child is unable to distinguish clearly between distresses caused and witnessed, the early forms of altruism and conscience may have similar conceptual origins and may be similarly "fused," to a certain degree, in the mind of the child. Altruism mediated by guilt would be one possible by-product of the early blurring of cause and consequence. Socialization experiences might differentially influence this learning process, depending upon how different caregivers focus on the child's behavior in these circumstances (Zahn-Waxler, Radke-Yarrow, & King, 1979).

Children's reactions to distresses they have *caused* to others (e.g., child steps on playmate and causes him or her to cry) were analyzed within the same framework as were responses to distresses witnessed. The descriptive data are presented in Table 5.2. It is significant that the same categories of response are seen in children's reactions to distresses they create, as were seen in children's reactions as bystanders to distress. (The category "seeks caregiver" was not coded for child-caused distresses.) Not only were the

Table 5.2

Children's Reactions to Distresses They Have Caused:
Average Percentage of Distress Incidents to Which the Child Responded

	Ages (in weeks)					
	38–61	62–85	62–85	86–109	86–109	110–134
	Cohort A T-1, %	Cohort A T-2, %	Cohort B T-1, %	Cohort B T-2, %	Cohort C T-1, %	Cohort C T-2, %
No response	15	9	12	6	6	5
Orients to emotion	12	15	7	8	3	2
Distress cries	55	40	26	27	22	19
Seeks caregiver						
Positive affect	20	19	17	19	13	13
Aggression	17	22	34	29	22	44
Imitation	10	14	10	8	24	24
Prosocial intervention	2	6	16	25	31	24

categories of responses similar, but there were some common developmental patterns as well. For example, signs of self-distress in response to victims' distress showed a reliable decrease with age, $F (2, 21) = 4.28$, $p < .05$, at Time 1. Prosocial interventions increased significantly across the age cohorts, $F (2, 21) = 13.61$, $p < .005$, at Time 1 and $F (2, 21) = 3.58$, $p < .05$, at Time 2. Imitation of victims' distresses increased reliably with age, $F (2, 21) = 3.59$, $p < .05$ at Time 1. A major difference in children's responses to the two types of distresses is that children's aggressions toward their victims increased with age in Time 2, $F (2, 21) = 3.65$, $p < .05$, in the child-caused distresses. In other words, children continued to violate their victims after the initial provocation with increasing frequency with age. Visual comparisons of Table 5.1A and B with Table 5.2 suggest some other differences between child-caused and child-witnessed distresses. Children's expressions of self-distress and of aggression were considerably higher in overall magnitude in child-caused distresses than in child-witnessed distresses, indicating that child-induced distresses were particularly aversive and conflictual. The communalities and differences in children's reactions to child-caused versus bystander distress events are intriguing. Sometimes children may be quite oblivious to the effects of their hurtful actions on others. These unintentional interpersonal harms may result in child behaviors parallel to those observed in bystander events, thus providing occasions for the early learning of altruism. These very young children can also be quite conscious and deliberate about the pain and distress they inflict, hence their aggressive tendencies are also evidenced. Just as there are early individual differences in children's prosocial behaviors, so too are there differences in these punitive behaviors that also seem to indicate awareness of the victim's plight.

Content of Children's Prosocial Responses

The developmental analyses have provided information on how children's prosocial interventions fit into a broader repertoire of affective and behavioral responses to victims in distress. All behaviors that appeared to be intended to alleviate the distress of the victim were coded as prosocial interventions. These efforts by children took many different forms. Children's very first prosocial initiatives almost invariably consisted of relatively undifferentiated positive physical contacts with the victim—of touching and patting or of presenting objects. All children in Cohort A showed this response pattern shortly after 1 year of age, and each child in Cohort B also showed this reaction at the time of entry into the study. These positive physical interventions remained prominent, but the content of physical reactions changed with age into more clearly definable categories of comforting (e.g., hugs and kisses). Many additional forms of intervention appeared in most of the children from the middle to the end of the second year of life. This was also the time period that showed the greatest increase in frequency of altruism. Descriptions and examples of the new prosocial interventions are given in Table 5.3.

Table 5.3 indicates variety and complexity in children's prosocial orientations toward victims in distress. Children in Cohorts B and C showed, on the average, eight of the ten types of prosocial responses described in the table. Often more than one form of prosocial behavior occurred within an incident. The affective accompaniments and motives for action appear to vary considerably, within and across response categories. There were still other forms of prosocial interventions that occurred less frequently (in between one-third and one-half of the children in Cohorts B and C). Often these interventions involved some elements of generalization. Prosocial actions were sometimes explicitly linked with aggressive, self-punitive behaviors; for example, one child would hurt another child, then hit herself on the head and hug her victim. Misplaced self-responsibility (perhaps guilt) was also reported to occur; for example, a child witnessing his mother cry, hugged the mother, then asked, "Did I make you sad?" Memories of events

Table 5.3

Categories of Prosocial Interventions[a]

I. *Verbal sympathy, reassurance, and concern (87%)*[b]
- A.   124 weeks—Sibling cries: "That's okay, Mary, you're all right; you'll be all right" (with concerned expression).
- B.   120 weeks—Mother cries: "Pick me up." Hugs mother's legs, "I love you. You're okay now, you'll be happy."
- C.   89 weeks—Hurts friend; Subject hugs friend: "All right? Mommy kiss, mommy fix. Oh, nice mommy. Nice johnny, better."

II. *Ambivalent prosocial intervention (i.e., alternation of prosocial and aggressive behaviors) (81%)*
- A.   128 weeks—Mother's pain: Runs, looks at source of pain, swats at mother, says "You cry," and kisses her fingers.
- B.   101 weeks—Subject hurts father: Hugs and kisses father, then slaps him in the face.

III. *Combative altruism, i.e., protecting or defending the victim (56%)*[c]
- A.   90 weeks—Child hurts another child: "No, no, not nice, sorry," and subject hits aggressor. Continues until aggressor apologizes, says "nice, nice," and pats aggressor.
- B.   92 weeks—Child hits another child: Subject pushes aggressor into the swimming pool.
- C.   79 weeks—Children fighting: "No, no," and subject stands between them as one goes to hit another; put pennies (that they had been fighting over) in the corner, said "Mommy," and brought her over to show her the fighting.

(continued)

Table 5.3 *(Continued)*

IV. *Prosocial actions that focus on the specific distress cue (100%)*
 A. 132 weeks—Mother cries: "What's the matter?" Asks to be picked up. "I'm kissing your eyes so they won't cry."
 B. 126 weeks—Mother angry at subject: "Don't talk loud and faster." Shortly after, she hugs mother and says "I love you."
 C. 86 weeks—Mother hurt foot: Concerned, ran over, said "hurt foot," and rubs mother's foot.

V. *Self-referential actions (i.e., providing the victim with that which would ostensibly comfort oneself; or, explicit comparisons of self and other in circumstances of distress) (87%)*
 A. 118 weeks—Mother's fatigue: "I'll get you my teddy bear," and does.
 B. 69 weeks—Mother's fatigue: Offers bottle to mother, lies down with her and pats mother, then drinks bottle.
 C. 103 weeks—Home visitor's "injured" foot: Subject says "Ow," and rubs own ankle: "Kiss it," and makes kissing noises in visitor's direction.

VI. *Prosocial actions containing evidence of hypothesis testing or ability to make appropriate inferences about what would help (75%)*
 A. 104 weeks—Baby sibling cries: "Sister is crying, let's go get her. Let me hold her. You'd better nurse her, mommy; does she have a burp?"
 B. 105 weeks—Sibling cries: "Brother is fussy." She puts a 7-Up bottle by him, saying "Brother likes that."

VII. *Instrumental help (81%)*
 A. 99 weeks—Child hurt, cries: Gets piece of toilet paper to clean injury and asks mother to get a Band-Aid.
 B. 113 weeks—Grandmother is chilly: Subject gets her a sweater.

VIII. *Indirect help—Enlists assistance of third party (62%)*
 A. 96 weeks—Baby crying: "Mommy, pick the baby up."
 B. 91 weeks—Baby crying: "Baby crying," tugs on his own mother and baby's mother.

IX. *Acts of sharing (94%)*
 A. 127 weeks—Playmate cries: Brings him a toy, "Here, Jimmy, here's a car; here's some coffee." Looks into his face, "Jimmy, are you okay?"
 B. 56 weeks—Father tired: Pulls hand away from father's head and tries to feed him his own cereal.

X. *Reparations for distresses caused by child (81%)[c]*
 A. 114 weeks—Mother cries: Subject is concerned, caresses mother's face, says "You're okay." (Mother—"Am I?") "Yes, you're okay. I take care of you. I take care of dad and I be nice. You're okay."
 B. 86 weeks—Mother angry about mess subject has made: Subject cries: "I want mommy," hugs, says "I wipe it up," and does.
 C. 136 weeks—Subject hurts mother: "I'm sorry, mommy, I'm sorry."

---

 [a] Illustrations are based on condensations of mother's narrative reports.
 [b] Percentage refers to the percentage of children for Cohorts B and C who manifested this type of prosocial response.
 [c] Category 3 pertains only to child-witnessed distresses, and Category 10 pertains only to child-caused distresses. The remaining response categories can be applied to distresses either caused or witnessed by children.

were reflected in some children's prosocial behavior. One child at 94 weeks observed her father being stung by a bee and several hours later came to rub the spot, saying, "Daddy's bee bite, I wash Daddy's bee bite." Sometimes children's recollections were of incidents occurring weeks or even months earlier. In other incidents a child would respond empathically to a total stranger. One youngster, upon seeing an unfamiliar man cry, said, "I want to make that man happy; I take care of him."

There is considerable face validity to support the interpretation that most of the prosocial behaviors studied reflect some level of understanding of the other person's experiences and of what would provide help or comfort to the victim in that particular situation. There is also a considerable range in children's abilities to make accurate inferences about the distress. At one extreme is the affective and cognitive precociousness of the child described earlier in the first illustration of a maternal incident report. At the other extreme, children sometimes show inappropriate behaviors, such as bringing a toy to a tired mother, or soothing a mother who is crying because she is peeling onions, or anxiously attempting to "heal" a dog that has just been combed by trying to patch the hair back on the dog. Some reactions are at once both appropriate and inappropriate to the other's plight, for example, the child who brings a bed sheet for the mother to blow her nose. Similar gradations of understanding of what is needed can often be seen in the prosocial behaviors of older children and adults as well.

In this discussion of findings, we have focused principally on similar developmental regularities across children; altruism was found to develop in virtually all of the children studied, and most children showed similarity in their total repertoire of prosocial responding. The very first signs of responding were remarkably similar in form from one child to the next, and they tended to occur within a narrow time frame shortly after the first year of life. These findings attest to the universality of the phenomenon, and suggest possible biological or maturational mechanisms. At the same time, clear and consistent individual differences in altruism emerge in terms of children's affects, behaviors, and apparent motives by the second half of the second year of life (Zahn-Waxler et al., 1979); and developmental pathways to altruism are different for different children (Radke-Yarrow & Zahn-Waxler, in press). Constitutional, temperamental, and environmental factors are probably also significant influences in determining the course of altruism.

Summary and Implications of Developmental Analysis of Altruism

Somewhere between 12 and 18 months of age, the majority of children studied progressed through developmental sequences moving from little interactive responding or diffuse affective responding to others' distress, to different positive forms of reaching out toward and caring for another person in need. Several hundred prosocial interventions were found for this sample of 24 children studied over a 9-month period of time. Children 18 months of age and older responded, on the average, with prosocial behavior to about one-third of all distresses witnessed. Similar levels of prosocial intervention in children of this age have been found in replication studies (Zahn-Waxler, Note 4) in which outside observers as well as mother–observers have been used.

Many children, it appears, are able to perform a caregiver function well by the age of 1½–2 years. Not only do they comfort another person by patting, hugging, or presenting an object, but also they have more sophisticated and complex methods of attempting to help. They express verbal sympathy, they give suggestions about how to handle problems, they are sometimes judgmental in their helping, they appear to try to cheer others up, and they sometimes try alternative helping responses when a given technique was not effective. According to the dictionary definition of altruism, it would seem appropriate to conclude that many (although by no means all) of these prosocial behaviors could be interpreted as containing elements of altruism. The behaviors appear to be intended to reduce suffering in others and to reflect concern for the victim in distress. Many of the acts would undoubtedly be judged as altruistic if an older child or adult were performing the very same behaviors. The use of parental reports provides evidence for many kinds of prosocial reactions in young children that would remain undetected or be underestimated by other procedures.

With few exceptions (Hoffman, 1975), these data on early altruism do not rest well with existing developmental theories of prosocial behavior, which usually posit a much later age of occurrence for "meaningful" prosocial behavior. In the words of Rheingold and Hay (1978), "current theories do not predict a prosocial infant [p. 105]." Choice of methods, too, has played a contributing role. In addition, other views of children's early social development have made it difficult to accept the idea that the very young child could perform caregiver functions. Often in studies of attachment and bonding, the child's helplessness, dependency, and inability to distinguish self from others were emphasized. In psychoanalytic theory, the infant's demanding, egocentric, and narcissistic attributes were highlighted. More recently, other characteristics of the young human offspring have come into focus. Increasingly, there are studies that corroborate very young children's understanding of others' internal states, children's abilities to cooperate and take turns with others, their willingness to share with peers and adults, and their capabilities for giving help (e.g., Bretherton, McNew, & Beeghley-Smith, 1981; Eckerman, Whatley, & Kutz, 1975; Rheingold et al., 1976; Ross & Goldman, 1977).

Why do children begin to perform prosocial interventions? The mechanisms used to explain older children's responses to victims in distress are mostly inapplicable to 1- and 2-year-old children. It is not viable, for example, to postulate for very young children mechanisms that involve (a) adoption of specific value systems; (b) adherence to learned norms of reciprocity, responsibility, or deservedness; (c) careful balancing of cost and gain or other sophisticated inferential processes; and so forth. And, as noted earlier, both cognitive and psychoanalytic theories mark altruism as a relative latecomer in development so they are not useful for understanding the prosocial behavior of young children. Hoffman's conceptual model (1975) is unique among theories of altruism in that it addresses early origins and does so within a developmental framework that highlights the role of both cognition and affect. He has hypothesized that a rudimentary form of altruism develops through a conditioning process in children between infancy and 2 years of age. It is motivated first by empathic distress and then by sympathetic distress, as self-other differentiation increases and the child's caring behaviors become progressively more oriented toward the emotional needs of the victim rather than those of the self. Early socialization experiences have also been implicated as potentially powerful determinants of the frequency and form of young children's prosocial behaviors (Rheingold & Hay, 1978; Zahn-Waxler et al., 1979; Grusec, Chapter 6). Observational learning, in which young children view significant others provide and receive comfort, may be an important contributor to altruism. So, too, might be children's own experiences with empathic caregiving: They themselves are distressed, and then experience comforting behavior from the caregiver. Also, children's potentials for responding to direct instructions, explanations, punishments, and reinforcements from caregivers about prosocial behaviors are relevant for understanding early altruism. However, knowledge of caretakers' actual socialization techniques regarding children's altruism is practically nonexistent.

In our own data on child-rearing practices based on home observations and parent reports (Zahn-Waxler et al., 1979), there was evidence of associations between maternal behaviors and children's prosocial behaviors. Mothers' empathic caregiving was related to children's altruism. Also, certain of mothers' disciplinary techniques in child-caused distress situations were linked with children's altruistic acts in bystander events. The rearing methods most effective were mothers' use of affective, sometimes moralistic, explanations about the negative consequences for others of the children's hurtful behaviors. The strong sanctions against hurting others contained in these explanations were also expressed in statements of principle and of love withdrawal, and in verbal prohibitions against hurting others. With respect to reinforcement theory, Grusec (see Chapter 6) provides naturalistic data

based on the reports of trained mother-observers on mothers' use of reinforcements for altruism; a number of different rewards, mostly social reinforcements that mothers use with their 4- and 7-year-old children were
identified (e.g., appreciation, smiles, hugs, praise). Our own analysis of
maternal reinforcements of altruism of younger children yielded similar reinforcement categories but with much lower frequencies of occurrence. Such
behaviors may well serve to encourage altruism.

Increased knowledge of the diversity, complexity, and ambiguity contained within the broad category of prosocial interventions can help investigators to begin to operationalize the phenomena with increased precision.
This, in turn, should aid in the construction of theories about altruism.
Procedures like those used here make it possible to obtain an unusually
comprehensive, descriptive base of data on altruism. To the extent that this is
done, it should become increasingly possible to uncover the multiple determinants and motives of prosocial acts: For example, different modes of
prosocial behavior could then be explored in relation to personality characteristics of children, parental socialization practices, and developmental
processes that might be especially relevant to altruism. This is a strategy
particularly important with young children for whom verbalizations about
their motives and reasons for prosocial interventions are not readily forthcoming.

An Analysis of Research Methods

*Children's Reactions to Natural versus
Simulated Distresses*

Comparisons of children's responses to natural versus simulated distress
emotions help to provide some perspective on the nature of the eliciting
stimuli used by the two methods. To a certain degree, the comparisons touch
on issues of validity of measurements as well. Do children respond with
similar relative frequencies to natural as opposed to simulated distresses?
Are there significant associations between children's reactions to the two
types of stimuli? Table 5.1A and B provide visual comparisons of children's
reactions to all naturally occurring distresses observed by the children and to
the simulated distresses of their mothers. The developmental analyses described earlier indicated some differences in children's reactions to these
two categories of stimuli. In addition, there were several significant main
effects of distress type as well. Children showed greater distress to natural
than to simulated distress at Time 1, $F (1, 18) = 36.79$, $p < .001$, and at
Time 2, $F (1, 18) = 20.25$, $p < .005$. Also, more aggression was seen in

response to the naturally occurring than to the simulated distresses at Time 2, $F (1, 18) = 5.18$, $p < .05$. More imitation of simulated distress than of naturally occurring emotion was seen at Time 1, $F (1, 18) = 5.01$, $p < .05$. Simulations of affect led to greater seeking out of the caregiver than did natural distresses at Time 1, $F (1, 18) = 8.10$, $p < .01$, and at Time 2, $F (1, 18) = 6.94$, $p < .05$. Simulations of distress also resulted in more positive affect than natural distresses at Time 1, $F (1, 18) = 11.07$, $p < .005$, and at Time 2, $F (1, 18) = 10.65$, $p < .005$. The relative frequencies of prosocial interventions to natural and to simulated distresses were remarkably similar, usually occurring on 30–35% of all distress occasions, once the response capability began to occur with significant frequency.

Correlations provide evidence of the degree to which there is congruence between children's responses to natural and simulated distresses. Intercorrelations of parallel response categories for natural and simulated distresses were computed separately for Cohort $A_{T2}B_{T1}$ and Cohort $B_{T2}C_{T1}$. Children who were nonresponsive to naturally occurring distresses also tended to be nonresponsive to simulated distresses, $r (15) = .47$, $p < .10$ (Cohort $A_{T2}B_{T1}$), and $r (14) = .58$, $p < .05$ (Cohort $B_{T2}C_{T1}$). Children's distress reactions to others' distress were also significantly interrelated across natural and simulated settings, $r (15) = .50$, $p < .05$, and $r (14) = .59$, $p < .05$. Prosocial responses to natural and simulated distresses were correlated, $r (14) = .63$, $p < .01$ in Cohort $B_{T2}C_{T1}$. The similar frequencies and the interdependencies of children's prosocial reactions to natural and simulated emotions suggest that (a) mothers' sampling of children's responses to naturally occurring emotion events is not unduly selective or biased; and (b) children's responses to simulations of distress may provide valid indexes of the young child's social behavior.

The patterns of difference between children's responses to natural and simulated distresses do not lend themselves well to simple interpretations. Also, there are confounds. Natural distresses include a wide range of distress victims, whereas simulated distresses were performed just by the mothers. That natural distresses elicited relatively more distress and aggression whereas simulated distresses elicited relatively more positive emotion indicates that, in certain respects, natural distresses are more compelling stimuli. Yet the two types of distress yielded equivalent rates of prosocial responding, so in this respect, on the average, children treat the two sets of circumstances with similar seriousness. The laughter and smiling in response to simulations were especially pronounced in the younger children (evidenced in the earlier reported interaction effect). The simulations sometimes may have been ambiguous stimuli for these younger children. The dramatic acting out of distress by mothers may, on occasion, have appeared as playful actions.

Also, laughter or smiling in response to distress can be a sign of tension. One is reminded of the sometimes fine line between comedy (distress that evokes humor) and tragedy (distress that evokes sorrow).

Children's Reactions to Mother versus Experimenter

How the child responds to different persons is of particular interest when one is exploring the early development of prosocial orientations. This was examined systematically in comparisons of children's responses to mothers' versus investigators' simulations of emotions: Responses to mother more nearly reflect the young child's day-to-day circumstances, whereas responses to an investigator would more likely be assessed in the typical research design. Comparisons were made of children's responses to the four simulations that were performed by both mother and investigator (negative affects of pain, choking cough, anger on the phone, and laughter). Prosocial interventions toward mother were significantly more frequent than those directed toward the investigator, $t(16) = 2.69$, $p < .05$ for Sample $A_{T2} B_{T1}$, and $t(15) = 2.30$, $p < .05$ for Sample $B_{T2} C_{T1}$, supporting a variant of the adage "charity begins at home." The average levels of prosocial actions for Samples $A_{T2} B_{T1}$ and $B_{T2} C_{T1}$ were 13% and 39% respectively (response to mother), and 3% and 9% respectively (response to home visitor). In addition, children in Sample $A_{T2} B_{T1}$ showed significantly more distress, $t(16) = 2.13$, $p < .05$, and more positive affect $t(16) = 2.52$, $p < .05$, to simulations of distress by mother than by the home visitor. Children also responded differentially to laughter expressed by the mother and by the home visitor. Children in Sample $A_{T2} B_{T1}$ laughed more frequently in response to mothers' laughter, $t(16) = 2.39$, $p < .05$, but smiled (only) more frequently in response to the home visitor, $t(16) = -2.59$, $p < .05$. Children in Sample $B_{T2} C_{T1}$ were more likely to imitate laughter expressed by their mother than by the home visitor, $t(15) = 2.30$, $p < .05$.

Given the attachment relationship of mother and child to each other, differences in children's responses to mother and to a relative stranger are not necessarily surprising. What is interesting is the constellation of differences. Children's heightened responding to mother included not only those attachment behaviors reflecting the child's dependency, but also behaviors of the child that illustrate the child's abilities: (a) to perform acts of care giving and comforting; and (b) to share positive emotional experiences with the mother. The findings also illustrate the importance of including family members in the research design to provide a veridical assessment of the extent to which the very young child is prosocial. If the study had used a relative stranger as the victim, the conclusion would have been that children between the ages of 1 and 2 are not capable of prosocial behavior. At the same time, it may be important to study children's responding in both types of settings, and to look for continuities of behavior that are not necessarily reflected in comparisons of identical response categories. For example, Weston and Main (Note 3) have studied children of this age and have reported correspondence between children's "concerned attending" to an adult actor in the laboratory and mothers' reports of children's prosocial interventions in the home.

Issues of Reliability and Validity

We were encouraged by the quality and quantity of data obtained through parents' reports. Mothers did not appear to try to put themselves or their children in a "good light," but rather attended responsibly to the requirements of the observing task. The estimates of observer and coder reliability also suggested that it was possible to train mothers to be reasonably accurate, reliable observers of their own children's behaviors. On the occasions when the mother, along with two independent investigators, made observations of children's responses to the same simulated events, reliability figures were just as high between mothers and investigators as they were between the two investigators (e.g., Cummings, Zahn-Waxler, & Radke-Yarrow, 1981). Sometimes there were behavior categories that did not yield good reliability. Positive emotion (laughter and smiles) in response to others' distress was difficult to observe reliably and, here, the inherent ambiguity of the meaning of this response may have contributed to the problem. In some instances, mothers' unique knowledge about their own children may help them to see behaviors that might be missed by someone less familiar with the research subject. There may also be occasions in which a given mother may be more affectively involved in an interaction in a way that make her less able to provide an accurate observation account.

For the major research questions regarding prosocial behaviors, mothers were asked to observe relatively moral, overt behaviors, for example, "Mary put her arms around Jimmy and hugged him and said 'Okay, now?'" Or, "When she saw Sally cry she started to fuss and cry, and then put out her arms for me to pick her up." A difficult area of observation for any trained observer, but relevant to theories of empathy (especially if one assumes that the face "mirrors" emotions), concerns descriptions of affective facial expressions that precede and accompany prosocial interventions. An upset facial expression is ambiguous. For example, it could variously indicate concern for self, concern for victim, empathy, guilt, or fear. Furthermore, different mothers may observe facial expressions with different levels of accuracy, just as some trained observers are better at this task than others. Very fine differentiations are required in order to make accurate discriminations between different emotions (Izard, 1977). The assessment of motives for altruism via measures of affect may require additional methodologies. Educational level of parent-observers might play some role in their differential abilities in general to make subtle and accurate observations. Within our own sample, there were no apparent differences in the observing abilities of mothers with high school and college educations.

How broadly or how narrowly should the observation framework be defined for the parent-observer? If it is too general, the observer may be faced with an overload of information and attempt to provide too much data. If it is too narrow, the observer may become unduly preoccupied with the behaviors in question. In the abstract, it would seem valuable to attempt to provide a framework that gives the parent-observer the full range of opportunities to describe all stimuli and reactions relevant to the research question, but, at the same time, one that does not make the parent acutely aware of the specific response patterns and contingencies under investigation. This might also help to minimize problems of social desirability in reporting. To the extent that the parent begins to ruminate on his or her behavior, it is possible that behaviors may begin to change, become selective, become questioned, and so forth. Some experimentation may be necessary in order to provide observing frameworks optimal for obtaining veridical data.

Convergent validation of findings from studies using very different procedures provides some basis for determining the validity of the phenomena that are studied. In this chapter our emphasis has been on the use of parental reporting for obtaining data relevant to the development of altruism in children. The methodology also made it possible to obtain data on parents' child-rearing and disciplinary practices in circumstances of distress. (Here, too, were indications that mothers did not attempt to "hold back" information, as they described their fights, their use of physical punishment and love withdrawal, and so forth.) When parental data are obtained in this manner and related to individual differences in children's altruism (Zahn-Waxler et al., 1979), there is significant correspondence between the results of the naturalistic study of socialization practices and those of an experimental study (Yarrow et al., 1973) of 3-5-year-old children in which different child-rearing environments were systematically varied (described in Radke-Yarrow & Zahn-Waxler, in press).

PROSOCIAL BEHAVIORS: NEW DIRECTIONS FOR RESEARCH

One strategy for assessing reliability and validity of data obtained with given procedures is to continue to study the sample of children over long periods of time, using both old and new research strategies. Here, the original 24 families were seen again 5 years later. Mothers reported on children's responses to naturally occurring and simulated emotions in the home for a 3-month period, and home visitors performed simulations. Children were also seen in a laboratory setting: Their responses to batteries of simulated distress incidents, their reasoning about hypothetical distress incidents, and their perspective-taking skills were measured. In addition to the reliability methods used previously, different reliability assessments were also made. Mothers viewed videotapes of children's responses to distress and used their standard reporting procedures to record the content of these incidents. Some of the incidents were naturally occurring prosocial and antisocial interactions filmed in a day care setting. Other incidents included simulations of children's responses to the distress of a peer: Different child confederates were seen responding to a peer's distress (a) with verbal sympathy and behavioral help; (b) with laughter and callous indifference; and (c) with no apparent reaction. With this technique mothers' reports can be compared with those of staff members trained in techniques of observation. The comparison of laboratory assessments of children in the longitudinal sample with a matched control group will also facilitate exploration of another methodological issue: namely, whether mothers trained to focus on their young children's functioning in affective encounters may have come to differ systematically from untrained mothers in what they are sensitized to, and hence what they communicate to their children about emotions. If differential communications about affect occur, these might be reflected in the behaviors of children in affective events.

Other extensions of research design and method are being pursued currently with a second sample of young children. One purpose is to explore further and to describe and explain different developmental processes associated with different kinds of altruism. A second but related purpose is to study some children from environments in which distress is a more pervasive, chronic stimulus. The empathy and prosocial behavior of children of clinically depressed parents is being investigated. If the distress of depressed parents is conveyed with special intensity, their children might be aroused similarly with special intensity. For example, some children might become particularly avoidant of others' distresses whereas others might become especially empathic. Twenty-seven children, each beginning at the age of 12 months, are being followed longitudinally. Mothers engage in the usual reporting and simulation procedures. New naturalistic and experimental procedures are used as well.

After several months of home visits and maternal reporting, children's reactions to mothers' simulations of distress were videotaped during a home visit (at 18 and 21 months of age). This provides a permanent visual record that can be used as a check on validity of mothers' reports. Many of the different responses to distress reported by mothers were observed to occur in the videotape accounts (Zahn-Waxler, Note 4). Furthermore, young children's different prosocial behaviors were remarkably similar to the early interventions described in the mother's reports. Videotapes also facilitate analyses of children's expressions of affect. It might then be possible, for example, to distinguish empathic arousal from fear by careful examination of the child's affective expression. Mothers' simulations can be assessed from the videotape records. Is there homogeneity or considerable variance in mothers' portrayals of distress? If there are individual differences in how mothers express emotions, are they reflected in systematic differences in children's behavior? Other procedures are introduced when children reach the age of 2–2½. The children and their mothers are seen in laboratory visits, and their responses to naturally occurring and simulated distresses are videotaped. Children are exposed to a range of distress stimuli interwoven with play activities. The distresses vary in terms of the specific affects, the actors, and whether the distresses are hypothetical or real (e.g., a mother crying, a tape-recorded infant cry, a distressed peer, a picture of a crying child). It will be informative to examine children's responses to distress when the mother is the reporter of behavior and when other research methods are used as well. Also, it will be possible with these independent measures to assess continuity–discontinuity further in children's orientations toward victims in distress over an extended period of time.

The research design also provides an opportunity to assess specific areas of accuracy and inaccuracy in mothers' retrospections. Currently, when the children are 2 years old, mothers are asked to recall some of the same maternal and child behaviors for which they had made specific observations 6 months to 1 year earlier. From these data it may be possible to distinguish areas of accurate recall from those where recollections are blurred or distorted.

In this chapter we have focused on the use of trained family members as observers as a primary tool for obtaining developmental data on children's altruism. These are not diary accounts and should not be referred to as such. That label would unduly alter the meaning of an observation record by implying bias, selectivity of reporting, and so forth before an evaluation is made of the parent's observing skills. Other investigators are also beginning to use parent–observers to study altruism (Grusec, Chapter 6; Crockenberg, Note 5). The procedures can be used for a broader, extended range of social and behavioral research questions, especially for the many variables not readily accessible to the experimenter or observer. As with any method, the viability of parental observation is increased if the method is used in juxtaposition with other research strategies. Any research problem that continues to rely exclusively on a single procedure, whether it is mothers' observations of behavior in the home setting, experimenters' assessments of children's responses to a hypothetical distress in the laboratory, a tester's coding of child's response to a story, or a single manipulation of mood states, and so on will ultimately fall short of the mark of ideal methodological requirements.

The principal aim of this chapter has been to outline the development of new response strategies for studying the early origins and ontogenesis of altruistic behaviors. The descriptive findings based on extensive samples of children's responses to multiple and real (or realistic) distress stimuli suggest that choices of methods may play a very critical role in determining the prosocial repertoire of young children; the data highlight the importance of making the natural environment more accessible. The early individual differences in altruism indicate that more than a stage theory approach will be required to understand the processes involved. Rather than continuing to construct contexts for altruism in the laboratory, we might do well first (or simultaneously) to obtain broader descriptive bases that generate greater depth, breadth, and sophistication of understanding of the phenomena (Mussen, Note 6; Baumrind, 1980). Otherwise, we may continue to create in our theories what Baldwin (1967) has referred to as mythologies of childhood.

Because of our interest in the origin of altruism, we chose to focus principally on children's responses to distress stimuli, reasoning that an implicit but central assumption in the definition of altruism is that the altruist is responding to a state of distress (real or perceived) in the victim. In the hundreds of investigations of children's prosocial behavior, measures of children's responses to the distresses of real other persons in distress are indeed rare (see review by Radke-Yarrow et al., in press). Often, the victims are hypothetical, the distresses are less than compelling, and the measures are few and unrepresentative of the phenomena. Many, although not all, of the behaviors we studied here appeared to indicate genuine regard for the other person. In our own research, too, we are still left with ambiguities and unfinished questions. There are other forms of prosocial behavior than those studied here. There are questions of interpretation of intent of some of the behaviors measured. For example, the early physical forms of prosocial intervention could reflect attempts by the child to give or receive comfort in circumstances of distress. Seeking the caregiver and distress reactions to others' distress, too, could reflect concern for self or empathy for the victim. Questions of motives and intent are not readily resolved. However, by using extensions of paradigms like those described here, it should now become possible to begin to distinguish empirically between different experiential and instigating factors that influence the different forms of prosocial behavior and the different motives for prosocial actions. With such an approach, it might be possible to apply the scientific process better to the study of children's compassion and aggression toward victims in distress.

ACKNOWLEDGMENTS

We wish to thank the mothers who served as observers. We are grateful to John Bartko, Claire Horowitz, Eunice Kennelly, Robert King, Marilyn Pickett, Frances Polen, Judy Smith, Maris Udey, and Jean Welsh for their assistance in various stages of the research. We express appreciation to Nancy Eisenberg, Mark Cummings, Joan Grusec, Ronald Iannotti, and Leon Kuczynski for their helpful comments on an earlier version of the manuscript. The training manual of instruction for parents' naturalistic reporting and simulations of affect and the coding manuals are available upon request. Requests should be sent to Carolyn Zahn-Waxler, Laboratory of Developmental Psychology, National Institute of Mental Health, 9000 Rockville Pike, Bethesda, Maryland 20205.

REFERENCE NOTES

1. Chandler, M. *Knowing the sort of help that is really needed: A consideration of developmental prerequisites to effective helping behavior.* Society for Research in Child Development, New Orleans, 1977.
2. Goldsmith, H. H., Campos, J. J., Benson, N., Henderson, C., & East, P. *Genetics of infant temperament: Parental report and laboratory observations.* International Conference on Infant Studies, New Haven, Conn., 1980.
3. Weston, D., & Main, M. *Infant responses to the crying of an adult actor in the laboratory: Stability and correlates of "concerned attention."* International Conference on Infant Studies, New Haven, Conn., 1980.
4. Zahn-Waxler, C. *Young children's responses to the emotions of others.* Workshop on infant reactions to emotional signals: 12–18 months. International Conference on Infant Studies, New Haven, Conn., 1980.
5. Crockenberg, S. Personal communication, June 1979.
6. Mussen, P. *Choices, regrets and lousy models (with reference to prosocial development).* American Psychological Association, San Francisco, 1977.

REFERENCES

Achenbach, T. M., & Edelbrock, C. S. Behavior problems and competencies reported by parents of normal and disturbed children aged 14 through 16. *Monograph of the Society for Research in Child Development,* 1981, *44*(No. 185).

Baldwin, A. *Theories of child development.* New York: Wiley, 1967.

Baumrind, D. New directions in socialization research. *American Psychologist,* 1980, *35*(7), 639–652.

Birch, H. G., Thomas, A., Chess, S., & Hertzig, M. E. Individuality in the development of children. *Developmental Medicine and Child Neurology,* 1962, *4*, 370–379.

Bretherton, I., McNew, S., & Beeghley-Smith, M. Early person knowledge as expressed in gestural and verbal communications: When do infants acquire a "theory of mind"? In *Infant social cognition*. Hillsdale, N.J.: Lawrence Erlbaum Associates, 1981.

Clifford, E. Discipline in the home: A controlled observational study of parental practices. *Journal of Genetic Psychology*, 1959, *96*, 45–82.

Cummings, E. M., Zahn-Waxler, C., & Radke-Yarrow, M. Young children's responses to expressions of anger and affection by others in the family. *Child Development*, 1981, *52*, 1274–1282.

Eckerman, C. O., Whatley, J. L., & Kutz, S. L. Growth of social play with peers during the second year of life. *Developmental Psychology*, 1975, *11*, 42–49.

Flavell, J. H. *The developmental psychology of Jean Piaget*. Princeton, N.J.: Van Nostrand, 1963.

Goodenough, F. *Anger in young children*. Minneapolis: University of Minnesota Press, 1931.

Hoffman, M. L. Developmental synthesis of affect and cognition and its implication for altruistic motivation. *Developmental Psychology*, 1975, *11*(5), 605–622.

Izard, C. E. Emergence of emotions and development of consciousness in infancy. In J. M. Davidson, R. J. Davidson, and G. E. Schwartz (Eds.), *Human consciousness and its transformations: A psychological perspective*. New York: Plenum Press, 1977.

Murphy, L. B. *Social behavior and child personality*. New York: Columbia University Press, 1937.

Parke, R. D. Interactional designs. In R. B. Cairns (Ed.), *The origins of social interactions*. Hillsdale, N.J.: Lawrence Erlbaum Associates, 1979.

Radke-Yarrow, M., & Zahn-Waxler, C. Roots, motives, and patterning in children's prosocial behavior. In J. Reykowski, D. Bar-Tal, & E. Staub (Eds.), *Origins and maintenance of prosocial behavior*. New York: Plenum Press, in press.

Radke-Yarrow, M., Zahn-Waxler, C., & Chapman, M. Prosocial dispositions and behavior. In P. Mussen (Ed.), *Manual of child psychology, Volume on personality and social development*. New York: Wiley, in press.

Reid, J. B. *A social learning approach to family intervention* (Vol. 2). *Observation in home settings*. Eugene, Ore.: Oregon Social Learning Center: Castalia Publishing, 1978.

Rheingold, H., & Hay, D. Prosocial behavior of the very young. In G. S. Stent (Ed.), *Morality as a biological phenomenon*. Berlin: Dahlem Konferenzen, 1978.

Rheingold, H., Hay, D., & West, M. Sharing in the second year of life. *Child Development*, 1976, *47*, 1148–1158.

Ross, H. S., & Goldman, B. D. Establishing new social relations in infancy. In T. Alloway, L. Krames, & P. Pliner (Eds.), *Advances in communication and affect* (Vol. 4). New York: Plenum Press, 1977.

Schaie, K. W. Methodological problems in descriptive developmental research on adulthood and aging. In J. Nesselroade & H. Reese (Eds.), *Life-span developmental psychology: Methodological issues*. New York: Academic Press, 1973.

Webster's Seventh New Collegiate Dictionary. Springfield, Mass.: G & C Merriam, 1965.

Wenar, C. The reliability of developmental histories. *Psychosomatic Medicine*, 1963, *25*, 505–509.

Yarrow, M., Campbell, J., & Burton, R. Recollections of childhood: A study of the retrospective method. *Monographs of the Society for Research in Child Development*, 1970, *35*(5, Serial No. 138).

Yarrow, M., Scott, P., & Waxler, C. Learning concern for others. *Developmental Psychology*, 1973, *8*, 240–260.

Zahn-Waxler, C., Radke-Yarrow, M., & King, R. A. Child rearing and children's prosocial initiations toward victims of distress. *Child Development*, 1979, *50*, 319–330.

JOAN E. GRUSEC

The Socialization of Altruism

The origins of altruism, or concern for others, are not obvious. It may be that children have a natural proclivity for empathizing with the needs of others, and so attempts to alleviate these needs may be fairly easy to encourage. No such natural predisposition may exist, however, and so the socialization of altruism may prove a somewhat more arduous task. However easy or difficult the task may be, it is usually considered desirable that children acquire, or have refined, the ability and tendency to help others. The subject of this chapter will be some of the techniques that are, or can be, used by agents of socialization in this learning process.

Altruism is usually defined as behaviors such as helping, sharing, comforting, and defending, which occur independent of any external benefit to the altruist, and which may even include self-sacrifice. It is difficult, of course, to be completely certain that a particular act is not followed by some kind of external positive consequence, although this consequence may be more obvious in some cases than others. Perhaps it is just that society, before labeling conduct as altruistic, demands that external rewards for prosocial conduct not be too obvious. Children who volunteer to help their mothers wash the dishes so that they will be taken to the park are not considered altruistic, but children who wash the dishes in order to have their mothers pleased with them may well be thought of as altruistic: The psychological reward of maternal approval seems less salient than the physical reward of being taken on an outing. The long-term goal of socialization, of course, is that our children wash the dishes purely for the intrinsic pleasure of knowing they have eased their mothers' household burdens, and that this intrinsic

139

THE DEVELOPMENT OF
PROSOCIAL BEHAVIOR

pleasure be just as strong if mothers never even know the identity of their benefactors.

This long-range goal has been labeled "internalization," the process whereby children take on society's values as their own. By this process society is relieved of the necessity to maintain constant surveillance over its citizens—an impossible task—and can be assured that people behave well because they experience such unpleasant but self-induced sensations as guilt when they deviate, or self-induced feelings of pleasure and pride when they conform. When behavior is attributed to internal rather than external causes, then internalization is complete, and the job of socialization has been successful. Such a state may not, in fact, be possible. But child-rearing techniques that most nearly produce such a state are of particular interest to the student of social development.

For a long time it was supposed that young children were incapable of showing concern for others. To the extent that egocentric thinking characterized children in the preoperational stage, they were thought to be unable to put themselves in the position of others in order to understand their needs and thereby be able to help. In the last several years it has become evident that even preschoolers have at least minimal skills in comprehending the point of view of others (e.g., Shatz & Gelman, 1973) and that they are quite capable of sharing, helping, and showing concern (e.g., Buckley, Siegel, & Ness, 1979; Rheingold, Hay, & West, 1976; Strayer, 1980; Zahn-Waxler, Radke-Yarrow, & Brady-Smith, 1977). Zahn-Waxler and Radke-Yarrow (1979) report that children as young as 12 months exhibit strong reactions to distress in others, and that the prototype for later reactions to the emotional distress of others can be seen as early as 2 years of age. Their intriguing work is discussed at length in Chapter 5 of this book.

Our own research, in which mothers record descriptions of their children's altruism, confirms that children as young as 4 years of age have well-developed and extensive helping repertoires. Some mothers report seeing their children engage in an average of more than one altruistic act per day, and it is quite evident that young children do show a remarkable degree of concern for others. Following are some typical examples of mothers' reports of their children's behavior that suggest that these children are capable of displaying some quite sophisticated examples of altruism:

> We were getting ready to go to friends for the rest of the day and preparations were becoming rather frantic. Cynthia (age 4) said to Richard (her younger brother), "Come on, I'll read you a story and we'll stay out of Mum and Dad's way." They sat together on the couch and Cynthia "read" (memorized) two books to him. When they were finished I said, "It was great being able to get ready without any interruptions."

David (age 4) has been playing at a neighbour's house for the afternoon. Michael (6) his next door neighbour and best friend has been playing at the neighbour's too. I'm taking both children home—Michael is riding his bike. David spots a car rounding the corner and shouts to Michael *"You should make a signal!"* David continues to lecture Michael on "safety" and then I realize that David is being overly concerned because Michael ran in front of a car this winter and was knocked down and since then David has shown a lot of concern about Michael's safety. When I catch up with David I say to him, *"You're concerned about Michael's safety—that's nice."*

THE TRAINING OF ALTRUISM

Researchers have investigated a variety of techniques that could be useful in developing children's altruism. In the material that follows these techniques will be described under three major headings: those that follow altruism, those that follow lack of altruism, and those that occur independent of the child's behavior but that subsequently facilitate concern for others. Each section will begin with a description of research that has been designed to assess the most effective way of inducing altruism: Most research has, in fact, been experimental in nature. This will be followed by a description of recent research from our own laboratory in which we have assessed altruism as it occurs in natural settings—primarily the child's home.

In our studies we have used a technique similar to that described by Zahn-Waxler and Radke-Yarrow (and first developed by Goodenough, 1931). We trained mothers in both group and individual sessions to record the behavior of their children. We were interested in any kind of helping act displayed by children and the reactions it elicited, so we asked them to write down, as soon after its occurrence as possible, a description of any altruism their child displayed and the reaction to that deed of anyone who was present. Mothers also were asked to record situations in which altruism should have occurred but did not, as well as any occasions on which they directly instructed their children about concern for others. Altruism was defined for them as any act in which their child intended to help another person or animal in a real situation (i.e., fantasy altruism was excluded)— especially, but not only, if some cost to the doer was involved. Behaviors that were considered regular duties (e.g., setting the table if it was part of the child's household responsibilities) were not to be recorded. Types of altruism included giving; sharing; helping; cooperating; protecting; encouraging; making restitution; comforting; and showing affection, concern, or consideration. To date, we have obtained records from the mothers of 11 male and 11 female 4-year-olds, and 8 male and 6 female 7-year-olds. Each mother collected data for approximately 4 weeks. The children were middle-class, primarily Caucasian, and generally had nonworking mothers.

In order to assess the reliability of mothers' observations, two different assessments were obtained. Just before they began their observations, mothers were shown a 20-minute videotape recording of a "typical" day in the life of a family. They were asked to observe the behavior of one specific child and to identify each instance of altruism that child displayed, each instance of lack of altruism, and each instance of direct instruction about altruism. There were 12 relevant incidents in the videotape. Overall, mothers correctly identified 96% of these incidents. Halfway through the data collection period, mothers were visited in their homes by a research assistant at a time when the child being observed was present. The mother had previously been asked to make two requests for altruism of her child sometime during the visit. The mother and the research assistant made independent records of the events that occurred after each request. Observer agreement for various categories of behavior will be reported in later parts of this chapter.

Immediate Consequences of Altruism

Reinforcement

The effects of reinforcement on altruism are extensively reviewed by Rushton in Chapter 4. A number of investigators have found that both material and social rewards will increase the occurrence of helping, sharing, and cooperating (Azrin & Lindsley, 1956; Fischer, 1963; Gelfand, Hartmann, Cromer, Smith, & Page, 1975; Hartmann, Gelfand, Smith, Paul, Cromer, Page, & Lebenta, 1976). Recall, however, that the aim of socialization is to encourage children to internalize the standards of society—in the case of altruism, to show concern for others "for its own sake." It is not at all clear from existing research that reinforcement produces internalization, that is, that children will eventually show concern for others even when reinforcement is discontinued.

In one recent study, Smith, Gelfand, Hartmann, and Partlow (1979) have provided some interesting insights into this problem. They followed the sharing of 7- and 8-year-old children with either praise ("That was a fine thing you did") or a material reward (a penny for each time the child shared). The children were then asked to give a reason for why they had shared. Those children who had been socially reinforced were likely to attribute their sharing to a desire to help or a concern for the welfare of the child with whom they had shared. Children who had received material reward said they had shared to get a reward. These data suggest, then, that behavior followed by a positive social consequence is seen by a child as compelled by some inner desire or value system—a major condition for internalization—whereas that followed by a positive material consequence is more likely to be seen as the result of external pressure from others. At the moment, however, the results of Smith *et al.* can only be considered suggestive, especially since the relationship between kind of attribution and subsequent sharing was weak.

Attribution of Prosocial Characteristics

Reinforcement is generally conceptualized as an outcome that is perceived as pleasant, at least by the recipient, and one that therefore leads to a greater probability that the response it follows will occur again. There is another event that can follow responding and that also has been shown to increase the probability of that responding, but that may be effective for reasons other than its pleasurable characteristics. This is the attribution of certain characteristics to the actor for his or her behavior. Thus Dienstbier, Hillman, Lehnhoff, Hillman, and Valkenaar (1975) labeled the emotions of children who had transgressed as either shame at having been found out or guilt due to the transgression itself. Subsequent deviation in which behavior could apparently not be detected was greater in the shame than in the guilt condition. Jensen and Moore (1977) administered a test to children and told them their performance suggested that they were either cooperative or competitive: The children's behavior changed in accord with the description they had been given. And, in another example of the effect, Toner, Moore, and Emmons (1980) reported that girls who had been told they were patient were able to delay gratification longer than those not given the label.

In our own laboratory we have explored the effects of attributional statements on children's altruism. In one study (Grusec, Kuczynski, Rushton, & Simutis, 1978a), we hypothesized that, if children who had shared were told they had done so because they were the kind of people who liked to help others whenever possible, they would subsequently share more than if they were told they had done so because they had been expected to. In the former case, sharing would be attributed to internal desires and values, and hence more likely internalized, whereas in the latter it would be attributed to external pressures—once the external pressure was removed, then altruism would no longer occur. An additional hypothesis of the study was that these attributional statements would have an effect on behavior only if children were really unsure about why they had behaved altruistically in the first place.

To test these hypotheses, we invited children to play a miniature bowling game in which they could, for good performance, win tokens that could be traded for prizes. Some children (in a modeling condition) first watched an adult who played the game and donated half his winnings to buy gifts for poor children. These subjects then played the game with the adult watching them, a procedure that was sufficient to induce them also to share half their winnings with the needy. Other children (in a direct instruction condition) were simply instructed when they played the game to share half their tokens with the poor children. We speculated that children in this latter condition would know why they had shared—they had been told to and so would be unaffected by subsequent attributions—whereas those in the modeling condition would be less sure about the reasons for their behavior, and so would be more responsive to different attributions. After children in all conditions had donated, the adult responded in one of three ways, either (a) suggesting that they had shared because they were the kind of people who really enjoyed helping others; (b) suggesting that they had shared because they thought the adult had expected them to; or (c) simply noting that they had shared quite a bit (a comment common to all conditions).

Children were then left alone to play the game again, and their donation was observed from an adjacent room through a one-way mirror. Subsequently children were given 12 colored pencils as a reward for taking part in the research, and were given the opportunity to share some of these pencils anonymously with other children in the school who would not have the opportunity to participate in the research. This latter procedure provided a test of how well the effects of the experimental manipulation would generalize to a related situation involving a somewhat different form of altruism.

The results of this study are summarized in Table 6.1. The effects of attributional statements on donation of tokens to poor children were evident only in the modeling condition, as predicted. In this condition, children who had had their sharing attributed to their own personality characteristics shared significantly more than children who had had sharing attributed to external pressure from an adult. Attributional statements had no effect on sharing in the direct instruction condition. (The high level of sharing in the direct instruction condition in the absence of surveillance should be noted

Table 6.1
Mean Number of Tokens Donated and Pencils Shared in Each Condition

		Internal attribution	External attribution	No attribution
Modeling	Tokens	6.07	2.72	4.14
	Pencils	4.22	4.21	4.13
Direct instruction	Tokens	5.64	4.78	4.36
	Pencils	5.79	4.36	3.99

and will be discussed later in this chapter.) Attributional statements did have an effect in both training conditions when the test was one of generalization: Here the amount of sharing was statistically significantly greater in the internal-attribution than the external-attribution or no-attribution conditions, regardless of whether donation had been induced originally by modeling or by direct instruction. Where no external coercion was operating, that is, when no one had instructed the children to share pencils, the effects of attribution were evident.

The results of this study provided support for the contention that following altruism with some kind of explanation for the behavior will modify future occurrences of that behavior, at least under conditions where the cause of altruism initially is ambiguous. But does the attribution of prosocial characteristics have any different effect on behavior than social reinforcement such as praise? Is the attribution of prosocial characteristics perhaps no more than a form of social reinforcement? This was the question addressed in a second study (Grusec & Redler, 1980).

In this study 8-year-olds were brought to a research trailer and were induced to share by an experimenter who suggested they could donate some of their winnings from the bowling game to poor children if they wished to. With the experimenter standing by, and with only the occasional repetition of the suggestion for some, all children donated half their tokens. They were then told, in a neutral tone of voice, "Gee, you shared quite a bit." To this was added either a prosocial attribution, "I guess you're the kind of person who likes to help others whenever you can; yes, you are a very nice and helpful person," social reinforcement, "It was good that you gave your tokens to those poor children; yes, that was a nice and helpful thing to do," or nothing at all.

A number of tests of altruism, both specific to the training situation and of a generalized nature, were then conducted. First children were left alone to play the bowling game, and the number of tokens they donated to the poor children was observed. They were then asked to share some pencils they had been given with other children in the school who would not be able to play the game. One week later the children returned to the research trailer, but to a different room and to work with a different experimenter. This time they were asked to help the new experimenter with some work she was doing that involved folding cardboard roofs. Following this, children were thanked and then received a prosocial attribution similar to that they had received earlier, or social reinforcement, or nothing at all. The children were then given the opportunity to play with an attractive toy or to continue helping the experimenter. Finally, 3 weeks later, children were visited in their classrooms by another adult who asked them to make drawings and collect craft materials for children who were hospitalized.

If attribution and social reinforcement are equivalent in their function, then they should have affected these various tests of altruism in the same way. That this was not the case is evident from Table 6.2. Both did increase the mean number of tokens subjects donated to poor children, relative to the number donated in the control group. On all tests of generalization, however, only the attribution of prosocial characteristics had an effect on children's altruism. Those in the attribution condition shared more pencils, helped the second experimenter more with her work, and made more drawings and collected more craft materials than children who had been reinforced for their initial altruism. There was no difference between the social reinforcement and control conditions in amount of generalized altruism.

From this study it seems clear that prosocial attributions are not just a variant of social reinforcement. They have their own special characteristics, one of which appears to be the ability to affect not only the behavior they follow but other members of that same class of behaviors. The mechanisms by which prosocial attributions function are not clear, but several suggestions will be discussed. The usefulness of each of these suggestions must be the subject of further research.

First, it is possible that attributions of concern for others may serve to change the self-concept of the individual to whom they are applied. Thus children who are told they are kind and helpful may come to think of themselves as having that particular set of personality characteristics. Such a change in self-concept may not occur when consequences are directed toward an act (social reinforcement) rather than toward a person. To the extent that individuals act consistently with their perceptions of their own dispositional characteristics, then, one would expect someone who had been labeled as altruistic to continue to behave in that manner. Children who had been told (on two different occasions) that they were kind and

Table 6.2

Mean Number of Tokens Donated, Pencils Shared, Cardboard Roofs Folded, and Drawings Made, and the Number of Children Collecting Craft Material in Each Condition[a]

	Attribution	Reinforcement	Control
Tokens	7.7	6.4	3.3
Pencils	5.8	2.8	2.3
Cardboard roofs	4.6	1.8	2.1
Drawings	2.7	1.6	1.4
Craft material	9	2	4

[a] $N = 20$ per condition.

helpful would thus continue to behave in that manner whenever the occasion arose. Those who had been told they had performed a kind and helpful act would be less inclined to widen the repertoire of their kind and helpful acts.

Perry, Perry, Bussey, English, and Arnold (1980) have extended this argument by hypothesizing that children experience self-criticism when they do not live up to prosocial dispositions that have been attributed to them. They suggest that children who are provided with prosocial attributions experience a change in their self-image, and that they consequently make higher demands on themselves for prosocial behavior. When these children fail to measure up to their own increased expectations, they undergo more dissatisfaction and self-recrimination than do children who never had high expectations of themselves in the first place. In order to avoid self-punishment, then, children who have a positive image of themselves behave in accord with this positive image. To test these notions, Perry et al. told children that, based on a previous interaction with them, they believed them to be capable of carrying out instructions, following rules, working hard, and avoiding distraction. The children were then asked to perform a boring task, but they were all successfully distracted from the task by an exciting cartoon that was played at the same time. Children who had been told they were capable of following rules and avoiding distraction failed, then, to live up to their self-expectations. When another adult (not the one who had delivered the prosocial attributions) suggested that the children might not be deserving of all the tokens they were subsequently given for their participation in the study, because they had been distracted, these children kept fewer tokens for themselves than did the children who had been treated identically except for not having had prosocial characteristics attributed to them. Perry et al. interpreted this finding as an indication that children who expected good behavior of themselves were more dissatisfied with their bad performance than were children whose expectations of themselves were not so high.

Yet another explanation of the effects of prosocial attribution might be entertained, one that derives from a levels-of-processing approach to the understanding of memory (Craik & Lockhart, 1972). According to this formulation, people process stimuli to different depths—the more deeply an event is processed the stronger the trace it produces and, therefore, the more easily it is recalled. Let us suppose that an attribution of behavior to the actor's altruistic characteristics is remembered better than some kind of specific praise for the act. If this were the case, then, children who had received prosocial attributions would be more responsive in subsequent situations demanding altruism than those who had received social reinforcement, because they would remember the importance of altruism better. In the Grusec and Redler (1980) study, for example, when someone entered their classroom soliciting materials for sick children, children in the attribution condition may have recalled the experimenter's earlier remarks better than children in the social reinforcement condition, so that a norm of altruism was more easily elicited in this new situation. Again, there are no data pertaining directly to this hypothesis. Rogers, Kuiper, and Kirker (1977), however, have reported that college subjects remembered words better when they were asked if they were descriptive of themselves than they remembered words they were asked to process at a structural ("Is this word written in big letters?"), phonemic ("Does this word rhyme with _____?"), or semantic ("Does this word mean the same as _____?") level. Until the relative levels of social reinforcement and attributional statements in a depth of processing hierarchy have been determined, however, this explanation must remain in the realm of hypothesis.

One final explanation for the apparent generalizability of the effects of prosocial attribution may lie simply in the nature of the inferences that can be made from statements that pertain to persons and those that pertain to acts. An attributed personality disposition is by its very nature relevant to a whole variety of situations, whereas praise of an act must be specific to that act. A nice and helpful person should be nice and helpful whenever the occasion demands, whereas someone praised for engaging in a helpful act need only engage in that one act again. In the former case a child may learn that it is good to be altruistic whenever possible, whereas, in the latter case, the child may learn only about being good in one particular situation.

Regardless of how prosocial attributions work, they do appear to be effective in promoting concern for others. It is well to note, however, that they may be particularly effective only at certain stages in the developmental sequence. If children at a certain point in development do not think of themselves as having enduring personality dispositions that direct consistent behavior across a variety of situations, then the attribution of certain dispositions may not be very effective. There is evidence, in fact, that such dispositional thinking does not begin until 7 or 8 years of age (Livesley & Bromley, 1973; Peevers & Secord, 1973). Redler and I assessed this possibility by repeating our study, but including, as well as a group of 8-year-olds, a group of 5-year-olds. As in the first study, we found for 8-year-olds that the effects of prosocial attributions generalized to a variety of altruistic behaviors whereas those of social reinforcement did not. For 5-year-olds, whereas attributional statements and social reinforcement increased donation to poor children—the specific behavior they followed—neither was effective in promoting generalized altruism. Thus, our hypothesis was confirmed.

The relative effectiveness of prosocial attribution and social reinforcement for older children is less clear. The evidence of Livesley and Bromley as well as Peevers and Secord suggests that children rather rapidly come to think of themselves as possessing certain personality characteristics. In this case, older children might be less affected by the attributions of someone else since they would already have a reasonably well-developed self-image. When we repeated part of our procedure (training for donation and testing on that task plus one other generalization task) with a group of 10-year-olds, however, our findings were not what we had expected. Attribution and social reinforcement increased donation to needy children: The effects of both were seen as well on the test of generalization. Ten-year-olds appeared capable, then, of extrapolating the information obtained from social reinforcement to another situation. We suggested this might be due to greater flexibility in the thinking of 10-year-olds than 8-year-olds, an example of developmental shifts in thinking from rigid, inflexible application of rules to more flexible extension of rules described by Nelson and Nelson (1978).

Maternal Reports of Consequences of Altruism

Laboratory research on the effects of different response consequences for the growth of altruism suggests how these consequences might operate if they were actually used. Data from maternal reports provide an idea of how frequently different consequences are actually used. They indicate whether mothers use some techniques whose effectiveness has not been studied in the laboratory, as well as suggesting if there are any relationships between the use of different techniques and the amount of altruism shown by different children.

According to our mothers' reports, the mean number of acts of altruism displayed per day by 4-year-olds was .68 for boys and .62 for girls; for 7-year-olds it was .41 for boys and .43 for girls. There were obviously no sex differences, and the larger number of acts reported for the younger children was no doubt due to the fact that the mothers of 7-year-olds, whose children were at school, saw a smaller proportion of their behavior. Reactions to altruism, which came from siblings, fathers, friends, neighbors, etc., as well as mothers, are summarized in Table 6.3. Indexes of observer reliability for the various categories of response ranged from .70 to .95, except for "praise the child," "mother feels pleasure," and "express personal appreciation." No examples of these behaviors were seen during assessment of reliability. Included in Table 6.3 are over 90% of the responses for both 4- and 7-year-olds, with the remainder of consequences being spread over a large variety of reactions that each occurred infrequently. For 4-year-olds our mothers reported a total of 425 acts of concern for others, whereas for 7-year-olds they reported 158 acts. Some altruism received more than one response—there were 645 responses in all for the 4-year-olds and 237 for the 7-year-olds.

Several things should be noted about Table 6.3. First of all, very few

Table 6.3
**Mothers' Reports of Reactions to Altruism and to Compliance to Requests for Altruism for
4- and 7-Year-Olds, Given in Percentages**

	Altruism		Requests for altruism	
	4-year-olds	7-year-olds	4-year-olds	7-year-olds
Acknowledge, thank	30	32	48	43
Smile, thank warmly, hug	17	18	20	21
Praise the act	13	11	8	12
Praise the child	6	5	6	4
Mother feels pleasure (accompanied by another response)	6	5	3	—
Altruism imitated	4	3	<1	1
No response	5	8	7	6
No response, but mother feels pleasure	3	<1	<1	1
Give explanation—no affect	3	1	<1	3
Express personal appreciation	3	5	2	—
Altruism	2	3	—	—

altruistic responses were followed by no response at all. Even if instances are included in which the mother stated that she made no response but felt pleasure at her child's behavior, and if we assume that the child was not in any way aware of her pleasurable feelings, the category of "no response" still includes fewer than 10% of all cases. Secondly, mothers, and others, virtually never responded to altruism with material rewards. In only six cases with 4-year-olds and one case with 7-year-olds did this occur. (An example of such material reward occurred when a mother peeled an orange for her daughter who was, for once, showing some interest in the welfare of her babysitter—this was accompanied, however, by praise for the child.) By far, the majority of responses to altruism were social in nature—hugging, praising, expressing personal appreciation, or just acknowledgment. Thus the mothers in our sample appeared to view concern for others as a behavior that should not be followed by material reward. Perhaps they viewed such a combining of events as inappropriate, or perhaps they had an intuitive appreciation of those conditions that might best facilitate internalization of concern for others.

Also evident from Table 6.3 is that responses to altruism are remarkably similar for 4- and 7-year-olds. Any changes in reactions that might occur as a reflection of children's increasing cognitive sophistication or changing environmental conditions or expectations were not revealed in these data. In view of the earlier discussion of prosocial attribution, it is of interest to look at changes in the use of this technique with age. The two reactions that parallel the conditions of the Grusec and Redler study are labeled in Table 6.3 as "praise the act" (e.g., "You did a great job") and "praise the child" (e.g., "Oh, what a good boy you are"). Both are used, although not frequently, and neither changes in its frequency of usage with age. Possibly the incidence of usage of "praise the child" might increase markedly with a slightly older sample where, according to our previous speculations, it should become more effective.

Children frequently are requested to help in some way, and the reactions they receive when they comply with these requests are also summarized in Table 6.3. (Here we are dealing with a total of 168 reactions for 4-year-olds and 67 reactions for 7-year-olds.) Again, the pattern of responding was similar for both age groups, and not very different from the pattern for responses to altruism.

Inspection of individual differences in consequences received for altruism revealed very little variability in our sample. Among the 4-year-olds, the two most frequent reactions for 19 of the 22 children came from three categories: acknowledgment of the act; smiling, hugging, or warm thanks; and praise for the act. A similar pattern existed for 7-year-olds. Quite evidently, it was not the types of consequences they received for altruism that produced different levels of the behavior in these children. Nor is the uniformity in reactions to altruism surprising in view of recent evidence from our own laboratory (Grusec & Kuczynski, 1980). We found that some transgressions are followed by the same disciplinary interventions in a large number of cases, and that consistency in response to given misdemeanors by a group of mothers can be greater than consistency across a variety of misdemeanors by one mother. Apparently there is also consistency of response when children display prosocial behavior.

In addition to acts of altruism and positive responses to requests for altruism, our mothers also recorded all instances in which their children offered altruism, regardless of whether or not the children followed through on these offers. For 4-year-olds there were 154 such acts reported, whereas there were 33 for 7-year-olds. Altogether there were 308 responses for 4-year-olds and 61 for 7-year-olds. Responses to offers of altruism are presented in Table 6.4. Indexes of observer reliability for the two new categories "accept offer" and "reject offer" were 1.00. The two most frequent reactions were to accept the altruism (e.g., by saying "Yes" or "Please do"), and to thank the child. Reactions were quite similar for 4- and 7-year-olds, although praise of the act tended to occur more for 7-year-olds.

Unlike altruism and compliance with requests for altruism, there did appear to be individual differences in the responses children received for

Table 6.4
**Mothers' Reports of Reactions to Offers of Altruism, Given
in Percentages**

	4-year-olds	7-year-olds
Accept offer	25	18
Acknowledge, thank	22	26
Smile, thank warmly, hug	13	8
Reject offer	12	11
Praise the act	8	21
Praise the child	4	—
Give reason for rejection	4	3
No response	4	3

their offers of altruism, at least for 4-year-olds. For those children above the median in offers of altruism, their offers were most frequently immediately followed by acceptance, whereas for those below the median offers were more frequently refused. It appears, then, that 4-year-olds who make frequent offers of help are those whose help is proportionately more often accepted and who are allowed to gain practice in helping others: Children whose help is refused (e.g., "Not now" in response to "Can I water the plants?" or "It's already done" in response to "I'll take out the garbage") make few offers. Moreover, if one looks at the relationship between number of offers to help and spontaneous acts of altruism, there was a rank order correlation of .78 ($p < .01$) for 4-year-olds: Children who offered to help tended as well to be children who engaged in spontaneous acts of altruism. For 7-year-olds the rank order correlation between offers to help and spontaneous altruism was not significant ($p = .41$).

Although there could be several explanations for these findings, the following seems particularly plausible. The children in our study received relatively uniform reactions to their altruism, and so there was little opportunity for the various response consequences discussed in earlier sections of this chapter to have a differential effect on their behavior. For 4-year-olds, however, there was a marked difference in how others responded to *offers* to help. Perhaps children who were allowed to put the majority of their offers into effect, who gained feelings of efficacy and ability, were those who subsequently displayed most spontaneous altruism—they had had practice in showing concern for others, and they knew they could do it. Children whose offers were not accepted did not have the opportunity to display altruism; indeed, they learned they were deemed incapable of behaving effectively in this way, or that their help was not needed. Thus they ceased in their efforts to show concern for others. Interestingly enough, this is one approach to the training of altruism that has received little attention in the research literature.

Immediate Consequences of Lack of Altruism

Sometimes children do not behave altruistically when others think they should. Our mothers were asked to report these incidents as well. There were not a great many of them, with an average per day per child ranging from 0 to .16 for 4-year-olds and from 0 to .11 for 7-year-olds. Here is a typical example:

> Mother preparing vegetables in kitchen. Kevin (age 4) playing within 2 feet of where mother is standing chopping carrots. One slice of carrot pops onto floor. Kevin very nonchalantly says, *"I can't pick that up for you—I'm too busy."* Mother, taken by surprise, replies, *"Well, O.K., Kevin. You are usually anxious to help when I'm busy—but maybe next time you will."* Kevin says, *"Maybe."*

In some cases requests for altruism are made but are not responded to, at least initially in a very cooperative manner. The following is an example:

> Mother asked Carol (age 7) for help in clearing the supper dishes. Carol said she didn't feel like it. I said that I didn't feel like it either, that's why I wanted some help. However, her next reply was *"Well, I'm not going to do it"*—quite saucy. I raised my voice and told her to get moving. She helped.

Punishment

One way socializing agents could attempt to modify lack of altruism is through the use of punishment. Punishment by itself does not appear to be a particularly effective way of training moral behavior (Hoffman, 1970). As with reinforcement, however, it may be useful to make a distinction between punishment of a material kind (spanking, loss of privileges) and punishment in the form of social disapproval. Smith *et al.* (1979), in the study described earlier in this chapter, included a condition in which children who did not share either were fined by losing pennies or were the subjects of social disapproval ("It's too bad you didn't help"). When asked later why they shared, children who had been fined reported that they did so to avoid losing money, whereas those in the social disapproval condition attributed their altruism to a desire to help others. It may be, then, that psychological punishment is conducive to the internalization of moral standards even if physical and material punishment are not. Again, however, it should be noted that the relationship between kind of attribution and subsequent sharing was weak.

Reasoning

Rather than, or as well as, using punishment as a disciplinary technique, socialization agents can turn to reasoning as a way of influencing behavior. Reasoning can take a number of forms, but that which has been most extensively investigated is a kind of reasoning that points out to a child the consequences for others of his or her misbehavior. Hoffman (1970) has proposed that this particular approach—described as "other-oriented induction"—is effective because it arouses a child's empathic capabilities. Children are thus encouraged to understand how other people feel and to see how they have played a role in producing distress in others. This awareness leads to a form of guilt that is inescapable—thus moral behavior will occur even in the absence of external surveillance since anxiety about deviation is self-imposed.

Some studies support this line of argument. Hoffman and Saltzstein (1967) reported that seventh grade girls whose parents used induction were rated by their peers as being considerate. For seventh grade boys, however, consideration was related not to the use of induction, but to the use of power assertion—physical punishment, withdrawal of privileges, and verbal censure. In a later study, Hoffman (1975a) found a correlation between peer ratings of fifth graders' consideration and use, by the parent of the opposite sex, of explicit suggestions for reparation after deviation, encouragement of apology, and expression of concern for the feelings of victims. Confirmation of a relationship between induction and concern for others was also provided by Dlugokinski and Firestone (1974), who carried out their research with 10-13-year-olds. All of these studies are, of course, correlational in nature, and alternative explanations can be offered for the relationship between altruism and other-oriented induction. Parents who are concerned with the effects of their children's actions on others, for example, may also model a great deal of altruism that their children imitate, and it may be the modeling that is the salient element in the socialization process. Nevertheless, a discipline technique that appears to encourage or train the empathic capacity of its recipient may well be a particularly useful approach to the training of altruism.

Moral Exhortation

People who deviate from expected behavior are often exhorted to change their ways. Children who fail to show adequate concern for others, then, may be urged to modify their selfish attitudes, or told that they *ought* to help, or share, or make amends for misdeeds. Bryan (1975) has demonstrated that under conditions in which an adult acts in one way but preaches that a child should act in another way—that is, under conditions of hypocrisy—actions will win out over words. To tell children that they ought to share and then to behave selfishly oneself is not an effective way to encourage sharing.

When exhortation is used by itself, however, it does appear to have a certain degree of effectiveness. In one study, for example, children were told in their classrooms over a period of several days either that they were neat and tidy individuals—an attribution condition—or that they *ought* to be neat and tidy—an exhortation condition (Miller, Brickman, & Bolen, 1975). Although the attribution condition was more effective in promoting tidiness than the exhortation condition, the latter did produce greater tidiness than a control condition in which children did not hear any kind of message about neatness. Whereas Miller *et al.* concerned themselves with the specific behavior of tidiness, there is no reason to believe their findings would not hold for altruism as well.

Some types of exhortation are more effective than others. Eisenberg-Berg and Geisheker (1979), for instance, compared normative exhortations in which they told 8- and 9-year-old children that people ought to share, and empathic exhortations in which they stated how happy and excited the beneficiaries of sharing would be. They found that children who had heard the empathic exhortation donated more money to poor children than did children who had heard the normative exhortation; presumably the latter had aroused children's sensitivity to the feelings and needs of others. The normative exhortation was not effective in increasing donation. Some kind of arousal, in fact, may be an important accompaniment to exhortation, necessary to facilitate its efficacy. Zahn-Waxler, Radke-Yarrow, and King (1979), for example, have reported that young children who are most altruistic have mothers who respond to their children's deviations (i.e., situations in which their children cause distress for others) with explanations about why they should not have done what they did. The explanations are described, however, as having a strong affective component, with the most effective explanations being those with a large component of moralizing, for example, "You made Doug cry. It's not nice to bite," and "It was bad for Jim to hit Mary."

In our own laboratory we have also assessed some of the effects of moral exhortation (Grusec, Saas-Kortsaak, & Simutis, 1978b). Children were given two different kinds of exhortations to share—a specific one in which they were urged to give half their winnings from a game to poor children since it would be a good thing to make the children happy by doing this, and a general one in which they were urged to share because it is a good thing to make other people happy by helping them in any way one can. In addition, a third group of children observed a model who donated half her winnings to the poor children. The effects of these three manipulations were assessed across a variety of situations—subsequent donation to poor children, willingness to help the experimenter pick up some objects she had "accidentally" dropped, number of special prizes (pencils) shared with other children who would not be able to participate in the study, donation to poor children 1–3 weeks later, and craft articles collected for hospitalized children. (The assessments of donation, pencil sharing, and collection of craft material were carried out in the same way as in the Grusec and Redler study described earlier.)

The effects of modeling and general and specific exhortations on these various measures of altruism are summarized in Table 6.5. Modeling was more effective on the immediate test of donation than was exhortation, although more children did share in the exhortation than control condition, where no attempt was made to induce sharing. The difference between modeling and exhortation disappeared, however, on the delayed test. We speculated that this occurred because children forgot over time whether they had actually seen someone donate or had merely heard someone exhort the importance of donation. This speculation was supported by the observation that, even immediately after training, whereas children in the modeling condition could accurately recall that the model had donated, many in the exhortation condition erroneously recalled that the adult who had preached had actually donated. Specific exhortations produced greater sharing of pencils among boys, and, in the no-modeling condition, children exposed to a general exhortation collected more craft materials for the sick children than did those in the control condition.

From these results we concluded that effective socialization must include training about generalized concern for others as well as about specific situations. The eventual superiority of exhortation over modeling is of interest, with one possible explanation of this superiority as follows. Exhortations may be encoded into memory as statements of what ought to be done, whereas example, or modeling, may be encoded as a description of what once happened. This distinction parallels that between episodic and semantic memory (Tulving, 1972), that is, between memory for specific events and

Table 6.5

Number of Children Who Donated Tokens Immediately and 3 Weeks Later, Number of Children Who Helped, Mean Number of Pencils Shared, and Number of Children Returning Craft Items (N = 16 per group)

	Model			No model		
Exhortation	Specific	General	None	Specific	General	None
Donation:						
Immediate	13	12	11	4	6	0
Delayed	5(15)[a]	3(14)[a]	4(14)[a]	2(13)[a]	3(13)[a]	0(15)[a]
Helping	7	4	2	3	4	9
Sharing:						
Boys	3.62	1.62	2.25	3.50	1.37	2.62
Girls	2.50	3.00	2.37	1.37	2.37	2.62
Craft items	4	2	3	4	9	2

[a] Number of children available for the follow-up.

memory for knowledge produced by the event, with the latter not tied to the situation in which it was first acquired. Exhortations, that is, materials encoded into semantic memory, may have a greater element of compulsion attached to them since they more nearly resemble a prescribed norm of behavior. Example, however, since it is attached to a specific situation, has much less of this element of coercion.

Although much remains to be learned about moral exhortation, it is evident that it has a role to play in the socializing process. One problem with its usage, however, is its tendency to produce reactance, or oppositional behavior, on the part of the recipient. Staub (1971a) reported that children who were exhorted to help others were *less* likely to help an experimenter pick up a box of paper clips he had "accidentally" dropped than were children who had not been subjected to preaching. Some evidence for reactance after exhortation can be seen in Table 6.5, if we consider the condition in which no modeling of altruism occurred, although this reactance clearly dissipated with time. It is possible that reactance is specific to the individual who does the exhorting, and that its form changes with age. The answer to this as well as other questions about moral exhortation must await further research.

Direct Instruction and Forced Appropriate Behavior

When reasoning and exhortation fail, agents of socialization may force compliance by imposing their greater power. Recall the example of Carol, cited earlier, in which she refused to help clear the supper dishes. Mother responded to her stubbornness by telling her, in a raised voice, to get going. The cryptic comment, "She helped" provides an indication of the success of this tactic. Presumably, of course, some threat lies behind the mother's command—if Carol fails to help now, one assumes that such a threat would be carried out. It is also possible, of course, that parents could literally physically force their children to engage in acceptable behavior.

The effectiveness of direct instruction has already been alluded to in a discussion of the Grusec et al. (1978a) study. Table 6.1 shows the high level of altruism that was achieved in this condition, regardless of attribution condition. White (1972) and White and Burnham (1975) found that direct instruction to donate was more effective than a permissive suggestion that children could donate if they wished to but that they did not have to. They also found it more effective than modeling of altruism on an immediate test and just as effective as modeling on a delayed test of altruism that took place several days after the original instruction. Staub (1975) has also emphasized the importance of children's learning to be altruistic by actual participation in positive behavior—one way of ensuring this, of course, would be to instruct them to do so.

Why direct instruction should be so effective is not immediately clear. It may work in the presence of a socializing agent, of course, because of the threat of punishment. But why should it work when a child is alone and presumably unobserved, that is, why should it lead to the internalization of altruism? Perhaps it is most effective when the threat is not too salient and, therefore, conditions are such as to allow a child to attribute compliance to internal value systems rather than to external pressure.

Maternal Reports of Consequences for Lack of Altruism

There were very few instances reported by our mothers of lack of altruism when they thought it should be forthcoming. Mothers of 4-year-olds reported 25 such incidents, whereas mothers of 7-year-olds reported 7 incidents. Reactions of mothers and others to lack of altruism are recorded in Table 6.6. This table includes all the reactions that any one act would receive. Indexes of rater reliability ranged from .75 to 1.00, except for scolding and frowning and direct instruction, which were not observed during reliability sessions. Often children's failure to show concern was followed by a request for such concern (22% of the immediate reactions for 4-year-olds and 33% for 7-year-olds); if this was unsuccessful it was followed by a stronger technique. Moral exhortation was, overall, the most frequently used technique for both age groups, closely followed by a request for altruism and then by verbal and social disapproval. Note that two techniques that have been of considerable interest to researchers—making children aware of the consequences of their behavior for others (empathy training) and direct instruction and forced appropriate behavior—are used much less frequently than moral exhortation and punishment. Although these techniques have been shown to be effective in the laboratory, they were, for some reason, avoided by those who attempted to influence the behavior of our sample of children.

Table 6.6
Mothers' Reports of Reactions to Lack of Altruism, Given in Percentages

	4-year-olds	7-year-olds
Moral exhortation	26 (.77)[a]	30 (.67)
Altruism requested	22 (.55)	30 (.50)
Scolding, frowning	18 (.67)	15 (1.00)
Empathy training	6 (.33)	5 (1.00)
Direct instruction, forced appropriate behavior	6 (1.00)	5 (1.00)
Lack of altruism accepted	8	5

[a] In parentheses is the probability that the reaction would produce altruism.

The minimal usage of forced appropriate behavior is also of interest in view of other findings about maternal discipline (Grusec & Kuczynski, 1980). In that study we played tape-recorded simulations of various misdemeanors to mothers of 4- and 7-year-olds and asked them to imagine it was their child who had committed this misdemeanor. We then asked them to describe how they would react to the misdemeanor. Ninety-five percent of these mothers reported that they would use forced appropriate behavior for at least one of the simulated misdemeanors, a marked contrast with our observer–mothers who reported on the actual reactions their children received when they showed lack of concern for others. Perhaps people are reluctant to force children to show concern for others, although they may be willing to force them to stop engaging in negative behaviors such as aggression and failure to obey. It is interesting to note Eisenberg-Berg and Hand's (1979) finding that preschoolers do not use punishment and authority-related reasoning in the judgments they make about prosocial moral conflicts. Perhaps this is a reflection of the fact that socializing agents do not force children to be altruistic.

The probability that a specific intervention would lead to immediate compliance is given in Table 6.6. Because so few children failed to behave altruistically, or did so more than once, it was impossible to characterize children as receiving predominant reactions to transgression.

Reactions to lack of compliance (including defiance, ignoring, or partial compliance) when children were *requested* to engage in an altruistic act is presented in Table 6.7. There were 43 such incidents for 4-year-olds and 21 such incidents for 7-year-olds. (Four-year-olds complied with requests for altruism on 130 occasions, and 7-year-olds complied on 52 occasions.) Again, as with lack of altruism, forced appropriate behavior and empathy

Table 6.7
Mothers' Reports of Reactions to Failure to Comply with Requests for Altruism, Given in Percentages

	4-year-olds	7-year-olds
Altruism requested	37 (.58)[a]	24 (.67)
Moral exhortation	15 (.55)	19 (.29)
Scolding, isolation withdrawal of privileges	14 (.20)	24 (.56)
Threat of punishment	13 (.56)	— —
Noncompliance accepted	11	22
Forced appropriate behavior	3 (1.00)	— —
Empathy training	1 (1.00)	3 (.50)

[a] In parentheses is the probability that the reaction would produce altruism.

training were rarely used. As well, moral exhortation was used somewhat less often than it was when children failed to behave altruistically in the absence of a specific request for such behavior. Those who unsuccessfully requested altruism from 4-year-olds even resorted occasionally to threats to withdraw privileges or objects, or not to comply with requests from the uncooperative child—something they never did for lack of altruism. There was, however, no report of physical punishment or threat of it. The proportion of times that various interventions were successful is also reported in Table 6.7.

Training Outside the Occurrence of Altruism

Children observe examples of altruistic behavior displayed by others, and this subsequently has an effect on their willingness to show concern for others. As well, they can be taught to feel empathy for others and to understand the perspective of others, even when they themselves are in no way responsible for the distress of those others. We did not ask our mothers to record instances where their children observed others engaging in altruism, since we felt this would make the burden of data collection too great for them. We did, however, ask them to record any situation in which they used some event their child had observed as an occasion to teach them about the importance of showing concern for others. There were few such occasions reported—five for 4-year-olds and three for 7-year-olds. Here is one example:

> Lisa (age 4) and a friend are getting ready to make collages. Lisa starts crying because Monica has taken the only red paper for background. Mother steps in and discusses giving friends first choice, sharing, etc., and encourages Lisa to choose another color. She finally does and proceeds quite happily. Mother sighs with relief that another catastrophe is solved!

Modeling

The effects of modeling on the development of altruism are discussed at length in Rushton's chapter in this volume. The observation of models is, of course, an ideal candidate for the internalization of the value of concern for others, since it is through identification with agents of socialization that children are supposed to adopt, or internalize, the standards of society. Certainly it is not obvious when one imitates the behavior of another person why one has done so; presumably it is therefore easy to attribute one's own behavior to internal causes (see, for example, Grusec et al., 1978a).

A number of investigators have demonstrated that children will match the altruistic behavior of those they observe (e.g., Bryan & Walbek, 1970;

Grusec, 1971; Grusec & Skubiski, 1970; Rice & Grusec, 1975; Rushton, 1976; Staub, 1971b). Yarrow, Scott, and Waxler (1973) gave nursery school children extensive exposure to either a helpful, supportive adult or a detached, minimally helpful adult. Both adults modeled altruism, either through the use of imaginary situations alone or through the use of imaginary situations combined with real behavioral examples. Modeling in all cases was accompanied by verbalizations of sympathy for the distress of the individual being helped, descriptions of the necessary aid, and expressions of pleasure at having helped. Symbolic modeling increased helping in imaginary situations, but only the extended training, carried out by the helpful and supportive adult, was effective in producing increases in real-life helping. It appeared, then, that the greatest facilitator of altruism was a model who exhibited kindness both to the child and to others. Note, as well, that the model accompanied her altruism with extensive verbalizations, and that these may have been necessary contributors to the effect.

Training Empathy and Knowledge of the Perspective of Others

Krebs' and Hoffman's chapters in this volume provide an extensive discussion of empathy and perspective taking in the development of altruism. In what follows, the term *empathy* will be used to refer to the child's ability to feel the same, or related, emotion as someone else is feeling. *Perspective-taking ability* will refer to the capability of knowing how others are feeling and/or thinking.

It has been suggested (e.g., Hoffman, 1975b) that through increasing empathy and perspective-taking ability young children grow increasingly more adept at showing concern for others. Thus a child may feel uncomfortably aroused when someone else is undergoing distress: By helping, this arousal is reduced and the altruism is thereby reinforced. In addition, knowing what someone in distress is feeling and thinking should enable a child to respond more effectively to that person's needs. A child who is upset by the crying of another child is motivated to reduce that child's distress as well as his or her own. Knowing that the child is crying because he or she cannot find mother will aid the would-be helper to reduce distress effectively by finding mother or by offering reassurances that she will return. One way, then, to encourage the development of altruism would be by training empathy and perspective-taking ability. It has already been noted that the use of other-oriented induction after deviation may facilitate the child's empathic capacities. But such empathy can also be encouraged independent of a specific behavior displayed by the child. It is to a brief discussion of studies of this particular influence technique that this chapter now turns.

One of the first reports on the training of children to understand the perspective of others was made by Staub (1971a). He had kindergarten children take turns acting out situations in which one child needed help and the other provided it. A day later the children were brought to a room where they heard (tape-recorded) cries of distress. Role-taking experience facilitated the helping of girls, but not of boys. Boys with role-taking training, however, were more altruistic in another situation—they shared more candy they had been given than did boys who had not had such training. Iannotti (1978) reported that playing roles in a series of skits involving some kind of dilemma, such as what to do when one finds a wallet with money inside it, and answering questions about the motives, feelings, and thoughts of the characters they were playing, increased the altruism of 6-year-old boys. This kind of training did not, however, increase altruism in 9-year-old boys. Friedrich and Stein (1975) had 5-year-olds watch excerpts from the television program *Mister Rogers' Neighborhood*, which attempts to teach prosocial behavior. The children were then instructed to use hand puppets to rehearse some of the prosocial scenes from the program. Such training proved to be successful, as evidenced by their greater willingness to help repair a damaged collage that another child had been making.

Maternal Reports of Training Outside
the Occurrence of Altruism

As noted earlier, mothers did not report many attempts to deliberately teach altruism. Certainly there were none of the kind assessed in the work of researchers like Staub, Iannotti, or Friedrich and Stein. More frequently, attempts to sensitize children to concern for others grew out of situations such as those discribed in the example at the beginning of this section— children were distressed or upset in some way and mothers used this as an excuse for talking to them about the needs of others. In only three of the cases did children have their attention directed to the feelings of other people. In the other six cases they heard a normative statement, for example, "It's good to share," or were given a reason for behavior that did not include a discussion of feelings. In sum, then, not much use was being made with these children of techniques that have been demonstrated in the laboratory to be effective in socializing altruism. Training in role playing and perspective taking may, indeed, be something done more naturally in a formal setting such as school or organized children's groups.

CONCLUSION

Some final points should be made about our study of the training of altruism as it actually occurs (among the sample of white, middle-class children we assessed). Although mothers were asked to report about a wide variety of situations, there are other situations they were not asked to tell us about but which no doubt have a major impact on the child's growth of concern for others. We know nothing about the examples of altruism these children observed, some of which laboratory and field experiments suggest they most certainly would have imitated. Nor do we know anything about how the children were disciplined in situations other than those directly related to altruism. Yet the work of Zahn-Waxler and Radke-Yarrow, and Hoffman, among others, indicates that events that occur in the discipline situation are critical for the growth of altruism. This was evident even in our own work during the training sessions we had with mothers. We had some difficulty when they protested that recording every instance of lack of concern for others was simply more than they could do. The source of the problem was clear when we discovered that their definition of lack of concern applied to virtually every misdemeanor. Thus playing with matches in the basement, as one child did, could be construed, in a broad sense, as lack of concern for others. And no doubt the consequences this particular child experienced taught him something about showing concern for others. The minimal use that our mothers reported of training that involved sensitizing the child to the feelings of others may simply reflect the narrow range of misdemeanors we sampled. The limited sampling of situations may also account for the minimal use of direct instruction.

Perhaps the most informative aspect of our data has to do with reactions to altruism and offers of altruism. The uniformity of response when children showed concern for others was striking, and an indication that the consistency in response to specific misdemeanors reported by Grusec and Kuczynski (1980) may be found as well in responses to prosocial behavior. One wonders what the effects would be if agents of socialization used other techniques such as the attribution of prosocial characteristics—techniques that have been shown to be effective in the psychological laboratory. Of particular note in the data was the strong relationship between the acceptance of offers of help and the number of such offers made, as well as the relationship between spontaneous help and offered help. Children who successfully offer to help will also help spontaneously. Children whose help is rejected, however, engage in few spontaneous acts of altruism. It was suggested earlier that children whose offers to help were accepted gained feelings of competence and mastery that motivated them to perform other such acts. It is possible, of course, that their offers of help were denied simply because they were unrealistic, and that children who offer forms of help they are actually incapable of giving will also be incapable of showing spontaneous altruism. Yet inspection of the actual incidents of denied altruism argues against this reasoning. Often children's offers were directed toward younger siblings who wanted their mothers rather than their older brothers or sisters to look after them. One child offered to vacuum a room that was dusty from his father's carpentry work in the basement, but his mother decided to wait until the father's project was completed. From the mother's reports, of course, we cannot ascertain the nature of the causal relationships that are operating. But the finding does suggest a new direction of inquiry for research concerned with the socialization of altruism.

REFERENCES

Azrin, N., & Lindsley, O. The reinforcement of cooperation between children. *Journal of Abnormal and Social Psychology*, 1956, *2*, 100-102.

Bryan, J. H. "You will be well advised to watch what we do instead of what we say." In D. J. DePalma & J. M. Foley (Eds.), *Moral development: Current theory and research*. Hillsdale, N.J.: Erlbaum, 1975.

Bryan, J. H., & Walbek, N. Preaching and practicing generosity: Children's actions and reactions. *Child Development*, 1970, *41*, 329-353.

Buckley, N., Siegel, L. S., & Ness, S. Egocentrism, empathy, and altruistic behavior in young children. *Developmental Psychology*, 1979, *15*, 329-330.

Craik, F. I. M., & Lockhart, R. S. Levels of processing: A framework for memory research. *Journal of Verbal Learning and Verbal Behavior*, 1972, *11*, 671-684.

Dienstbier, R. A., Hillman, D., Lehnhoff, J., Hillman, J., & Valkenaar, M. C. An emotion-attribution approach to moral behavior. Interfacing cognitive and avoidance theories of moral development. *Psychological Review*, 1975, *82*, 299-315.

Dlugokinski, E. L., & Firestone, I. J. Other centeredness and susceptibility to charitable appeals: Effects of perceived discipline. *Developmental Psychology*, 1974, *10*, 21-28.

Eisenberg-Berg, N., & Geisheker, E. Content of preachings and power of the model/preacher: The effects on children's generosity. *Developmental Psychology*, 1979, *15*, 168-175.

Eisenberg-Berg, N., & Hand, M. The relationship of preschoolers' reasoning about prosocial moral conflicts to prosocial behavior. *Child Development*, 1979, *50*, 356-363.

Fischer, W. F. Sharing in preschool children as a function of amount and type of reinforcement. *Genetic Psychology Monographs*, 1963, *68*, 215-245.

Friedrich, L. K., & Stein, A. H. Prosocial television and young children: The effects of verbal labeling and role playing on learning and behavior. *Child Development*, 1975, *46*, 27-38.

Gelfand, D. M., Hartmann, D. P., Cromer, C. C., Smith, C. L., & Page, B. C. The effects of instructional prompts and praise on children's donation rates. *Child Development*, 1975, *46*, 980-983.

Goodenough, F. *Anger in young children*. Minneapolis: University of Minnesota Press, 1931.

Grusec, J. E. Power and the internalization of aversive behaviors. *Child Development*, 1971, *42*, 93-105.

Grusec, J. E., & Kuczynski, L. Direction of effect in socialization: A comparison of the parent vs. the child's behavior as determinants of disciplinary techniques. *Developmental Psychology*, 1980, *6*, 1-9.

Grusec, J. E., Kuczynski, L., Rushton, J. P., & Simutis, Z. Modeling, direct instruction, and attributions: Effects on altruism. *Developmental Psychology*, 1978, *14*, 51-57. (a)

Grusec, J. E., & Redler, E. Attribution, reinforcement, and altruism. *Developmental Psychology*, 1980, *16*, 525-534.

Grusec, J. E., Saas-Kortsaak, P., & Simutis, Z. M. The role of example and moral exhortation in the training of altruism. *Child Development*, 1978, *49*, 920-923. (b)

Grusec, J. E., & Skubiski, L. Model nurturance, demand characteristics of the modeling experiment, and altruism. *Journal of Personality and Social Psychology, 1970, 14,* 352-359.

Hartmann, D. P., Gelfand, D. M., Smith, C. L., Paul, S. C., Cromer, C. C., Page, B. C., & Lebenta, D. V. Factors affecting the acquisition and elimination of children's donating behavior. *Journal of Experimental Child Psychology, 1976, 21,* 328-338.

Hoffman, M. L. Moral development. In P. H. Mussen (Ed.), *Manual of child psychology*. New York: Wiley, 1970.

Hoffman, M. L. Altruistic behavior and the parent-child relationship. *Journal of Personality and Social Psychology, 1975, 31,* 937-943. (a)

Hoffman, M. L. Developmental synthesis of affect and cognition and its implications for altruistic motivation. *Developmental Psychology, 1975, 11,* 607-622. (b)

Hoffman, M. L., & Saltzstein, H. D. Parent discipline and the child's moral development. *Journal of Personality and Social Psychology, 1967, 5,* 45-57.

Iannotti, R. J. Effect of role-taking experiences on role taking, empathy, altruism, and aggression. *Developmental Psychology, 1978, 14,* 119-124.

Jensen, A. M., & Moore, S. G. The effect of attribute statements on cooperativeness and competitiveness in school-age boys. *Child Development, 1977, 48,* 305-307.

Livesley, W. J., & Bromley, D. B. *Person perception in childhood and adolescence.* London: Wiley, 1973.

Miller, R. L., Brickman, P., & Bolen, D. Attribution versus persuasion as a means for modifying behavior. *Journal of Personality and Social Psychology, 1975, 31,* 430-441.

Nelson, K. E., & Nelson, K. Cognitive pendulums and their linguistic realization. In K. E. Nelson (Ed.), *Children's language* (Vol. 1). New York: Gardner, 1978.

Peevers, B. H., & Secord, P. F. Developmental changes in attribution of descriptive concepts to persons. *Journal of Personality and Social Psychology, 1973, 27,* 120-128.

Perry, D. G., Perry, L. C., Bussey, K., English, D., & Arnold, G. Processes of attribution and children's self-punishment following misbehavior. *Child Development, 1980, 51,* 545-551.

Rheingold, H. L., Hay, D. F., & West, M. J. Sharing in the second year of life. *Child Development, 1976, 47,* 1148-1158.

Rice, M. E., & Grusec, J. E. Saying and doing: Effects on observer performance. *Journal of Personality and Social Psychology, 1975, 32,* 584-593.

Rogers, T. B., Kuiper, N. A., & Kirker, W. S. Self-reference and the encoding of personal information. *Journal of Personality and Social Psychology, 1977, 35,* 677-688.

Rushton, J. P. Socialization and the altruistic behavior of children. *Psychological Bulletin, 1976, 83,* 898-913.

Shatz, M., & Gelman, R. The development of communication skills: Modification in the speech of young children as a function of listener. *Monographs of the Society for Research in Child Development, 1973, 38* (5, Serial No. 152).

Smith, C. L., Gelfand, D. M., Hartmann, D. P., & Partlow, M. E. Y. Children's causal attributions regarding help giving. *Child Development, 1979, 50,* 203-210.

Staub, E. The use of role playing and induction in children's learning of helping and sharing behavior. *Child Development, 1971, 42,* 805-817. (a)

Staub, E. A child in distress: The influence of nurturance and modeling on children's attempts to help. *Developmental Psychology, 1971, 5,* 124-132. (b)

Staub, E. To rear a prosocial child: Reasoning, learning by doing, and learning by teaching others. In D. J. DePalma & J. M. Foley (Eds.), *Moral development: Current theory and research.* Hillsdale, N.J.: Erlbaum, 1975.

Strayer, J. A naturalistic study of empathic behaviors and their relation to affective states and perspective taking skills in preschool children. *Child Development, 1980, 51,* 815-822.

Toner, I. J., Moore, L. P., & Emmons, B. A. The effect of being labeled on subsequent self-control in children. *Child Development,* 1980, *51,* 618-621.

Tulving, E. Episodic and semantic memory. In E. Tulving & W. Donaldson (Eds.), *Organization and memory.* New York: Academic Press, 1972.

White, G. M. Immediate and deferred effects of model observation and guided and unguided rehearsal on donating and stealing. *Journal of Personality and Social Psychology,* 1972, *21,* 139-148.

White, G. M., & Burnham, M. A. Socially cued altruism: Effects of modeling, instructions, and age on public and private donations. *Child Development,* 1975, *46,* 559-563.

Yarrow, M. R., Scott, P. M., & Waxler, C. Z. Learning concern for others. *Developmental Psychology,* 1973, *8,* 240-260.

Zahn-Waxler, C., & Radke-Yarrow, M. *A developmental anaysis of children's responses to emotions in others.* Paper presented at the biannual meeting of the Society for Research in Child Development, San Francisco, March 1979.

Zahn-Waxler, C., Radke-Yarrow, M., & Brady-Smith, J. Perspective-taking and prosocial behavior. *Developmental Psychology,* 1977, *13,* 87-88.

Zahn-Waxler, C., Radke-Yarrow, M., & King, R. A. Child rearing and children's prosocial initiations toward victims of distress. *Child Development,* 1979, *50,* 319-330.

DONNA M. GELFAND
DONALD P. HARTMANN

Response Consequences
and Attributions:
Two Contributors
to Prosocial Behavior[1]

This chapter concerns children's intuitive or commonsense psychology of prosocial behavior and its relationship to some of the demonstrable environmental determinants of helping, sharing, and donating. The questions we will consider are as follows: To what extent are children's and adults' causal attributions accurate when they seek to explain helpful behavior? What types of attributional errors are people likely to make? Are psychological theorists and researchers sometimes prey to the same types of attributional errors as those made by children and psychologically naive adults? These classic issues will be addressed in this chapter, and they are the ones that have helped guide our research over the past decade.

In the sections that follow we first will examine some frequently offered definitions of a particular prosocial behavior—altruism—often believed to be purely self-sacrificial. Then we will assess the possibility that these definitions contain attributional errors because they ignore the possibility that "altruistic" behavior in actuality is reinforced in some manner. Next, we will describe research demonstrations of several external reinforcement contingencies and other environmental manipulations such as instructions that powerfully affect generous and helpful behavior but that may escape the notice of an actor or observer seeking to explain the behavior. The causal perceptions of actors and observers will be examined, and we will attempt to

1. Our work described in this chapter was supported in part by National Institutes of Health Grant no. HD06914.

trace the developmental course of various attributions regarding the sources of helpful and generous behavior (henceforth referred to as prosocial behavior). Finally, we will explore the perennial issue of the relationship between cognition and behavior, and will argue that the relatively powerful situational and social learning factors most often outweigh causal attributions in directing behavior.

DEFINITIONS OF ALTRUISM

Most major theories of behavior assign a prominent role to self-interest; for example, operant theory (Skinner, 1953) holds that behavior is maintained by its consequences. These reinforcing consequences may be real or anticipated, externally or self-produced, and positively or negatively valenced. Despite an emphasis on consequence control by operant theory and a recognition of its importance by other social learning theory approaches, many investigators have defined sharing, aiding, and donating as independent of reinforcement processes (e.g., Bar-Tal, 1976, pp. 5-7). According to Krebs and Wispé (1974), altruistic behaviors not only are performed "without concern for one's self-interest," but also necessarily involve self-sacrifice (p. 194). Similarly, Bryan and London (1970) maintain that altruistic behaviors must "have a high cost to the actor with little possibility of material or social rewards [p. 200]."

Much human learning appears to involve rewards, and yet altruism supposedly requires the sacrifice of rewards, a phenomenon that has been called the *altruistic paradox* (Rosenhan, 1978). Definitions such as those offered by Krebs and Wispé and by Bryan and London also are troublesome on other accounts. These authors' definitions involve nonobservable factors such as estimation of self-interest and of likelihood of reinforcement. Thus, it is difficult to know whether observed behaviors meet these definitional requirements. Under what conditions could it be concluded confidently that helpful behavior was engaged in with no thought of reward from self or others now or in the future?

Our social learning theory orientation caused us to doubt the utility of definitions of altruism that excluded the possibility of external reinforcement, and suggested instead that these definitions should be stripped of their nonobservable characteristics. Moreover, a social learning perspective suggests that charitable behaviors are responsive to the environmental events found to control other voluntary social behaviors such as cooperation, aggression, and competition (e.g., Arzin & Lindsley, 1956; Bandura, 1973; Vogler, Masters, & Morrill, 1970).

CONTROL BY POSITIVE CONSEQUENCES

Praise and other positive consequences are the reinforcing events most likely to be overlooked by psychologically naive observers. Charitable and helpful behaviors that are maintained by praise may be attributed incorrectly to altruistic motivation. Therefore, it is important to determine whether fairly subtle incentives such as praise could reinforce children's helpfulness. In some early studies investigators failed in their attempts to demonstrate that unaccompanied parise could increase children's helpful behavior (e.g., Aronfreed & Paskal, 1965; Fischer, 1963; Midlarsky & Bryan, 1967). However, procedural inadequacies may have produced the negative results. The children participating in these studies may have received few training trials and were given very vague statements of approval. Some apparently never received praise because they never performed the helping response.

To provide a better test of the effects of praise we employed a reversal or ABAB, $N = 1$ design that would (a) assess each child's baseline rate of donation; (b) expose each child to many training trials; (c) employ explicit praise for donations; and (d) reveal the unique contribution of praise as a consequence separate from instructions and prompts to donate. In addition, the reversal design allowed us to tailor the experimental procedures to each child's performance level and to make each child's responding a unique demonstration of the effects of praise on donating (e.g., as recommended by Gelfand & Hartmann, 1975).

In our study (Gelfand, Hartmann, Cromer, Smith, & Page, 1975) kindergarten and first grade children individually played a marble-drop game to earn pennies for prizes. Each child received periodic opportunities to contribute pennies to aid another child who was supposedly having poor luck with a similar marble-drop game in a nearby room. Our subjects were the two-thirds of the children who donated no pennies to help the other child during the baseline trials. Next, each of these children was verbally prompted to donate "once or twice." Those children who responded briefly to this prompt, but reverted to not donating were prompted once more and subsequently praised for donating (e.g., "Good! You're really helping her [him]"). The next two phases repeated first the no-praise baseline and then the praise conditions. The children who completed the entire sequences of experimental phases responded similarly to the subjects whose data are shown in Figure 7.1. These results demonstrated that praise can increase the generosity of young children, a phenomenon also reported by Midlarsky, Bryan, and Brickman (1973) and by Rushton and Teachman (1978).

Some reviewers (e.g., Mussen & Eisenberg-Berg, 1977) have questioned the durability and generality of the behavioral effects produced in laboratory

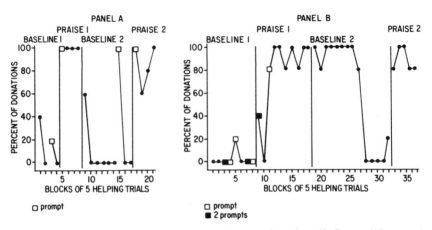

Figure 7.1. **Representative data for children who participated in all phases of the experiment. Subject 32, a first grade boy whose data are shown in Panel A, was prompted to donate during both Baseline 2 and Praise 2 phases. Subject 3, a kindergarten girl whose data are shown in Panel B, was not prompted to donate during either Baseline 2 or Praise 2 phases. Open squares (□) indicate trials that included a single prompt; solid squares (■) indicate blocks that included two prompts. From Gelfand, Hartmann, Cromer, Smith, & Page (1975), © The Society for Research in Child Development, Inc.**

studies employing praise. Therefore, it is important to note that the same results have been reported by investigators working in more naturalistic settings. For example, Slaby and Crowley (1977) instructed nursery school teachers to make their attention contingent on their students' prosocial statements. Not only did the children make more friendly and cooperative statements as a result of the contingent attention, but their *physical* prosocial responding (e.g., helping) also increased when the contingency for verbally helpful behavior was in effect. These results are consistent with the notion that verbal and physical prosocial behavior belong to the same response class, either because of their shared reinforcement history (Lövaas, 1961) or because the reinforcers served as cues that both types of behavior were permissible (Bandura, 1973).

Other results have indicated that verbal and physical helping are not coequal members of a common response class, however. Barton and Ascione's (1979) study found that preschool children trained in verbal sharing (verbal compliance with requests to share) increased their rates of both verbal and physical sharing. In contrast, children trained only in physical sharing increased their rates of physical sharing. These results are inconsistent with the traditional learning theory model of response class, which holds that the generalization of effects is bidirectional. Reinforcement of either verbal or physical responses should strengthen the other, unreinforced response. Instead, as Luria (1961) has suggested, verbal behavior may have a unique and unidirectional role in regulating physical behavior.

Other behavioral studies (e.g., Barton, Olszewski, & Madsen, 1979; Cooke & Apolloni, 1976) have provided additional evidence that natural socializing agents such as teachers can produce relatively durable increases in children's sharing and other prosocial behaviors. However, monitoring and reinforcing children's behavior can be awkward and demanding for adult caretakers. Some investigators have attempted to develop more efficient methods for increasing children's prosocial behavior. For example, Rogers-Warren and Baer (1976) used modeling and correspondence training to increase preschool children's sharing and praising. The correspondence-training procedure used by these investigators involved reinforcing the children with praise and treats at the end of each training session for accurate reports of their sharing with or praising of playmates. This method was effective in increasing the targeted prosocial behaviors, suggesting that periodic monitoring and delayed reinforcement of accurate reporting can be substituted for procedures that are more disruptive and less efficient, such as the teacher's continuous identification and reinforcement of ongoing student behavior. Correspondence training is a promising training technique and deserves further study to determine the conditions that allow its efficient use, such as the children's verbal skills and their repertoires of prosocial behavior (Israel, 1978).

Rogers-Warren, Warren, and Baer (1977) also performed a component analysis of the treatment procedures they used to increase preschool children's sharing, including the modeling of sharing, vicarious reinforcement of reports of sharing, self-report of sharing, reinforcement for reported sharing, and reinforcement for accurate reports of sharing. Only reinforcement for accurate reports of sharing produced increased sharing and high levels of accurate reporting for all subjects. However, design limitations made it unclear which treatment component, besides reinforcement for true reports of sharing, was responsible for the changes in the children's behavior.

The previously described investigations demonstrated that the contingent use of positive reinforcers such as praise, trinkets, and treats alone or in combination with other treatment procedures can produce generalized and enduring improvements in young children's praising, sharing, and donating (also see Gelfand & Hartmann, 1980). Whether these facilitative effects result from feedback, incentive, or response-strengthening functions (e.g., Bandura, 1977) of positive consequences is not clear. Recently a fourth and paradoxical function of rewards has been suggested by research conducted on the overjustification effect. Rewards may have response-weakening effects because of the coercive or control implications they convey. Thus, under some circumstances, salient external consequences for prosocial behavior such as unusually generous offers of money or toys may produce performance decrements by undermining children's interest in the rewarded activity (Lepper, 1981), by eliciting reactance (Bem, 1967; Staub, 1979), or by causing devaluation of the rewarded activity (Deci, 1975).

Although this paradoxical effect of rewards has been demonstrated for a variety of behaviors (Condry, 1977; Lepper, 1981), only a single study has suggested that rewards may weaken children's prosocial behavior (Garbarino, 1975). Nevertheless, socializing agents should exercise care in attempting to promote children's helping, sharing, and donating through offers of rewards. According to Lepper's (1981) principle of minimal sufficiency, effective but nonsalient rewards, such as praise, should be preferred over more obvious response consequences, which might possibly decrease children's propensities to help. However, not all children find praise reinforcing and not all adults praise children effectively. Maternal praise may function as a punishing stimulus for some children (Herbert, Pinkston, Hayden, Sajwaj, Pinkston, Cordua, & Jackson, 1973). Similarly, Midlarsky et al. (1973) found that social approval for donating coming from a selfish model actually resulted in a reduction of subsequent donating. Nevertheless, under many circumstances praise probably increases and maintains most young children's generous and helpful behavior.

CONTROL BY AVERSIVE CONSEQUENCES

Alternatively, helpful responses may be strengthened by following them with escape from or avoidance of a variety of unpleasant experiences such as social disapproval for failure to help, worry over violating a personal norm of helping, and vicarious discomfort resulting from the observation of unalleviated pain in others (Staub, 1978, 1979). The second of the series of studies conducted in our laboratory investigated the effects of one such unpleasant event—a fine—on children's donations (Hartmann, Gelfand, Smith, Paul, Cromer, Page, & LeBenta, 1976).

Our decision to investigate the effect of negative events in an escape-avoidance learning paradigm primarily was based on two considerations. First, escape-avoidance learning may be particularly illuminating in the study of a behavior such as altruism that appears to occur in the absence of identifiable reinforcers (Goldiamond, 1968). When the aversive consequences used in training are avoided successfully, the trained response may appear, to an external observer, to occur in the absence of any reinforcers. A second reason for using the escape-avoidance training paradigm was that similar training procedures have been implicated by some theories of altruism that propose that *not* helping produces negative self-evaluation (e.g.,

Rawlings, 1970) or empathic emotional distress (Aronfreed, 1976). Enacting helpful behavior would then be negatively reinforced by reduction or relief from these aversive feelings (e.g., Cialdini, Darby, & Vincent, 1973). In support of such a view, Zahn-Waxler, Radke-Yarrow, and King (1979) found that certain maternal disciplinary actions were associated with toddlers' altruism and with their reparation attempts after they had harmed others. The mothers of the most altruistic children were nurturant, but they also responded to their children's transgressions with dramatic explanations of the distress their children had caused to others. Thus, the children could escape feelings of guilt or anxiety by attempting to make amends for their own socially harmful behavior. This line of reasoning led us to expect that aversive consequences could be used to promote children's prosocial responding.

The procedures used in our study were similar to those used in our earlier study of the effects of positive consequences. Ten-year-old children individually played the marble-drop game in order to earn pennies, and were given periodic opportunities to donate a penny to assist another child. Following baseline trials, we exposed the ungenerous children to a training procedure in which their failure to donate resulted in a loss of two pennies. Some of the children were also given explicit instructions regarding the contingency between not donating and the loss of pennies; other children were not so instructed until a later phase of the study. Children informed of the response–consequence contingency showed a remarkable increase in responding, donating on almost every available opportunity (see Figure 7.2). Most of these children never experienced the contingency, and would appear to an uninformed external observer to be engaged in repeated altruistic acts in the absence of any reinforcement.

The results were quite different for children who were not apprised of the response–consequence contingency. Only one of the seven subjects in this condition acquired the donating response, despite receiving between 30 and 90 opportunities to donate (and losing between 60 and 180 pennies because of their failure to help). When these children were informed of the contingency, five of the six previous nondonors quickly began donating to help their needy peer (see Figure 7.3).

These findings dramatically substantiate the suggestion by Bandura (e.g., 1977) that conditioning procedures that are unmodified to take advantage of children's rapidly expanding language skills and cognitive capacities may be inefficient and sometimes ineffective methods of producing behavior change. The results also indicate that modified escape–avoidance training procedures can be highly effective in promoting high rates of prosocial behavior. Other aversive procedures have also been used to strengthen children's helpful behaviors. Rushton and Teachman (1978) found that so-

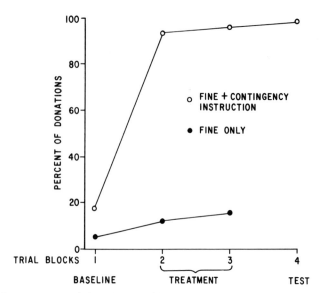

Figure 7.2. **Percentage of donations per block of ten donating trials for children in the fine-only ($n = 7$) and fine-plus-contingency instructions conditions ($n = 28$). From Hartmann, Gelfand, Smith, Paul, Cromer, Page, & LeBenta (1976).**

cial disapproval for failure to donate can strengthen children's donating, and that the effects of training persist over a 2-week period. In addition, positive practice, a mildly aversive forced rehearsal procedure, was employed successfully by Barton and Osborne (1978) to increase children's physical sharing.

The preceding studies indicate that prosocial behavior can be acquired and strengthened in the laboratory by means of training procedures that involve aversive stimuli. However, one might question whether the same procedures commonly operate in children's natural environments. Some social learning theorists suggest that prosocial behavior is more likely to be maintained by positive than by negative consequences (e.g., Aronfreed, 1976; Staub, 1979). According to Patterson and Cobb (1971), "positive social reinforcers are prime determinants for most children's prosocial behaviors [p. 82]." This hypothesis was investigated in another study conducted in our laboratory by Tonick, Gelfand, Hartmann, Cromer, and Millsapp (1977).

In this seminaturalistic study, we observed the prosocial and antagonistic behaviors of nine groups of three interacting nursery school children. The videotaped observations were conducted at a nursery school during three 15-minute play periods while the children were presented with a single toy.

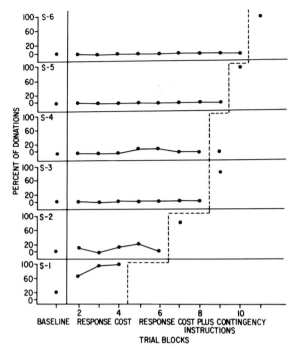

Figure 7.3. **Multiple baseline data for the seven subjects in the fine-contingency only condition (10 donating trials per trial block) before and after being informed of the contingency. From Hartmann, Gelfand, Smith, Paul, Cromer, Page, & LeBenta (1976).**

The videotapes were subsequently scored for verbal and nonverbal prosocial and coercive attempts to gain possession of the toy, prosocial and coercive responses to these requests by the possessor, and a variety of other disruptive and socially appropriate behaviors including expressions of gratitude for other children's sharing. The results were quite complex, but two findings stand out with some clarity. The sharing we observed was likely to be preceded by increasingly negative and forceful interactions between the possessor and nonpossessor children, and appeared to represent attempts on the part of the nonpossessors to coerce the possessor to share the toy. Coercive requests in the form of grabbing, complaining, and demanding were 10 times more common than were pleasant attempts to gain possession of the toy. Verbal demands were more likely to lead to sharing than were verbal requests, and grabbing and other forms of physical "requesting" were almost twice as likely to precede sharing immediately than were any other nonpossessor behaviors. The picture that emerges is that sharing represented a means of escape from an increasingly menacing social situation. If positive consequences maintained the children's sharing, the nature of these consequences was not at all apparent to us. For example, fewer than 2% of shares were followed by any form of verbal recognition such as a "thank you." These results are consistent with other naturalistic studies conducted with preschoolers that also failed to observe positive consequences such as smiling and praise following prosocial behavior (e.g., Barton et al., 1979).

Taken together, the results of several studies cast doubt on the hypothesized match (e.g., Patterson & Cobb, 1971) between the valence of social behaviors and of their consequences (i.e., positive consequences for positive behaviors). Despite the frequent report of reciprocity in social relations (Staub, 1978), it would appear, at least with preschool children, that aversive rather than positive control from peers may be more common in maintaining at least some forms of prosocial behavior, especially compliant as opposed to spontaneous responses. These results may be restricted to young children, since it is widely held that both the nature and locus of maintaining stimuli for helpful responding change with advancing age. Presumably the prosocial behaviors of older children increasingly come under the control of self-administered consequences, such as feelings of pride and guilt (e.g., Bar-Tal, 1976; Mussen & Eisenberg-Berg, 1977).

CAUSAL ATTRIBUTIONS REGARDING PROSOCIAL ACTS

The research we have reviewed has identified some environmental events that affect prosocial behavior, but that may not appear to do so. We believe that definitions of altruistic behavior that exclude the possibility of extrinsic reinforcement are unnecessarily narrow and probably misguided. Such definitions may stem from insufficiently detailed functional analyses of the behavioral impact of events that precede and follow the helpful behavior. Unfortunately, inadequate analyses and flawed definitions can prove socially costly by deterring investigators from searching for situational determinants of prosocial behavior. The resulting ignorance of environmental interventions that could increase helping, sharing, and donating unduly limits opportunities to promote prosocial behavior in the population, and particularly in the young.

Thus, it is important to assess whether the causes of prosocial behavior are accurately perceived. As an initial step in this assessment, we interviewed the children who had participated in our studies of the effects of instructions, prompts, and rewards on donating. The children were questioned concerning their understanding of the experimental procedures and of the factors influencing their behavior. These informal interviews revealed that the children readily detected some of our influence tactics, but remained unaware of others. Specifically, the children noticed and remembered the tangible consequences for donating and the threats of fines for failure to donate, and they attributed their increased generosity to the tangible reward and fine contingencies. However, they failed to detect other, equally potent behavior influences—instructions and praise and reproof statements (Smith, Gelfand, Hartmann, & Partlow, 1979). We believe that modeling also would go undetected as a behavioral constraint, as Lepper (1981) has recently suggested and as Bandura (1969) has long maintained. Why would this be so, and how might the limited detectability of certain procedures and the obviousness of others affect children's behavior? These questions have been the focus of our recent research efforts.

These attributional questions are not new; in one or another form they have stimulated psychological research and theoretical conjecture for decades (Frieze & Bar-Tal, 1979). The naive or "person-in-the-street" psychology of Heider (1958) addressed just such issues. According to Heider, the average person continuously makes attributional judgments concerning his or her own behavior and the conduct of others. Some behavioral effects are commonly attributed to personal dispositions and others to environmental inducements or constraints. Attribution theorists such as Kelley (1967, 1973), Jones (1979), and Bem (1972) have developed models or schemata of the causal attributions made by adults under varying circumstances. Jones (1979) has claimed that: "Understanding how people make inferences about others' stable characteristics from observations of their behavior is . . . one of the most fundamental problems in social and clinical psychology [p. 107]." In addition, Bem (1972) has stimulated the study of self-perceptions, or the process of making causal inferences about our *own* characteristics based on observations of our own behavior.

In the simplest case a behavioral outcome might have a single dominant cause. For example, regardless of their personality characteristics, everyone in a theater audience would leave as quickly as possible upon hearing that the building was on fire. In this instance situational factors clearly govern behavior. In other cases, such as in response to an invitation to speak before a large group, personal tastes, skills, or predispositions may be paramount. However, most often some combination of personal dispositions and situational factors determines behavior.

Kelley's Causal Schemata

Kelley (1971, 1973) has described two major types of causal attributions involving both extrinsic and internal causes—the multiple *necessary* causal schema and the multiple *sufficient* causal schema. In Kelley's view, observers seek covariation between different types of potential causes and a particular behavioral outcome. In the *multiple necessary causal schema,* more than one factor must be operative for the behavior to result. As an example, a child must wish to help others and must have received permission to do so if the child is to engage in some form of helping (the behavioral result).

More extensively studied is the *multiple sufficient causal schema,* in which any of two or more causes could produce a behavioral effect. As a case in point, either altruistic motivation (an internal disposition or intrinsic cause) or extrinsic environmental factors such as material or social benefits could suffice to motivate a person to act helpfully. When one potential cause is observed to be present, then the other may or may not be operative. When visible and presumably potent causal factors are present, observers are inclined to discount the operation of other types of causal influences. This phenomenon is sometimes called discounting, or use of the *discounting principle.* Most often when extrinsic incentives or constraints are apparent the actor's intrinsic motivation is discounted or questioned (Kelley, 1967, 1973). A child who is promised a treat or other extrinsic incentive for helping a disabled neighbor with household chores is presumed to lack sufficient altruistic or intrinsic motivation to behave helpfully in this situation without being rewarded. That is, the child's helpfulness is attributed to the extrinsic incentive.

Discounting the possible intrinsic motivation of externally constrained actors may occur simply because extrinsic factors often are extremely *salient.* Taylor and Fiske (1978) suggested that observers will perceive situational factors as causally important to the degree that situations are salient, and information about external incentives or constraints is made available to the observer. Features such as perceptual salience (e.g., movement, brightness, and novelty) and type of cognitive encoding (e.g., both in images and semantically) may focus observers' attention on material rewards and punishments as probable explanations for a child's behavior, as Taylor and Fiske (1978) have speculated. However, unlike many writers (e.g., Nisbett & Ross, 1980; Taylor & Fiske, 1978), we believe that motivational as well as perceptual and cognitive factors must be used to account for causal attributions of prosocial behavior. We will return to this issue later for more extended consideration.

ATTRIBUTIONAL ERRORS

In the absence of very obvious external or situational determinants, behavior is often explained by reference to dispositional factors. In fact, both

Jones (1979; Jones & Davis, 1965) and Taylor and Fiske (1978) accept Heider's (1958, Chapter 2) notion that situational factors often are ignored and personality factors are used erroneously to explain actors' behavior. There is overwhelming empirical evidence that even behavior that is clearly constrained (e.g., is controlled by instructions) is often attributed to personal dispositions rather than to the nonsalient situational factors (Miller, Mayerson, Pogue, & Whitehouse, 1977). This attributional bias probably occurs partly because of the perceptual salience of actions as opposed to instructions or other situational factors (Jones, 1979). Thus, observers are likely to make the "*fundamental* attributional error [Ross, 1977, p. 183]" of attributing situationally controlled behavior to the actor's personal characteristics. In contrast to highly salient material rewards and punishments, many social control processes are subtle and not likely to attract observers' attention. In these latter situations attributional errors are probable.

Misperception of Social Incentives

Like a number of other investigators (e.g., Deci, 1971, 1972; Anderson, Manoogian, & Reznick, 1976), our research group has found that social consequences such as praise and reproof are not seen as behavioral controls even when they do, in fact, influence children's behavior. Bem (1972) and Deci (1975), among others, have attempted to explain why social consequences are not generally thought to control people's behavior. Using Skinner's (1957) terminology, Bem (1972) described social consequences (such as praise for good behavior) as appearing to be *tacts,* or descriptions of the actor's personality or behavior. An example would be the statement: "It is nice of you to help." In contrast, material incentives are viewed as *mands,* or coercive controls over the actor's behavior. Both actor and observer may fail to realize that social consequences (which appear to be simple behavior or character descriptions) are actually determining the actors' behavior; this interpretive error is made by children and adults alike. To illustrate this process, Smith *et al.* (1979) employed the marble-drop game procedure with second and third grade children. All children were induced to donate at every opportunity to do so by receiving permissive-sounding, but actually very compelling instructions that perhaps it would be nice to help the other child "once or twice." Then each child received the same sequence of opportunities to donate. On some trials the children successfully donated because they were given time to do so, and on other trials, through experimental manipulations, the opportunity passed before the child could make a donation. All children received the same sequence of successes and failures in their attempts to make donations. Children were randomly assigned to groups which received differing consequences for donating and for failing to donate, including (a) social punishment in the form of a mild rebuke from the experimenter (e.g., "Too bad you didn't set his marble free"); (b) rebuke accompanied by material punishment (a two-penny fine); (c) a fine only; (d) social reward or praise (e.g., "Good thing you set her marble free"); (e) praise accompanied by a two-penny reward; (f) the two-penny reward only; and (g) no consequences for donating or for failing to donate. Then each child was questioned to determine the child's recall of what the experimenter had done and the child's beliefs concerning his or her own reasons for donating.

As shown in Figure 7.4, the children who received material consequences such as penny rewards for donating or fines for not donating attributed their generosity to these material consequences. However, the children who received only social consequences (praise or rebuke) attributed their behavior to a desire to help or to concern about the other child, as did children who received no experimenter-delivered consequences. The children's recall of the experimenter's behavior lends support to the perceptual saliency model. The participants accurately recounted the tangible rewards and fines they had received, but were considerably less accurate in their recall of the social consequences provided by the experimenter. The children were especially inaccurate in describing the experimenter's praise or reproof in the combined material and social consequences conditions, as is shown in Table 7.1. Their inaccuracy in reporting the experimenter's comments in the combined conditions may have been due to the high salience of the material consequences, which may have distracted the children's attention from the praise and reproof statements. In a similar vein, Dienstbier and

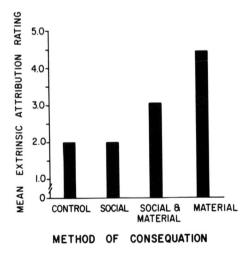

Figure 7.4. **Mean ratings of attributional statements as a function of type of consequences received. Higher numbers denote judges' ratings of children's more extrinsic motivation. Adapted with permission from Smith, Gelfand, Hartmann, & Partlow (1979), © The Society for Research in Child Development, Inc.**

Table 7.1
Percentage of Children Reporting Receiving Various Consequences as a Function of Experimental Condition

Reported consequence	Experimental condition						
	Control	Praise	Rebuke	Praise and reward	Rebuke and fine	Reward	Fine
Nothing	92	33	17	—	—	—	—
Praise	—	58	—	—	—	—	—
Rebuke	8	—	50	—	8	—	—
Praise and rebuke	—	8	33	—	—	—	—
Praise and reward	—	—	—	0	—	—	—
Rebuke and fine	—	—	—	—	8	—	—
Reward	—	—	—	100	—	100	—
Fine	—	—	—	—	83	—	100

Note. Accurate reporting of consequences is reflected by italicized values in the principal diagonal. From Smith, Gelfand, Hartmann, & Partlow (1979), © The Society for Research in Child Development, Inc.

his associates (Dienstbier, Hillman, Lehnhoff, Hillman, & Valkenaar, 1975) have suggested that, unlike more salient material rewards, unobtrusive social rewards fail to distract children from the task at hand. Thus, distraction may cause the children to make external attributions when they receive salient material response consequences. In contrast, they may make internal attributions when praised for good behavior because the praise does not disrupt ongoing behavior sequences. In addition, children may come to accept adults' descriptions of them as helpful (Grusec, Kuczynski, Rushton, & Simutis, 1978) and patient (Toner, Moore, & Emmons, 1980). These acquired self-descriptions may guide the child's future conduct, especially in the presence of the labeling adult (Toner et al., 1980). Whatever the mediational process in operation, it is clear that, like adults, 7–9-year-old children perceive material rewards and consequences as molding their behavior, but mistakenly consider equally compelling instructions, descriptions, and social consequences as motivationally impotent.

ACTORS' AND OBSERVERS' CAUSAL ATTRIBUTIONS

It appears that children and adults hold implicit causal theories or world views regarding the extent to which a particular stimulus is a plausible cause of a particular response. They attribute their own prosocial behavior to the most likely causes—to altruistic motivation when no salient extrinsic incentives can be observed, and to extrinsic factors when salient tangible rewards and punishments are present. However, what happens to the *observer's* causal attributions when an actor receives tangible consequences (which generate extrinsic attributions) together with social consequences (which generate intrinsic consequences)? The Smith *et al.* (1979) study revealed that children's interpretations of their own reasons for donating tended to be more intrinsic when they received social together with material consequences (e.g., a rebuke and a fine) than when they received material consequences alone. This was true regardless of whether the consequences constituted rewards or punishments. Later we will present evidence that actors' and observers' attributions tend to differ systematically when actors receive combined material and social consequences for engaging in prosocial behavior. As will be seen, motivational factors seem best able to account for these differences in actor–observer causal analyses of prosocial actions.

There is an extensive social psychology literature on attributional differences between actors and observers. In a review of this literature, Jones and Nisbett (1971) concluded that actors are likely to attribute their own behavior to situational requirements, whereas observers more often see stable personal dispositions as determining actors' behavior. Jones and Nisbett viewed these actor–observer discrepancies as due to actors' greater and more precise information regarding their own emotions and intentions.[2] Also, observers tend to focus their attention on the most salient environmental stimulus—the actor's behavior. In contrast, the actor's attention is more likely focused outward on situational stimuli and their motivational properties.

Our research has revealed a significant exception to the original Jones and Nisbett (1971) formulation of actor–observer attribution differences. When prosocial acts are considered, actors may be *more* likely than observers to attribute their helpful behavior to intrinsic prosocial motivation. That is, the Jones and Nisbett position requires an adjustment in order to account for the type of behavior presently under consideration. Socially undesirable behaviors may be evaluated very differently from highly socially desirable acts. In the previously described study by Smith *et al.* (1979), children made attributions about their own prosocial behavior. In this situation adding social consequences to material ones produced more intrinsic attributions than did material consequences alone. That is, although the children did not recall the experimenter's praise or reproof clearly, their attributions about

2. Nisbett has since concluded that actors may have different, but not necessarily more accurate, information regarding their own motives than do observers (Nisbett & Ross, 1980; Nisbett & Wilson, 1977).

their own donating reflected the influence of the experimenter's comments. However, in two other experiments in which children made causal attributions about *others'* helpfulness, they attributed helping to extrinsic factors (material consequences) in the combined material and social consequences conditions (Experiments 1 and 2 in Cohen, Gelfand, & Hartmann, 1981). In the presence of material consequences alone or with social consequences, the observers attributed the actors' helpfulness to external factors. (Because they chiefly address developmental differences in attribution, the Cohen *et al.* experiments will be described more fully in a later section of this chapter on developmental trends.)

When viewing their own socially neutral or socially desirable activities, children tend toward internal attributions. For example, Swann and Pittman (1977) found that 6–9-year-old children's intrinsic interest in a game was *not* reduced when they received verbal reinforcement along with material rewards for playing the game. In contrast, material rewards alone *did* reduce subsequent involvement in the game. Swann and Pittman interpreted their results as supporting Deci's (1975) contention that material rewards are perceived as controlling a person's behavior, and praise is perceived simply as providing information about the appropriateness of the behavior. That is, praise is seen as informative, not as manipulative. Although useful in many respects, Deci's control-versus-information theory does not explain why children should attribute their own desirable behavior to dispositional factors in the presence of both material and social consequences, but fail to do so in interpreting the prosocial behavior of others. Nor does the alternative perceptual saliency hypothesis explain the self–other attributional differences. Material consequences should be at least as obvious to actors as to observers (and perhaps even more obvious to the actors whose attention supposedly is focused outward). Yet children tend to see their own prosocial activity as motivated by altruism, and the helpfulness of others as motivated by rewards or punishments.

A MOTIVATIONAL INTERPRETATION

Taken alone, cognitive and perceptual explanations fail to account for actor–observer differences in causal interpretations of prosocial behavior that is followed by combined social and material inducements. Motivational variables must be considered in order to explain and predict causal attributions in such cases. Consider the potential heightening of self-esteem when viewing one's own donations, rescue attempts, and other helpful acts as due to a helpful disposition rather than to mercenary motives. Self-image maintenance and self-esteem are better served by viewing one's own helpfulness as due to altruistic motivation than to crass materialism. Consequently, given a choice of possible sufficient motivators (e.g., extrinsic consequences or intrinsic prosocial motives), actors will tend to attribute their own behavior to the nobler cause. However, there is no particular incentive for doing so when analyzing the behavior of others. In fact, self-perceptions are best served by viewing others' prosocial acts as due to desire for rewards or escape from punishment and one's own helping as due to benevolence and consideration for others. In addition, correctly perceiving the causes of other people's behavior allows the observer to manipulate incentives in order to modify others' behavior effectively, which may be highly beneficial to the manipulator. Thus, accurate attributional analysis of the behavior of others is socially functional. Future research may provide an empirical basis for selection among these alternative explanations of actor and observer differences in the causal analysis of behavior that receives joint social and material reward or punishment. However, we are convinced that motivational factors cannot reasonably be ignored in the study of social perception.

DEVELOPMENTAL TRENDS IN
CAUSAL ATTRIBUTIONS

To this point we have implied that children and adults reason alike, and that there are no developmental differences in the causal attributions made by children of different ages. Such a view is incorrect; in fact, there are large and highly reliable age differences in styles of reasoning about the sources of helpful behavior. Long ago Piaget (1965/1932) observed that adults and older children reason differently about moral issues than do young children. Piaget focused on children's solutions of moral dilemmas and their evaluations of the culpability of story characters who had caused damage accidentally, either during a mischievous act or a well-intended one. Unfortunately, Piaget's stories confounded the amount of damage done and the actor's intentions (Karniol, 1978). For example, in one story a child accidentally broke 15 cups while attempting to be helpful, and a second child accidentally broke 1 cup during a raid on the jam jar. Thus, the story characters with good intentions always caused more damage than did the disobedient ones. Methodological problems notwithstanding, Piaget concluded that younger children fail to base their judgments on actors' intentions, and instead mete out punishment according to the extent of the damage done (e.g., smashing 15 cups as compared to just 1 cup).

More recent research has examined the separate effects of actors' intentions and of the amount of havoc they wreak. When intentions and damage are evaluated separately, it appears that even preschool children can utilize intention cues in judging the severity of an offense (Karniol, 1978). For instance, kindergarten children have been found to ponder longer when judging accidentally harmful rather than intentionally harmful acts (Imam-öglu, 1975). Kindergarteners also attribute greater hostility to actors who cause harm intentionally than to those who do so accidentally (Rotenberg, 1980); and, like adults, they recommend clemency for those who do harm under mitigating circumstances (Darley, Klosson, & Zanna, 1978). Thus, the reasoning of young children resembles that of older children under certain circumstances. However, younger children are more likely to impute intentionality to *all* acts than are children older than 5 (Sedlak, 1979; Smith, 1978), making it difficult to reach any general conclusions about the interpretive abilities of young children. Despite the increasing volume of research on the subject, we know far less about the reasoning processes of preschool and kindergarten children than that of older ones. However, the research just described would suggest that young children have an incomplete understanding of the role of intentions in the control of prosocial behavior.

REPLICATABLE DEVELOPMENTAL FINDINGS IN CAUSAL ATTRIBUTIONS

Certain developmental trends have been discovered repeatedly in studies conducted independently in various research laboratories. The robust developmental differences found in attributional analyses are as follows. Most older children and adults discount the intrinsic altruistic motivation of helpers who are offered rewards or other inducements for helping. In contrast, many preschool children view extrinsic material incentives as *increasing* the actor's desire to help. Cohen and her associates (Cohen et al., 1981) conducted two studies that examined causal attributions regarding story characters who were offered a variety of inducements to act helpfully, ranging from no inducements to promised social and material rewards for helping and punishments for not helping. Participants ranging in age from 5 years to young adulthood heard brief descriptions of pairs of child story characters. In each story one character was offered one type of consequence for helping, and the other character was offered a contrasting consequence (e.g., social reward for one and no inducement for the other actor). Figure 7.5 shows the mean number of times subjects of various ages selected each consequence as being associated with a greater desire to help. As predicted, most kindergarten children perceived material rewards and punishments as enhancing actors' internal motivation to help. They appeared to use an *additive principle* in interpreting the behavior of materially rewarded or

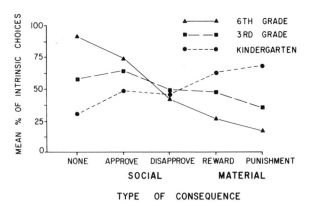

Figure 7.5. **Mean percentage of times children selected a consequence as being associated with a greater intrinsic desire to help. Adapted with permission from Cohen, Gelfand, & Hartmann, 1981, © The Society for Research in Child Development, Inc.**

punished actors, according to which material consequences add to actors' preexisting altruistic motivation making them especially highly motivated to help. In contrast, most older subjects use a discounting principle (the *multiple sufficient causal schema*), and fail to credit altruistic motivation to actors who behave prosocially after receiving obvious extrinsic incentives for engaging in such behavior (Karniol & Ross, 1976; Leahy, 1979; Smith *et al.*, 1979).

In the Cohen *et al.* studies, use of the discounting principle increased with age until 12 or 13 years, but not thereafter. Also, the third graders tended to discount the altruism of actors threatened with punishment, but to credit altruism to those offered material rewards. This suggests that recognition of the coercive intent of adults who threaten punishment developmentally precedes detection of the manipulativeness of adults who offer rewards. This same result has been reported by Hill and Enzle (1977), and indicates that the recognition of the manipulative intent of authority figures may be a necessary prerequisite to children's use of the discounting principle. This and other explanations of age trends in the use of the additive and the discounting principles are receiving increasing research scrutiny.

BASIS OF DEVELOPMENTAL TRENDS IN CAUSAL ATTRIBUTIONS

Possible explanations of developmental shifts in children's causal attributions include explanations based on random responding or biased responding by the younger children, their inability to understand the questions asked of them, their role-taking deficits, their overreliance on perceptual salience, and their belief in immanent reward as well as immanent punishment.

Random Responding

It is possible that younger subjects do not understand questions addressed to them regarding causal relationships. A likely result of such a deficit in comprehension would be random responding. However, about two-thirds of the kindergarten children tested by Cohen et al. (1981) responded *consistently,* not randomly (see also the similar results of Karniol & Ross, 1976; Kun, 1978; Shultz & Mendelson, 1975; and Wannemacher & Ryan, 1978). Thus, random responding is an unlikely explanation of the developmental trends.

Artifact

Perhaps the age differences in responding occur because the younger children share a common misinterpretation of the particular attribution question asked. That is, the results might be due to a procedural artifact. This explanation, too, is unlikely, because other investigators (Clark, 1973; Feldman, Klosson, Parsons, Rholes, & Ruble, 1976; Leahy, 1979) and our group (Cohen et al., 1981) all have found that rewording the questions does not alter the nature of the children's answers.

Dominance of Perceptual Salience

It is well established that young children's interpretations of physical and social phenomena are dominated by simple perceptual salience, as their limited conservation abilities demonstrate. With advancing age and experience, children begin to think more abstractly and to realize that some events may be multiply and subtly determined. During the early years, however, children may be highly affected by the perceptual salience of extrinsic incentives. Nevertheless, the perceptual salience explanation fails to account for preschoolers' attributing a greater desire to help to rewarded and punished actors than to those who do not receive obvious extrinsic incentives. Why should intrinsic desire to help be inferred in the presence of highly salient inducements?

Immanent Punishment and Reward

In our studies, the younger children sometimes appeared to employ a version of the immanent justice principle suggested by Piaget (1965/1932).

That is, they seemed to believe that good actions are always rewarded immediately or always result in immediate avoidance of punishment. According to this line of reasoning story characters who are offered rewards invariably merit them because of their good intentions as well as their good deeds. In addition, the character who successfully avoids punishment must be truly altruistic at heart. What a simple and just world (Lerner, 1980) some of these young children believe in! Our results and those of other investigators suggest that immanent punishment probably should be extended to include the concept of immanent reward. Moreover, further research is needed to establish the origins of the belief in immanent reward and punishment and of the development with increasing age of a certain amount of skepticism regarding people's motivation to behave in a helpful manner.

Social Role-Taking Deficits

When asked whether the actors would help even without extrinsic incentives, the younger children we studied believed that everyone would help (but see Eisenberg-Berg & Hand, 1979, for contradictory findings). In contrast, the older children and adults perceived that offers of reward and threats of punishment are methods of coercing reluctant actors to behave helpfully (Cohen et al., 1981). Older children and adults seem to imagine themselves in the position of a socialization agent, and to calculate that such a person must have believed that the actors would not help unless bribed or coerced. That is, older subjects deduce that child actors are threatened or offered rewards only in situations in which they are unlikely to help if left to their own devices. However, most children younger than 7 years fail to appreciate the probable motivation of caretakers who offer reward or threaten punishment in order to influence children to donate, share, or help. This interpretation receives empirical support from at least three sources. First, Karniol and Ross (1979) found that young children who discounted rewarded actors' intrinsic interest in an activity also inferred manipulative intent on the part of the caretakers who offered the rewards. Those children who recognized the caretakers' manipulativeness also tended to discount the rewarded actors' intrinsic interest in the activity that earned them reward. Second, Cohen et al. (1981) concluded that the children who employed the discounting principle in their studies engaged in a two-part reasoning process: (a) they deduced that adults offered incentives to make children help; and (b) they deduced that the adults were doubtful that the children would help if not offered incentives. Data from the Cohen et al. study suggest that both deductive steps are necessary prerequisites for use of the discounting principle. In another recent study by Benson, Hartmann, and Gelfand (1981), 6- and 8-year-olds heard stories that either explicitly described or only implied caretakers' manipulative intent. As an example of an explicit manipulative intent statement, one story read, "Tim's teacher thought Tim would not help on his own. Tim's teacher said, 'Tim, I'll give you a new box of crayons if you help the new boy find his way around the school.'" Most of the 6-year-olds used the discounting principle only if the teacher or parent of one of the two story characters explicitly stated the belief that the child would not help if not rewarded or threatened. When this information was only implied (e.g., "Sally's mother said, 'Sally, you can have an ice cream cone if you help Mrs. Jones rake her lawn.'"), the first graders perceived rewarded actors, and those threatened with punishment as wanting and liking to help more than nonthreatened and unrewarded actors. In contrast, as shown in Table 7.2, the older children tended to use the discounting principle whenever actors were externally induced to behave prosocially. These older children did not require specific explanations of caretakers' manipulative intent in order to discount the altruistic motivation of coerced actors, whereas the younger children did require such explanations. As Table 7.2 also indicates, the first graders discounted story characters' altruistic motivation in the explicit rationale conditions whether the stories involved simple comparisons (both story characters received the same type of incentive) or more complex ones (each of the two characters received a different type of incentive). Nevertheless, it is possible for a child to recognize adult caretakers' manipulative motives, but still to employ the additive rather than the discounting principle in explaining the motivation of rewarded and punished actors. As Cohen et al. (1981) concluded, the inference of manipulative intent may be a necessary, but is not a sufficient condition for the use of the discounting principle and the multiple sufficient causal schema. In summary, the research evidence points to several possible

Table 7.2

Children's Choices of More Altruistic Story Character as a Function of Subject Grade and Type of Story Comparison

	Type of story comparison		
Subject grade	Explicit rationale same incentives	Explicit rationale differing incentives	Implicit rationale differing incentives
First grade	1.38^{α}	1.29^{α}	$.64^{\beta}$
Third grade	1.63^{α}	1.92^{α}	1.69^{α}

Note. Scores range from 2.0 (consistent use of discounting principle) to 0.0 (failure to use discounting principle). All column means are significantly different ($p < .05$). Row means not sharing a superscript are significantly different ($p < .01$). From Benson, Hartmann, & Gelfand (1981).

explanations of younger children's reliance on the additive principle. An appreciation of adults' probable reasons for offering children rewards for compliance and punishment for noncompliance can lead to increasing use of discounting processes as the child grows older.

CAUSAL PERCEPTIONS AND PROSOCIAL BEHAVIOR

Now we come to the central, thorny issue of the impact of people's causal perceptions on their prosocial behavior. Do perceptions determine behavior and, if so, how? Very few writers take the position that causal attributions are uninfluential in directing behavior. In fact, Nisbett and Ross (1980) have claimed that the point essentially is not in dispute: "People's judgments often affect their behavior, and both their judgments and their behavior reflect inferential errors [p. 11]." Yet these authors avoid consideration of the next question—*How* do people's judgments affect their behavior?—stating that the inability to bridge the gap between cognition and behavior is not theirs alone, but is "the most serious failing of modern cognitive psychology [Nisbett & Ross, 1980, p. 12]." Perhaps it is premature to conclude that behavior reflects causal attributions when the supporting evidence is quite modest and when the manner of action, if any, remains unknown. Let us consider the possible types of relationships between attributions and behavior and the potential means of bridging the two.

The View That Judgment Directs Behavior

This is a popular position among some cognitive developmental writers and certain social learning theorists as well. In the cognitive-developmental tradition, Blasi (1980) has maintained that moral cognition plays a central role in moral behavior and that only those beneficial acts that are altruistically intended and altruistically motivated truly qualify as moral. Blasi reviewed a large body of research, much of it unpublished and thus of unknown quality, to support his contention that prosocial behavior is based upon moral judgment.

In addition to moral judgment, other cognitive processes such as attribution formulation are believed to guide prosocial behavior. Indeed, some rigorously conducted research has lent support to the position that attributions can influence prosocial behavior. Grusec and her associates (Grusec *et al.,* 1978; see Rushton's chapter in this volume) produced high rates of donating by exposing children to a model who made donations. Those children who were told that they imitated the adult's donating because they were generous, later acted more altruistically in another situation than did children who were told that they shared only because it was expected of them. Note, however, that the actual cause of the children's initial donating was simple observational learning. Later, their manipulated self-perceptions did affect their helpfulness. Thus, there is some evidence to support the notion of attributions as direct determinants of behavior.

At other times, however, only weak links or none have been found between attributions and subsequent behavior. For example, Smith et al. (1979) found a correlation of only $r = .24$ (.26 when corrected for attenuation) between internality of self-judged prosocial motivation and donations made anonymously. In some experimental conditions the correlation between attributions and donations closely approximated zero. This and other negative evidence has led many writers to minimize the magnitude of the relationship to be expected between thought and deed. In fact, Mischel and Mischel (1976) have concluded that, far from preceding and directing behavior, moral reasoning often follows behavior and is distorted so as to provide justification for whatever course of action the person pursued. That is, attributions and other judgments may represent rationalizations. But if judgment does not guide behavior, what does?

Attributions and Behaviors Have Different Determinants

Jones (1979) addressed the question of why people's behavior so often seems to be at variance with their stated motives, intentions, and attributions. The answer, Jones suggested (see also Dreman, 1976), may be that overt behavior is responsive to a broader range of causal influences than are interview and questionnaire responses. What might this range of causal influences include?

We suggest that behavior is affected by a variety of incentive conditions and social learning experiences. Prosocial behavior is also mediated by the helper's altruistic motivation, by adherence to prosocial norms and rules including reciprocity norms, by self-efficacy beliefs as regards one's own ability to help, and by other cognitive and motivational factors (e.g., see the elaborate social learning explanations of prosocial behavior offered by Rushton, 1980, and Staub, 1978, 1979). Only when situational and social learning influences are relatively weak and ineffectual will other elements such as causal attributions emerge to direct behavior. Such situations may be relatively uncommon. Therefore, in attempting to predict behavior, one must analyze the relative power of the situational factors at work and of the cognitive ones.

Insofar as cognitive psychologists minimize or ignore the power of situational variables, they will present an inadequate model of human functioning; their humans will remain lost in thought much like Tolman's rats. Excessive mentalism robs psychology of the ability to understand and predict actions. Our minds are not simply computers any more than our bodies are simply machines. A complete and accurate account of prosocial behavior must draw upon learning and motivational principles as well as on cognitive psychology's illumination of the processes of attention, encoding, memory, retrieval, and script and schema construction. In addition, the early development of cognitive and behavioral repertoires must be traced. To do any less is to present a misleading caricature of humans and of their capacities for selfless as well as for self-serving behavior.

ACKNOWLEDGMENTS

Thanks are due our students, past and present, who have aided in the preparation of this manuscript either by their research participation (Nina Benson, Esther Cohen, Cindy Cromer, Lizette Peterson, Carol Shigetomi, Cathy Smith, & Illene Tonick), or by their helpful comments on the manuscipt itself (Lynne Zarbatany & Sigurdur Gretarsson).

REFERENCES

Anderson, R., Manoogian, S. T., & Reznick, J. S. The undermining and enhancing of intrinsic motivation in preschool children. *Journal of Personality and Social Psychology*, 1976, *34*, 915-922.

Aronfreed, J. Moral development from the standpoint of a general psychological theory. In T. Lickona (Ed.), *Moral development and behavior theory, research, and social issues.* New York: Holt, Rinehart & Winston, 1976.

Aronfreed, J., & Paskal, V. *Altruism, empathy and the conditioning of positive affect.* Unpublished manuscript, University of Pennsylvania, 1965. Cited in J. Aronfreed. *Conduct and conscience: The socialization of internalized control over behavior.* New York: Academic Press, 1968.

Azrin, N., & Lindsley, O. The reinforcement of cooperation between children. *Journal of Abnormal and Social Psychology*, 1956, *52*, 100-102.

Bandura, A. *Principles of behavior modification.* New York: Holt, Rinehart & Winston, 1969.

Bandura, A. *Aggression: A social learning analysis.* Englewood Cliffs, N.J.: Prentice-Hall, 1973.

Bandura, A. *Social learning theory.* Englewood Cliffs, N.J.: Prentice-Hall, 1977.

Bar-Tal, D. *Prosocial behavior: Theory and research.* New York: Halstead, 1976.

Barton, E. J., & Ascione, F. R. Sharing in preschool children: Facilitation, stimulus generalization, response generalization, and maintenance. *Journal of Applied Behavior Analysis*, 1979, *12*, 417-430.

Barton, E. J., Olszewski, M. J., & Madsen, J. J. The effects of adult presence on the prosocial behavior of preschool children. *Child Behavior Therapy*, 1979, *1*, 271-286.

Barton, E. J., & Osborne, J. G. The development of classroom sharing by a teacher using positive practice. *Behavior Modification*, 1978, *2*, 231-249.

Bem, D. J. Self-perception: An alternative interpretation of cognitive dissonance phenomena. *Psychological Review*, 1967, *74*, 183-200.

Bem, D. J. Self-perception theory. In L. Berkowitz (Ed.), *Advances in experimental social psychology* (Vol. 6). New York: Academic Press, 1972.

Benson, N. C., Hartmann, D. P., & Gelfand, D. M. *Intentions and children's moral judgments.* Paper presented at the biennial meeting of the Society for Research in Child Development, Boston, 1981.

Blasi, A. Bridging moral cognition and moral action: A critical review of the literature. *Psychological Bulletin,* 1980, *88,* 1–45.

Bryan, J. H., & London, P. Altruistic behavior by children. *Psychological Bulletin,* 1970, *73,* 200–211.

Cialdini, R. B., Darby, B. L., & Vincent, J. E. Transgression and altruism: A case for hedonism. *Journal of Experimental Social Psychology,* 1973, *9,* 502–516.

Clark, E. V. How children describe time and order. In G. A. Ferguson & D. I. Slobin (Eds.), *Studies of child language development.* New York: Holt, Rinehart & Winston, 1973.

Cohen, E. A., Gelfand, D. M., & Hartmann, D. P. Causal reasoning as a function of behavioral consequences. *Child Development,* 1981, *52,* 514–522.

Condry, J. Enemies of exploration: Self-initiated versus other-initiated learning. *Journal of Personality and Social Psychology,* 1977, *35,* 459–477.

Cooke, T., & Apolloni, T. Developing positive social–emotional behaviors: A study of training and generalization effects. *Journal of Applied Behavior Analysis,* 1976, *9,* 65–78.

Darley, J. M., Klosson, E. C., & Zanna, M. P. Intentions and their contexts in the moral judgments of children and adults. *Child Development,* 1978, *49,* 66–74.

Deci, E. Effects of externally mediated rewards on intrinsic motivation. *Journal of Personality and Social Psychology,* 1971, *18,* 105–111.

Deci, E. The effects of contingent and noncontingent rewards and controls on intrinsic motivation. *Organizational Behavior and Human Performance,* 1972, *8,* 217–229.

Deci, E. *Intrinsic motivation.* New York: Plenum, 1975.

Dienstbier, R. A., Hillman, D., Lehnhoff, J., Hillman, J., & Valkenaar, M. C. An emotion-attribution approach to moral behavior: Interfacing cognitive and avoidance theories of moral development. *Psychological Review,* 1975, *82,* 299–315.

Dreman, S. B. Sharing behavior in Israeli school children: Cognitive and social learning factors. *Child Development,* 1976, *47,* 186–194.

Eisenberg-Berg, N., & Hand, M. The relationship of preschoolers' reasoning about prosocial moral conflicts to prosocial behavior. *Child Development,* 1979, *50,* 356–363.

Feldman, N. S., Klosson, E. C., Parsons, J. E., Rholes, W. S., & Ruble, D. N. Order of information presentation and children's moral judgments. *Child Development,* 1976, *47,* 556–559.

Fischer, W. F. Sharing in preschool children, as a function of amount and type of reinforcement. *Genetic Psychology Monographs,* 1963, *68,* 215–245.

Frieze, I. H., & Bar-Tal, D. Attribution theory: Past and present. In I. H. Frieze, D. Bar-Tal, & J. S. Carroll (Eds.), *New approaches to social problems.* San Francisco: Jossey-Bass, 1979.

Garbarino, J. The impact of anticipated rewards on cross-age tutoring. *Journal of Personality and Social Psychology,* 1975, *32,* 421–428.

Gelfand, D. M., & Hartmann, D. P. *Child behavior analysis and therapy.* New York: Pergamon, 1975.

Gelfand, D. M., & Hartmann, D. P. The development of prosocial behavior. In R. L. Ault (Ed.), *Developmental perspectives.* Santa Monica, Calif.: Goodyear, 1980.

Gelfand, D. M., Hartmann, D. P., Cromer, C. C., Smith, C. L., & Page, B. C. The effects of instructional prompts and praise on children's donation rates. *Child Development,* 1975, *46,* 980–983.

Goldiamond, I. Moral behavior: A functional analysis. *Psychology Today,* 1968, *2,* 31–34.

Grusec, J. E., Kuczynski, L., Rushton, J. P., & Simutis, Z. Modeling, direct instruction, and attributions: Effects on altruism. *Developmental Psychology,* 1978, *14,* 51–57.

Hartmann, D. P., Gelfand, D. M., Smith, C. L., Paul, S. C., Cromer, C. C., Page, B. C., & LeBenta, D. V. Factors affecting the acquisition and elimination of children's donating behavior. *Journal of Experimental Child Psychology,* 1976, *21,* 328–338.

Heider, F. *The psychology of interpersonal relations.* New York: Wiley, 1958.

Herbert, E. W., Pinkston, E. M., Hayden, M. L., Sajwaj, T. E., Pinkston, S., Cordua, G., & Jackson, C. Adverse effects of differential parental attention. *Journal of Applied Behavior Analysis,* 1973, *6,* 15–30.

Hill, K., & Enzle, M. Interactive effects of training domain and age on children's moral judgments. *Canadian Journal of Behavioral Science,* 1977, *9,* 371–381.

Imamŏglu, E. O. Children's awareness and usage of intention cues. *Child Development,* 1975, *46,* 39–45.

Israel, A. C. Some thoughts on correspondence between saying and doing. *Journal of Applied Behavior Analysis,* 1978, *11,* 271–276.

Jones, E. E. The rocky road from acts to dispositions. *American Psychologist,* 1979, *34,* 107–117.

Jones, E. E., & Davis, K. E. From acts to dispositions: The attribution process in person perception. In L. Berkowitz (Ed.), *Advances in experimental social psychology* (Vol. 2). New York: Academic Press, 1965.

Jones, E. E., & Nisbett, R. E. The actor and the observer: Divergent perceptions of the causes of behavior. In E. E. Jones et al. (Eds.), *Attribution: Perceiving the causes of behavior.* Morristown, N.J.: General Learning Press, 1971.

Karniol, R. Children's use of intention cues in evaluating behavior. *Psychological Bulletin,* 1978, *85,* 76–85.

Karniol, R., & Ross, M. The development of causal attributions in social perception. *Journal of Personality and Social Psychology,* 1976, *34,* 455–464.

Karniol, R., & Ross, M. Children's use of a causal attribution schema and the inference of manipulative intentions. *Child Development,* 1979, *50,* 463–468.

Kelley, H. H. Attribution theory in social psychology. In D. Levine (Ed.), *Nebraska Symposium on Motivation* (Vol. 15). Lincoln: University of Nebraska Press, 1967.

Kelley, H. H. Causal schemata and the attribution process. In E. E. Jones et al. (Eds.), *Attribution: Perceiving the causes of behavior.* Morristown, N.J.: General Learning Press, 1971.

Kelley, H. H. The process of causal attribution. *American Psychologist,* 1973, *28,* 107–128.

Krebs, D. L., & Wispé, L. G. On defining altruism. *Journal of Social Issues,* 1974, *30*(2), 194–199.

Kun, A. Evidence for preschoolers' understanding of causal direction in extended causal sequences. *Child Development,* 1978, *49,* 218–222.

Leahy, R. L. Development of conceptions of prosocial behavior: Information affecting rewards given for altruism and kindness. *Developmental Psychology,* 1979, *15,* 34–37.

Lepper, M. R. Intrinsic and extrinsic motivation in children: Detrimental effects of superfluous social controls. In W. A. Collins (Ed.), *Minnesota Symposia on Child Psychology* (Vol. 14). Hillsdale, N.J.: Erlbaum, 1981.

Lerner, M. J. *The belief in a just world.* New York: Plenum, 1980.

Lövaas, O. I. Interaction between verbal and nonverbal behavior. *Child Development,* 1961, *32,* 329–336.

Luria, A. *The role of speech in the regulation of normal and abnormal behavior.* New York: Liveright, 1961.

Midlarsky, E., & Bryan, J. H. Training charity in children. *Journal of Personality and Social Psychology,* 1967, *5,* 408–415.

Midlarksy, E., Bryan, J. H., & Brickman, P. Aversive approval: Interactive effects of modeling and reinforcement on altruistic behavior. *Child Development,* 1973, *44,* 321–328.

Miller, A. G., Mayerson, N., Poque, M., & Whitehouse, D. Perceivers' explanations of their attributions of attitude. *Personality and Social Psychology Bulletin*, 1977, *3*, 111–114.

Mischel, W., & Mischel, H. N. A cognitive social-learning approach to morality and self-regulation. In T. Lickona (Ed.), *Moral development and behavior*. New York: Holt, Rinehart & Winston, 1976.

Mussen, P. H., & Eisenberg-Berg, N. *Roots of caring, sharing, and helping*. San Francisco, Calif.: Freeman, 1977.

Nisbett, R., & Ross, L. *Human inference: Strategies and social judgment*. Englewood Cliffs, N.J.: Prentice-Hall, 1980.

Nisbett, R. E., & Wilson, T. D. Telling more than we can know: Verbal reports on mental processes. *Psychological Review*, 1977, *84*, 231–259.

Patterson, G. R., & Cobb, J. A. A dyadic analysis of aggressive behaviors: An additional step toward a theory of aggression. In J. P. Hill (Ed.), *Minnesota Symposia on Child Psychology* (Vol. 5). Minneapolis: University of Minnesota Press, 1971.

Piaget, J. [*The moral judgment of the child*] (Marjorie Gabain, trans.). New York: Free Press, 1965. (First published in London: Kegan Paul, 1932.)

Rawlings, E. I. Reactive guilt and anticipatory guilt in altruistic behavior. In J. Macauley & L. Berkowitz (Eds.), *Altruism and helping behavior*. New York: Academic Press, 1970.

Rogers-Warren, A., & Baer, D. M. Correspondence between saying and doing: Teaching children to share and praise. *Journal of Applied Behavior Analysis*, 1976, *9*, 335–354.

Rogers-Warren, A., Warren, S. F., & Baer, D. M. A component analysis: Modeling, self-reporting, and reinforcement of self-reporting in the development of sharing. *Behavior Modification*, 1977, *1*, 307–322.

Rosenhan, D. L. Toward resolving the altruism paradox: Affect, self-reinforcement, and cognition. In L. Wispé (Ed.), *Altruism, sympathy, and helping: Psychological and sociological principles*. New York: Academic Press, 1978.

Ross, L. The intuitive psychologist and his shortcomings: Distortions in the attribution process. In L. Berkowitz (Ed.), *Advances in experimental social psychology* (Vol. 10). New York: Academic Press, 1977.

Rotenberg, K. J. Children's use of intentionality in judgments of character and disposition. *Child Development*, 1980, *51*, 282–284.

Rushton, J. P. *Altruism, socialization, and society*. Englewood Cliffs, N.J.: Prentice-Hall, 1980.

Rushton, J. P., & Teachman, G. The effects of positive reinforcement, attributions, and punishment on model induced altruism in children. *Personality and Social Psychology Bulletin*, 1978, *4*, 322–325.

Sedlak, A. J. Developmental differences in understanding plans and evaluating actors. *Child Development*, 1979, *50*, 536–560.

Shultz, T. R., & Mendelson, R. The use of covariation as a principle of causal analysis. *Child Development*, 1975, *46*, 394–399.

Skinner, B. F. *Science and human behavior*. New York: Macmillan, 1953.

Skinner, B. F. *Verbal behavior*. New York: Appleton-Century-Crofts, 1957.

Slaby, R. G., & Crowley, C. G. Modification of cooperation and aggression through teacher attention to children's speech. *Journal of Experimental Child Psychology*, 1977, *23*, 442–458.

Smith, C. L., Gelfand, D. M., Hartmann, D. P., & Partlow, M. E. P. Children's causal attributions regarding help giving. *Child Development*, 1979, *50*, 203–210.

Smith, M. C. Cognizing the behavior stream: The recognition of intentional action. *Child Development*, 1978, *49*, 736–743.

Staub, E. *Positive social behavior and morality* (Vol. 1). New York: Academic Press, 1978.

Staub, E. *Positive social behavior and morality* (Vol. 2). New York: Academic Press, 1979.

Swann, W. B., Jr., & Pittman, T. S. Initiating play activity of children: The moderating influence of verbal cues on intrinsic motivation. *Child Development,* 1977, *48,* 1128-1132.

Taylor, S. E., & Fiske, S. T. Salience, attention, and attribution: Top of the head phenomena. In L. Berkowitz (Ed.), *Advances in experimental social psychology* (Vol. 11). New York: Academic Press, 1978.

Toner, I. J., Moore, L. P., & Emmons, B. A. The effect of being labeled on subsequent self-control in children. *Child Development,* 1980, *51,* 618-621.

Tonick, I. J., Gelfand, D. M., Hartmann, D. P., Cromer, C. C., & Millsapp, R. *A naturalistic study of children's prosocial behavior.* Paper presented at the meeting of the American Psychology Association, San Francisco, August 1977.

Vogler, R. E., Masters, W. M., & Morrill, G. S. Shaping cooperative behavior in young children. *Journal of Psychology,* 1970, *74,* 181-186.

Wannemacher, J. T., & Ryan, M. L. "Less" is not "more": A study of children's comprehension of "less" in various task contexts. *Child Development,* 1978, *49,* 660-668.

Zahn-Waxler, C., Radke-Yarrow, M., & King, R. A. Child rearing and children's prosocial initiations toward victims of distress. *Child Development,* 1979, *50,* 319-330.

III

THE ROLE OF
COGNITION

DANIEL BAR-TAL
AMIRAM RAVIV

A Cognitive-Learning Model of Helping Behavior Development: Possible Implications and Applications

INTRODUCTION

Most psychologists agree that the ability to perform altruistic behavior is not primarily inborn, but is, in part, a product of development (e.g., Campbell, 1972; Freud, 1933; Hoffman, 1975; Kohlberg, 1976; Rosenhan, 1978; Staub, 1979). Although children perform helping acts from an early age, young children are incapable of performing helping behavior of the highest quality—the altruistic act. Helping behavior is defined in this chapter as an act that benefits others with no external rewards promised a priori in return. A person who benefits another being when promised a reward in return performs an exchange act, but not helping. Helping behavior, which is one category of prosocial behavior, encompasses acts such as sharing, aiding, or donating. Prosocial behavior, as an antithesis of negative forms of social behavior, is a wide category that encompasses such behaviors as helping, cooperation, or exchange. It is defined as behavior that benefits another person. In this framework, helping behavior may be performed as a result of various motives such as feelings of obligation, indebtedness, conformity with others' expectations, expectation of external rewards, or altruism. Altruism, as one type of helping act that is at the highest level of quality, is defined as voluntary and intentional behavior carried out for its own end to benefit a person, as a result of moral conviction in justice and without expectations for external rewards.

There exist various forms of helping behaviors that are distinguishable from one another with regard to the quality of the act. Furthermore, we

199

THE DEVELOPMENT OF
PROSOCIAL BEHAVIOR

suggest that these behaviors develop sequentially. That is, with age, the extent and the quantity of helping behavior increase and, in addition, the quality of helping behavior increases. This means that at older age levels more children offer help than at the younger age levels and, in addition, more helping acts are performed. Moreover, changes in quality are reflected in children's motives for helping: Whereas young children help mostly because of hedonistic motives, primitive empathy, or compliance with adults' demands, older children may help as a result of high-level empathy, sympathetic distress, or internalization of norms prescribing help. The present chapter proposes a framework for the development of helping behavior. Specifically, it will suggest a cognitive learning model for the development of helping behavior. Empirical evidence supporting the model will be presented, implications of the model will be discussed, and, in conclusion, we shall offer several possible applications of the proposed model.

COGNITIVE LEARNING MODEL FOR THE DEVELOPMENT OF HELPING BEHAVIOR

The prerequisite condition for the performance of any helping act and, more specifically, high-quality helping acts, is the acquisition of various skills. For example, in order to perform an altruistic act, the highest level of helping behavior, it is suggested that the following skills are necessary: (a) the ability to consider a variety of alternative acts; (b) the ability to predict the outcome of one's own behavior; (c) the ability to understand the importance of intention to act; (d) the ability to recognize the other person's needs; (e) the ability to empathize; (f) the ability to reason morally according to postconventional principles; and (g) the ability to self-regulate one's behavior. Lower-level quality helping acts require less skills.

The development of the aforementioned first six skills is contingent upon the development of cognition, social perspective, and morality. The acquisition of these skills provides the competence to perform altruistic behavior. However, in order to activate this competence, there is a need to consider the specific motivational and performance conditions in the psychological situation. Acquisition of self-regulatory skill enables self-control—that is, the ability to perform even sacrificing helping behavior in accordance with one's own set of standards by means of self-rewarding or self-punishing reactions. During the early years of development, the child's helping behavior is directed by tangible or social rewards and punishments, which constitute the motivational forces for behavior. Thus, the sequence of the development of helping behavior is *determined by the level of the cognitive-motivational development of the child. Different levels of the de-*

velopment of helping behavior are qualitatively distinguishable from one another, and this is indicated in the differential motivations for the performance of the helping act.

Phases of Helping Behavior Development

We suggest that there exist six phases in the development of helping behavior, and that they are distinguishable from one another in terms of the differential motivations for the performance of a helping act. In our analysis we have disregarded cases of mechanistic helping acts which may merely be an expression of imitation or play. The proposed phases are based upon a previous conceptualization by Bar-Tal, Sharabany, and Raviv (1981). The proposed phases were selected on the basis of empirical evidence regarding the development of the skills necessary for the performance of various types of helping behavior, and specifically for the performance of altruistic behavior, which reflects the highest level of development. However, we are aware of the fact that other researchers may find it preferrable to add to or to subtract from the six phases we propose.

The following represents a summary of the phases.

Phase 1: Compliance—Concrete and defined reinforcement. During this phase children perform a helping act because they have been requested or commanded to do so, and this request or demand is accompanied by the promise of a concrete reward or an explicit threat of punishment. Helping behavior during this phase is, in fact, exchange behavior. The children do not perform the behavior because of a sense of responsibility or duty, or even because of a respect for authority, but rather the behavior is guided solely by the promise of reward (pleasure) or the threat of punishment (pain). During this phase, the children are egocentric in their perspective; that is, they do not realize that others may think or feel differently from themselves. Behavior at this phase is directed mostly by well-defined, concrete rewards and punishments.

Phase 2: Compliance. During the second phase the motive for the performance of helping behavior is compliance with authority. The children do not initiate the helping act; rather, they obey the commands or requests of others who are superior to them in power or prestige. They recognize that others may think or feel differently from them, and are prepared to comply with the requests or commands of others. The children perform the act in order to gain approval or to avoid punishment. Concrete reinforcements are not necessary, since the children recognize authority. However, the reinforcement is still well defined—approval or disapproval.

Phase 3: Internal initiative—Concrete reward. During this phase the children initiate the helping act voluntarily and spontaneously. However, they perform helping behavior because they anticipate the receipt of a defined and concrete reward in return. The children's orientation during this third phase is egoistic in nature, since they are motivated by the desire for reinforcement; however, they are capable of recognizing others' needs.

Phase 4: Normative behavior. During the fourth phase, the motivation underlying performance of helping behavior is compliance with societal demands. The children are aware of the behavioral norms with which they are expected to conform, and they know that conformity leads to positive sanctions, whereas violation of the norms leads to negative sanctions. The children will help even dissimilar others merely because they feel that it is expected of them to do so. The reward they anticipate is well defined but not concrete, such as approval by others. During this phase the children are capable of adopting the role of a person in need and of feeling sympathetic distress. At this level, however, sympathetic distress cannot be considered by itself a motivating factor.

Phase 5: Generalized reciprocity. During the fifth phase, helping behavior is governed by universal principles of exchange. Individuals are aware of a regulated system that controls helping behavior, and they help others in the belief that when they are in need others will offer them help in return. A reciprocal social contract underlies the performance of helping acts; thus, the rewards are undefined and nonconcrete. The rules of the system are internalized, and the individuals help in order to ensure the smooth running of the system.

Phase 6: Altruistic behavior. In the final phase the individuals initiate the helping act spontaneously and voluntarily with no motive other than to benefit another person. They do not anticipate or expect any reward; rather they perform the behavior out of a moral conviction in justice. Thus, in this phase the individuals' helping behavior is intentional and it is selected by them from among various alternative behaviors. The individuals are able to assess another's needs, they can adopt the other's role, they experience sympathetic distress when another is in need, and they are concerned for the other's welfare. Although the individuals do not anticipate the receipt of any reward, they may experience self-satisfaction or raised self-esteem as a result of the performance of the act.

EMPIRICAL EVIDENCE

The following is a summary of the empirical evidence that supports the suggested model:

1. A positive relationship has been found between age and the extent and quantity of helping behavior.

2. A positive relationship has been found between the extent of helping behavior and the level of cognitive, social perspective-taking, and moral judgment development.
3. A relationship has been found between age and the type of motivators (reinforcements) that enhance helping behavior.
4. It has been found that age is positively correlated with the quality level of the expressed motives for helping behavior.
5. It has been found that there exists a positive relationship between the extent of helping behavior and the level of motivations for helping behavior, as represented in a situation.

Age

Several researchers have obtained results indicating that the extent, or the quantity, of helping behavior increases with age during the first years of life, especially during the late childhood (e.g., Elliott & Vasta, 1970; Emler & Rushton, 1974; Green & Schneider, 1974; Handlon & Gross, 1959; Midlarsky & Bryan, 1967). One possible explanation that accounts for these results suggests that the frequent performance of helping acts depends upon the level of children's cognitive, social perspective-taking, and moral judgment development. Thus, in order to perform different types of helping behavior, the child has to increase and develop a variety of capacities related to helping behavior, especially of high quality.

Cognitive, Social-Perspective, and Moral Development

Several empirical studies have found a relationship between helping behavior and cognitive, social perspective-taking, and moral judgment development. An extensive review of these studies can be found in Staub (1979), and this chapter will only describe a few. Larsen and Kellogg (1974) and Zwolinski, reported in Reykowski (1977), investigated the relationship between a conservation task, as a reflection of cognitive development, and helping behavior among young children. The results of their study indicate that the ability to perform helping acts is consolidated only after sufficient cognitive restructuring has taken place, and the child enters into the stage of concrete operations at about the age of 8 or 9. Krebs and Sturrup (1974) investigated the existence of a relationship between the development of social perspective and helping behavior and found a positive correlation between role-taking ability and helping behavior. In a more recent experiment, Iannotti (1978) trained children to take roles of others and thereafter assessed the effect of the training on sharing behavior. The results indicated that the understanding of others' perspective facilitates helping behavior.

Recently, Buckley, Siegel, and Ness (1979) investigated the relationship between helping behavior and egocentrism and empathy. Their findings indicated that children who exhibited helping behavior had significantly higher scores on the measures of perspective taking and empathy than did children who did not display helping behavior. In addition, a number of studies have investigated the relationship between moral judgment and helping behavior (e.g., Dreman, 1976; Emler & Rushton, 1974; Rubin & Schneider, 1973). These studies have shown that the higher the children's score on moral judgment tests, the greater the extent of helping behavior they exhibit.

In order to understand the development of helping behavior, it is necessary to survey the findings in the area of prosocial moral judgment. Prosocial moral judgment involves reasoning in moral conflict situations in which positive justice must be applied (Mussen & Eisenberg-Berg, 1977). These dilemma situations are structured in such a way that the individuals' own desires and needs come into conflict with those of others, and there is a deemphasis on laws, authority figures, punishments, and formal obligations. An example of such a dilemma situation could be to present the individuals with a real or hypothetical situation in which they or the person in the story have an opportunity to perform a costly helping act, and, thereafter, they are asked whether help would be provided and why. The reasoning offered by the individual may serve as an important indicator of the motives underlying helping behavior and could aid in differentiating the quality of helping acts on the basis of differential motives.

In a study by Eisenberg-Berg (1979), the prosocial moral judgment of elementary and high school students was investigated. Subjects were presented with four stories, each containing a conflict between the actor's own needs and the needs of others. Subjects' answers were coded into 10 major categories (23 categories altogether). The results obtained indicated that children's reasoning about prosocial moral dilemmas changes with age. Whereas elementary school children's reasoning tends to be hedonistic, stereotyped, involving the labeling of others' needs, and approval and interpersonally oriented, high school students tended more to use reasoning that reflected strongly empathic, more abstract, and/or more internalized moral concerns. In this vein, Eisenberg-Berg and Mussen (1978) presented high school students with prosocial moral dilemmas in order to assess their empathic ability and measure their helping behavior. The findings indicated that the level of prosocial moral judgment was related positively to empathic ability and that, among adolescent males only, prosocial moral reasoning was related positively to a willingness to help the experimenter. In a more recent study, Eisenberg-Berg and Hand (1979) observed the helping behavior of preschool children and presented them with four dilemma situations in order to assess the level of their prosocial moral judgment. The results showed that young children tended, in general, to use hedonistic and needs-oriented reasoning for offering help. In addition, it was found that children's observed frequency of spontaneous sharing, involving cost for the helper, was related negatively to hedonistic prosocial moral reasoning, and positively to needs-oriented reasoning.

Finally, Bar-Tal, Raviv, and Shavit (1981) compared the prosocial moral judgment of kindergarten and second grade children using the categories described in the phases of helping behavior development. The children in this study were presented with three pictures, each describing two children, one of them in a state of need. The children were asked whether the second child in the picture would help the other child and why. Whereas the majority of the children in both age groups thought that the second child would help, the responses to the second question varied according to age. That is, the younger children believed that the first child would receive a concrete reward in return, immediately following the helping act. The older children suggested that the second child would help because the first child would reciprocate in the unspecified future.

Types of Motivators (Reinforcements)

Studies have shown that whereas young children are especially motivated to perform helping behavior for tangible rewards, older children perform it for social rewards. Only later in life do individuals acquire the ability of self-rewarding—the ability to regulate one's own behavior without external motivators. For example, Fischer (1963) investigated how various reinforcement conditions affect the acquisition of sharing behavior in 4-year-old children. He found that for the great majority of the children who acquired the behavior only tangible reinforcement was effective. Other studies that have investigated older children have found that social rewards (i.e., social approval) increased the extent of helping behavior (e.g., Gelfand, Hartman, Cromer, Smith, & Page, 1975; Midlarsky, Bryan, & Brickman, 1973). In accordance with these results, White and Burnam (1975), who studied donation behavior of fourth and fifth grade children, found that the two age groups responded differently to social cues. For example, in private situations (without the possibility of receiving external rewards), the older children tended to donate more money than the younger children. In the public situation (with possibility of receiving social rewards), no difference was observed between the two groups. Finally, Guttmann, Bar-Tal, and Leiser (1979) investigated the effect of four experimental conditions (promise of tangible reward in return for a helping act, promise of a social reward, promise of undefined rewards, and no promise of any reward) on helping behavior of kindergarten and second grade children. The results showed that whereas only a few of the younger children agreed to help without the promise of reward, about half of the older children agreed to help in this condition. The difference between the two age groups was reduced in the other experimental conditions.

Quality of Expressed Motives and Age

Several studies have investigated children's reasoning regarding their motives for helping, following an actual act of helping. The results of these studies have shown in general that children's expressed motives for helping behavior change with age. These findings provide empirical support for the contention that the quality of helping behavior as reflected in expressed motives develops with age.

Levin and Bekerman-Greenberg (1980) studied the development of reasoning about sharing in a situation in which children were given the opportunity to share pretzels with other children. They were then asked to explain why they did or did not share. The subjects were children from kindergarten and second, fourth, and sixth grades. The results of this study showed a positive relationship between age and the number of pretzels shared. In addition, the subjects' responses to the question regarding why they shared were categorized into five levels: (a) generosity due to immediate automatic reward; (b) generosity due to "good boy/girl" morality; (c) conditional generosity, which depends on the relationship between the helper and helpee; (d) generosity due to empathy; and (e) functional generosity due to the value of positive justice. The findings showed that the justifications expressed by the subjects for sharing were related positively to age. Whereas the majority of the kindergarten and second grade children expected or anticipated an immediate reward for their sharing act, the majority of fourth and sixth grade children shared because they recognized the importance of societal demands (Category c).

In another study by Ugurel-Semin (1952), children between ages 7 and 11 were required to divide an unequal number of nuts between themselves and another child. After sharing, the children were asked to state the reasons that they divided the nuts as they did. The children's responses were classified into seven major categories arranged in the following order from low to high level of justification: egocentrism, sociocentrism (obedience to moral and religious rules and customs), awareness of social reaction (fear or shame of public opinion), superficial reciprocity, deeper and enlarged reciprocity, altruism, and justice. The results of this study showed that the children justified their sharing behavior differently at different age levels: the older the children, the higher the level of justification they used.

Expressed Motives and Helping Behavior

Several studies have investigated the relationship between expressed motives and the quantity of helping behavior. Dreman and Greenbaum (1973), Levin and Bekerman-Greenberg (1980), and Ugurel-Semin (1952) found that the higher the level of the motives the children expressed, the more helping behavior they exhibited.

Motivation and Helping Behavior

There are two major shortcomings in those studies whose findings regarding motives for helping behavior are based upon children's verbal reports. First, the answers of the children may be distorted in accordance with social desirability, and, second, the children do not necessarily behave according to the motives they express. In order to overcome these shortcomings, an experimental paradigm that enables the determination of children's motives for helping behavior in a specific behavioral context was developed. In this experimental paradigm children are presented with the opportunity to be helpful; and the motive underlying the helping act is determined on the basis of the situation in which the behavior takes place. In this paradigm, different situations are constructed in which children have the opportunity to help. Each situation consists of specific conditions for the performance of the helping act which reflect the motive to help. The situations are arranged in a regressive order in such a way that a child who does not help in the situation reflecting an advanced motive (e.g., altruistic) has the opportunity to help in another situation which reflects a less advanced motive (e.g., to gain social reward). In two studies that utilized the described paradigm (Bar-Tal, Raviv, & Leiser, 1980; Raviv, Bar-Tal, & Lewis-Levin, 1980) the constructed situations corresponded to the phases of helping behavior development, as proposed in this chapter. The results of these studies showed that as children grow older more of them help, and the quality of the helping acts changes. That is, the older the children, the greater the extent of initiation of sharing behavior without any promise of external reward. In the advanced condition, the older children initiated sharing without even being reminded of the social norm involved. In contrast to this, the younger the children the greater the number that helped under the condition of compliance with the promise of a concrete, defined reward in return for help.

Summary

The reviewed evidence seems to support the suggestion that as children develop more advanced cognitive, social-perspective, and moral levels and as they acquire self-regulatory skills, they perform more helping acts, each of greater cost and of a higher quality. It is assumed that these relationships reflect the fact that the development of high-quality behavior is contingent upon the development of skills that develop within the domain of cognition, social perspective-taking, moral judgment, and motivation. Helping behavior develops sequentially as a child acquires the ability to recognize the needs of the person in need, to take the role of the person in need, to empathize, to understand the meaning of intending to act, to delay gratification, to reason according to high-level moral orientation, and to regulate one's own behavior.

IMPLICATIONS

There are at least two implications of the proposed model. These implications and its applications will now be discussed.

Parameters of Helping Behavior

The proposed approach to helping behavior development suggests that helping behavior should be viewed as a multifaceted concept. The assessment of helping behavior can be done not only with regard to its extent (how many children helped) and quantity (how much each of the children helped), but also with reference to its quality (why each of the children helped). The quality of the helping act is determined on the basis of the individual's motives for the behavior. The level of motivation to perform helping acts can be assessed in accordance with the developmental phases of helping behavior, as outlined in this chapter. The phases indicate whether the act is intentional, whether it is voluntary, whether the individual expects any rewards in return, and what are the real motives behind the performance of the act. Individuals perform helping acts that differ with regard to their quality. Some help in order to receive future rewards, some are forced to help, some reciprocate past favors, some help in order to compensate for harm done previously, some do it accidentally, and some help altruistically. In order to analyze the helping behavior, it is necessary to distinguish among the different motives underlying the behavior. Whereas the altruistic helping act reflects motives of the highest quality, helping behavior performed as a consequence of a promise of reward reflects the lowest-quality motives.

Consideration of the three parameters previously discussed is necessary to determine the level of helping behavior development. The evidence indicates that its development is positively related to the level of cognitive, social perspective-taking, moral judgment development and the development of self-regulatory skills. A model of helping behavior development that emphasizes the three parameters enables recognition of individual differences in the performance of helping behavior, and, moreover, it enhances our understanding of the nature of its development.

Teaching Helping Behavior

The proposed model suggests that the development of the ability to perform high-quality helping behavior depends on the maturational process and the influence of the social environment where the child lives. Although the cognitive-developmental approach emphasizes the maturational process of the cognitive, social perspective-taking and moral judgment development, it also recognizes the influence of the social environment. In contrast, traditional social learning theory has focused mainly on the environmental conditions that foster the development of altruistic behavior. The present cognitive learning model recognizes equally the influence of both factors. By recognizing the significance of social environment, in general, and specifically the importance of reinforcements, the present model implies that appropriate teaching can accelerate the development of high-quality helping behavior. That is, agents of socialization may play an active role in the development of altruism.

The teaching can assume two complementary forms: first, direct stimulation for the development of high-quality helping behavior, in accordance with the individual's level of cognitive, social perspective-taking, moral judgment, and motivational development, that is, teaching the children to perform high-quality helping behavior with different techniques in the framework of their capacities; second, facilitation of the development of high-level cognition, social perspective-taking, and/or moral judgment. Such facilitation might indirectly contribute to the development of high-quality helping behavior, because the achievement of high-level development in these domains is the prerequisite for the development of altruism. In the present chapter we shall discuss only the first form. Several techniques have been suggested that appear to be effective for the direct teaching of helping behavior:

1. Reinforcement: Reinforcing consequences serve to inform performers what they should do in order to gain beneficial results or to avoid punishment. Reinforcements may take the form of tangible objects such as goods or money, or they may include aspects of social interactions such as approval or praise. Through the use of various forms of reinforcements children acquire self-regulatory skills.

2. Modeling: Children who have the opportunity to observe a helping model learn what is appropriate and how it is possible to carry out helping acts. In addition, through observation, the children can learn the consequences of performing this act. Modeling serves as one of the principal techniques by which the child learns new modes of helping behavior.

3. Induction: This technique refers to the offering of an explanation why a child should act in a certain way or why the child's action was inappropriate. The emphasis in this technique is on reasoning and on specific content that stresses the importance of helping behavior (Staub, 1975, 1979).

4. Role playing: In this technique children are instructed to enact the role of helper or helpee in various situations. Through role playing children learn to view events from a variety of points of view. In addition, such experiences may also increase the vicarious experience of the emotions with others' experience, that is, enhance empathy.

5. Use of story contents: In this technique the child is exposed to verbal, visual, or written content, which describes helping acts from the point of view of the helper and/or helpee. Such content might appear in instructional materials, literature, or visual media. This technique requires not merely reading but also use of the content in further discussions, elaborations, and directions.

One important question derived from the proposed model is what techniques should be used in each of the described phases of helping behavior development. At present, there is no direct empirical evidence that can provide a basis for the answer to this question. However, several speculations are offered that can function as hypotheses for further research. During the first phase, *Compliance—Concrete and defined reinforcement,* in accordance with the description of the phase, it seems that mainly a person who uses tangible reinforcements may bring the child to behave helpfully. Children at the first phase rarely initiate helping acts by themselves. They have to be directed to helpful acts and either promised a reward for helping or threatened to be punished for not helping. It is not clear how much induction or modeling is effective at the first phase. In the second phase, *Compliance,* helping behavior is still rarely initiated by the children. Significant figures direct children's helping behavior, using the social reinforcement technique. It seems that at this phase the children become responsive to the influence of the model and to the use of induction. In the third phase, *Internal initiative—Concrete reward,* the children tend to initiate the helping acts by themselves. They are able to predict the outcomes of their behavior, choose alternatives, take the role of the person in need, and understand the importance of intention. However, the children at this phase still often act as a consequence of egoistic orientation. Thus, there is a need to increase the awareness of others' needs, enhance feelings of empathy, and communicate the normative expectations to help. Induction, role playing, and use of story contents can be effective techniques to achieve those objectives. In addition, the use of social reinforcement can be an effective technique to facilitate the emergence of helping behavior. During the fourth phase, *Normative behavior,* the children become aware of the social expectations to perform helping acts, even when they do not receive tangible reward in return. In this phase, the children should be stimulated to perform helping acts without expecting social rewards. The effectiveness of role playing and use of story contents increases, since they nondirectly foster the development of helping behavior. Through these techniques the child is stimulated to use advanced moral reasonings and develop empathy. Other techniques, such as induction or reinforcement, may become less effective, since they might be perceived as pressure, extortion, or manipulation. Significant moral models can also play an important role in stimulating high-quality helping behavior in this phase.

Few individuals reach the sixth phase of altruism. Thus, it is not simple to move a person from Phase 5, *Generalized reciprocity,* to Phase 6. Such movement can occur as a result of a personal insight into the principles of justice, equality, and others' welfare. Only indirect techniques such as role playing, identification with moral models, or story content can facilitate the development of altruism. Use of rewards at this phase may be detrimental to the development of altruism.

APPLICATIONS

Helping behavior can be viewed as one of the elementary behaviors necessary for the survival of human beings, in view of their biological and physical limitations. Throughout their lives human beings function numerous times as helpers and helpees. In fact, it is almost impossible to imagine any social group in which individuals do not help one another. The importance of helping behavior has been long recognized, and even the ancient religions placed special emphasis upon the value of helping others. In the modern world, helping behavior can be found at every level of human social functioning. For example, at the intersocietal level, countries provide aid to other countries; at the intrasocietal level, society has established various institutions that help the poor, sick, weak, or deprived; and at the interpersonal level, individuals help one another as part of the functional ongoing interactions.

Because of its importance, helping behavior (i.e., availability of supportive, helping individuals and institutions) is considered to be one of the aspects of a high level of "quality of life." Improvement of the quality of life has become one of the major objectives of modern society. It is therefore not surprising that individuals try to build interpersonal relationships based upon concern for others, understanding, sensitivity, and willingness to extend help.

This view can be supported by the findings of clinical and epidemiological research. Such research indicates the significance of interpersonal support for the development of the adaptively functioning individuals and for the maintenance of their physical and mental health (e.g., Caplan, 1974; Cobb, 1976; Froland, Brodsky, Olson, & Steward, 1979). For example, social support has been identified as one of the important factors predicting longevity (Rowland, 1977). In view of these findings, a preventive approach, which is widely accepted in the area of mental health (see Caplan, 1964; Cowen, 1973), can also be used with regard to promoting helping behavior as an antidote against undesirable behaviors.

On the basis of the described functionality and significance of helping behavior, we suggest that society should actively encourage the development of high-quality helping behavior. The present model recognizes the possibility of facilitating and encouraging high-quality helping behavior. Such facilitation and encouragement can take the form of active intervention. In this section we shall describe possible methods of intervention by different socialization agents. The proposed intervention techniques, as described in the previous section, include reinforcement, modeling, induction, role playing, and use of appropriate story contents. These techniques are discussed with reference to their potential users. Three potential categories of users are identified: parents, teachers, and peers. In addition the role of television as an influential agent also will be described. Table 8.1 depicts the possible usage of different techniques by different agents of socialization.

Table 8.1

Possible Uses of Teaching Techniques by Different Socialization Agents

Teaching techniques	Agents of socialization			
	Parents	Teachers	Peers	Television
Reinforcement	+ +	+ +	+	−
Modeling	+ +	+	+	+ +
Induction	+ +	+ +	+	+
Role playing	−	+ +	−	−
Story contents	+	+ +	−	+ +

Note. The sign + + indicates a frequent use of the technique. The sign + indicates a possible but infrequent use of the technique. The sign − indicates that the agent does not use the technique.

Parents

Parents exert a most significant influence upon the socialization outcomes of their children. Parents are likely to use primarily three techniques to teach their children altruistic behavior: reinforcement, modeling, and induction. The use of reinforcement of helping behavior at the younger ages determines whether this behavior will be repeated or not. Parents can use different types of reinforcements in accordance with their children's age. Whereas at the early age the parents can use tangible rewards to motivate their children to perform helping behavior, at older age levels social rewards should be used. Ultimately, however, the principal goal to which training is directed is to motivate the child to perform helping behavior without expecting any external rewards. Achievement of this goal indicates a development of self-regulatory skills.

The development of the child's helping behavior is influenced also by observation of the parents' helping behavior. Parents who want their children to behave altruistically should themselves behave in this manner. In addition, the use of verbal directions to perform helping acts and explanations as to why individuals should help are important techniques that can be used by parents to teach their children high-quality helping behavior. By means of these techniques, parents can indicate the desirable directions of helping behavior and can stimulate moral reasoning as to why this behavior should be performed. Also, by directing children's attention to the harmful consequences of their behavior, parents sensitize their children to the needs of others and thus enhance their capacity for empathy (Hoffman, 1970).

Parents do not usually use role-playing techniques, since special training is required for their use. They might, though, use story contents, especially by reading and telling stories to their children. But, also, this technique requires some degree of professional training in using the materials, and therefore it is used only incidentally. (Parents usually do not discuss or elaborate upon the story contents.)

Teachers

Although the family is the primary agent of socialization, and the child, until the time of entering a school, is exposed for a lengthy period of time to the family influence, the school has a significant influence upon the child's behavior (Bar-Tal, 1978; Dreeben, 1968). In school, teachers may facilitate the development of high-quality helping behavior by using all the techniques suggested in this chapter. Although they might not always be able to establish meaningful relationships with the child, they may be trained and directed in the effective use of these techniques. They can reinforce helping behavior, they may provide behavioral examples, and they may use induction. (It should be pointed out that the children do not have many opportunities to observe the helping behavior of their teachers.) Teachers can also utilize role-playing techniques and the use of story contents, both of which require special training and preparation. Role playing techniques provide the child with the opportunity to learn the situations in which helping behavior is required, to learn how to execute this behavior, and to learn the consequences of helping and not helping (Staub, 1979). In addition, role playing develops sensitivity to the needs of others and increases role-taking ability and empathy. Role playing may be a useful technique for the teaching of altruistic behavior, since it involves cognitive and affective processes, as well as behavioral reactions (see Ahammer & Murray, 1979, as an example).

As part of their formal role definition, teachers have the opportunity to direct children to specific story contents in different subject matters. Through the use of appropriate contents, children may learn to behave altruistically by symbolic modeling. Story contents about altruistic behavior or the needs of other people, exhortation to perform a helping act, or explaining the importance of helping behavior may stimulate helping acts. Story contents provide information about when and how to perform helping acts, as well as why to carry them out. In addition, story contents may develop empathy and the ability to take others' roles (Wolf, 1975).

Peers

The influence of peers on the individual's behavior, especially during the adolescent period, has been noted (e.g., Bronfenbrenner, 1970; Coleman, 1961; Staub, 1979). As the child grows older, the social group becomes the primary source for obtaining information, and it sets the example for desirable behavior. Although peer groups rarely perceive of their goals as the active teaching of helping behavior, they can facilitate its development through the use of reinforcement, modeling, and induction.

Durkheim (1961) has suggested that moral education has its basis in group dynamics. Bronfenbrenner (1970) has provided an interesting illustration of the possible functions of peer groups. He showed that in the Soviet Union identification with the peer group serves as the primary mechanism for moral behavior: Identification with the peer group leads to an automatic internalization of the group values.

Through the peer group, the influence of another agent of socialization can be represented, that of the teacher. The teacher can guide the group norms in the direction of encouraging helping behavior.

Television

Television not only entertains, it also serves as an important agent of socialization. Although most of the research about the influence of television has been focused on the observation of aggressive rather than helping models, recently concern has been shown regarding the effect of television on the development of prosocial behavior (Rushton, 1979; Staub, 1979). Through the use of prosocial contents, the primary technique by which television exerts influence upon the viewer is modeling. Children may imitate helping behavior by identifying with the characters seen in the television programs. By viewing the programs, children also can learn what is the appropriate behavior in given situations (see, for example, Ahammer & Murray, 1979). Furthermore, television may not only teach children to consider a variety of alternative acts, to recognize other persons' needs, or to perform helping behaviors, but it also may facilitate the development of empathy (see Rushton, 1979).

Summary

In this section we have discussed different techniques that can be used in teaching helping behavior of high quality. These techniques facilitate the development of skills that, according to the proposed model of helping behavior development, are necessary prerequisites for the development of altruistic behavior.

Different agents of socialization can facilitate the development of altruistic behavior. We believe that, although the parents have the most significant influence upon altruistic development, especially in early childhood, teachers play an important role in teaching this behavior. Teachers as agents of society can, by role definition, be instructed to promote the development of altruism. As professionals, who can be trained to use the various techniques, they may actively facilitate the development of altruism by using these techniques in different combinations and also by directing other agents of socialization.

REFERENCES

Ahammer, I. N., & Murray, J. P. Kindness in the kindergarten: The relative influence of role playing and prosocial television in facilitating altruism. *International Journal of Behavioral Development,* 1979, 2, 133-157.

Bar-Tal, D. Social outcomes of schooling process and their taxonomy. In D. Bar-Tal & L. Saxe (Eds.), *Social psychology of education: Theory and research.* New York: Halsted, 1978.

Bar-Tal, D., Raviv, A., & Leiser, T. The development of altruistic behavior: Empirical evidence. *Developmental Psychology,* 1980, 16, 516-525.

Bar-Tal, D., Raviv, A., & Shavit, N. Motives for helping behavior expressed by kindergarten and school children in kibbutz and city. *Developmental Psychology,* 1981, 17, 766-772.

Bar-Tal, D., Sharabany, R. & Raviv, A. Cognitive basis of the development of altruistic behavior. In V. Derlega & J. Grzelak (Eds.) *Cooperation and helping behavior: Theories and research:* New York: Academic Press, 1981.

Bronfenbrenner, U. Reaction to social pressure from adults versus peers among Soviet day school and boarding school pupils in the perspective of an American sample. *Journal of Personality and Social Psychology,* 1970, *15,* 179–189.

Buckley, N., Siegel, L. S., & Nees, S. Egocentrism, empathy, and altruistic behavior. *Developmental Psychology,* 1979, *15,* 329–330.

Campbell, D. T. On the genetics of altruism and the counter-hedonic components in human culture. *Journal of Social Issues,* 1972, *28,* 31–38.

Caplan, G. *Principles of preventive psychiatry.* New York: Basic Books, 1964.

Caplan, G. *Support system and community mental health.* New York: Behavioral Publications, 1974.

Cobb, S. Social support as a moderator of life stress. *Psychosomatic Medicine,* 1976, *38,* 300–314.

Coleman, J. S. *The adolescent society.* New York: Free Press, 1961.

Cowen, E. L. Social and community interventions. *Annual Review of Psychology,* 1973, *24,* 423–472.

Dreeben, R. *On what is learned in school.* Reading, Mass.: Addison-Wesley, 1968.

Dreman, S. B. Sharing behavior in Israeli school children: Cognitive and social learning factors. *Child Development,* 1976, *47,* 186–194.

Dreman, S. B., & Greenbaum, C. W. Altruism or reciprocity: Sharing behavior in Israeli kindergarten children. *Child Development,* 1973, *44,* 61–68.

Durkheim, E. *Moral education.* New York: Free Press, 1961.

Eisenberg-Berg, N. Development of children's prosocial moral judgment. *Developmental Psychology,* 1979, *15,* 128–137.

Eisenberg-Berg, N., & Hand, M. The relationship of preschoolers' reasoning about prosocial moral conflicts to prosocial behavior. *Child Development,* 1979, *50,* 336–363.

Eisenberg-Berg, N., & Mussen, P. Empathy and moral development in adolescence. *Developmental Psychology,* 1978, 14, 185–186.

Elliott, R. E., & Vasta, R. The modeling of sharing: Effects associated with vicarious reinforcement, symbolization, age, and generalization. *Journal of Experimental Child Psychology,* 1970, *10,* 8–15.

Emler, M. P., & Rushton, J. P. Cognitive-developmental factors in children's generosity. *British Journal of Social and Clinical Psychology,* 1974, *13,* 277–281.

Fischer, W. F. Sharing in preschool children as a function of amount and type of reinforcement. *Genetic Psychology Monographs,* 1963, *68,* 215–245.

Freud, S. *New introduction lectures on psychoanalysis.* New York: W. W. Norton, 1933.

Froland, C., Brodsky, F., Olson, M., & Stewart, L. Social support and social adjustment: Implications for mental health professionals. *Community Mental Health Journal,* 1979, *15,* 82–93.

Gelfand, D. M., Hartman, D. P., Cromer, C. C., Smith, C. L., & Page, B. C. The effects of instructional prompts and praise on children's donation rates. *Child Development,* 1975, *46,* 980–983.

Green, F. P., & Schneider, F. W. Age differences in the behavior of boys on three measures of altruism. *Child Development,* 1974, *45,* 248–251.

Guttmann, J., Bar-Tal, D., & Leiser, P. *The effect of various reward situations on children's helping behavior.* Unpublished manuscript. Tel-Aviv University, 1979.

Handlon, B. J., & Gross, P. The development of sharing behavior. *Journal of Abnormal and Social Psychology,* 1959, *59,* 425–428.

Hoffman, M. L. Moral development. In P. H. Mussen (Ed.), *Carmichael's manual of child psychology* (Vol. 2). New York: Wiley, 1970.

Hoffman, M. L. Developmental synthesis of affect and cognition and its implications for altruistic motivation. *Developmental Psychology,* 1975, *11,* 607–622.

Ianotti, R. J. Effect of role taking experience on role taking, empathy, altruism and aggression. *Developmental Psychology,* 1978, *14,* 119-124.

Kohlberg, L. Moral development from the standpoint of a general psychological theory. In T. Lickona (Ed.), *Moral development and behavior: Theory, research, and social issues.* New York: Holt, Rinehart & Winston, 1976.

Krebs, D., & Sturrup, B. Role-taking ability and altruistic behavior in elementary school children. *Personality and Social Psychology Bulletin,* 1974, *1,* 407-409.

Larsen, G. Y., & Kellogg, J. A developmental study of the relation between conservation and sharing behavior. *Child Development,* 1974, *45,* 849-851.

Levin, I., & Beckerman-Greenberg, R. Moral judgment and moral behavior in sharing: A developmental analysis. *Genetic Psychology Monographs,* 1980, *101,* 215-230.

Midlarksy, E., & Bryan, J. H. Training charity in children. *Journal of Personality and Social Psychology,* 1967, *5,* 408-415.

Midlarsky, E., Bryan, J. H., & Brickman, P. Aversive approval: Interactive effects of modeling and reinforcement on altruistic behavior. *Child Development,* 1973, *44,* 321-328.

Mussen, P., & Eisenberg-Berg, N. *Roots of caring, sharing, and helping.* San Francisco: W. H. Freeman, 1977.

Raviv, A., Bar-Tal, D., & Lewis-Levin, T. Motivations for helping behavior by children of three different ages. *Child Development,* 1980, *51,* 610-613.

Reykowski, J. Cognitive development and prosocial behavior. *Polish Psychological Bulletin,* 1977, *8,* 35-45.

Rosenhan, D. L. Toward resolving the altruism paradox: Affect, self-reinforcement, and cognition. In L. Wispé (Ed.), *Altruism, sympathy, and helping.* New York: Academic Press, 1978.

Rowland, K. F. Environmental events predicting death for the elderly. *Psychological Bulletin,* 1977, *34,* 349-372.

Rubin, K. H., & Schneider, F. W. The relationship between moral judgment, egocentrism, and altruistic behavior. *Child Development,* 1973, *44,* 664-665.

Rushton, J. P. Effects of prosocial television and film material on the behavior of viewers. In L. Berkowitz (Ed.), *Advances in experimental social psychology* (Vol. 12). New York: Academic Press, 1979.

Staub, E. To rear a prosocial child: Reasoning, learning by doing, and learning by teaching others. In D. DePalma & J. Folley (Eds.), *Moral development: Current theory and research.* Hillsdale, N.J.: Erlbaum, 1975.

Staub, E. *Positive social behavior morality* (Vol. 2). New York: Academic Press, 1979.

Ugurel-Semin, R. Moral behavior and moral judgment of children. *Journal of Abnormal and Social Psychology,* 1952, *47,* 463-474.

White, G. M., & Burnam, M. A. Socially cued altruism: Effects of modeling instructions and age on public and private donations. *Child Development,* 1975, *46,* 559-563.

Wolf, L. L. Children's literature and the development of empathy in young children. *Journal of Moral Education,* 1975, *5,* 45-49.

NANCY EISENBERG

The Development of Reasoning regarding Prosocial Behavior

Although definitions of prosocial behavior and altruism vary (see Introduction), most theorists would agree that altruistic behaviors in humans are voluntary acts intended to benefit another, and that they are ends in themselves rather than means to obtaining external rewards (Bar-Tal, 1976; Krebs, 1970; Mussen & Eisenberg-Berg, 1977; Staub, 1978, 1979). However, whereas many theorists and researchers concerned with behaviors that benefit another are interested primarily in altruistic behaviors, behaviors that appear to be altruistic frequently do not meet the criteria for the above definition of altruism. For example, an apparently altruistic behavior may, in reality, be motivated by the desire for social or concrete rewards, or may have been done involuntarily or unintentionally. Since an observer usually cannot clearly discern the motives behind an act, a particular helping behavior often cannot be classified as altruistic, but only as either a positive behavior (behavior that benefits another, Staub, 1978) or as a prosocial behavior (a voluntary behavior that apparently is intended to benefit another regardless of the individual's motive for desiring to benefit the other).

Since individuals' positive behaviors are frequently not altruistic, the researcher who desires to understand the development of altruistic behavior must differentiate behaviors motivated by altruistic concerns from behaviors motivated by baser concerns. Furthermore, since the development of altruistic behavior is enmeshed with the development of other types of positive behavior, it is important to understand the development of, and motivations behind, less altruistic positive behaviors.

In brief, it is clear that the issue of motivation is critical to the study of

219

prosocial and altruistic behavior. But how does one differentiate between various motivations underlying different modes of positive behavior, and how can these motives be assessed? One way to approach the problem is to examine people's moral reasoning regarding prosocial behaviors. Whereas a person's reasoning about moral issues is not necessarily the motivational bases for behavior in moral conflicts, the individual's conceptualization of an issue helps to determine what motives are elicited in a given situation. In fact, as will be illustrated in this chapter, research on prosocial moral reasoning has proved useful in at least four ways: (a) for clarifying how individuals conceptualize and make attributions about the kindness of an actor; (b) for determining the possible range of cognitive, conscious motivations that may engender children's positive actions; (c) for the prediction of prosocial behavior; and (d) for the examination and modification of preexisting theory and knowledge on moral judgment.

RESEARCH APPROACHES

Researchers have used a variety of methods to study the development of reasoning regarding prosocial behaviors. Since the procedures employed in a particular study affect both the form and content of the resultant data, it is useful to delineate differences in various types of studies.

The major methodological variation in the research reflects a distinction evident throughout the moral judgment literature. This variation originates in the different procedures used by the two most famous researchers in the area of moral development—Piaget and Kohlberg. Piaget (1948) studied the development of moral judgment partly by presenting children with two stories involving moral behavior. The children were then requested to compare the scenarios, make a decision (e.g., decide which of the protagonists was naughtier or which story solution was fairer), and justify their decisions. Thus, Piaget frequently requested children to indicate a preference for one of two or more criteria underlying a moral decision by choosing between predetermined alternatives.

In contrast to Piaget's procedure, Kohlberg (1969, 1971) and his colleagues have elicited moral judgments by presenting subjects with stories (actually a series of stories presented one at a time) that contain a conflict between two or more moral issues. A typical story involves the conflict between saving the life of one's wife and stealing. Subjects are requested to resolve the moral conflict and then explain their reasoning. The subjects' reasoning, rather than their story resolution, is used to obtain a moral judgment score. The emphasis is thus on the mode and diversity of reasoning used by people to resolve moral conflicts, not on the subjects' preference for one of two moral criteria chosen by the experimenter.

Researchers who have examined children's concepts of prosocial behavior using Piaget's paradigm generally have sought to clarify the criteria used by people to label an act as "kind" or "nice" (Baldwin & Baldwin, 1970; Baldwin, Baldwin, Castillo-Vales, & Seegmiller, 1971; Baldwin, Baldwin, Hilton, & Lambert, 1969; Leahy, 1979). In contrast, researchers who have modeled their investigations after Kohlberg's technique have attempted to delineate the reasons used by people to resolve moral dilemmas in which one possible outcome is prosocial behavior; they generally seek to determine the *reasons* people use to justify either prosocial behavior or the decision not to act in a prosocial manner. Thus, research based on Kohlberg's paradigm deals, in part, with reasoning and judgments regarding motives for behavior, whereas data obtained with Piagetian techniques concern the formation of the concept of "kindness" and how individuals make attributions regarding the kindness of another's behavior.

THE DEVELOPMENT OF CONCEPTS OF KINDNESS

Much of the work on the development of concepts of "kindness" has been done by Clara and Alfred Baldwin and their colleagues. According to the Baldwins, "kindness is a motivation that is sometimes inferred from the fact that one person benefits another, provided the circumstances are appropriate [Baldwin & Baldwin, 1970, p. 30]." Some of the circumstances that they hypothesized would influence an observer's judgments of a beneficial act were (a) intentionality of the act; (b) whether or not the benefactor has a choice; (c) whether or not the benefactor is acting in obedience to a request or command from an authority; (d) whether or not the benefactor is acting in his or her own self-interest (for example, helping in an attempt to bribe another or to promote trade); and (e) whether or not the benefactor is acting in accordance with a social obligation. Important social obligations the Baldwins discussed were the obligation (a) to benefit an invited guest; (b) to return a favor; (c) to equalize the total benefits in a situation; and (d) to help someone who is in serious trouble. The Baldwins hypothesized that a particular act that benefits another will be judged as less kind if the act is not by choice and not intentional, and if the act satisfies a social obligation.

The Baldwins tested their hypotheses with a picture story technique. Subjects in kindergarten, in second, fourth, sixth, and eighth grades and in college were presented with a set of 10 story pairs. In each pair of stories, the actual benefit of the protagonist's behavior for another was the same, but some feature of the context was varied to provide a contrast that, according to the Baldwins' hypotheses, should make the behavior in one story seem kinder than in the other. For example, to test the role of intentionality, in one story the benefit was intentional (a boy helped another boy recover a ball after being requested to do so), whereas in the other story the benefit was unintentional (a boy accidentally and unknowingly helped another boy recover a ball). The subjects were presented with each story pair, asked to select the story in which the child was kinder, and then requested to explain their choices.

In general, the Baldwins' data were consistent with their hypotheses. Among adults, an act was judged as kinder if it was intentional and by choice, involved a self-sacrifice, did not benefit the actor, and did not fulfill a social obligation. Furthermore, there were developmental changes in children's reasoning regarding kindness. By second grade, children's reasoning regarding intentionality was like that of adults, as was their evaluation of the kindness of an act done to promote a trade. By fourth grade, children did not differ from adults in their inferences regarding the role of choice, obedience to authority, self-sacrifice, obligation to a guest, or a bribe. By eighth grade, children did not differ from adults in attributions regarding the role of returning a favor. Only the evaluation of one social obligation (equalization of benefits) changed from eighth grade to adulthood. These findings generally were replicated in a cross-cultural study involving Mexican children (Baldwin et al., 1971), although the Mexicans were somewhat slower than Americans to view acts involving obedience to authority, obligations to a guest, trade, bribery, no self-sacrifice, or the equalization of benefits as less kind than acts not involving these factors. Contrary to expectations, in neither of the studies did children or adults view helping someone in minor trouble as more kind than helping someone in serious trouble (the Baldwins had reasoned that a serious need for help would create a social obligation to help).

Several researchers have expanded on the Baldwins' research by identifying other variables that influence people's attributions regarding kindness. Jensen and Hughston (1973) found that good acts (e.g., attending to one's baby brother) that were followed by rewards were viewed by preschoolers as more positive than good acts that were punished. Thus, consistent with Piaget's (1948) research, young children's judgments of "goodness" of an act seemed to be influenced by the consequences of the behavior for the actor, that is, by adults' rewards and sanctions for the act—although children do seem to distinguish between good and bad motives as early as age 3 (Keasey, 1978). Furthermore, in a study of 4-, 6-, 8-, and 10-year-olds, Shure (1968) found that older children were more likely than younger children to judge people as nice if they helped or shared when norms of fairness did not demand such behavior (e.g., a child who helped clean up a mess he or she did not make was judged kinder than a child who cleaned up after making the mess, and a child who shared his or her own toy was viewed as nicer than a child who shared a class toy). Similarly, Peterson,

Hartmann, and Gelfand (1977) found that kindergarteners through third graders (but especially the older children) rewarded more stars to hypothetical actors who helped a dependent needy than to actors who helped someone who had previously assisted them (although they themselves were more likely to assist someone who had helped them than a dependent other). Peterson (1980) obtained similar findings when kindergarteners, and third and sixth graders judged the kindness of helping a needy individual versus someone who might reciprocate help in the future. Thus, helpers who were acting in ways consistent with a social obligation based on the norm of reciprocity were judged less positively than those who assisted someone when there was no prior obligation to do so.

With a somewhat modified version of Piaget's methodology, Leahy (1979) examined a variety of causal schemes used by children and adults to make inferences regarding the kindness of an act. Leahy presented first grade, fifth grade, and adult subjects with 10 short descriptions of situations that always ended in one child's giving another child his or her lunch. The details of the scenarios were varied to manipulate consistency (if the individual acted consistently toward the same stimulus) and distinctiveness (if the individual acted in the same way toward many different stimuli) of the protagonists' behaviors, as well as factors relating to rewards and punishment for sharing. Subjects were asked to award nickels to each story protagonist based on the kindness of his or her actions.

According to the resultant data (and consistent with Jensen & Hughston's study), young children, but not fifth graders or adults, viewed an act as kinder if it was rewarded than if it was not rewarded. In contrast, fifth graders and adults believed an act less kind if it resulted in either reward or avoidance of punishment. Fifth graders and adults also rewarded actions occurring under the threat of harm more than actions consistent with the avoidance of physical harm. Furthermore, adults, unlike the first or fifth graders, rewarded an individual more if he or she helped when there was a reciprocity-related reason not to assist—for example, when the potential recipient had not shared with the potential benefactor on the previous day. Finally, subjects of all ages allocated higher rewards to story protagonists who were consistent in their behavior and helped more than one individual.

To summarize the research on conceptions of kindness, whereas some aspects of people's understanding of kindness (and attributions regarding an individual's kindness) are developed by age 5 or 6, there are further changes in these conceptions throughout the elementary school years. First graders as well as adults seem to make inferences regarding an individual's disposition to be kind based on his or her tendency to act kindly consistently. Furthermore, even young elementary school children consider the actor's intentions when evaluating the kindness of an act. By middle childhood an act is judged as more kind if it is done by choice rather than involuntarily or as an act of obedience to authority. However, young children, but not older children or adults, also judge an act as more kind if it is rewarded. In contrast, older children and adults view an act as less kind if it benefits the benefactor in some manner, and as more kind if it is done despite potential costs to the self and despite social obligations. Thus, with age, the definition of kindness more closely approximates the standard definition of altruism, that is, voluntary behavior done to benefit another with no expectation of external rewards for the benefactor.

THE DEVELOPMENT OF REASONING ABOUT ACTUAL AND HYPOTHETICAL PROSOCIAL MORAL DILEMMAS

Conceptualization of reasoning regarding prosocial behavior has been influenced greatly by the work of Kohlberg and his colleagues. Kohlberg's research generally concerns prohibition-oriented moral reasoning— reasoning about situations in which one salient course of action involves a transgression, that is, violation of authorities' dictates, rules, laws, or formal obligations. For example, in Kohlberg's well-known Heinz dilemma, he presents the conflict between Heinz's stealing a drug to save his wife's life and allowing his wife to die. However, despite Kohlberg's neglect of purely prosocial issues, his stages of moral judgment have provided valuable information regarding the types of reasoning that individuals might use with prosocial dilemmas. Kohlberg's six stages, which are believed by Kohlberg to be universal and invariant in sequence, are presented in Table 9.1 (although Kohlberg has recently suggested that there may be no Stage 6 distinct from Stage 5 [1978]).

Table 9.1
Definition of Moral Stages

I. Preconventional Level

At this level the child is responsive to cultural rules and labels of good and bad, right or wrong, but interprets these labels in terms of either the physical or the hedonistic consequences of action (punishment, reward, exchange of favors), or in terms of the physical power of those who enunciate the rules and labels. The level is divided into the following stages:

Stage 1: The punishment and obedience orientation. The physical consequences of action determine its goodness or badness regardless of the human meaning or value of these consequences. Avoidance of punishment and unquestioning deference to power are valued in their own right, not in terms of respect for an underlying moral order supported by punishment and authority (the latter being Stage 4).

(continued)

Table 9.1 (*Continued*)

Stage 2: The instrumental relativist orientation. Right action consists of that which instrumentally satisfies one's own needs and occasionally the needs of others. Human relations are viewed in terms like those of the market place. Elements of fairness, of reciprocity, and of equal sharing are present, but they are always interpreted in a physical pragmatic way. Reciprocity is a matter of "you scratch my back and I'll scratch yours," not of loyalty, gratitude, or justice.

II. Conventional Level

At this level, maintaining the expectations of the individual's family, group, or nation is perceived as valuable in its own right, regardless of immediate and obvious consequences. The attitude is not only one of *conformity* to personal expectations and social order, but of loyalty to it, of actively *maintaining*, supporting, and justifying the order, and of identifying with the persons or group involved in it. At this level, there are the following two stages:

Stage 3: The interpersonal concordance or "good boy‑nice girl" orientation. Good behavior is that which pleases or helps others and is approved by them. There is much conformity to stereotypical images of what is majority or "natural" behavior. Behavior is frequently judged by intention—"he means well" becomes important for the first time. One earns approval by being "nice."

Stage 4: The "law and order" orientation. There is orientation toward authority, fixed rules, and the maintenance of the social order. Right behavior consists of doing one's duty, showing respect for authority, and maintaining the given social order for its own sake.

III. Postconvention, Autonomous, or Principled Level

At this level, there is a clear effort to define moral values and principles which have validity and application apart from the authority of the groups or persons holding these principles, and apart from the individual's own identification with these groups. This level again has two stages:

Stage 5: The social-contract legalistic orientation, generally with utilitarian overtones. Right action tends to be defined in terms of general individual rights, and standards which have been critically examined and agreed upon by the whole society. There is a clear awareness of the relativism of personal values and opinions and a corresponding emphasis upon procedural rules for reaching consensus. Aside from what is constitutionally and democratically agreed upon, the right is a matter of personal "values" and "opinion." The result is an emphasis upon the "legal point of view," but with an emphasis upon the possibility of changing law in terms of rational considerations of social utility (rather than freezing it in terms of Stage 4 "law and order"). Outside the legal realm, free agreement and contract is the binding element of obligation. This is the "official" morality of the American government and constitution.

Stage 6[a]: The universal ethical principle orientation. Right is defined by the decision of conscience in accord with self-chosen *ethical principles* appealing to logical comprehensiveness, universality, and consistency. These principles are abstract and ethical (the Golden Rule, the categorical imperative); they are not concrete moral rules like the Ten Commandments. At heart, these are universal principles of *justice,* of the *reciprocity* and *equality* of human *rights,* and of respect for the dignity of human beings as *individual persons.*

Source: Kohlberg, 1971.
[a]Kohlberg recently has suggested that there may be no Stage 6 that is distinct from Stage 5 (Kohlberg, 1978).

Researchers interested in prosocial behavior who have adapted Kohlberg's methodology generally have presented children and adults with hypothetical moral conflicts involving prosocial or altruistic behavior. The subjects are then asked to resolve the dilemma, and are questioned regarding their reasoning. A common modification of this procedure is to elicit children's reasoning regarding real-life rather than hypothetical moral dilemmas, for example, regarding their own prosocial behaviors. In both types of procedures, it is the individual's reasoning about the issues involved in the moral dilemma that is examined, not the individual's definition of kindness.

Research regarding Children's Reasoning about Their Own Prosocial Behavior

One of the earliest studies about children's reasoning regarding prosocial behavior was done by Ugurel-Semin (1952). Ugurel-Semin contrived a situation in which each of 291 Turkish children aged 4–16 divided nuts between himself or herself and a peer. The children were then asked why they divided the nuts as they did. Based on the children's responses, Ugurel-Semin coded the children's reasoning for sharing into the following categories: egocentrism (mean age 7 years, 3 months); sociocentrism (obedience to moral and religious rules and customs; mean age 9 years, 2 months); awareness of social reaction (e.g., shame; mean age 9 years, 3 months); superficial reciprocity (emphasis on equality; mean age 9 years, 5 months); deeper and enlarged reciprocity and cooperation (mean age 10 years, 5 months); altruism (sympathy, sacrifice; mean age 10 years, 5 months); and justice (justice and right demand equal sharing; mean age 10 years, 10 months). Thus, when one considers the age trends in responses, the following pattern emerges. The child first reasons in an egocentric manner, that is, he or she exhibits a purely selfish attitude or confuses self with other, or the material with the moral. Then (at approximately 9 years of age), the child reasons primarily in terms of obedience to stereotypic, socially accepted rules (about equality and when and with whom one shares) and shame for violation of these rules. Finally, at around age 10½, children shift to an emphasis on maintaining interpersonal relationships and helping motivated by empathy or internalized values regarding justice. While Ugurel-Semin's sequence of reasoning is not entirely consistent with Kohlberg's (note the absence of authority and punishment reasoning characteristic of Kohlberg's Stage 1), there is some similarity in the sequences of development.

In a small study involving 12 preschool children, Damon (1971) allowed children an opportunity to share with a peer and questioned the children regarding their motives. The two types of reasoning most frequently used by the children were "empathic" (concern about consequences to others) and "pragmatic" (concern about reciprocal consequences of sharing for the friendship or to oneself). Some instances of the latter type of reasoning would perhaps be more accurately labeled as "hedonistic" (self-oriented) and "reciprocity-oriented."

Dreman and Greenbaum (1973), like Ugurel-Semin and Damon, elicited children's reasoning regarding their own prosocial behavior in contrived settings. After giving kindergarteners the opportunity to share with classmates, those who did so were questioned regarding their reasons for sharing. The children's reasons were coded into four categories: (a) reciprocity—"the donor feels obligated to help because of immediate services rendered or the possibility of future interpersonal reward or punishment"; (b) in group—"the donor feels obligated to help people he likes because assumedly he wants to perpetuate the friendship and/or repay friends for past services rendered"; (c) social responsibility—"the donor feels obligated to give to the dependent recipient because of the prevailing social norms"; and (d) altruism (empathic)—"the donor wants the recipient to be happy: No interpersonal profit or loss is supposedly involved [pp. 65–66]." According to the data, amount of sharing was related to reasoning; the amount of candy shared increased across categories from reciprocity to altruism. More importantly, Dreman and Greenbaum found that kindergarteners justified their sharing with reciprocity-oriented ($N = 5$), interpersonally oriented ($N = 17$), norm-directed ($N = 35$), and empathic reasons ($N = 21$) (Dreman, 1976; Dreman & Greenbaum, 1973).

Bar-Tal and his colleagues, in a series of studies in Israel, have examined children's motives about their own prosocial behavior across a variety of settings (see Chapter 8). In general, their paradigm has involved presenting children with a series of opportunities to share or help, proceeding from the least explicit (with regard to pressure and/or the offer of a reward) to the most explicit. For example, in one study (Bar-Tal, Raviv, & Leiser, 1980) children played a game with a peer, won candy, and then were provided with successive opportunities to share the candy (until the child shared). The opportunities were designed to represent various types of positive behavior: (a) altruistic condition (the child was left alone for 3 minutes with the loser); (b) normative condition (the child was allowed to share after the experimenter referred to the norm of sharing); (c) internal initiative and concrete reward (the experimenter told the child that he or she would get a reward for sharing); (d) compliance (the experimenter told the winner to share with the loser); and (e) compliance and concretely defined reinforcement (the experimenter told the winner to share and, in return, promised the winner a big prize). Finally, after a child shared in any of the above conditions, the child was interviewed regarding his or her reasons for sharing.

In these studies, the children's reasoning about their motives was coded into a variety of categories that were identical or similar to those used by Bar-Tal et al. (1980) and Raviv, Bar-Tal, and Lewis-Levin (1980): (a) concrete reward—prosocial behavior occurred because of the promised reward; (b) compliance—prosocial behavior occurred because the experimenter told the child to do so; (c) internal initiative with concrete reward—prosocial behavior occurred because the child believed that he or she would receive a concrete reward for performing the act; (d) normative—prosocial behavior occurred because of a normative belief prescribing sharing with other children (conformity with this norm brings social approval, e.g., "It's nice to share"); (e) generalized reciprocity—prosocial behavior occurred because of a belief in a generalized social rule that people who act prosocially will receive aid when they are in need; (f) personal willingness without external reward but with expressions of self-satisfaction (e.g., "I like to share to give others satisfaction"); (g) personal willingness to act prosocially without any reward (e.g., "Candy should be shared to make the other children happy").

Bar-Tal and his colleagues viewed the above stages as comprising a developmental sequence, with the former reasons being less mature than the latter. However, the data on the issue are contradictory. In a study involving fourth, sixth, and eighth graders, mode of reason was unrelated to age (Raviv et al., 1980). In two other studies involving kindergarteners and elementary school children up to the fourth grade, use of reasons similar to those listed previously changed with age (Bar-Tal et al., 1980; Guttman, Bar-Tal, & Leiser, 1979). Furthermore, since Bar-Tal and his colleagues often combined infrequently used reasoning categories with frequently used ones, or used fewer than all the categories, it is unclear whether the stages actually develop in the sequence delineated, or if the relationships to age were due to changes in the use of only a few of the categories. For example, in one study, only three categories were used frequently: internal initiative with concrete reward, normative, and personal willingness without any reward (Bar-Tal et al., 1980). Nevertheless, according to Bar-Tal and his colleagues' data (which consist of reasoning primarily from children who did not share until explicitly requested to do so), it does appear that from kindergarten through the fourth grade, reasoning related to concrete rewards is the least developmentally mature and is used primarily by kindergarteners; normative reasoning is used most frequently by all children; and reasoning expressing a personal willingness to share without reference to any reward or specific norm was used more frequently by fourth graders than by younger children (though not that frequently) (Bar-Tal et al., 1980). Furthermore, the above sequence of reasoning appears to be related to the type of situation in which children shared. Children who shared for both a reward and because they were told to do so expressed lower level reasoning than children who shared on their own or after the experimenter referred to the norm of sharing (without explicitly requesting the child to share) (Bar-Tal et al., 1980; Raviv et al., 1980).

Like Ugurel-Semin, Dreman and Greenbaum, and Bar-Tal and his colleagues, Eisenberg-Berg and Neal (1979) examined children's reasoning about their own real-life prosocial behavior. Unlike other researchers, however, Eisenberg-Berg and Neal explored children's reasoning about their naturally occurring positive behaviors rather than behaviors in contrived situations. In this study, a familiar experimenter questioned 22 children in preschool classes regarding positive behaviors performed by the children toward peers (without adult instigation) during free-play periods. According to the data, the children most frequently explained their own prosocial behavior with reference to the needs of others (simple expressions of empathic reasoning) and pragmatic concerns. Authority and punishment reasoning analogous to Kohlberg's Stage 1 was not used by any of the children, and stereotyped justifications ("It's nice to help") and hedonistic and approval-oriented reasoning were also verbalized infrequently. Thus, these children did not use as much reward-oriented (hedonistic) or normative reasoning (including stereotyped reasoning) as did Bar-Tal and his colleagues' younger children (Bar-Tal et al., 1980; Guttman et al., 1979), but expressed more pragmatic and/or empathic concerns. The differences in reasoning are probably due to age differences and variations in methodology. Bar-Tal's and Guttman's subjects were slightly older. Furthermore, Bar-Tal and Guttman used a methodology in which (a) most children heard an adult refer to norms of sharing or helping before they acted prosocially and/or were told by an adult to assist the needy other; and (b) many children shared only after being offered a material or social reward (a hedonistic incentive) for prosocial action. In Eisenberg-Berg and Neal's study, prosocial behavior instigated by adults was not examined.

Because of substantial differences in the methodologies and coding systems used by researchers investigating children's reasoning about their own prosocial behavior, there is considerable variation in the results. Overall, however, it appears that preschoolers' and young school-aged children's reasoning regarding why they act prosocially is pragmatic, empathic, and hedonistic or self-oriented (including being oriented to reciprocity and helping someone important to the child), and frequently involves references to norms requiring prosocial behavior (including stereotypic conceptions of these norms) (Bar-Tal et al., 1980; Damon, 1971; Dreman & Greenbaum, 1973; Eisenberg-Berg & Neal, 1979; Guttman et al., 1979; Ugurel-Semin, 1952). Normative reasoning is verbalized by young children primarily in studies in which an adult either is present during the prosocial act or instigates the behavior. In none of the studies did children frequently verbalize judgments analogous to Kohlberg's Stage 1 authority and punishment-oriented reasoning, even when an adult suggested that the child share or help. In elementary school, children appear to use decreasing amounts of reward-oriented reasoning (Bar-Tal et al., 1980; Ugurel-Semin, 1952). They also increasingly develop reasoning that is more altruistic, that is, which involves a willingness to share without the expectation of external rewards, and frequently reflects role taking and/or empathic responding or an emphasis on equality and justice (Bar-Tal et al., 1980; Guttman et al., 1979; Ugurel-Semin, 1952). To summarize, as for children's conceptions of kindness, children's motives regarding their own sharing and helping behaviors appear to become more consistent with mature conceptions of altruism with age.

Reasoning regarding Prosocial Behavior in Hypothetical Dilemmas

Researchers whose goals have included delineating the development of judgments about prosocial behavior and comparing such reasoning to Kohlberg's prohibiton-oriented reasoning have tended to use hypothetical moral dilemmas (e.g., Eisenberg-Berg, 1979b; Eisenberg-Berg & Hand, 1979; Higgs, 1975; Levin & Bekerman-Greenberg, 1980; Mussen & Eisenberg-Berg, 1977; O'Connor, Cuevas, & Dollinger, 1979). Much of this research has been done using dilemmas devised by Eisenberg-Berg.

Eisenberg-Berg explicitly differentiated between what she called prohibition moral reasoning and prosocial moral reasoning. She pointed out that Kohlberg's moral dilemmas deal with only one domain of moral judgment—the prohibition-oriented domain. In nearly all of Kohlberg's dilemmas, laws, authorities, rules, punishment, and formal obligations are salient concerns. Whereas Kohlberg's dilemmas may include potential instances of prosocial action, potential prosocial behavior is nearly always cast in a prohibition-oriented context in which a prosocial act necessarily constitutes the violation of a prohibition or an authority's dictates. For example, in the Heinz dilemma, to help his wife, Heinz must break the law by stealing, whereas in another dilemma regarding euthanasia, the protagonist must kill (which is a transgression) to assist another person. According to Eisenberg-Berg, Kohlberg's dilemmas do not tap prosocial moral reasoning; that is, reasoning about conflicts in which the individual must choose between satisfying his or her wants or needs and those of others in a context in which the role of laws, punishment, authorities, formal obligations, and other external prohibitions is irrelevant or de-emphasized. In brief,

Kohlberg's dilemmas do not deal with situations in which the primary cost of helping another is personal, and prosocial action does not necessarily entail committing a transgression and/or violating authorities, rules, or laws.

In a series of studies, Eisenberg-Berg and her students have examined preschoolers' and school-aged children's prosocial moral reasoning (Eisenberg-Berg, 1979a, 1979b; Eisenberg-Berg & Hand, 1979; Eisenberg-Berg & Neal, 1981; Eisenberg-Berg & Roth, 1980; Mussen & Eisenberg-Berg, 1977). The typical procedure has involved individual interviews during which the child is read three or four prosocial moral dilemmas. In each story dilemma, the needs or wants of one individual or group conflict with those of another in a context in which the roles of laws, rules, authorities, punishment, and formal obligations are irrelevant or minimal. An example of a story used with younger children is as follows:

> One day a girl (boy) named Mary (Eric) was going to a friend's birthday party. On her (his) way she saw a girl (boy) who had fallen down and hurt her (his) leg. The girl asked Mary to go to her house and get her parents so the parents could come and take her to the doctor. But if Mary did run and get the child's parents, she would be late for the birthday party and miss the ice cream, cake, and all the games. What should Mary do? Why?

In a study involving 125 second, fourth, sixith, ninth, eleventh, and twelfth graders, Eisenberg-Berg examined developmental changes in prosocial moral reasoning (Eisenberg-Berg, 1979b; Mussen & Eisenberg-Berg, 1977). In this study, the children's reasoning was coded into a variety of moral judgment categories, many of which resembled aspects of Kohlberg's stages (examples of some of the categories are presented in Table 9.2). These types of reasoning, like Kohlberg's, reflect components of both the content (topic) and structure (form of reasoning, based on level of differentiation and integration, perspective taking, and cognitive operations) (although Kohlberg emphasizes structure more than Eisenberg-Berg).[1] Then the types of reasoning the children used to justify helping or sharing were subjected to correlational analyses, a factor analysis, and multivariate and univariate linear trend analyses. Next, types of reasoning that were intercorrelated and/or factored together were grouped into "orientations." Finally, based on the multivariate and univariate linear trend analyses (performed for indi-

---

1. Whereas Kohlberg more clearly differentiates between content and structure of reasoning than does Eisenberg-Berg, the differences in their actual stages and coding are not so great as it might seem. Definitions of Kohlberg's stages, despite efforts to the contrary, still are based, in part, on content (the "norm-element" aspect of Kohlberg's coding system), whereas the prosocial moral reasoning categories reflect varying levels of structure. For example, the higher-level prosocial reasoning categories obviously involve more perspective taking and cognitive differentiation.

Table 9.2
Frequently Used Prosocial Moral Reasoning Categories[a]

1. *Obsessive and/or magical view of authority and/or punishments*

Avoidance of punishment and unquestioning deference to power are valued in their own right. The physical consequences of action determine its goodness regardless of human values and needs (similar to Kohlberg's Stage 1). An example for this type of reasoning is the statement, "If I didn't help, someone would find out and punish me."

2. *Hedonistic reasoning*

(a) *Pragmatic, hedonistic gain to the self:* orientation to selfish gain for oneself (besides gain resulting from direct reciprocity), for example, "I wouldn't help because I might be hungry."

(b) *Direct reciprocity:* orientation to personal gain due to direct reciprocity (or lack of it) from the recipient of an act, for example, "She'd help because they'd give her food the next time she needed it."

(c) *Affectional relationship:* The individual's identification with another, his or her liking for the other, and the other's relation to his or her own needs are important considerations in the individual's moral reasoning, for example, "She'd help because she'd probably have friends in the town."

3. *Nonhedonistic pragmatism*

Orientation to practical concerns that are unrelated to selfish considerations, for example, "I'd help because I'm strong."

4. *Concern for others' physical, material, or psychological needs*

Orientation to the needs of another when these needs conflict with one's own needs, for example, "He needs food," or "They'd be happy if they could swim."

5. *Reference to and concern with humanness*

Orientation to the fact that the other is a human, a living person, for example, "You'd share because they're people."

6. *Stereotyped reasoning*

Stereotypes of a good or bad person: orientation to stereotyped images of a good or bad person, for example, a child would help because "it's nice."

7. *Approval and interpersonal orientation*

Orientation to others' approval and acceptance in deciding what is the correct behavior, for example, "His parents would be proud of him if he helped."

8. *Overt empathic orientations*

(a) *Sympathetic orientation:* expression of sympathetic concern and caring for others, for example, "He would feel sorry for them."

(b) *Role taking:* The individual takes the perspective of the other and explicitly uses this perspective in his or her reasoning, for example, "I'm trying to put myself in his or her shoes."

9. *Internalized affect*

(a) *Simple internalized positive affect and positive affect related to consequences:* The individual simply states that he or she would feel good as a result of a particular course of action without giving a reason, or says he or she would feel good because of the consequences of his or her act for the other person. The affect must be used in a context that appears internalized, for example, "She'd help because seeing the villagers fed would make her feel good."

(b) *Internalized positive affect from self-respect and living up to one's values:* orientation to feeling good as the result of living up to internalized values, for example, "I'd feel good knowing that I had lived up to my principles."

(continued)

Table 9.2 (*Continued*)

(c) *Internalized negative affect due to loss of self-respect and/or not living up to one's values:* orientation to feeling bad as the result of not living up to internalized values, for example, "He'd think badly of himself if he didn't do the right thing."

10. *Other abstract and/or internalized types of reasoning*

    (a) *Internalized law, norm, and value orientation:* orientation to an internalized responsibility, duty, or need to uphold the laws and accepted norms or values, for example, "She has a duty to help needy others."

    (b) *Concern with the rights of others:* orientation to protecting individual rights and preventing injustices that violate another's rights, for example, "I'd help because her right to walk down the street was being violated."

    (c) *Generalized reciprocity:* orientation to indirect reciprocity in a society (i.e., exchange that is not one-to-one but eventually benefits all), for example, "If everyone helps one another, we'll all be better off."

---

[a]Less frequently used categories are omitted. See Eisenberg-Berg (1979b); Eisenberg-Berg & Hand (1979). Adapted from Eisenberg-Berg (1979b).

vidual moral reasoning categories) and chi-squares (examining differences between elementary school and high school students' use of "orientations"), age-related "stages" or prosocial moral reasoning were delineated. These stages, modified slightly as a result of longitudinal research with young children (Eisenberg-Berg & Roth, 1980), are presented in Table 9.3. According to the stages, hedonistic (self-oriented) reasoning is the least developmentally mature type of judgment, followed by needs-oriented (primitive empathic) reasoning, stereotyped and interpersonal and approval-oriented reasoning, and then overtly empathic reasoning. The most advanced stage of reasoning includes judgments based on internalized values, norms, or responsibilities, and guilt or positive affect relating to maintenance of self-respect by living up to these values. Whereas use of less mature types of reasoning decreased in frequency with age, childhood modes of reasoning were used occasionally even by the oldest subjects, particularly when justifying decisions not to assist a needy other. This research model does not involve the assumption that the stages are invariant in sequence and universal; rather, it delineates a descriptive, age-related sequence of development with middle-class American children.

    The results of this early study and subsequent research with young children (Eisenberg-Berg & Hand, 1979; Eisenberg-Berg & Neal, 1981; Eisenberg-Berg & Roth, 1980) can be compared with data on prohibition moral reasoning. According to this comparison, prosocial moral judgment and prohibition-oriented moral judgment differ, in the early years, in sequence of development. For example, Kohlberg's Stage 1 authority and punishment orientation is virtually absent in preschoolers' prosocial moral

Table 9.3
"Stages" of Prosocial Moral Reasoning

Stage 1: Hedonistic, pragmatic orientation: The individual is concerned with selfish, pragmatic consequences rather than moral considerations. "Right" behavior is that which is instrumental in satisfying the actor's own needs or wants. Reasons for assisting or not assisting another include consideration of direct gain to the self, future reciprocity, and concern for others whom the individual needs and/or likes.

Stage 2: "Needs of others" orientation: The individual expresses concern for the physical, material, and psychological needs of others even though the other's needs conflict with one's own needs. This concern is expressed in the simplest terms, without clear evidence of role taking, verbal expressions of sympathy, or reference to internalized affect such as guilt ("He's hungry" or "She needs it").

Stage 3: Approval and interpersonal orientation and/or stereotyped orientation: Stereotyped images of good and bad persons and behavior and/or considerations of others' approval and acceptance are used in justifying prosocial or nonhelping behaviors. For example, one helps another because "it's nice to help" or because "he'd like him more if he helped."

Stage 4a: Empathic orientation: The individual's judgments include evidence of sympathetic responding, role taking, concern with the other's humanness, and/or guilt or positive affect related to the consequences of one's actions. Examples include "He knows how he feels," "She cares about people," and "I'd feel bad if I didn't help because he'd be in pain."

Stage 4b: Transitional stage: Justifications for helping or not helping involve internalized values, norms, duties, or responsibilities, or refer to the necessity of protecting the rights and dignity of other persons; these ideas, however, are not clearly and strongly stated. References to internalized affect, self-respect, and living up to one's own values are considered indicative of this stage if they are weakly stated. Examples include "It's just something I've learned and feel."

Stage 5: Strongly internalized stage: Justifications for helping or not helping are based on internalized values, norms, or responsibilities, the desire to maintain individual and societal contractual obligations, and the belief in the dignity, rights, and equality of all individuals. Positive or negative affects related to the maintenance of self-respect and living up to one's own values and accepted norms also characterize this stage. Examples of Stage 5 reasoning include "She'd feel a responsibility to help other people in need" or "I would feel bad if I didn't help because I'd know that I didn't live up to my values."

reasoning even though, according to Kohlberg and his colleagues, it is the major mode of prohibition-oriented moral reasoning early in childhood (Kohlberg, 1969). This conclusion is consistent with research concerning children's reasoning about their own naturally occurring prosocial behavior (Eisenberg-Berg & Neal, 1979), and with Bar-Tal and his colleagues' research in which compliance-oriented reasoning was infrequent (e.g., Bar-Tal et al., 1980; Guttman et al., 1979). Whereas O'Connor et al. (1979) found 1.1–11.8% of school-aged children's reasoning to be authority-oriented, they assessed children's moral reasoning with a preference method (children chose one of several predetermined reasons as being best) rather than elicit-ing the children's self-generated reasoning. Since children can say they prefer reasoning that they do not really use spontaneously (because it sounds good or because the child simply is not attending), O'Conner et al's data are not necessarily inconsistent with Eisenberg-Berg's results.

Not only is Kohlberg's Stage 1 reasoning virtaully absent in prosocial moral reasoning, but the development of prosocial reasoning also is more advanced than that of prohibition-oriented reasoning. For example, stereotyped moral judgments seem to emerge earlier in prosocial moral reasoning than in prohibition moral judgment (Eisenberg-Berg, 1979b). Fur-thermore, children use much needs-oriented, empathic moral judgment in the preschool years (Eisenberg-Berg & Hand, 1979; Eisenberg-Berg & Neal, 1981), even though Kohlberg includes empathic moral reasoning in Stage 3 (a stage of reasoning that does not become salient until early adolescence).[2] The use of empathic needs-oriented judgments in the preschool years is consistent with research indicating that even young children are empathic (Zahn-Waxler & Radke-Yarrow, 1979). Only when prohibitions were in-volved in issues related to prosocial behavior and the subjects were adults has a researcher found that prosocial moral reasoning is no more advanced than prohibition-oriented moral reasoning (Higgs, 1975).

It is not clear why prosocial moral reasoning is more advanced and somewhat different than prohibition moral reasoning. Perhaps the dif-ferences in use of authority and punishment reasoning and needs-oriented judgments are due, in part, to the patterns of child-rearing practices that are associated with prosocial acts and transgressions. According to recent re-search, parents sometimes use physical techniques (physical restraint and physical punishment) and unexplained verbal prohibitions (which provide no other basis for obeying but the parent's authority) when a child transgres-ses (e.g., bites a peer or snatches a toy), but seldom use such power-based techniques when a child merely views another's distress (Zahn-Waxler, Radke-Yarrow, & King, 1979). Thus, children may associate prohibition and authority-related issues with prohibition but not prosocial aspects of morality. Furthermore, needs-oriented reasoning may occur earlier in proso-cial moral reasoning because, during the early phases of socialization, the child is exposed to both sides of a prosocial conflict; that is, he or she is a helper at times and a recipient of aid at other times. In contrast, the child is

2. Alternatively, it may be that Kohlberg codes needs-oriented reasoning, even when the needs of others are in conflict with the story protagonist's own needs, as pragmatic rather than empathic reasoning. This may occur because Kohlberg views needs-oriented reasoning when the other's needs do not conflict with one's own as pragmatic Stage 2 reasoning.

almost always on one side of a prohibition issue; children must follow the rules and obey authorities but seldom make or enforce prohibitions. Thus, the child may be better able to role take about prosocial dilemmas and, consequently, may be better equipped both to conceptualize and to empathize when dealing with prosocial conflicts.

As was true with respect to developmental sequences, the internal structures of prosocial and prohibition moral judgment are not identical. For example, empathic types of reasonings appear to be particularly salient in prosocial moral reasoning. Furthermore, empathic reasoning is not related to stereotypic, interpersonal and approval-oriented reasoning in prosocial moral judgments, although Kohlberg implied that these types of judgments are interrelated when he grouped them together in his Stage 3.

Whereas there are differences in the sequence of development for prosocial and prohibition moral reasoning, there are also similarities (Eisenberg, 1977, Eisenberg-Berg, 1976; Higgs, 1975). Different types of hedonistic reasoning (e.g., reasoning concerning selfish gains and potential reciprocity from the recipient of assistance) cluster together in both prosocial and prohibition moral reasoning, and occur early in the developmental process (Eisenberg-Berg, 1979b; Kohlberg, 1969; Mussen & Eisenberg-Berg, 1977). Similarly, stereotyped reasoning and interpersonal, approval-oriented reasoning cluster together in both types of judgments, and develop subsequent to hedonistic reasoning. Furthermore, for both types of judgments, verbalizations or statements of highly internalized values and principles develop later in childhood and do not occur frequently until adolescence (Eisenberg-Berg, 1979b; Kohlberg, 1969, 1971).

In summary, Eisenberg-Berg and her students delineated a sequence of "stages" of prosocial moral reasoning that is reminiscent of, but not identical to, Kohlberg's stages of prohibition-oriented moral judgment. When discussing prosocial moral dilemmas, the 4-year-old verbalizes much hedonistic and some needs-oriented reasoning. By early elementary school, the use of hedonistic reasoning is on the decline (although it is still frequently used), whereas needs-oriented and approval-oriented reasoning has increased in frequency of use. In the middle and later elementary school years, children's judgments are stereotyped, interpersonal and approval-oriented, and overtly empathic, as well as somewhat hedonistic. From the elementary to high school years, use of stereotypic and interpersonal and approval-oriented reasoning declines, whereas references to empathic and internalized factors increase. It thus appears that children's prosocial moral judgment with age becomes more overtly empathic, less hedonistic, and more oriented toward internalized principles and self-respect with regard to these principles.

THE RELATIONSHIP OF PROSOCIAL MORAL
REASONING TO PROSOCIAL BEHAVIOR

A logical question that immediately arises in the study of moral judgment concerns the relationship of judgment to behavior. Obviously, the significance of studying moral judgment is much greater if information regarding reasoning can aid in the understanding of moral behavior.

A simple and direct relationship between behavior and moral judgment cannot be expected. This is because any single behavior may spring from a variety of motives. Nevertheless, a positive association between moral judgment and prosocial behavior might be found if people who are more empathic and internalized in their moral judgment behave in a prosocial manner more consistently than people who verbalize less advanced reasoning.

In general, there does seem to be some relationship between an individual's prosocial behavior and his or her moral reasoning (although reasoning does not always predict behavior, see Table 9.4). Eisenberg-Berg found that more mature prosocial moral reasoning was related to increased incidence of helping an experimenter with a dull task among high school boys (but not girls, Eisenberg-Berg, 1979a), and to spontaneous sharing in the preschool class (Eisenberg-Berg & Hand, 1979). These data are consistent with research in which increased incidence of prosocial behavior has been associated with more sophisticated justifications for actually occurring sharing behavior (Dreman & Greenbaum, 1973). It is also consistent with Bar-Tal and his colleagues' finding that children who shared or donated without adult pressure and without the promise of reward expressed more mature motives for their behavior than children who assisted only when they were told to do so and/or were promised rewards (Bar-Tal *et al.*, 1980; Raviv *et al.*, 1980). Furthermore, Levin and Bekerman-Greenberg (1980) found that incidence of sharing with a peer was related to reasoning about situations similar to the sharing situation (but not to reasoning about dissimilar situations when the effects of grade level were controlled); however, they did not provide adequate justification for their sequence of stages. Finally, the fact that level of reasoning about prosocial behaviors and actual prosocial actions frequently are related is consistent with research indicating a similar relationship between helping behavior and mature Kohlbergian, prohibition-oriented reasoning (Blasi, 1980; Harris, Mussen, & Rutherford, 1976; Kohlberg, 1969; McNamee, 1972; Staub, 1974). Thus, whereas cause and effect are not clear, information regarding maturity of prosocial moral reasoning can aid in the prediction of prosocial behavior. This relationship increases our confidence that individuals' moral judgments actually provide information regarding their motivations for positive or selfish behaviors.

Table 9.4

Studies Examining the Relationship between Prosocial Behavior and Reasoning about Prosocial Behavior: Methods and Results

Study	Subjects	Measure of prosocial behavior[a]	Measure of reasoning	Relationship	Direction and comments
Bar-Tal et al., 1980	Israeli M & F in K and grades 2 and 4	Sharing candy won in a guessing game with a peer	Categories outlined on p. 228	Between level of reasoning and amount of sharing	+
Dreman, 1976	Israeli M, grades 1, 4, 7	Sharing candy won for doing a drawing; conditions varied subjects' anonymity and likelihood of reciprocity	Reasons for sharing, opportunity to share, categories outlined on p. 227	Between amount of candy and justification level (did not look at each justification separately)	0 —Complex interaction with situation; subjects gave more reciprocity reasons in reciprocity condition
Dreman & Greenbaum, 1973	Israeli M & F, K	Sharing an odd number of candies; conditions varied anonymity and likelihood of reciprocity (if donor would be known)	Reasons for sharing after opportunity to share; categories outlined on p. 227	Between reasoning justification and mean number of candies shared	+ —The relationship is positive if the sequence of development (from higher level to lower) is altruism, social responsibility in group, and reciprocity reasoning (it is unclear which type of reasoning is seen as most mature)

238

Eisenberg-Berg, 1979b	M & F, grades 9, 11, 12	Volunteering and actually donating an hour to help the experimenter with a dull task	Prosocial moral reasoning stages; similar to those in Table 9.3	Between volunteering and level of reasoning	+—for boys, 0 for girls
Eisenberg-Berg & Hand, 1979	M & F, preschoolers	Spontaneous or "asked for" (compliant) naturally occurring prosocial behaviors	Categories of reasoning derived from those in Table 9.2	Between frequency of prosocial behaviors and amount of various modes of reasoning	+—for spontaneous sharing (+ with needs-oriented reasoning; – with hedonistic) 0 for other prosocial behaviors
Levin & Bekerman-Greenberg, 1980	Israeli M & F, grades K, 2, 4, 6	Sharing pretzels won in a lottery with a peer	Reasoning about a hypothetical situation similar to the sharing assessment, a somewhat similar situation, or a very different situation dealing with distributive justice; level of reasoning (from high to low): positive justice, empathy, conditional generosity; good boy–girl morality; immediate reciprocity, egocentrism	Between level of reasoning and number of pretzels shared	+—for all types of stories; + relation with similar situation when the effects of grade were controlled; – with distributive justice when age controlled

(continued)

Table 9.4 (Continued)

Study	Subjects	Measure of prosocial behavior[a]	Measure of reasoning	Relationship	Direction and comments
Raviv et al., 1980	Israeli M, grade 4, 6, 8	Donation of prize money to crippled children; children proceeded through a series of conditions, varying in amount of normative cues, promise of concrete reward, and/or adult command for sharing	Reasoning levels (high to low): altruism, generalized reciprocity, normative, internal initiative with concrete reward, compliance	Between level of reasoning and which condition the children donated in	+
Rubin & Schneider, 1973	M & F, age 7	Sharing candy with poor children; helping a younger child with a task rather than playing	Story dilemmas concerning prosocial acts	Between sharing and helping and level of moral judgment	+—for both sharing and helping
Wright, 1942a	M & F, grade 3	Opportunities to share an attractive toy with friend or stranger	Reasons for preferring friend or stranger after sharing	Between sharing with stranger (associated with higher sharing) and reason given	+—Fewer self-oriented reasons were given for sharing with a stranger
Wright, 1942b	M & F, ages 8, 11	Sharing attractive and unattractive toys with peer	Reasons about hypothetical situation involving distribution of toys (few details given)	Reasons for sharing and actual sharing	+—Ideology and behavior related (few details given)

[a]Maturity of attributions regarding prosocial behaviors (as measured with Baldwin & Baldwin's, 1970, instrument) has been positively, significantly associated with prosocial behavior in two studies (Dlugokinski & Firestone, 1973, 1974), and with cooperation but not helping in another study (Seegmiller & Suter, 1977).

THE ROLE OF SITUATIONAL VARIATION IN
PROSOCIAL MORAL REASONING

In real life, situations that call for prosocial action vary on many dimensions. Different prosocial behaviors (e.g., sharing, helping, and comforting) require different skills and involve different configurations of costs and benefits (Eisenberg-Berg, Cameron, Tryon, & Dodez, 1980). Furthermore, the costs and benefits for a particular type of behavior (e.g., helping) vary across contexts. For example, sharing scarce food is quite different in meaning from sharing excess candy. Moreover, the significance of a prosocial act changes as a function of many situational factors such as the presence or absence of authorities, and the manner in which a prosocial act is initiated (if it is spontaneous, in response to a request, or in response to vivid cues depicting the needy others' distress). Thus, since one would not necessarily expect an individual's behavior to be consistent across a variety of situations, it is reasonable to assume that people's reasoning will vary across moral dilemmas that differ in various aspects.

It is likely that much of the inconsistency in the research on moral reasoning about prosocial behavior is due to differences in the situations about which the subjects reason. For example, in most of the studies done by Bar-Tal and his colleagues, the majority of children reasoned about sharing or helping that was requested and/or directly rewarded by an adult authority, whereas Eisenberg-Berg and Neal (1979) explicitly avoided eliciting reasoning about these types of situations. Furthermore, in some studies, children reasoned about situations in which reciprocity from a peer was a realistic possibility (e.g., Dreman & Greenbaum, 1973; Eisenberg-Berg & Neal, 1979); however, in other studies involving hypothetical stories or a prize belonging to only one person, immediate reciprocity by a recipient was unlikely (e.g., Bar-Tal et al., 1980, Eisenberg-Berg, 1979b; Eisenberg-Berg & Hand, 1979; Raviv et al., 1980). These and other situational variations undoubtedly could be related to selective use of various modes of prosocial moral reasoning.

Research examining the effects of situational factors on children's reasoning about prosocial behaviors is very scarce. However, Eisenberg-Berg and Neal (1981) have conducted two studies relating to this issue. In research with preschoolers and first graders, they manipulated the cost of a prosocial behavior in moral dilemmas and the reasoner's perspective (first person versus third person). According to their data, children's prosocial judgments were more hedonistic and less needs-oriented when they reasoned about costly prosocial behaviors, particularly if they were making judgments about what they themselves rather than third person others should do. Thus, Eisenberg-Berg's data are consistent with the commonsense notion that reasoning, as well as behavior, is influenced by subtle situational variables. Furthermore, these data are reminiscent of Eisenberg-Berg's finding that when children said that the story protagonist should not assist the needy other, they usually justified their decision with immature hedonistic reasoning (relating to the cost of helping) regardless of their modal level of reasoning (Eisenberg-Berg, 1979b). Indeed, it is likely that differences in moral judgment across moral dilemmas are due, in part, to individuals' sensitivity to dissimilar configurations of circumstances (e.g., costs and benefits) in different contexts.

IMPLICATIONS

Implications of the Research for an Understanding of Prosocial Behavior

Although moral judgments are obviously just that—judgments and not behavior—research on reasoning regarding prosocial behaviors is useful for delineating the range of conscious motives that underlie children's behavior at a given age. Whereas it has not been proved that young children's behaviors are usually motivated by the considerations they express in their reasoning, the fact that there is often an association between prosocial behavior and reasoning is consistent with the assumption that children's reasoning frequently reflects their motivations.

According to the data, the young child does not define "kindness" with the same criteria as do adults. Specifically, children are less likely than adults to view positive acts as kind only if they meet the criteria of the definition of altruism, that is, if they are voluntary (intentional) and unlikely to be motivated by external benefits. Furthermore, in the preschool years, the decision of whether or not to act prosocially appears to be motivated by a more limited range of concerns than for older children, that is, primarily by empathic, hedonistic, and pragmatic considerations. The ability of the young child to be responsive to others' needs, however, suggests that even young children may assist another for internal, altruistic reasons.[3]

By the school years, it appears that the repertoire of motives and reasons underlying the child's prosocial behavior broadens. The child is now attuned to stereotypic images of social norms, and may desire to act in accordance with these norms. The school-aged child also frequently expresses reasoning reflecting the desire for social approval, personal gains achieved

3. However, some theorists would argue that people who are empathic help others to reduce an aversive state (empathic distress) and, thus, that empathically motivated prosocial behavior is not altruistic (and that altruism is actually hedonism).

through reciprocity, and concern for the needs of others identified with the self. As children's role-taking skills are refined, their emotional empathic reactions appear to involve more than mere orientation to another's needs. Their concerns are expressed more explicitly, and with greater self-awareness. During the school years, children's definitions of kindness become very similar to those of adults. Kind acts are intentional, voluntary behaviors that are not motivated by hedonistic gains (reinforcements or avoidance of punishment) or social obligations. Finally, by high school, adolescents justify prosocial behavior with a wide variety of reasons, including (for a few adolescents) commitment to internalized principles and values, and maintenance of positive self-regard for living up to one's own values. Empathic concerns and conformity with societal norms are salient aspects of the adolescent's reasoning, and likely underlie many of their prosocial behaviors. Even adolescents, however, frequently verbalize less developmentally advanced concerns, and, like young children, justify decisions not to assist another primarily with hedonistic considerations. With age, thus, the child's range of considerations related to prosocial actions becomes more abstract and varied.

The developmental changes in children's moral reasoning are consistent with age-related cognitive advances (in role-taking abilities and the capacity to reason abstractly) that occur during childhood and adolescence (Inhelder & Piaget, 1958; Shantz, 1975). More sophisticated types of moral reasonings require that the individual adopt another's or society's perspective (Kohlberg, 1969, 1971; Selman, 1976), and consider abstractions like "justice" and "equality." Thus, it is not at all surprising that mature forms of reasoning about prosocial behaviors parallel developmental changes in these capacities.

Although it is possible to delineate developmental trends in children's reasoning about prosocial behaviors, it is important to note that there can be large individual differences in children's judgments at a given age level. Such differences underscore the potential contributions of personality and socialization experiences (as well as individual rates of cognition development) to the development of reasoning about positive behaviors. Differences in socialization experiences most likely affect the child in a variety of ways, for example, by providing differential opportunities for role taking, by shaping the child's general feelings and attitudes toward people, and by influencing the development of characteristics such as empathic responding and autonomy, which may be related to the use of autonomous moral reasoning (Eisenberg, 1977; Eisenberg-Berg & Mussen, 1978). Thus, although there appear to be similarities among children in the development of reasoning about prosocial behaviors, it would be ill-advised for psychologists to ignore the role of individual differences in this process.

The fact that moral reasoning changes as a function of situational variation is consistent with the conclusion that motives underlying prosocial behavior also vary depending on the situation. Indeed, there are probably many types of positive behaviors, each characterized by a different configuration of costs, benefits, and implications for the individual (Eisenberg-Berg, et al., 1980). For example, positive behaviors spontaneously performed by children when confronted with a needy other are probably quite different in meaning from positive behaviors instigated by an adult's suggestions or demands. By eliciting children's moral reasoning about different types of prosocial behaviors, it should be possible to clarify further the meaning of different types of prosocial behaviors for children of varying ages.

Research on reasoning regarding prosocial behaviors is in its infancy. At present, work on this issue is so limited that conclusions from the research must be quite tentative. Furthermore, many important questions have yet to be asked. For example, there is little research on how children's reasoning about their own behavior relates to judgments about hypothetical situations. There is also a great need to attend to how children's reasoning is influenced by their ability to discriminate and weigh the subtle differences in various modes of prosocial behavior and in the situations in which potential prosocial acts are embedded.

A multifaceted research program is needed to address the many unanswered questions. Research in which children's reasoning about their own naturally occurring real-life prosocial behavior is elicited or observed in the natural setting would be particularly useful for providing information about children's motives for and judgments about everyday behaviors. As yet, this technique has not been used to examine differences in reasoning concerning various modes of prosocial behavior, for example, spontaneous versus compliant prosocial acts, and acts directed toward adults versus children. Such an approach should prove valuable. Methods such as that used by Bar-Tal (which involve putting a child in a series of different situations in which he or she can share, and eliciting the child's reasoning when sharing occurs) are useful because they provide a means of obtaining real-life reasoning but in controlled situations. In the future, however, it would be profitable to determine children's reasoning for *not* sharing in specific situations, and to ensure that all children in the sample are exposed to each situation. Then the reasoning obtained from children in a specific situation (e.g., when the child is reminded of the norm of social responsibility) would not come from a subsample of children who shared for the first time in that situation. Finally, because of the ease with which situational characteristics and cues can be altered in hypothetical dilemmas, this methodology could be exploited for the examination of the role of situational factors in moral judgment. A combination of these techniques should prove most effective in future research on prosocial reasoning, especially if the findings on moral judgment are related to individual differences in performance of a variety of prosocial behaviors.

Implications for the Study of Moral Judgment

Research relating to moral judgments about prosocial behavior has several implications for theory concerning the general domain of moral judgment. First, according to the research, reasoning regarding different types of moral dilemmas may vary in structure and developmental course. It is therefore not wise to assume without empirical verification that Kohlberg's stages of moral judgment apply equally well to all types of moral issues. Second, the level of reasoning verbalized by an individual is often highly related to how the individual resolves a moral conflict. For example, children of all ages tend to justify the decision not to assist a needy other with hedonistic reasoning, although judgments regarding decisions to help others vary in structure considerably. Thus, reasoning will vary, depending on the story resolution most likely in a particular dilemma. Furthermore, contrary to Kohlberg's (1969) assertions, it is likely that a particular child's reasoning can be quite varied. Whereas Kohlberg has claimed that 50% of the child's reasoning is at one stage with nearly all of the rest being only one stage above or below the modal stage, the child's reasoning need not be restricted to such a narrow range (e.g., children may reason at a much lower level in some situations than in others). In prosocial moral reasoning, developmentally immature types of reasoning do not die out entirely, but may be used in certain situations. Thus, it may be incorrect to conceptualize moral judgments as developing through an invariant sequence of stages with little use of reasoning more than one level below the individual's modal stage (see Selman, 1980, for a similar conclusion).

In view of the research on moral reasoning concerning prosocial behavior, how might stages of prosocial moral reasoning be viewed? The stages are probably conceptualized most accurately as constituting an age-related sequence of development through which many (but not all) individuals progress. Further claims of universality and invariance would seem to be unjustified. Thus, the study of prosocial moral judgment stages currently provides primarily information regarding which types of reasonings develop early and which develop later, and what types of judgments are characteristic at various ages in western society.

Both the ordering of the stages and the age of emergence of various modes of reasoning undoubtedly are dependent, in part, on the development of cognitive abilities over the years. Thus, the sequence and timing of development are partially fixed. However, experiential factors also must play a role. For example, the role of punishment in relation to various moral issues most likely varies across families, socioeconomic classes, and societies. The strength of association of punishment with a particular moral behavior or issue in a given group should thus influence group members' moral judgments with regard to that issue.

Even though moral judgments in some (and perhaps all) domains may not develop in an invariant, universal sequence and may vary as a function of specific situational variables (such as costs of helping), by sampling an individual's moral judgment with several stories, one frequently can determine the type (or types) of reasoning most characteristic of the individual's thinking at that point in development. Such information contains clues regarding variables that are important to the individual (e.g., the importance of social approval), and thus provides the researcher with insights to the individual's hierarchy of motives and values. These insights are essential if we are to predict and understand the development and maintenance of prosocial behavior better.

ACKNOWLEDGMENTS

The author wishes to express her appreciation to Daniel Bar-Tal, Robert B. Cialdini, Susan Sommerville, and Carolyn Zahn-Waxler for their suggestions regarding the content of this chapter.

REFERENCES

Baldwin, A., & Baldwin, C. Children's judgments of kindness. *Child Development,* 1970, *41,* 29–47.

Baldwin, A., Baldwin, C., Hilton, I., & Lambert, N. The measurement of social expectations and their development in children. *Monographs of the Society for Research in Child Development,* 1969, *34* (4, Serial No. 128).

Baldwin, A. L., Baldwin, C. P., Castillo-Vales, V., & Seegmiller, B. Cross-cultural similarities in the development of the concept of kindness. In W. W. Lambert & K. Weisbrod (Eds.), *Comparative perspectives.* Boston: Little, Brown, 1971.

Bar-Tal, D. *Prosocial behavior: Theory and research.* New York: Halsted, 1976.

Bar-Tal, D., Raviv, A., & Leiser, T. The development of altruistic behavior: Empirical evidence. *Developmental Psychology,* 1980, *16,* 516–524.

Blasi, A. Bridging moral cognition and moral action: A critical review of the research. *Psychological Bulletin,* 1980, *88,* 1–45.

Damon, W. *A developmental analysis of the positive justice concept from childhood through adolescence.* Unpublished Master's thesis, University of California, Berkeley, 1971.

Dlugokinski, E., & Firestone, I. J. Congruence among four methods of measuring other-centeredness. *Child Development,* 1973, *44,* 304–308.

Dlugokinski, E. L., & Firestone, I. J. Other centeredness and susceptibility to charitable appeals: Effects of perceived discipline. *Developmental Psychology,* 1974, *10,* 21–28.

Dreman, S. B. Sharing behavior in Israeli school children: Cognitive and social learning factors. *Child Development,* 1976, *47,* 186–194.

Dreman, S., & Greenbaum, C. W. Altruism or reciprocity: Sharing behavior in Israeli kindergarten children. *Child Development,* 1973, *44,* 61–68.

Eisenberg, N. The development of prosocial moral judgment and its correlates (Doctoral dissertation, University of California, Berkeley, 1976). *Dissertation Abstracts International,* 1977, *37,* 4753B. (University Microfilms No. 70–44, 184)

Eisenberg-Berg, N. The relationship of political attitudes to constraint and prosocial moral reasoning. *Developmental Psychology,* 1976, *12,* 6, 552–553.

Eisenberg-Berg, N. The relationship of prosocial moral reasoning to altruism, political liberalism, and intelligence. *Developmental Psychology,* 1979, *15,* 87–89. (a)

Eisenberg-Berg, N. The development of children's prosocial moral judgment. *Developmental Psychology,* 1979, *15,* 128–137. (b)

Eisenberg-Berg, N., Cameron, E., Tryon, K., & Dodez, R. *Prosocial behavior in the preschool years: Methodological and conceptual issues.* Paper presented at the International Conference on the Development and Maintenance of Prosocial Behavior, Warsaw, Poland, June 29–July 3, 1980.

Eisenberg-Berg, N., & Hand, M. The relationship of preschoolers' reasoning about prosocial moral conflicts to prosocial behavior. *Child Development,* 1979, *50,* 356–363.

Eisenberg-Berg, N., & Mussen, P. Empathy and moral development in adolescence. *Developmental Psychology,* 1978, *14,* 185–186.

Eisenberg-Berg, N., & Neal, C. Children's moral reasoning about their own spontaneous prosocial behavior. *Developmental Psychology,* 1979, *15,* 228–229.

Eisenberg-Berg, N., & Neal, C. Effects of identity of the story character and cost of helping on children's moral judgment. *Personality and Social Psychology Bulletin,* 1981, *1,* Vol. 7, 17–23.

Eisenberg-Berg, N., & Roth, K. The development of children's prosocial moral judgment: A longitudinal follow-up. *Developmental Psychology,* 1980, *16*(4), 375–376.

Guttman, J., Bar-Tal, D., Leiser, P. *The effect of various reward situations on children's helping behavior.* Unpublished manuscript, University of Tel-Aviv, 1979.

Harris, S., Mussen, P., & Rutherford, E. Some cognitive, behavioral, and personality correlates of maturity of moral judgment. *Journal of Genetic Psychology,* 1976, *128,* 123–135.

Higgs, A. C. An investigation of the similarities between altruistic and moral judgments (Doctoral dissertation, University of Maryland, Baltimore, 1974). *Dissertation Abstracts International,* 1975, *35,* 4629B. (University Microfilms No. 75–7336, 158)

Inhelder, B., & Piaget, J. *The growth of logical thinking from childhood to adolescence.* New York: Basic Books, 1958.

Jensen, L. C., & Hughston, K. The relationship between type of sanction, story content, and children's judgments which are independent of sanction. *Journal of Genetic Psychology,* 1973, *122,* 40–54.

Keasey, C. B. Children's developing awareness and usage of intentionality and motives. In H. E. Howe, Jr. (Ed.), *Nebraska Symposium on Motivation* (Vol. 26). Lincoln: University of Nebraska Press, 1978.

Kohlberg, L. Stage and sequence: The cognitive developmental approach to socialization. In D. Goslin (Ed.), *The handbook of socialization theory and research.* Chicago: Rand McNally, 1969.

Kohlberg, L. From is to ought: How to commit the naturalistic fallacy and get away with it in the study of moral development. In T. Mischel (Ed.), *Cognitive development and epistemology.* New York: Academic Press, 1971.

Kohlberg, L. Revisions in the theory and practice of moral development. In W. Damon (Ed.), *New directions for child development: Moral development.* (Vol. 2). San Francisco: Jossey-Bass, 1978.

Krebs, D. L. Altruism—An examination of the concept and a review of the literature. *Psychological Bulletin,* 1970, *73,* 258-303.

Leahy, R. L. Development of conceptions of prosocial behavior: Information affecting rewards given for altruism and kindness. *Developmental Psychology,* 1979, *15,* 34-37.

Levin, I., & Bekerman-Greenberg, R. Moral judgment and moral reasoning in sharing: A developmental analyses. *Genetic Psychological Monographs,* 1980, *101,* 215-230.

McNamee, S. M. Moral behavior, moral development, and needs in students and political activists with special reference to the law and order stage of development. (Doctoral dissertation, Case Western Reserve, 1972). *Dissertation Abstracts International,* 1972, *33*B, 1800-1801. (University Microfilms No. 72-25, 303.).

Mussen, P., & Eisenberg-Berg, N. *The roots of caring, sharing, and helping.* San Francisco: Freeman, 1977.

O'Connor, M., Cuevas, J., & Dollinger, S. *Understanding intentions behind prosocial acts: A developmental analysis.* Unpublished paper (Children's Memorial Hospital, Chicago), 1979.

Peterson, L. Developmental changes in verbal and behavioral sensitivity to cues of social norms of altruism. *Child Development,* 1980, *51,* 830-838.

Peterson, L., Hartmann, D. P., & Gelfand, D. Developmental changes in the effects of dependency and reciprocity cues on children's moral judgments and donation rates. *Child Development,* 1977, *48,* 1331-1339.

Piaget, J. *The moral judgment of the child.* New York: Free Press, 1948.

Raviv, A., Bar-Tal, D., & Lewis-Levin, T. Motivations for donation behavior by boys of three different ages. *Child Development,* 1980, *51,* 610-613.

Rubin, K. H., & Schneider, F. W. The relationship between moral judgment, egocentrism, and altruistic behavior. *Child Development,* 1973, *44,* 661-665.

Seegmiller, B. R., & Suter, B. Relations between cognitive and behavioral measures of prosocial development in children. *The Journal of Genetic Psychology,* 1977, *131,* 161-162.

Selman, R. L. Social-cognitive understanding: A guide to educational and clinical practice. In T. Lickona (Ed.), *Moral development and behavior: Theory, research, and social issues.* New York: Holt, Rinehart & Winston, 1976.

Selman, R. *The growth of interpersonal understanding: Developmental and clinical analyses.* New York: Academic Press, 1980.

Shantz, C. V. The development of social cognition. In E. M. Hetherington (Ed.), *Review of child development research* (Vol. 5). Chicago: University of Chicago Press, 1975.

Shure, M. B. Fairness, generosity, and selfishness: The naive psychology of children and young adults. *Child Development,* 1968, *30,* 857-886.

Staub, E. Helping a distressed person: Social, personality, and stimulus determinants. In L. Berkowitz (Ed.), *Advances in experimental social psychology* (Vol. 7). New York: Academic Press, 1974.

Staub, E. *Positive social behavior and morality: Social and personal influences.* New York: Academic Press, 1978.

Staub, E. *Positive social behavior and morality: Socialization and development.* New York: Academic Press, 1979.

Ugurel-Semin, R. Moral behavior and moral judgment of children. *Journal of Abnormal and Social Psychology,* 1952, *47,* 463-474.

Wright, B. Altruism in children and the perceived conduct of others. *Journal of Abnormal and Social Psychology,* 1942, *37,* 218-233. (a)

Wright, B. The development of ideology of altruism and fairness in children. *Psychological Bulletin*, 1942, *39*, 485. (b)

Zahn-Waxler, C., & Radke-Yarrow, M. *A developmental analysis of children's response to emotions in others.* Paper presented at the Biennial Meeting of the Society for Research in Child Development, San Francisco, March, 1979.

Zahn-Waxler, C., Radke-Yarrow, M., & King, R. A. Child rearing and children's prosocial initiations toward victims of distress. *Child Development,* 1979, *50,* 319–330.

RACHEL KARNIOL

Settings, Scripts, and Self-Schemata: A Cognitive Analysis of the Development of Prosocial Behavior

This chapter has as its basic premise that all social behavior, including prosocial behavior, is cognitively mediated. The foregoing assumption implies that individuals who engage in prosocial behavior respond to stimuli that they have interpreted in a specific way. Ordinarily, in prosocial behavior, the stimulus is a situational context in which another person is presumed to need some ameliorative action. The two critical questions that need to be answered about prosocial behavior and its development are (a) How do individuals who observe the particular setting or events become aware of another's need for help?; and (b) How does this awareness of the other's need become translated into a concern about the other's need? Both of these questions focus on the processes that intervene between the time the situation is perceived and the helping response is undertaken. The first question, that of becoming aware of need, concerns a perceptual and inferential process on the part of the observer. In most theoretical analyses, need awareness has been presumed to be the consequence of engaging in role-taking activities (e.g., Hoffman, 1975, Staub, 1979). The second question, that of need concern, refers to the motivational process that is presumed to be contingent on need awareness and is ordinarily labeled empathy (e.g., Hoffman, 1975; Staub, 1979; Stotland, 1969). These two processes are thought to be necessary but not sufficient for the observer to seek to ameliorate the other's state of need.

Our task in this chapter is to present a cognitive analysis of prosocial behavior that recasts the process of role taking and empathy, thereby depriving them of their unique status as ordinarily conceptualized. Our analysis is

THE DEVELOPMENT OF
PROSOCIAL BEHAVIOR

based on information processing models in which individuals are assumed to respond to stimuli only after finding a context of interpretation for the observed stimuli. This interpretational context is found by conducting a memory search. If the memory search yields a prestored interpretational context, this context provides a rich knowledge structure that is then used to interpret the situation and to guide the observer's reaction to it. Within these retrieval models, the prestored knowledge structures have been diversely labeled frames (Charniak, 1978; Minsky, 1975), schemata (Bobrow & Norman, 1975), scripts (Schank & Abelson, 1977), and commonsense algorithms (Rieger, 1976). Whatever particular label they use in referring to the knowledge structures accessed in response to stimuli, these models all suggest that situations can be responded to only after a fair amount of cognitive work which is initiated by the situational context. Hence, to apply these models, we must examine both the stimulus situations and the responses that have been subsumed under the rubric of prosocial behavior.

Before we consider the implications of these models, we will briefly summarize the settings and responses used in prosocial research. The responses that have been subsumed under the heading of prosocial behavior we conceptualize as *rescue, sharing,* and *donation. Rescue* we use to refer to the rendering of physical service or aid to someone in need; *sharing,* to the distribution of goods and services among interacting individuals; and *donation,* to the allotment of goods to those defined as needy by virtue of some characteristic that is not limited to the observed situation (e.g., blindness).

The stimuli used to elicit these three types of helping response have been quite diverse. Studies of rescue have often employed either taped simulated emergencies in which individuals have an accident and cry out for help (e.g., Staub, 1971) or collapsed individuals who presumably need help (e.g., Darley & Batson, 1973; Piliavin & Piliavin, 1972). Lost wallets, broken grocery bags, and stranded motorists who phone for help also abound in the literature (e.g., Gaertner & Bickman, 1971). All these rescue settings have in common the fact that the need is situation-specific, and observers must respond by giving of their time, and possibly physical strength, in order to help. Because of their inherent complexity, few such studies have been conducted with children (for an exception, see Staub, 1971).

Sharing situations, however, have ordinarily involved interacting children, one of whom is given some goods and the other is not (e.g., candy). The "rich" child is then provided with an opportunity to share the bounty with the other child (e.g., Staub & Sherk, 1970). One variation on this procedure is to tell the "rich" children of other, nonpresent children whom they can share their goods with (e.g., Cialdini & Kenrick, 1976; Ugurel-

Semin, 1952). Sharing situations have in common the fact that the person with whom the child is to share is not presented as needy in general, but only with respect to the goods to be distributed.

The common element in donation studies is the symbolic presentation of some chronically needy segment of the population (e.g., crippled children, orphans). Although they could presumably ask for the donation themselves, the needy individuals are ordinarily introduced either pictorially (e.g., a March of Dimes can) or verbally by the experimenter or model (e.g., Grusec & Skubiski, 1970; Midlarsky, Bryan, & Brickman, 1973). The majority of such studies have been conducted with children who were asked to donate out of their game winnings. Thus, in both sharing and donation settings, there are usually only quantitative differences in the dependent measure (i.e., how much is given), whereas in rescue situations, qualitative differences are possible as well (e.g., the type of help given).

Why should these diverse types of response be treated as homologous under the heading of prosocial behavior? It appears to us that their bond lies in their all being responses to another person's need and the presumed uniformity of the processes that the presentation of need stimuli precipitate. The first of these processes is need awareness.

NEED AWARENESS

How do we become aware of another person's need for help? We indicated earlier that need awareness is an inferential process. We see a given social situation and infer that there is someone who needs our help. The process invoked to explain how inferences are drawn and result in need awareness has usually been that of role taking. The act of role taking has been conceptualized as a cognitive process in which one imaginatively transfers him- or herself into the other's perspective in order to experience what the other is presumably experiencing. For instance, Feshbach (1978) defines role taking as the "imaginative transposing of oneself into the thinking and acting of another." Shantz (1975) similarly refers to role taking as the "ability to take the position of another person and thereby infer his perspective." Selman (1976) more stringently views role taking as the coordination of one's real perspective with another's inferentially derived perspective.

Young children's inability to role take, and hence their lack of awareness of need in others, has been explained with reference to the Piagetian concept of egocentrism, defined as the inability to take divergent psychological roles (Flavell, Botkin, Fry, Wright, & Jarvis, 1968). This inability is presumed to underlie many of young children's cognitive limitations, as well as to prevent their awareness of other people's needs, thoughts, and feelings.

Specifically, egocentrism is presumed to prevent children from recognizing that others have divergent inner psychological processes and to be responsible for their being insensitive to others' need states.

From Piaget's perspective, the child's liberation from egocentrism is a gradual process that depends on both cognitive development and social interaction opportunities. The establishment of peer relations in the elementary school years facilitates the decline of egocentrism. As children become able to differentiate psychological perspectives, this ability in turn helps them in their interpersonal relationships. The ability to role take is presumed to be basic to the ability to comprehend and predict others' behavior (Hartup, 1970) and is therefore a prerequisite to adequate social interaction.

Although much has been written about role taking (e.g., Selman, 1976), 1980), we know little about how the process occurs. For instance, what initiates a role-taking episode? What information is used in the process of role taking, and how is the relevance of such information determined for the specific problem at hand? Current models of role taking (e.g., Selman, 1976, 1980) discuss transitions and stage-like progressions in the *content* of role-taking acts (i.e., variations in the inferences children draw once they engage in role taking), but they do not answer these questions about the *process* itself.

Flavell (1974) and Flavell *et al.* (1968) have presented a model of role taking that does address the process issue more directly while building on four concepts. In Flavell's model, children must first become aware of the fact that others have covert psychological processes. Second, they must become aware of the need to determine what the other person's perspective is in a given context. Third, they must determine what the other's point of view is, and last, they must use this knowledge to modify their behavior appropriately. Flavell suggests that children's inferences in role-taking situations are done via a synthesis of (a) stored knowledge about people and behavior in situations; and (b) perceptual information from overt behavior and situational cues. Although Flavell's model is elegant, it does not solve the problem of *how* role taking is done. Specifically, how do children become aware of the fact that others have covert psychological processes or what the content of these psychological processes is? The problem as we see it is that Flavel assumes as well that role taking is qualitatively a different and unique sort of inferential process.

It seems to us, however, that if role-taking inferences are based on stored knowledge and overt cues, they are analogous to other inferential processes and there would seem to be little reason to conceptualize role taking as an imaginative transposition of oneself into the other's perspective. What is role taking then? It is first of all an inferential process that uses stored knowledge. It would appear critical, then, to examine how children store knowledge about persons and events and how this knowledge is retrieved by them when they are exposed to a given social setting. Consequently, to understand need awareness, we must examine the informational sources, both stored and situational, that are available to the child for making the inference that need for help may be present.

**NEED AWARENESS AND
INFORMATION PROCESSING**

What are the informational sources that are explicitly available to the child in helping situations? First, in all three types of helping situations, it is possible to attain awareness of need in the observer by directly requesting help. In rescue situations, there are often outright expressions of need on the part of the individual who requires it (e.g., "Help! Fire!"). Similarly, in both sharing and donation situations, there are often individuals who can directly alter need awareness in others. In sharing, the interactants may explicitly convey their need for the goods to be distributed (e.g., "Can I have some too?"). In donation situations, either the victim or a representative may approach the observer specifically in order to obtain a donation (e.g., "We're collecting on behalf of crippled children. Would you like to give?").

Ordinarily it is assumed that once a direct request for help has been made, awareness of need is equivalent in all those to whom the request is delivered. Consequently, when young children are found less likely to help under direct request conditions, developmental differences are explained as being due to the increasing socialization to altruism of older children. It is possible, however, that differences in need awareness may exist even when direct requests are involved. For instance, young children may not know why orphans or crippled children need money or what their donation would do to alleviate the need (i.e., do orphans stop being orphans when you give them money?). The possibility that differences in the perception of needy people produce variations in need awareness and underlie developmental differences in helping has not been examined. Nonetheless, it is clear that direct requests for help are the most effective means of attaining need awareness.

What informational sources are available to the child when no direct requests for help are made in helping contexts? Rescue situations that do not involve outright expressions of need ordinarily contain clear situational cues that convey the need. The sight of a person falling, a stranded motorist, and a carton of eggs breaking all convey the need for help. Similarly, in donation situations, the individual can become aware of need by observation, without an explicit request on anyone's part (e.g., seeing someone disheveled sitting on the sidewalk with a tin can beside him). Even more illustrative is the case of beggars who expose a crippled limb as if to say "This is why I need your help." What is it about these situations that conveys the need for help even though there is no direct request for help? As well, does the observer's becoming aware of need in these contexts also imply that he or she understands how the need can be alleviated? Current models of helping do not appear to answer these questions.

We would like to suggest that awareness of need in others is based on the understanding of *situations*. Our contention is that the inference of need in others does not depend on role-taking activities but on information retrieval processes that are initiated by situational stimuli. Specifically, we contend that the observation of social stimuli such as another person's behavior in a given setting initiates cognitive processes in which the observer attempts to match the observed event with some prestored chunk of stereotyped knowledge. In many ways, this stereotyped knowledge (often called a prototype) is analogous to a preexisting theoretical structure (Rumelhart & Ortony, 1977). Once the appropriate knowledge store or theoretical structure is accessed, the observer is in possession of adjunct information that has either been prestored or inferentially derived, and that is relevant to the situation. This adjunct knowledge may include information about the motivation of actors, the internal psychological processes they would experience as a consequence of either achieving or failing to achieve the goal that motivated their behavior, and knowledge about how goal attainment can be facilitated or circumvented. Becoming aware of need, then, can be thought of as the problem of finding appropriate matches among prestored knowledge structures and observed events. From the current perspective, need awareness depends on the scope of these prestored knowledge structures and the adjunct information they yield once accessed.

We will now elaborate on this viewpoint with reference to research and theorizing in artificial intelligence and human information processing. We will start with Bobrow and Norman (1975), who have recently discussed stimulus-initiated information processing as an "event-driven schema." Within this perspective, schemata are knowledge structures that specify typical relationships between events, behavior, objects, and persons. Bobrow, Norman, Rumelhart, and Ortony argue that all input data (i.e., environmental stimuli that are perceived) automatically invoke processing activity, and that all such input must be accounted for. Within this framework, being accounted for means that the individual must find a context of interpretation for the stimuli being processed. For most human actions, the context of interpretation is found by fitting actions to a goal that seems to be logically implicated (Bruce, 1975; Lichtenstein & Brewer, 1980; Schmidt, Sridharan, & Goodson, 1978). Helping situations are usually situations in which the goal of an individual has been frustrated, and giving help could presumably bring the individual closer to his or her goal. Need awareness, then, is essentially the understanding of the intended goal, awareness of the existence of a frustrator, and an understanding that the goal could be approximated through human action.

In any context, then, the amount of processing to which an input event is subject depends on the speed with which the individual finds an interpretational context or schema for the stimulus events and the total processing load on the system. In general, the first interpretational context into which events can be embedded will be accepted. When this context is proved to be inadequate, the interpretation can then be expanded or modified by reanalyzing the inferred goal (e.g., opening the refrigerator door is usually a prelude to eating, but can serve to initiate cooking, baking, or cleaning activity).

From this perspective, the situation itself creates awareness of need by initiating information processing activities. As part of the individual's processing of stimuli, situation-related scripts are accessed. Scripts are structures of knowledge consisting of a coherent sequence of actions and events expected by the individual in goal-seeking contexts that tend to recur, and involve the individual either as a participant or as an observer (Abelson, 1976). Schank and Abelson (1977) suggest that understanding is knowledge-based in that to understand the actions that are going on in a given context, the person must have been in that situation before (cf. Hoffman, 1975).[1] The actions of others only make sense if "they are part of a stored pattern of actions that have previously been experienced [p. 67]." Consequently, understanding is a process by which people match what they see and hear to prestored groupings of actions that they have already experienced.

Schank and Abelson assume not only that information is stored in episodic form but that it is also acquired that way. Thus, when children enter novel situations, they immediately assume that the event sequence is a script, and expect it to recur in the same way on subsequent occasions.[2] As a consequence, the definition of the object is not only its physical description but its place in the script sequence of which it formed a part. Schank and Abelson claim that "first experiences with objects tend to define the object by establishing an initial script. This serves as the basis of an adult script that evolves from it [p. 225]."

The understanding of scripts and the formation of expectations about

1. Vicarious experience with situations would of course also serve the same function (e.g., hearing others describe their experiences, seeing events portrayed on television).
2. Notice that this is quite similar to the Piagetian concept of assimilation.

likely events are based on the understanding of human goals. Future actions are predicted and understood in terms of the goals inferred to be active in the situation. As Bransford and McCarrell (1974) have illustrated, the sorting of cloths into piles of whites and nonwhites only makes sense if we understand the goal of washing in such a fashion as to prevent colors from running. Since most of the goals that activate mundane behavior are not biological, the learning of such goals is a developmental phenomenon. Thus, we learn achievement goals, enjoyment goals, and instrumental goals that are only preconditions to satisfying more distant goals. Schank and Wilensky (1978) also identify preservation goals (P-Goals), which are set up to handle serious and imminent threats to valued persons and objects. Examples of such goals are P-Health, P-Property. The arousal of such goals is assumed to preempt any lesser goals the individual may have had in the situation prior to the activation of P-Goals. We would not understand an ambulance driver who stopped on an emergency call to buy tickets to a football game. Schank and Abelson (1977) suggest that the means for realizing P-Goals are scripts such as $Ambulance, $Fire extinguisher (where $ stands for script). The failure of P-Goals to be realized is understood to lead to strong emotional reactions, the strength of which is determined by the value and type of object affected.

The set of goals that individuals have can be ranked in terms of their normative importance to a prototypical member of any given culture. Carbonell (1980) has recently suggested that these goals can be presented as a goal tree, and that different personality types are really expressions of deviations between a socially defined normative goal tree and the ordering of goals by the particular personality type. As well, personality types set up expectations for the planning strategies that will be selected by personality types in given goal-oriented settings and their responses to the failure or success of their strategies. Socialization teaches us the normative goal tree in our culture and the definition of personality types that deviate from normative goal trees. Hence, if we know that certain people are ambitious, we can infer how they will rank order their goals, how they will behave in a given setting and how they will react in the face of obstacles (e.g., the play *What Makes Sammy Run*, the book *The Apprenticeship of Duddy Kravitz*.)

Because individuals can infer the plans of others by observing their behavior, they can detect obstacles in others' plans (Allen & Perrault, 1980). Obstacles, in this context, are goals that the other can probably not achieve without assistance. Helpful behavior can then be conceptualized as an observer's assuming the goal of overcoming an obstacle in the other's goal plan. Engaging in such behavior requires the individual to reconstruct the plan of the other person, based on the other's actions. This process depends on both the observer's knowledge of how plans are constructed and original beliefs about what goals the other is likely to have in the first place.

Whereas the above theorists have not elaborated how inferences about others' affective reactions are drawn, in his model of commonsense algorithmic knowledge—that is, knowledge about actions, states, and causality in mundane activities—Rieger (1976) has advanced the idea of inducement networks, whose purpose is to determine for a given event or state those internal psychological states that could be induced in an actor as a consequence of the event. Such networks relate what an actor experiences to what he or she might feel internally as a reaction to those experiences. Rieger suggests that as each new thought enters, the observer applies the appropriate inducement networks to it across all potential actors in the situation. The inducement network selectively probes relevant aspects of the situation by asking questions that can then constrain the alternative affective reactions that are plausible in that setting (cf. Anderson & Pichert, 1978; Fiske, Taylor, Etcoff & Laufer, 1979).

Rieger provides the example of "Igor kisses Natasha" with Boris as the observer. In attempting to find the psychological reactions to this scene, the inducement network will question what the emotional ties between the three are (e.g., Boris loves Natasha who loves Igor), how old they are (e.g., jealousy may be an age-linked affect), and other relevant questions. The inducement network for Boris' mental state will take his emotional ties to Natasha into account, and hence may infer jealousy on his part. The inducement network for Natasha's mental state will not take her relationship with Boris into account but rather her relationship with Igor. Rieger suggests that the information that is thereby derived is then fed into prediction networks that relate the internal state of actors to new goals they may want to reach as a function of their inferred affective state.

In Rieger's example, we would not be surprised if Boris reacted to the above scene with a subsequent murder attempt. Why not? Schmidt and his colleagues have suggested that understanding requires the activation of three domains of knowledge—knowledge about persons, the world, and about plans. Observers have commonsense theories about the kind of psychological states that activate persons to choose certain goals. These commonsense theories contain rules which specify the feelings, sentiments, needs, etc. that humans believe motivate the pursuit of particular goals. These rules of motivation form part of the knowledge kept in the person domain and are accessed to comprehend and predict human action.[3]

Inducement networks, then, are activated by the need to predict others' behavior, and depend on such prestored commonsense theories about how people react in certain situations. Notice that from this perspective, the

3. Schmidt's concept of commonsense theories is quite similar to the concept of implicit personality theory (Schneider, 1973), which has had a fairly long history in social psychology.

inferences drawn by actors and observers need not be different from each other, as long as the informational store on which the inferences are based is similar. In Rieger's example of the perpetual triangle, we would be unable to infer jealously on the part of Boris unless we had information about his sentiments toward Natasha. Ordinarily, however, observers and actors have different information stored and hence their inferences may differ.

How does all the above relate to helping situations: First, helping situations can be conceptualized as activators of preservation goals in the actor. Whenever they are exposed to a social setting, observers who process the situation access situational scripts that may contain information about the other's need for help, the preservation goals in the situation, the means for the attainment of the goals, and inducement network information about the emotional reactions of the actor whose P-Goal has been activated.

We are suggesting, then, that need awareness is reached through the accessing of stored situational information which provides an interpretational context for the sequence of actions and goals in the situation. Thus, need awareness is not dependent on imaginative attempts to understand what the other is thinking, feeling, or experiencing. We "simply know" that help is needed because of previously stored information that is accessed by exposure to the relevant scene. We do not need to put ourselves into the other's place, try to understand what he or she feels, and then conclude that help is needed.

For instance, on seeing a child with a broken doll, we may access a "children cry over broken objects" script. The script may tell us what to do in general, but it will not tell us what to do for this particular child in order to stop his or her crying. The success of the helping attempt may then depend on additional nonscripted knowledge about the specific setting and individual in question. For instance, children who did not have the information that substituting other attractive toys may make the other feel better would be unable to respond by bringing the crying child a teddy bear. Furthermore, as Flavell suggests, stored knowledge about the particular target person can be used to decide how best to solve the problem (e.g., "Billy doesn't like stuffed toys. I'd better get a train"). Thus, the difference between a child who can stop the other's tears by finding the appropriate placating object and one that is unable to do so may not lie in differential need awareness (cf. Hoffman, 1975), but rather in the richness of the given observer's script repertoire and the ability to relate scripted to script-relevant information.

How do inducement networks differ from role taking processes? Inducement networks use *general* knowledge about people's motives and reactions. This knowledge is presumed to be stored and to be activated when the need to predict the internal psychological reactions of others arises. Although this viewpoint is similar in some respects to that of Flavell *et al.* (1968), it is quite different from most formulations of role taking as dependent on analogical operations in which one imaginatively transfers him- or herself into the other's perspective in order to experience what the other is experiencing. Ordinarily, role taking is conceptualized as an "as if" process in that the child attempts to imagine what he or she would experience in the other's position. From an inducement network perspective, no analogical transposition is required. Children simply "consult" their activated stored knowledge in order to find an appropriate experience, given the current situation. Children may, of course, be less likely to activate inducement networks (cf. Flavell, 1974) and, second, they may be limited in their available memory store and hence in the information that inducement networks can yield if they are applied.

As children develop, they build up scripts for helping situations (Abelson, 1975). These scripts develop through the child's own personal experience and through vicarious experiences. Obviously, the more experience a child has with a given situation, the more likely he or she is to have a script for it and hence to become aware of need in it. The finding that children's familiarity with situations facilitates their recognition of need and emotion in others (Shantz, 1975) may well be a function of script development as well.

Children's scripts may not only differ in quantity but in their scope. Thus, children would be expected to be much less knowledgable about the types of help that can be given in many situations. This would be expected to lead to developmental differences in help giving (e.g., Green & Schneider, 1974), even when need awareness is equivalent across the ages tested.

As well, it is highly likely that not only do children process situational cues differently, but that they are less sensitive to those cues that are interpreted as need cues by adults. For instance, in research in which the needy individual is portrayed pictorially, there is an assumption that the child processes the need cues in the picture in the same manner as do adults. It may well be, however, that children do not perceive such cues (e.g., ragged cloths, gaunt cheeks) as indicative of need, and that socialization teaches them this correlative information. In other words, not only do children have a limited script repertoire, but need scripts may not be accessed by exposing children to the same stimuli that do call up such scripts in adults.

Let us now summarize this section on need awareness. We have been arguing that need awareness is attained through the processing of stimulus situations and the accessing of situation-related scripts. These scripts contain adjunct information that informs the observer about the state of need and the possible paths by which such need can be alleviated. To the extent that such scripts are less available to younger children, we would expect them to become less aware of need than older children. Presumably awareness of need can be stimulated through both direct and indirect exposure to need situations. Since scripts are based on one's experiences, individual differences in script formation would be expected and would lead to individual differences in need awareness. Nonetheless, many scripts are "culturally overlearned" (Abelson, 1976) and are virtually universal within any given culture. Hence, there should be much overlap in general expectations for how others will behave and react in given settings.

VICARIOUS AROUSAL IN HELPING CONTEXTS

It is commonly accepted that helping in rescue situations is mediated by empathy, commonly defined as an emotional reaction to another person's emotional experience (e.g., Berger, 1962; Feshbach, 1978; Stotland, 1969). Empathy is presumed to be a learned response. Two major explanations for its development have been offered. Aronfreed (1968) has posited a conditioning theory of the development of empathy. Within this approach, there is an implicit assumption that need awareness is a nondevelopmental phenomenon. That is, it is assumed that awareness of another's experiencing of distress is only limited by one's own experiencing of distress in similar settings but not by one's cognitive developmental level.

Aronfreed argues that need concern arises as a consequence of a history of repeated pairings of the child's own distress with that of another's distress. As children learn that the suffering of others often foreshadows their own suffering, they develop an emotional reaction to the distress cues emitted by others. This vicarious reaction, which Aronfreed calls empathy, eventually comes to be experienced by children even when they do not anticipate the other's distress to have any implications for their own future. As Aronfreed (1968) states, "the cues which transmit the experience of others will acquire their own independent value for the elicitation of changes in the child's affectivity under conditions where these are no longer perceived by the child as signals of other events which it will experience directly [p. 111]." Since this empathic experience is aversive, altruistic behavior is engaged in to reduce the empathic reaction that the child experiences at the sight of the other's distress.

Hoffman (1975, 1976), in his theory of altruistic motivation, builds on Aronfreed's conditioning analysis of empathy development, but also tries to account for developmental differences in need awareness. First, Hoffman argues that young children can only react to distress cues they have emitted in the past. Consequently, need awareness in young children is limited to those situations the child is familiar with through past experience. Hoffman suggests that the surface cues associated with the elements of children's own past determine their awareness of need. From this perspective, young children project onto others on the basis of their own experiences but do so by using situational cues in the need context. Only in preadolescence does Hoffman suggest that children are able to transcend the situational cues and become aware of need states that are not reflected in the immediate situation. Hoffman also argues that egocentrism is responsible for the young child's inability to transcend the situation in inferring need in others.

In attempting to account for need concern, Hoffman, in opposition to Aronfreed, distinguishes between empathic and sympathetic distress. Empathic distress is an automatic reaction to others' distress cues. With the development of role taking and the ability to understand others' distress, Hoffman suggests that sympathetic distress develops. According to Hoffman, sympathetic distress is a transformed version of empathic distress, so that whereas the motivation for helping in empathic distress is hedonistic, to relieve one's own distress, in sympathetic distress the motivation is to relieve the other's distress. Hoffman attempts to explain this transition by using the concept of role taking and presents anecdotes of young children who attempt to reduce others' distress by providing objects that reduce their own distress. Only older children who can presumably role take in a mature fashion can apparently find more appropriate objects to relieve the other's distress. This distinction seems tenuous, however, since, as Hoffman admits, the affective aspect of the distress in the child is the same, the only distinction is that the child experiencing sympathetic distress uses new inputs "as specific information about which acts can alleviate the other's distress and which cannot [p. 146]." From our viewpoint, the difference between the two types of distress would appear to be only in the success of the helping act taken to relieve the distress and would seem to be accountable for by script development. Nonetheless, as in Aronfreed's approach, Hoffman assumes that there is an aversive state that helping is presumed to reduce. Once the other's distress cues are no longer being emitted, the vicarious distress experienced by the child is reduced, and helping is thereby reinforced. From Hoffman's perspective, the ability to role take becomes critical for the child's ability to experience sympathetic distress.

We argued earlier that role taking is not necessary for need awareness since such awareness can be attained by processing of situational cues and accessing of situation-related scripts. If role taking does not need to occur for the experience of need awareness, then sympathetic distress cannot be a function of role-taking ability. How, then, is sympathetic distress produced? It is our contention that need situations can be responded to without any reference to the other's distress state. We will present data to demonstrate that the processing of stimuli produces changes in arousal level *independently* of any effects these stimuli may have had on the emotional reactions of others. Hence empathy would not appear to be dependent on others' emotional reactions, whether displayed or inferred.

In our discussion of need awareness, we argued that environmental stimuli automatically invoke processing, the aim of which is to find an interpretational context for the observed events and to allow for the prediction of behavior. In the area of research known as social psychophysiology (Harris & Katkin, 1975), there is evidence that both direct and indirect exposure to stimuli produce changes in physiological arousal and cardiac rate in particular. Thus, subjects who view unpleasant slides of homicides and car wrecks (Hare, Wood, Britain, & Shadman, 1971; Libby, Lacey, & Lacey, 1973), or nudes (Burdick, 1978), listen to white noise, or "empathize" to a tape about a dying man (Lacey, Kagan, Lacey, & Moss, 1963) all evidence cardiac deceleration. Demands to do mental arithmetic in response to visually presented material (Kahneman, Tursky, Shapiro, & Crider, 1979; Tursky, Schwartz, & Crider, 1970), the generation of thoughts to affective-valued words like murder and sex (May & Johnson, 1973; Schwartz, 1971), and other cognitive tasks all lead to significant heart rate acceleration. The amount of heart rate acceleration in response to cognitive tasks is apparently a function of the difficulty of the cognitive task, such that the more difficult the task, the greater the acceleration. On the other hand, the direction of change cannot be predicted in advance, since there is evidence that subjects may respond differentially to the same stimuli (e.g., Lacey & Lacey, 1970; Valins, 1967). For instance, subjects who are afraid of spiders show cardiac acceleration when they view slides of spiders, whereas those who are not afraid of spiders show cardiac deceleration (Hare, 1973).

In all discussions of empathy, it is assumed that vicariously experienced arousal is similar to the arousal experienced directly by subjects who are suffering, and that it is this similarity in arousal that serves to motivate helping behavior. We are arguing, however, that the arousal experienced in need-related contexts is not specific to the other's need state. If our argument is valid, it would be expected that watching another person in distress would lead to a divergent arousal pattern than either being in distress or imagining oneself in distress. On the other hand, an empathy argument would suggest that imagining oneself in distress and watching another person's real distress would yield similar arousal patterns. In support of our point of view, it has been found that experiencing or imagining one's own suffering leads to cardiac acceleration, whereas watching another person's suffering leads to cardiac deceleration (Barber & Hahn, 1964; Craig, 1968).[4] In general, all cognitive processing has been found to lead to cardiac acceleration, and it has been suggested that an increase in heart rate facilitates

---

4. Although we do not mean to imply that there is no processing during observation, there seems to be a clear distinction between the cardiac pattern during intake of stimulus information and the processing of such information, the former leading to deceleration and the latter to acceleration (Lacey et al., 1963).

information processing (Cacioppo, Sandman, & Walker, 1978). Moreover, imagining one's own emotional reactions to verbally depicted scenes produces an increase in heart rate (Lang, Kozak, Miller, Levin, & McLean, 1980).

Given that all imaginative activity seems to produce an increase in heart rate, Stotland's (1969) finding that similar vasoconstriction patterns occur in an "imagine yourself suffering" and an "imagine him suffering" condition is not particularly surprising. We are arguing, then, that the imaginative activity engaged in does not need to focus on the other's presumed emotional experience, since imaginative activity per se, or any other cognitive activity, can equally well produce heart rate changes. For our purposes, these data are important since they indicate that physiological reactions are an *automatic* function of stimulus intake and processing.

Moreover, there is evidence that arousal has effects on both stimulus processing and subsequent retrieval from memory (Eysenck, 1975; Kleinsmith & Kaplan, 1963). Easterbrook (1959) has argued that emotional arousal has the effect of progressively restricting the use of cues in the situation. Arousal has also been found to enhance the probability of sampling information from dominant sources (Broadbent, 1971). The above suggests that arousal leads to the activation of fewer scripts by a number of dominant stimuli that are highly associated with these scripts. Furthermore, as Norman (1979) has argued, the fewer the scripts active at any time, the more processing resources remaining for those that are active, and the more quickly each can pursue its activities. Hence, we are suggesting that arousal facilitates the retrieval of highly dominant scripts and speeds up the rate at which these scripts are "read through." It is important to note in this context that all rescue studies use highly scripted need situations as stimuli (i.e., people falling and screaming).

There is some evidence consistent with our line of analysis. First, Gaertner and Dovidio (1977) measured heart rate changes in response to a simulated emergency in which someone was heard falling and screaming. In keeping with our predictions, the greater the cardiac acceleration experienced by the subjects, the more quickly subjects went to the victim's aid. In their second study, Gaertner and Dovidio attempted to alter the subjects' attributions for their arousal state by informing them that a placebo pill would increase their arousal. In our view, such misinformation should serve to hinder the accessing of situation-related scripts. Telling subjects that a pill is producing their arousal should slow down their search for relevant situation-related scripts and alter their reaction time to helping. In keeping with this interpretation, the misinformed group helped the victim significantly more slowly than the group not given the additional misinformation. An attribution explanation can explain a lower *rate* of helping in the misinformation group, but cannot account for reaction time differences. Harris and Huang (1973) also found less help in the first minute after the presentation of a screaming fallen woman by subjects who were told that their arousal was due to white noise. These data can be interpreted as indicating that misinformation about the sources of arousal serves to slow down processing of the stimulus situation, and thereby impedes retrieval of situation-related scripts that can direct subjects as to what the required helping act might be.

How does our analysis differ from an attributional one? An attributional analysis suggests that only subjects who are aroused and who attribute this arousal to the other's need state will be likely to help. From our perspective, subjects may, but need not, become aware of their changed arousal state when they access situational scripts that include both need and need-elimination information. The variations in arousal that the observer experiences and becomes aware of in such situations may then be attributed to the particular script accessed (e.g., "My heart is racing. It must be the fire alarm"). If the script accessed is one that involves need, the subject may decide to help the other person. If the script accessed is one that does not involve need (e.g., "My heart is racing. It's probably the blond I saw in the window before the fire alarm went off"), it is highly unlikely that even aroused subjects will help.

Folkman, Schaefer, and Lazarus (1979) suggest that when we hear the scream "Fire!" there is a concomitant change in arousal since "we recognize instantly through experience that the alarm means danger [p. 271]." We would argue that the recognition of danger is subsequent to the accessing of a "fire" script. This script, plus the adjunct information associated with it, may contain sufficient information to make the experienced arousal attributable logically to the situational context.

Whether or not the changed arousal is attributed to the situational context depends on many factors, including the observer's script repertoire (i.e., does he or she have a script that links the current situation to arousal states?), the richness of the scripts accessed, the observer's awareness of a changed arousal state, and the likelihood of his or her engaging in a causal search process as a consequence of such awareness.

The sequence we posit as occurring under arousal conditions, then, is as follows. First, the processing of complex stimuli produces physiological changes that the observer experiences and may, or may not, be aware of. Second, arousal serves to facilitate retrieval of situation-related scripts. The accessing of scripts involving P-Goals increases arousal, and most probably serves to delimit the number of scripts that are activated. Third, the observer may attribute his or her changed arousal state to the particular script accessed. If the individual attributes his or her changed arousal to a script that contains need and need elimination information, the individual may become motivated to help the other person.[5] We do not wish to imply, however, that the self-attribution of arousal to need-related scripts is a necessary part of the sequence, only that it is a possible or concomitant one.

This analysis of the role of arousal in helping has serious developmental implications. First, whereas there is evidence that children also experience cardiac changes to both perceptual and cognitive tasks (Elliott, 1966; Jennings, 1971), we do not know how such arousal changes affect their retrieval of situation-related scripts. Given that scripts become more coherent over time, arousal may interfere with the accessing of scripts that are not well formed. Thus, whereas the argument has been made that adults retrieve information in an all-or-none fashion from a single location (Johnson, 1972), the same may not be true of children who are aroused. Second, we have no evidence as to whether or not children actually become aroused in those settings in which P-Goals are involved and adults do evidence arousal. Third, we do not know how likely children are to become aware of their changed arousal states or to engage in a causal search process in order to attribute the arousal. Whereas Abelson (1976) has argued that scripts are coded for experienced affect, young children appear to have relatively few affectively coded scripts (Karniol, Note 1). As a consequence, they may be less able to find appropriate situational scripts to account for their changed arousal state, even if such arousal does in fact occur. Because of the fact that most of the processes we have been discussing would be expected to be developmental ones, differences in prosocial behavior may well reflect the development of these processes.

DECIDING TO HELP

Assuming that subjects can access the appropriate situation-related scripts and that these scripts do inform them what the needed ameliorative act would be, what is the motivational mechanism that induces subjects to help the other person? From a script-theoretic point of view, the decision to help another person must be linked to "something" that has been activated by the processing activity in which the subject has engaged. This "something," we suggest, is the self-schema (Markus, 1977). The self-schema is defined as a "cognitive generalization about the self, derived from past experience, that organizes and guides the processing of self-related informa-

---

5. From this line of analysis, the motivation to help is not a function of the need to reduce arousal but, as we shall elaborate subsequently, it is the outcome of involvement of the self-system by arousal.

tion [p. 64]." Bower and Gilligan (1979) suggest that the self is a cognitive structure that is active at the time of data input and data retrieval. Events in the world not only serve to activate stored episodic information, but this episodic information can then activate self-related information. This activation of self-related information is evident in people's tendency to relate information to themselves (e.g., "Your story reminds me of the time I . . ."). As Rogers and his colleagues have recently noted (Rogers, Kuiper, & Kirker, 1977), "the self acts as a background or setting against which incoming data is interpreted or coded [p. 678]."

How does situational information activate the self-schema? Bower suggests that the same networks are used to record both specific episodic information and generic information about the self. If a person has a self-schema of being kind, he or she is able to retrieve episodes of kindness in the past (e.g., "I helped the lady with the parcels last week"). Similarly, episodes and scripts can activate the self-schema if they have links to generic descriptive terms that are part of the self-schema. Bower gives the example illustrated in Figure 10.1. Thus, an episode of helping an old woman is generically described as being kind and the self-schema of "kindness," can be activated by the episode. Assuming that one had a self-schema of being kind, activation of episodes that are semantically defined as involving kindness should also activate the kindness self-schema. Only when the person has a "kindness" self-schema (or some other generic description of the self

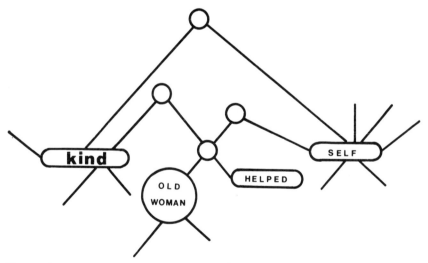

Figure 10.1. **The hypothetical structure of a kindness self-schema (adapted from Bower & Gilligan, 1979).**

that can relate to helping—e.g., moral, generous, sympathetic) and that schema is activated by the processing of situational information thereby yielding appropriate scripts, will the person be likely to help. To the extent that individuals differ in their use of generic labels for their self and for situations, individual differences in helping will arise.

Moreover, persons who do not have links between the self-schema and the category of kindness—called aschematic by Markus—would not access a self-schema when episodes of kindness occur. As well, individuals may not have a generic description of kindness linked to episodes that are so defined by most people. Hence, both types of individuals would be unlikely to help others in need. Of course, there is an assumption above that people want to maintain behavior that is consistent with certain self-schemata.

Evidence for the activation of self-schemata by arousal comes from recent studies on self-awareness. Fenigstein and Carver (1978) found that subjects who were aware of their heartbeats took longer to say the names of the colors on a Stroop color test containing self-relevant words printed in different colors. This finding suggests that self-relevant aspects of memory are activated by awareness of arousal. Yet another study (Wegner & Giuliano, 1980) that measured heart rate found that subjects who were more aroused used more personal pronouns on a sentence completion task. The latter authors suggest that changes in arousal initiate an epistemic search that scans stimuli that could produce emotions in the self and memories of such stimuli, as well as emotion-specific internal sensations. Such a search ordinarily terminates rapidly, since "stimulus conditions indicate clearly how the arousal is to be construed [p. 720]."

Direct evidence for the role of self-schemata in helping comes from a misattribution study (Coke, Batson, & McDavis, 1978). In this study, subjects were given false feedback about their arousal to a taped request for volunteer subjects. Those subjects who were misinformed that they were aroused indicated that they were softhearted, empathic, warm, concerned, and compassionate as opposed to upset, troubled, or alarmed. It appears that subjects informed about their state of arousal sought generic descriptions about their self that would account for their apparent arousal. People who are compassionate, warm, etc., would be expected to experience arousal in need-related situations. Thus, experiencing arousal in need-related contexts activated these subjects' self-schema for being the kind of individuals who react to other people in need. Activation of the self-schema subsequently would be expected to lead these subjects to help. As Coke and his colleagues did in fact find, greater helping was evident only in those subjects who were aroused and whose self-schema of kindness was activated. Aroused subjects who did not have their "kindness" schema activated did not offer to help the needy individual.

This view of the role of self-schemata in helping is consistent with a recent model (Nelson, 1978) of children's conceptual structure. Nelson argues that the self is the central core of young children's memory since "the conceptual network of the young child is derived from personal experience [p. 70]." This structure relates the self to sets of objects, people, and settings by way of particular functions or actions the self performs on them. Wood (1976) has also argued that children use the self as a reference for classifying episodes. Thus, they have labels for situations by the type of behavior that is appropriate for each situation. "Be careful," "be forceful," and "be concerned" are generic descriptions that the child uses to classify situations. In other words, it is the self's action that provides the common bond between diverse situations that would not otherwise be labeled in the same manner.

The above suggests that self-schemata can be activated not only when arousal is experienced but also whenever cues serve to focus attention to the self. As Carver (1979) has recently argued, if the schemata that the environmental stimuli activate have an implication for self, self-schemata are accessed by the very process of classifying the environmental input. In keeping with this, a number of studies have found that self-relevant memory can be activated by directing attention to the self (Geller & Shaver, 1976) and that self-reports that are given under self-focus are much more accurate (Pryor, Gibbons, Wicklund, Fazio, & Hood, 1977; Scheier, Buss, & Buss, 1978). Presumably, self-attention produces not only activation of self-relevant memory but also leads to more thorough or veridical access to such memory.

This analysis of the role of self-schemata has ramifications for the development of prosocial behavior. First, it suggests that children must learn generic labels for situations and actions as well as for the self. It is clear that certain generic labels are socially recommended for adoption whereas others are not. Children learn which generic labels are considered important for them to apply to themselves and what behaviors lead to the application of such labels by others (Bem, 1981). Horrocks and Jackson (1972) suggest that such labeling is dependent on socialization practices of parents and is dependent on the child's ability to adapt the parents' use of such generic labels. The importance of affective labeling in particular has been discussed by Gold (1976), who found that children identified as having difficulties in self-control showed a significant deficit in affective labeling. Gold argues that parental socialization practices are critical for the development of children's appropriate labeling of affective states and situations that induce them. Parents who expose children to conflicting labels, or inappropriate labels, may enhance the likelihood of behavior disorders in children.

Livesley and Bromley (1973) have documented children's lack of usage of generic labels to describe themselves. In fact, such use was hardly evident until after the age of 10. There was, however, a tendency to describe others by using generic labels associated with kindness and helpfulness from age 7 onward. The above suggests that helping in younger children is not a function of self-schema activation since such self-schemata are apparently not available, but develop with age.

This interpretation is supported by a recent study (Grusec & Redler, 1980) in which children who were told that *they*, as opposed to their actions, were helpful and nice were found to be significantly more altruistic. This effect was found for 8- and 10-year-olds but not for 5-year-olds. Thus, it seems that the provision of generic labels for the self can only induce helping if it activates the self-schema. Since in younger children the self-schema is not linked to these generic labels, the provision of such labels does not enhance prosocial behavior.

PRIMING OF SELF-SCHEMATA

We have argued that as situational stimuli are processed, they activate self schemata that may be relevant for need contexts and that may therefore lead to helping. By the same token, the prior activation of self-schemata by diverse experimental means may also lead to subsequent helping.

For instance, Isen, Shalker, Clark, and Karp (1978) have recently argued that thoughts associated with good mood or mood inducing events may serve to cue other positive material in memory. Their data, however, seem to be consistent with the notion of self-schemata activation. In fact, Isen *et al.* found that trait words that are pleasant (and presumably self-descriptive) were recalled better after winning a game. Unpleasant words that were presumably more self-descriptive when negative aspects of the self were attended to were better recalled after losing a game. This is in accord with the notion that the activation of different schemata or foci tends to lead to the recall of different elements (Anderson & Pichert, 1978).

In the same manner, asking children to reminisce about sad and happy experiences differentially leads to their helping others (Moore, Underwood, & Rosenhan, 1973). Our research (Karniol, Note 1) has shown that when children think of happy experiences, younger children's most frequent response is one involving the receipt of gifts. Hence, even children who do not yet have a self-schema of "kindness" may help others more after thinking happy thoughts by virtue of the activation of the "receiving and giving things" script. For reminiscence about sad experiences, the most common experience children tended to cite was one involving lost objects. The activation of such a schema by thinking sad thoughts would not be expected to lead to helping, since it does not serve to prime any aspect of the helping script.

In general, then, experimental manipulations may lead to increased helping to the extent that such manipulations serve to facilitate the accessing of need-related or helping scripts.

HELPING SCRIPTS IN CHILDREN

What types of scripts for helping do children actually have? Whereas no study has directly examined this issue, there is some evidence suggesting that the reason young children do not help in many experimental settings is because their helping scripts are not activated within the situation. Specifically, we would argue that for young children, both helping and sharing are activities that are engaged in (a) for your friends; and (b) to get others to like you. Only in situations wherein these variables are implicated in the situation will children offer help or share with the other person (e.g., nursery school or kindergarten where both of these factors are relevant).

Evidence for this comes from studies that have examined children's perceptions of people they like and of friendship formation. Thus, children ages 6-12 state explicitly that they only share or help people they know and like (Damon, 1977), that they share to attain and retain friends (Damon, 1977; Youniss & Volpe, 1978), and that they only expect those who like them and want to retain their friendship to help and share with them (Damon, 1977). One recent study (Strayer, Wareing, & Rushton, 1979) has also found that most spontaneous helping by preschoolers tends to be directed only toward friends.

Hence, we would argue that unless the situation is such that for some reason a friendship script has been activated or a "get others to like you" script has been activated, it is highly unlikely that children will share or help the other. In view of this, in settings in which children are required to help a stranger, we would anticipate that unless the child wants the other to like him or her, expects future interaction with the other, or expects to have the other give him or her something in return, he or she would be unlikely to help.

There is one other script for helping that children appear to have. This involves children's perceptions that from an adult authority perspective, helping is defined as being good, and if one wants to be good, one has to help these adult authorities (Selman, 1976). This would suggest that in many settings where social desirability factors are strong (e.g., many modeling studies), children's helping may well be a function of their wanting to be "nice" as defined by the adult in the setting.

CONCLUSIONS

We have outlined a model of prosocial behavior that assumes that such behavior is the outcome of information processing activities initiated by the stimulus situation. Different situations activate different schemata and scripts and hence are differentially likely to lead to helping.

First, we have suggested that need awareness is contingent on the accessing of situation-related scripts that inform us about the particular goals that have been thwarted and that we could assist in attaining. To a large extent, the awareness of need is dependent on possessing a wide repertoire of scripts that can be cued off by the observed behavioral events. There is little doubt that this is a developmental phenomenon, and hence we would expect developmental differences in need awareness.

Second, we suggested that need concern is a possible but not necessary part of the behavioral sequence in helping. The accessing of situation-related scripts induces arousal changes since cognitive activity per se produces such changes automatically. The more elaborate the cognitive activity engaged in, the more arousal change there is. As well, the more time devoted to the processing of the stimulus situation, the more likely is the individual to find a script to which the changes in arousal can be attributed. As we indicated, we have no empirical evidence regarding these issues in children.

However, we suggested that the changes in arousal that the individual experiences need not occur, and they need not be attributed to the need-related scripts for a decision to help to be made. Specifically, the individual may find a generic label for the situation. If this generic label has relevance for the self-schema, the self-schema is activated and there will then be a tendency to help in order to maintain the self-schema.[6] We thus suggest that the decision to help is dependent on the child's acquisition of generic descriptions of situations and self. To the extent that such generic descriptions are a function of development, we would argue that young children's helping undergoes a change when such generic labels are learned.

The implications of our approach are twofold. First, it suggests that to understand children's helping we must examine their scripts for helping situations. We could, for instance, use the procedure employed by Nelson (1978), who asks her subjects to tell "What happens when . . . ?" We could ask "What happens or what do you do when someone shouts for help," or "asks you for candy," or "asks you to give money to the poor," etc. It is

---

6. We do not mean to imply that a helping act will occur in every instance when the self-schema is activated. There are situational factors that can deter helping (e.g., the cost of helping, presence of others).

possible that an act of rescue, sharing, or donation is not even part of the child's script for such situations, although we are not arguing that this is the case.

Second, we are suggesting that children must learn generic descriptions for the self and for situations. Only after they have done so would we expect helping to occur in the absence of social pressure. This could be examined by asking children to describe situations that are considered "generous" or "helpful" (e.g., "Tell me a story about someone who did something 'nice', 'helpful', 'generous' "). We would expect that children, and adults, who use the same generic label for their self will behave altruistically in those situations for which they employ the same generic label. In our current research, we are investigating these issues. Overall, our model suggests that we must examine the individual's phenomenology when we are trying to predict responses to stimulus settings that involve need-related cues. To the extent that similar cultures promote a similar understanding of goal structures, lead to the activation of similar scripts, and encourage the acquisition of similar links between generic labels for the self and certain scripts, our model implies that, to understand prosocial behavior within any given culture, these cognitive structures and the relationships among them must first be elaborated.

REFERENCE NOTES

1. Karniol, R. Being happy, sad, and afraid: Children's scripts for affect inducing contexts. Unpublished manuscript, University of Tel-Aviv, 1980.

REFERENCES

Abelson, R. P. Concepts for representing mundane reality in plans. In D. G. Boborow & A. Collins (Eds.), *Representation and understanding.* New York: Academic Press, 1975.

Abelson, R. P. Script processing in attitude formation and decision making. In J. S. Carroll & J. W. Payne (Eds.), *Cognition and social behavior.* Hillsdale, N.J.: Erlbaum, 1976.

Allen, J. F., & Perrault, C. R. Analyzing intention in utterances. *Artificial Intelligence,* 1980, *15,* 143–148.

Anderson, R. C., & Pichert, J. W. Recall of previously unrecallable information following a shift in perspective. *Journal of Verbal Learning and Verbal Behavior,* 1978, *12,* 1–12.

Aronfreed, J. *Conduct and conscience: The socialization of internalized control over behavior.* New York: Academic Press, 1968.

Barber, T. X., & Hahn, K. W. Experimental studies in "hypnotic" behaviour: Physiological and subjective effects of imagined pain. *Journal of Nervous and Mental Disease,* 1964, *134,* 416–425.

Bem, S. L. Gender schema theory: A cognitive account of sex typing. *Psychological Review,* 1981, *88,* 354–364.

Berger, S. M. Conditioning through vicarious instigation. *Psychological Review,* 1962, 69, 450–466.

Bobrow, D. G., & Norman, D. A. Some principles of memory schemata. In D. G. Bobrow & A. Collins (Eds.), *Representation and understanding*. New York: Academic Press, 1975.

Bower, G. H., & Gilligan, S. G. Remembering information related to one's self. *Journal of Research in Personality*, 1979, *13*, 420–432.

Bransford, J. D., & McCarrell, N. S. A sketch of a cognitive approach to comprehension: Some thoughts about understanding what it means to comprehend. In W. B. Weimer & D. S. Palermo (Eds.), *Cognition and the symbolic process*. Hillsdale, N.J.: Erlbaum, 1974.

Broadbent, D. E. *Decision and stress*. London: Academic Press, 1971.

Bruce, B. C. Belief systems and language understanding. PBN Report No. 2973. Cambridge, Mass.: Bolt Beranek and Newman, Inc., 1975.

Burdick, J. A. Heart rate, tonic cardiac variability and evaluation. *Journal of Psychosomatic Research*, 1978, *22*, 69–77.

Cacioppo, J. T., Sandman, C. A., & Walker, B. B. The effects of operant heart rate conditioning on cognitive elaboration and attitude change. *Psychophysiology*, 1978, *22*, 330–338.

Carbonell, J. G. Towards a process model of human personality traits. *Artificial Intelligence*, 1980, *15*, 49–74.

Carver, C. S. A cybernetic model of self focus. *Journal of Personality and Social Psychology*, 1979, *37*, 1251–1281.

Charniak, E. On the use of framed knowledge in language comprehension. *Artificial Intelligence*, 1978, *11*, 225–265.

Cialdini, R. B., Kenrick, D. T. Altruism as hedonism: A social developmental perspective on the relationship on negative mood states and helping. *Journal of Personality and Social Psychology*, 1976, *34*, 907–914.

Coke, J. S., Batson, C. D., & McDavis, K. Empathic mediation of helping: A two stage model. *Journal of Personality and Social Psychology*, 1978, *36*, 752–766.

Craig, K. D. Physiological arousal as a function of imagined, vicarious, and indirect stress experiences. *Journal of Abnormal Psychology*, 1968, *73*, 513–520.

Damon, W. *The social world of the child*. San Francisco: Jossey-Bass, 1977.

Darley, J., & Batson, C. "From Jerusalem to Jericho": A study of situational and dispositional variables in helping behavior. *Journal of Personality and Social Psychology*, 1973, *27*, 100–108.

Easterbrook, J. A. The effect of emotion on cue utilization and the organization of memory. *Psychological Bulletin*, 1959, *66*, 183–201.

Elliott, R. Physiological activity and performance in children and adults. *Journal of Experimental Child Psychology*, 1966, *4*, 58–68.

Eysenck, M. W. Effects of noise, activation level, and response dominance in retrieval from memory. *Journal of Experimental Psychology: Human Learning and Memory*, 1975, *104*, 143–148.

Fenigstein, A., & Carver, C. S. Self-focusing effects of heartbeat feedback. *Journal of Personality and Social Psychology*, 1978, *36*, 1241–1250.

Feshbach, N. D. Studies of empathic behavior in children. In B. A. Maher (Ed.), *Progress in Experimental Personality Research*, Vol. 8. New York: Academic Press, 1978.

Fiske, S. T., Taylor, S. E., Etcoff, N. L., & Laufer, J. K. Imaging, empathy, and causal attribution. *Journal of Experimental Social Psychology*, 1979, *15*, 378–396.

Flavell, J. The development of inferences about others. In T. Mischel (Ed.), *Understanding other persons*. Oxford: Blackwell, 1974.

Flavell, J. H., Botkin, P. T., Fry, C. L., Wright, J. W., & Jarvis, P. E. *The development of role taking and communication skills in children*. New York: Wiley, 1968.

Folkman, S., Schaefer, C., & Lazarus, R. S. Cognitive processes as mediators of stress and coping. In V. Hamilton & D. M. Warburton (Eds.), *Human stress and cognition*. New York: Wiley, 1979.

Gaertner, S. L., & Bickman, L. Effects of race on the elicitation of helping behavior: The wrong numbers technique. *Journal of Personality and Social Psychology*, 1971, *20*, 218-222.

Gaertner, S. L., & Dovidio, J. F. The subtlety of white racism, arousal and helping behavior. *Journal of Personality and Social Psychology*, 1977, *35*, 691-700.

Geller, V., & Shaver, P. Cognitive consequences of self-awareness. *Journal of Experimental Social Psychology*, 1976, *12*, 99-108.

Gold, G. H. Affective behaviorism: A synthesis of humanism and behaviorism with children. In A. Wandersman, P. Poppen, & D. Ricks (Eds.), *Humanism and behaviorism: A dialogue and growth*. Oxford: Pergamon, 1976.

Green, F. P., & Schneider, F. W. Age differences in the behavior of boys on three measures of altruism. *Child Development*, 1974, *45*, 133.

Grusec, J. E., & Redler, E. Attribution, reinforcement, and altruism: A developmental analysis. *Developmental Psychology*, 1980, *16*, 525-534.

Grusec, J. E., & Skubiski, S. L. Model nurturance, demand characteristics of the modeling experiment and altruism. *Journal of Personality and Social Psychology*, 1970, *14*, 352-359.

Hare, R. D. Orienting and defensive responses to visual stimuli. *Psychophysiology*, 1973, *10*, 453-464.

Hare, R. D., Wood, D., Britain, S., & Shadman, J. Autonomic responses to affective visual stimulation. *Psychophysiology*, 1971, *7*, 408-417.

Harris, M. B., & Huang, L. C. Helping and the attribution process. *Journal of Social Psychology*, 1973, *90*, 291-297.

Harris, V. A., & Katkin, E. S. Primary and secondary emotional behavior: An analysis of the role of autonomic feedback on affect, arousal and attribution. *Psychological Bulletin*, 1975, *82*, 904-916.

Hartup, W. Peer interaction. In P. H. Mussen (Ed.), *Carmichael's manual of child psychology*, Vol. 2. New York: Wiley, 1970.

Hoffman, M. L. The development of altruistic motivation. In D. S. DePalma & J. M. Foley (Eds.), *Moral development*. Hillsdale, N.J.: Erlbaum, 1975.

Hoffman, M. L. Empathy, role-taking, guilt, and development of altruistic motives. In T. Lickona (Ed.), *Moral development and behavior*. New York: Holt, Rinehart, & Winston, 1976.

Horrocks, J. E., & Jackson, D. W. *Self and role: A theory of self-process and role behavior*. Boston: Houghton Mifflin, 1972.

Isen, A. M., Shalker, T. E., Clark, M., & Karp, L. Affect, accessibility of material in memory and behavior: A cognitive loop? *Journal of Personality and Social Psychology*, 1978, *36*, 1-12.

Jennings, J. R. Cardiac reactions and different developmental levels of cognitive functioning. *Psychophysiology*, 1971, *8*, 433-450.

Johnson, N. F. Organization and the concept of a memory code. In A. W. Melton & E. Martin (Eds.), *Coding processes in human memory*. Washington, D.C.: Winston & Sons, 1972.

Kahneman, D., Tursky, B., Shapiro, D., & Crider, A. Pupillary, heart rate and skin resistance during a digit transfer task. *Journal of Experimental Psychology*, 1969, *79*, 164-167.

Kleinsmith, L. J., & Kaplan, S. Paired-associate learning as a function of arousal and interpolated interval. *Journal of Experimental Psychology*, 1963, *5*, 190-193.

Lacey, J. H., Kagan, J., Lacey, B. C., & Moss, H. A. The visceral level: Situational determinants and behavioral correlates of autonomic response patterns. In P. H. Knapp (Ed.), *Expression of emotions in man*. New York: International Universities Press, 1963.

Lacey, J. H., & Lacey, B. C. Some autonomic-central nervous system interrelationships. In P. Black (Ed.), *Physiological correlates of emotion*. New York: Academic Press, 1970.

Lang, P. J., Kozak, M. J., Miller, G. A., Levin, D. N., & McLean, A., Jr., Emotional imagery, conceptual structure and pattern of somatovisceral response. *Psychophysiology,* 1980, *17,* 179–195.

Libby, W. L., Lacey, B. C., & Lacey, J. H. Pupillary and cardiac activity during visual attention. *Psychophysiology,* 1973, *8,* 433–450.

Lichtenstein, E. H., & Brewer, W. F. Memory for goal-directed events. *Cognitive Psychology,* 1980, *12,* 412–445.

Liveseley, W. J., & Bromley, D. B. *Person perception in childhood and adolescence.* New York: Wiley, 1973.

Markus, H. Self schemata and the processing of information about the self. *Journal of Personality and Social Psychology,* 1977, *35,* 63–79.

May, J. R., & Johnson, H. J. Physiological activity to internally elicited arousal and inhibitory thoughts. *Journal of Abnormal Psychology,* 1973, *82,* 239–245.

Midlarsky, E., Bryan, J. H., & Brickman, P. Aversive approval: Interactive effects of modeling and reinforcement on altruistic behavior. *Child Development,* 1973, *44,* 321–329.

Minsky, M. A. A framework for representing knowledge. In P. H. Winston (Ed.), *The psychology of computer vision.* New York: McGraw-Hill, 1975.

Moore, B. S., Underwood, B., & Rosenhan, D. L. Affect and altruism. *Developmental Psychology,* 1973, *8,* 99–104.

Nelson, K. Semantic development and the development of semantic memory. In K. E. Nelson (Ed.), *Children's language,* Vol. 1. New York: Gardner, 1978.

Norman, D. Perception, memory, and mental processes. In L. G. Nilsson (Ed.), *Perspectives on memory research.* Hillsdale, N.J.: Erlbaum, 1979.

Piliavin, J., & Piliavin, I. Effects of blood on reactions to a victim. *Journal of Personality and Social Psychology,* 1972, *23,* 353–361.

Pryor, J. B., Gibbons, F. X., Wicklund, R. A., Fazio, R., & Hood, R. Self-focused attention and self-report validity. *Journal of Personality,* 1977, *45,* 513–527.

Rieger, C. An organization of knowledge for problem solving and language comprehension. *Artificial Intelligence,* 1976, *7,* 89–127.

Rogers, T., Kuiper, N., & Kirker, W. Self reference and the encoding of personal information. *Journal of Personality and Social Psychology,* 1977, *35,* 63–79.

Rumelhart, D. E., & Ortony, A. The representation of knowledge in memory. In R. C. Anderson, R. J. Spiro, & W. E. Montague (Eds.), *Schooling and the acquisition of knowledge.* Hillsdale, N.J.: Erlbaum, 1977.

Schank, R. C., & Abelson, R. P. *Scripts, plans, and knowledge.* Hillsdale, N.J.: Erlbaum, 1977.

Schank, R. C., & Wilensky, R. A goal-directed production system for story comprehension. In D. A. Waterman & F. Hayes-Roth (Eds.), *Pattern-directed inference systems.* New York: Academic Press, 1978.

Scheier, M. F., Buss, A. H., & Buss, D. M. Self consciousness, self report of aggressiveness, and aggression. *Journal of Research in Personality,* 1978, *12,* 133–140.

Schmidt, C. F., Sridharan, N. S., & Goodson, J. L. The plan recognition problem: An intersection of psychology and artificial intelligence. *Artificial Intelligence,* 1978, *11,* 45–83.

Schneider, D. J. Implicit personality theory: A review. *Psychological Bulletin,* 1973, *79,* 294–309.

Schwartz, G. E. Cardiac responses to self induced thoughts. *Psychophysiology,* 1971, *8,* 462–467.

Selman, R. L. Social-cognitive understanding: A guide to educational and clinical practice. In T. Lickona (Ed.), *Moral development and behavior.* New York: Holt, Rinehart, & Winston, 1976.

Selman, R. L. *The growth of interpersonal understanding.* New York: Academic Press, 1980.

Shantz, C. U. The development of social cognition. In E. M. Hetherington (Ed.), *Review of child development research*, Vol. 5. Chicago: University of Chicago Press, 1975.

Staub, E. Helping a person in distress: The influence of implicit and explicit "rules" of conduct on children and adults. *Journal of Personality and Social Psychology*, 1971, *17*, 134-144.

Staub, E. *Positive social behavior and morality*, Vol. 2. New York: Academic Press, 1979.

Staub, E., & Sherk, L. Need for approval, children's sharing behavior, and reciprocity in sharing. *Child Development*, 1970, *41*, 243-253.

Stotland, E. Exploratory investigations of empathy. In L. Berkowtiz (Ed.), *Advances in experimental social psychology*, Vol. 4. New York: Academic Press, 1969.

Strayer, F. F., Wareing, E., & Rushton, J. P. Social constraints on naturally occurring preschool altruism. *Ethology and Sociobiology*, 1979, *1*, 3-11.

Tursky, B., Schwartz, G. E., & Crider, A. Differential patterns of heart rate and skin resistance changes during a mental task. *Journal of Experimental Psychology*, 1970, *83*, 451-457.

Ugurel-Semin, R. Moral behavior and moral judgment of children. *Journal of Abnormal and Social Psychology*, 1952, *47*, 463-474.

Valins, S. Emotionality and autonomic reactivity. *Journal of Experimental Research in Personality*, 1967, *2*, 41-48.

Wegner, D. M., & Guiliano, T. Arousal-induced attention to self. *Journal of Personality and Social Psychology*, 1980, *38*, 719-721.

Wood, B. S. *Children and communication*. Englewood Cliffs, N.J.: Prentice-Hall, 1976.

Youniss, J., & Volpe, J. A relational analysis of children's friendships. In W. Damon (Ed.), *New directions in child development: Social cognition*. San Francisco: Jossey-Bass, 1978.

IV

THE ROLE OF AFFECT

MARTIN L. HOFFMAN

Development of Prosocial Motivation: Empathy and Guilt

Recent years have seen intensified research interest in altruism, which may be defined generally as behavior such as helping or sharing that promotes the welfare of others without conscious regard for one's own self interest. Although a lot of the research has been done with children, there is very little theory about how altruism develops. One reason for this may be that most of the research on altruism has been carried out in a social learning tradition that assumes that altruistic responses, like other behaviors, are acquired through processes like reinforcement and imitation that remain virtually the same throughout the life cycle. With such an approach, a developmental theory may seem unnecessary.

My interest has been less in altruistic responses and more in altruistic motivation, and I have been working for several years on a developmental model that does not depend on reinforcement and imitation but on the interaction between affective and cognitive processes that change with age (Hoffman, 1963, 1970b, 1975a, 1977b). The basic concept in the model is empathy, defined as a vicarious affective response, that is, as an affective response that is more appropriate to someone else's situation than to one's own situation. This definition, the advantages of which are discussed elsewhere (Hoffman, in press–c), is unlike many others since it does not require an exact match between the observer's and the model's affect.

A second concept having prosocial motivational qualities is guilt. This is not the Freudian guilt, based on hostile impulses repressed in the past, but a more realistic response to the harm one has done to others in the present.

What follows is the most recent version of my theoretical model for the

281

THE DEVELOPMENT OF
PROSOCIAL BEHAVIOR

development of empathy, along with my current, somewhat more speculative notions about the development of guilt.

DEVELOPMENT OF EMPATHIC AND
SYMPATHETIC DISTRESS

In this theoretical model, empathy, although an affective response, has
cognitive and motivational components. The focus is on empathic
distress—the empathic response to another person's pain or discomfort—
which is pertinent to altruistic motivation, although the model may also bear
on other empathically aroused affects.

Modes of Empathic Arousal

There are at least six distinct modes of empathic arousal. They vary in
the degree to which perception and cognition are involved, in the type of
eliciting stimulus (e.g., facial, situational, symbolic), and in the amount and
kind of past experience required. They are here presented roughly in order of
their appearance developmentally.

1. *Reactive Newborn Cry.* It has long been known that infants cry to
the sound of someone else's cry. The first controlled study of this reactive cry
was done by Simner (1971), who found it in 2- and 3-day-olds. He also
established that the cry was not simply a response to a noxious physical
stimulus, since the infants did not cry as much to equally loud and intense
nonhuman sounds. There thus appears to be something especially unpleasant about the sound of the human cry. Simner's findings have been replicated in 1-day-olds by Sagi and Hoffman (1976), who report in addition
that the subject's cry is not a simple imitative vocal response lacking an
affective component. Rather, it is vigorous, intense, and indistinguishable
from the spontaneous cry of an infant who is in actual distress. No one yet
knows the reason for this reactive cry, although I can see three possible
explanations: (a) it is innate; (b) it is a primary circular reaction. Since the
infant cannot tell the difference between the sound of his or her own cry and
the sound of someone else's cry, the sound of someone else's cry produces a
cry response in the infant. The infant then cries to the sound of his or her
own cry, and so on; (c) the sound of the infant's cry is associated with his or
her own past distress—perhaps at birth. Consequently, the sound of the
infant's cry serves as a conditioned stimulus for the infant's own cry response. Since the infant cannot tell the difference between the sound of his
or her own and someone else's cry, the sound of someone else's cry may
also serve as a conditioned stimulus for the infant's cry response.

Regardless of which explanation is correct, the fact remains that infants respond to a cue of distress in others by experiencing distress themselves. This reactive cry must therefore be considered as a possible early, rudimentary precursor of empathy, though not a full empathic response since it lacks any awareness of what is happening. It is also possible that the reactive cry may actually contribute to empathic distress later on because the frequent co-occurrence of distress cues in others and actual distress in self may lead to an expectation of distress in self when one perceives distress cues in others. This leads to the next mode.

2. *Classical Conditioning.* The second mode requires some perceptual discrimination capability, and therefore appears a bit later developmentally than the reactive newborn cry. It is a type of direct classical conditioning of empathy that results from the experience of observing the distress of another person at the same time that one is having a direct experience of distress. The result is that distress cues from others become conditioned stimuli that evoke feelings of distress in the self. Aronfreed and Paskal (Note 1) demonstrated this kind of empathic conditioning with school children in the laboratory. It often occurs in real life, too, as when the mother's affective state is transferred to the infant through physical handling. For example, if the mother feels anxious or tense her body may stiffen, and the child may also experience distress. Subsequently, the mother's facial and verbal expressions that accompanied her distress can serve as conditioned stimuli that evoke distress in the child even in the absence of physical contact. Furthermore, through stimulus generalization, similar expressions by other persons may evoke distress feelings in the child.

3. *Direct Association.* The third mode was described some time ago by Humphrey (1922). When we observe people experiencing an emotion, their facial expression, voice, posture, or any other cue in the situation that reminds us of past situations in which we experienced that emotion may evoke a similar emotion in us. The usual example cited is the boy who sees another child cut himself and cry. The sight of the blood, the sound of the cry, or any cue from the victim or the situation that reminds the boy of his own past experiences of pain may evoke an empathic distress response. This mode does not require the co-occurrence of distress in self and distress cues from others. The only requirement is that the observer have *past* experiences of pain or discomfort. The feelings of distress that accompanied those past experiences are then evoked by distress cues from the victim that call up any of them. It is thus a far more general associative mechanism than the first, one which may provide the basis for a variety of distress experiences with which children, and adults as well, may empathize.

4. *Mimicry.* A fourth mode of empathic arousal was described over 70 years ago by Lipps (1906). For Lipps, empathy is an innate, isomorphic

response to another person's expression of emotion. There are two steps: The observer automatically imitates the other with slight movements in facial expression and posture ("motor mimicry"). This then creates inner kinesthetic cues in the observer that contribute (through afferent feedback) to the observer's understanding and feeling the same emotion. This conception of empathy has been neglected in the literature perhaps because it seemed too much like an instinctive explanation. There is some recent research (reviewed by Hoffman, 1977b), however, suggesting its plausibility.

5. *Symbolic Association.* The fifth mode, like the third, is based on the association between the victim's distress cues and the observer's past distress. In this case, though, the victim's distress cues evoke empathic distress not because of their physical or expressive properties but because they symbolically indicate the victim's feelings. For example, one can respond empathically to someone as a result of seeing a picture of him or her in an emotional situation, reading a letter from that person, or hearing someone else describe what happened to him or her. The empathy-eliciting cue can be an emotional label or a description of the event. This is obviously a relatively advanced mode of arousal since it requires the ability to interpret symbols. It is still largely involuntary, however, and the words or pictures serve mainly as a mediator between the victim's distress and the observer's empathic response. That is, once the observer understands the other's affective situation—once he or she reads the letter, for example—the person can usually be expected to respond empathically.

6. *Role Taking.* The previous modes are largely involuntary and minimally cognitive, requiring only enough perceptual and cognitive discrimination ability to detect the relevant cues from the model (e.g., mimicry) or the model's situation (e.g., association). The sixth mode is different in that it usually involves a deliberate cognitive act of imagining oneself in another's place. More specifically, the research suggests that empathic affect is most likely to be generated when we try to imagine how we would feel if the stimuli impinging on the other person were impinging on us (Stotland, 1969). Why should this happen? I would suggest that associative connections are made between the stimuli impinging on the model and similar stimulus events in the observer's own past. That is, imagining oneself in the other's place may produce an empathic response because it has the power to evoke associations with real events in one's own past in which one actually experienced the emotion in question. The process may thus have something in common with the associative modes discussed previously. The important difference is that in this case the evoking stimulus is the mental representation of oneself in the other's situation. That is, the arousal is triggered by a cognitive restructuring or transformation of events (what is happening to the other is viewed as happening to the self) and thus is more subject to conscious control.

These six modes of empathic arousal may not form a stage sequence in the sense of each one encompassing and replacing the preceding. The first mode typically drops out after infancy, owing to controls against crying, although even adults feel sad when they hear a cry and some adults even feel like crying themselves, though they usually control it. The sixth mode, being deliberate, may be relatively infrequent—used at times, for example, by parents and therapists who believe it is important to feel some of what the child or patient is feeling. The intermediate four modes, however, enter in at different points in development and may continue to operate through the life-span.

Which of these arousal modes operate in a given situation presumably depends on the cues that are salient. If the expressive cues from the victim are salient, then mimicry may be the predominant mode. Conditioning and association are apt to predominate when situational cues are salient. Cues based on pictorial or verbal communication will of course require symbolic association. And, in any of these cases, the possibility exists for additional arousal if the observer gives thought to how he or she would feel in the other's situation. In other words, an arousal mode exists for whatever type of cue about the other's feelings may be present, and mulitple cues may increase the level of arousal (although they may at times work at cross purposes, as noted later). This is important because it indicates that empathy may be an overdetermined response in humans. Empathy may also be a self-reinforcing response. That is, as already mentioned in connection with the newborn's reactive cry, every time we empathize with someone in distress the co-occurrence of our own distress and distress cues from another person may increase the strength of the connection between the cues of another's distress and our own empathic response, thus increasing the likelihood in the future that distress in others will be accompanied by empathic distress in ourselves. Another aspect of these arousal modes worth noting is that most of them require very little cognitive processing and are largely involuntary. With several such arousal modes in the human repertoire, the evidence that empathy may be a universal response that had survival value in human evolution should perhaps not be surprising (Hoffman, 1981).

Cognitive Transformation and Developmental Levels of Empathy

Although empathy may usually be aroused by the predominantly simple, involuntary mechanisms just described, the subjective experience of empathy is rather complex. The literature on empathy often stops with the idea that the observer feels vicariously what the model feels through direct experience. This is the essential feature of empathy, to be sure, but a mature adult who observes another person in pain, for example, may also feel sympathy for the victim and a desire to reduce the victim's distress. More about that later. For now, the important point is that the experience of empathy also has a significant cognitive component, at least in older children and adults. Thus, regardless of the arousal mechanism, mature empathizers know that their arousal is due to a stimulus event that is impinging on someone else, and they have some idea of what the other person is feeling. Young children who lack the distinction between self and other may be empathically aroused without these cognitions. In other words, how people experience empathy depends on the level at which they cognize others. This suggests that the development of empathic distress must correspond at least partly to the development of a cognitive sense of the other, which undergoes dramatic changes developmentally and thus provides a conceptual basis for a developmental scheme for empathy.

Although extensive work has been done on role taking, there is as yet no formal literature on a broader, life-span conception of a cognitive sense of the other. I have attempted to work out such a life-span conception, with an approximate timetable, drawing on concepts from several different bodies of research. This scheme is presented in detail elsewhere (Hoffman, 1975a). I will summarize it here briefly.

1. For most of the first year children appear to experience a fusion of self and other.
2. By about 12 months, they attain "person permanence" and become aware of others as physical entities distinct from the self.
3. By 2 or 3 years of age, they acquire a rudimentary sense of others as having inner states (thoughts, perceptions, feelings) independent of their own, although they cannot yet discern the other's inner states. This is the initial step in role taking. Later they become able to discern what the other's inner states are, progressing from simple to complex states.
4. By late childhood or early adolescence, they become aware of others as having personal identities and life experiences beyond the immediate situation.

Empathy may thus be viewed as having an affective component that is experienced differently as the child progresses through these four social-cognitive stages. I will now describe four hypothetical levels of empathic distress that may result from this coalescence of empathic affect and the cognitive sense of the other, as exemplified by empathizing with another person in distress.

1. *Global Empathy.* For most of the first year, before the child has acquired "person permanence," distress cues from others may elicit a global

empathic distress response—a fusion of unpleasant feelings and of stimuli that come from the infant's own body, from the dimly perceived "other," and from the situation. Since infants cannot yet differentiate themselves from the other, they must often be unclear as to who is experiencing any distress that they witness, and they at times may behave as though what is happening to the other is happening to them. For example, a colleague's 11-month-old daughter who saw another child fall and cry responded as follows: She first stared at the victim, looking as though she were about to cry herself, and then put her thumb in her mouth and buried her head in her mother's lap, which is what she does when she hurts herself. Kaplan (1977) describes a very similar response in a 9-month-old girl, and Radke-Yarrow & Zahn-Waxler (Note 2) report that the same pattern is characteristic of 10-14-month-old infants.

The transition to the second level begins as the child approaches person permanence. At first, children are probably only vaguely and momentarily aware of the other person as distinct from the self, and the mental image of the other, being transitory, may often slip in and out of focus. Consequently, children at this intermediate stage probably react to another's distress as though the dimly perceived self and the dimly perceived other were somehow simultaneously, or alternately, in distress. This is a difficult concept to grasp, and examples may help. One child I know, whose typical response to both his own and another's distress, beginning late in the first year, was to suck his thumb with one hand and pull his ear with the other—an example of Level "1" functioning. Something new happened at 12 months. On seeing a sad look on his father's face, he proceeded to look sad and suck his thumb, while pulling on his father's ear—as though he was just beginning to recognize the difference between self-in-distress and other-in-distress but the distinction was not yet clear. In a similar example, Zahn-Waxler, Radke-Yarrow, and King (1979) describe a child whose first positive overture to someone in distress, at 12 months, involved alternating between gently touching the victim and gently touching himself.

2. *"Egocentric" Empathy.* The second level is clearly established when the child is fully aware of the self and other as distinct physical entities and thus able for the first time to experience empathic distress while also being aware that another person, and not the self, is the victim. Children cannot yet fully distinguish between their own and the other person's inner states, however, and are apt to confuse them with their own, as illustrated by their efforts to help others, which consist chiefly of giving the other person what they themselves find most comforting. Examples are a 13-month-old who responded with a distressed look to an adult who looked sad and then offered the adult his beloved doll; and another who ran to fetch his own mother to comfort a crying friend, even though the friend's mother was

equally available. In labeling this empathic level, I used quotations because the term *egocentric* is not entirely accurate. Although the child's attempts to help indicate a confusion between what comforts him or her and what comforts the other, these same acts, nevertheless, together with his or her facial responses, indicate that the child is also responding with appropriate empathic affect.

3. *Empathy for Another's Feelings.* With the beginning of a role-taking capability, at about 2 or 3 years, children become aware that other people's feelings may sometimes differ from theirs, and their perspectives are based on their own needs and interpretation of events. More important, because children now know that the real world and their perceptions of it are not the same thing, and that the feelings of others are independent of her own, they become more responsive to cues about what the other is feeling. By 3 or 4 years, children can recognize and respond empathically to happiness or sadness in others in simple situations (e.g., Borke, 1971; Feshbach & Roe, 1968; Strayer, Note 3). And, with the development of language, which enables children for the first time to derive meaning from symbolic cues of affect, not just its facial and other physical expressions, they can begin to empathize with a wide range of emotions, including complex emotions like disappointment and feelings of betrayal. Eventually, they become capable of empathizing with several, sometimes contradictory emotions at once. Thus, while empathizing with the victim's distress, one may also empathize with the victim's feelings of inadequacy and low self-esteem—hence the victim's desire *not* to be helped. And, finally, children can be aroused empathically by information pertinent to someone's feelings even in that person's absence. This leads to the fourth empathic level.

4. *Empathy for Another's General Plight.* By late childhood, owing to the emerging conception of self and other as continuous persons with separate histories and identities, one becomes aware that others have feelings beyond the immediate situation. Consequently, though one may continue to be empathically aroused by another's immediate distress, one's empathic concern may be intensified when one knows that the other's distress is not transitory but chronic. This fourth level, then, consists of empathically aroused affect combined with an image of another's general life condition (general level of distress or deprivation, opportunities available or denied, future prospects, etc.).

This is a rather complex level, as one may be responding to a network of information—expressive cues from the other, immediate situational cues, knowledge of the other's life condition—utilizing several of the arousal modes described earlier. The separate sources of information may ordinarily be congruent although they are at times contradictory, as when knowledge about the other's life condition conflicts with the immediate situational or expressive cues. When this happens, the situational or expressive cues may lose much of their force for the observer who knows that they only reflect a transitory state. Imagine a child, for example, who is having a good time playing and laughing but who does not know that he or she is mentally retarded or has a terminal illness. An observer who has attained the fourth empathic level may be more likely to respond with sadness than with joy, to mingle joy and sadness or to suppress sadness so as to share the child's joy.[1] A less mature observer, however, might simply respond with joy. In other words, I am hypothezing that if the image of the model's general life falls short of the observer's standard of well-being, the observer's response may include varying degrees of empathic distress even if contradicted by the other's apparent momentary state; that is, the image may to some extent override contradictory cues in the present. This fourth level then may involve a certain amount of distancing—responding partly to one's mental image of the other rather than to the stimulus immediately presented by the other. Indeed, once this level is attained one may never again respond totally in terms of the other's actual feelings, but always at least partly in terms of one's knowledge of the other's general condition. This is in keeping with our definition of empathy not as an exact match with another's feelings but an affective response more appropriate to another's situation then to one's own.[2]

As an extension of the fourth level, children eventually can be empathically aroused by the plight of an entire group or class of people (e.g., poor, oppressed, outcast, retarded). Because of different backgrounds, one's specific distress experience may differ from theirs. All distress experiences probably have a common affective core, however, and this, together with the individual's high cognitive level, may allow for a generalized empathic distress capability. The combination of empathic affect and the perceived plight of an unfortunate group may be the most developmentally advanced form of empathic distress. It may also provide a motive base, especially in adolescence, for the development of certain social and political ideologies centered around alleviation of the plight of unfortunate groups (Hoffman, 1980).

Sympathetic Distress

Thus far, I have suggested that empathic distress includes both an affective component, and a cognitive component that are derived from the ob-

---

1. An example of the last is the parent who eventually accepts the child's condition and can then experience joy when the child does.
2. An exact-match definition would have difficulty explaining this phenomenon.

server's cognitive sense of the other. Many affect theorists (e.g., Schachter & Singer, 1962) suggest that how a person labels or experiences an affect is heavily influenced by certain pertinent cognitions. These writers are explaining how we distinguish among different affects (e.g., anger, fear, joy) aroused *directly*. Whether or not they are right, the cognitive sense of others appears to be so intrinsic to *empathically* aroused affect as to alter the very quality of the observer's affective experience. More specifically, once people are aware of the other as distinct from the self, their own empathic distress, which is a parallel response—a more or less exact replication of the victim's presumed feeling of distress—may be transformed at least in part into a more reciprocal feeling of concern for the victim. That is, they continue to respond in a purely empathic, quasi-egoistic manner—to feel uncomfortable and highly distressed themselves—but they also experience a feeling of compassion, or what I call sympathetic distress for the victim, along with a conscious desire to help because they feel sorry for him or her and not just to relieve their own empathic distress. In short, I am suggesting that the affective and cognitive components of empathy combine to produce a qualitatively different feeling in the observer. The developmental process involved may be the one pertaining to the co-occurrence of distress in the emerging "self" and the emerging "other," discussed earlier.

This transformation hypothesis is difficult to test. As yet the evidence is circumstantial: As already noted, (a) children seem to progress developmentally from responding to someone's distress first by seeking comfort for the self, and later by trying to help the victim and not the self; and (b) there appears to be an in-between stage, in which they feel sad and comfort both the victim and the self, which occurs at about the same time that they gain person permanence. Insofar as this transformation does occur, the four levels previously described may be said to apply to sympathetic as well as empathic distress. (From here on, the term *empathic distress* will be used generically to refer to both empathic and sympathetic distress).

EMPATHY AS MOTIVE

The relevance of empathic distress to altruism of course is that it is assumed to form the basis of a motive to help others. This is not a new idea, going back at least two centuries to utilitarian philosophers like Hume, Mill, Rousseau, Shelley, and Adam Smith (see review by Hoffman, in press-d). We may ask, why should empathic distress lead to helping? The answer may be simple: The best way to reduce one's empathic distress may ordinarily be to get rid of its source, namely, the other's actual distress. The best way therefore may be to help. It is true that one can sometimes get rid of empathic distress by perceptual or cognitive strategies such as directing one's attention elsewhere. Very young children sometimes do this. These strategies may provide only limited relief for older children and adults, however, because of the human tendency to form mental images. Turning away from the victim or covering one's ears does not remove the image of the victim (at least for observers who have attained "person permanence"), except perhaps temporarily; and the empathic distress is therefore likely to return. Regardless of where one is looking, one knows that the other is in distress. (Furthermore, as I will suggest later, efforts to avoid empathic distress may produce feelings of guilt.)

In the earliest empirical study, Murphy (1937) found a positive correlation between empathic behaviors such as "responding to another child's distress by staring with an anxious expression," and behaving in a comforting manner. Empathy also related positively to aggression, however. Murphy suggested that the pattern may simply reflect the child's social activity level. Highly active children are more empathic, helpful, and aggressive. Feshbach and Feshbach (1969), in a more controlled study, replicated Murphy's aggression findings for boys: Four- to five-year-old boys who obtained high empathy scores on a measure in which subjects report how they feel after looking at story slides depicting children in situations representing different emotions (Feshbach and Roe, 1968) were rated as more aggressive by nursery school teachers than boys with low empathy scores. For 6–7-year-old boys there was a negative relation between empathy and teacher ratings of aggressiveness, which suggests that by this age empathy may have begun to take hold as an inhibitor of aggression. There was no relation between empathy and aggression for girls at either age.

Levine and Hoffman (1975) examined the relation in 4-year-olds between the Feshbach and Roe measure of empathy and a modified version of Kagan and Madsen's (1971) measure of cooperation. No correlation was found between empathy and cooperation for either sex. In this study the cooperative subjects were asked why they cooperated. Only a few answered in empathic terms (e.g., "Because he wanted me to help him," or "Because he would cry if I didn't"); most referred to the requirements of the game, or to reciprocity. Thus, the emotional state of the other child was not salient during the game, which suggests that young children's empathic capability may sometimes not be engaged because their attention is easily captured by task demands and other irrelevant stimuli.[3]

In a study of kindergarten boys, Kameya (1976) examined the relation

3. Marcus, Telleen, and Roke (1979) report a positive correlation between empathy and cooperative behavior in the preschool, but their definition of cooperation—playing with others as opposed to playing alone—is questionable.

between the Feshbach and Roe measure and several indexes of helping behavior, which included helping an experimenter who dropped a pile of paper clips and expressed pain after bumping his knee, donating candy to poor children, and volunteering to color pictures for hospitalized children. Empathy did not correlate with any of these behaviors. Among subjects who did volunteer to color pictures for hospitalized children, however, those who actually took the pictures with them and showed signs of following through on their promise had higher empathy scores than those who showed no signs of following through. This "follow-through" behavior is the only altruism index involving considerable self-sacrifice over a prolonged period (the subjects were told they would have to do the coloring during two successive recess periods while the other children were outside playing). This suggests that although empathy may not often be engaged in young children, when it is engaged it may serve as a rather effective prosocial motive.

These somewhat inconsistent correlational findings stand in contrast to the rather clear pattern that seems to be emerging in naturalistic observations (Main, Weston, & Wakeling, Note 4; Murphy, 1937; Sawin, Note 5; Zahn-Waxler et al., 1979) and experimental research. Thus, during the first year children tend to cry in response to distress cues from others, including unfamiliar adults. This empathic cry decreases during the second year, and the decrease appears to be closely associated with an increase in overt attempts to comfort the victim, although many children this age do nothing, probably because they lack the necessary coping skills. By 3 or 4 years of age most children show both empathic distress and some form of helpful action. And, there is also evidence that children (9-year-olds) who respond empathically (show a sad look on their face) are more apt to make a sacrifice to help a victim than those who do not respond empathically (Lieman, Note 6). Finally, the experimental research on adults also shows a clear pattern (see review by Hoffman, 1977b): When exposed to someone in distress, adults are invariably aroused empathically (as indexed physiologically). The arousal is typically followed by helping action, and the latency of the act decreases with both the intensity of empathic arousal and magnitude of the pain cues from the victim.

Why is there a discrepancy between the correlational and other research? One possible explanation is that empathic distress is unlikely to be activated in young children unless certain conditions exist, for example, distress cues from the victim are salient, as they often are not in the correlational research, or the children are in an appropriate mood from the start. Regarding the children's mood, consider the study by Barnett, King, Howard, and Dino (1980) who found a positive correlation between empathy and volunteering to make coloring books for hospitalized children in a group that was first asked to discuss a sad incident about another person. No correlation was obtained in a control group in which a sad mood was not induced.

Another possible explanation for the discrepancy between the correlational and other research is that the Feshbach and Roe measure, which was used in all the correlational studies, has problems that I have noted elsewhere (Hoffman, in press -c). The main problem lies in the assumption that empathy is a unitary trait, which underlies a scoring system in which responses reflecting empathic fear, anger, sadness, and happiness are summed to produce a subject's empathy score. A measure specifically of empathic sadness or distress might yield more consistent findings. The results obtained by Main et al. (Note 4) and Sawin (Note 5) fit this view: Main found that 12-month-old infants who showed empathic sadness in response to the cry of an adult stranger in a laboratory situation were described by their parents as actively attempting to comfort distressed persons in the home environment. Sawin used the Feshbach and Roe measure and found that whereas the overall empathy score did not relate to helping in first and third grade children, the subscore for empathic sadness did significantly for the first grade group. The correlational method may thus be consistent, after all, with the naturalistic and experimental, adding credence to the generalization that empathy leads to helping action.

When the findings are arranged developmentally, the result is a rather neat package: In response to someone's being hurt, children below 1 year of age typically stare at the victim, appear agitated, often cry empathically, and sometimes seek comfort for themselves; in the second year they cry less but show empathic distress in their facial responses, begin to make tentative approaches to the victim, and sometimes attempt to comfort him or her; by 3 or 4 years they continue to show empathic distress and in most instances can be counted upon to make a relatively appropriate attempt to help. Beyond the preschool years, children continue to respond empathically, and with more consistently appropriate helping behavior. The latency of the helping act also decreases with the intensity of the victim's distress cues, and the helping action is followed by a drop in empathic arousal. These findings all fit the pattern to be expected if empathic distress is a prosocial motive.

Three qualifications are in order: The first is implied in my earlier point that people at the fourth, most advanced level might respond empathically to a victim's general condition even if this contradicted the victim's feelings in the immediate situation. If this is true, it follows that responding in the most direct empathic manner might not always lead to the most appropriate (highest level?) helping response. The other qualifications are the phenomenon of empathic overarousal, and the fact that empathic distress is related to perceived similarity between observer and victim.

Empathic Overarousal

There is evidence that altruistic action may require a certain amount of need fulfillment in observers, so as to reduce their self-preoccupation and leave them open and responsive to cues signifying the other's affect and need for help. For example, the arousal of deprived need states such as concerns about failure, social approval, and even physical discomfort due to noise has been found to interfere with altruistic action (e.g., see review by Hoffman, 1977b). Since empathic distress may itself be extremely aversive under certain conditions, it may at times direct the attention of observers to themselves and thus actually decrease the likelihood of an altruistic act. Consider one of the experimental groups in the study of kindergartners by Kameya (1976), who were presented with several stories involving children who were ill, deprived, in pain, or suffering combinations of these. The subjects took turns playing each of the roles and then discussed the feelings of the story children. In this group empathy was found to relate *negatively* to one of several helping behaviors (it did not relate to the others). These results suggest that the experimental treatment, although designed to improve role-taking skills, may instead have evoked extreme empathic distress, especially in the high-empathy subjects. These subjects may then have attended to their own distress, thus accounting for the negative relation. Perhaps there is an optimal range of empathic arousal—determined by people's levels of distress tolerance—within which they are most responsive to others. Beyond this range, they may be too preoccupied with their own aversive state to help anyone else.

Another possibility is that once over their threshold of distress tolerance, observers may employ certain mechanisms to reduce the level of arousal itself. They might avoid interacting with people in pain, like the empathic nursing students in a study by Stotland, Mathews, Sherman, Hansson, and Richardson (1979). They might employ certain perceptual and cognitive strategies such as looking away from the victim or thinking about other things, as did Bandura and Rosenthal's (1966) subjects, who were given a strong dose of epinephrine before observing someone receive electric shock. I noted earlier that strategies like these may not be as effective as helping in reducing empathic distress. They may nevertheless be employed in intense empathy-arousing situations in which helping is not possible, as in the studies just cited. Still another possible response that observers may make is to derogate the victims, for example, by making negative attributions about their motives or blaming them for their plights. Like other motives, then, empathic distress may operate as a prosocial motive only within certain intensity limits. Beyond that point, it may be transformed into an egoistic motive. (This transformation may have been adaptive in human evolution because it often occurred when the victim's situation was hopeless. In preserving one's energies rather than helping when the situation is hopeless, the individual continues to be available to help others when helping will be more effective.)

Empathy and Perceived Similarity

There is evidence that children respond more empathically to others of the same race or sex (Feshbach & Roe, 1968; Klein, 1971). And adults have been found to empathize more with others perceived as similar to themselves in abstract terms (e.g., similar "personality traits") (Krebs, 1975). These findings indicate that empathic morality may be particularistic, applied more to one's group than to others, although the findings are also compatible with the idea that moral education programs that point up the similarities among people, at the appropriate level of abstraction, may help foster a more universalistic morality.

OTHER AFFECTIVE RESPONSES TO VICTIMS

Before moving on, it is necessary to point out that empathic distress must be viewed in the perspective of all the emotional responses a person may make when observing someone in distress. In focusing on empathy, it is easy to lose sight of the fact that an observer's emotional response to a victim may not always be empathic. For example, it may be a direct reaction to something noxious, such as the sight of the victim's blood. It may be a startle response to sudden movements by the victim. It may be due to feeling afraid that what happened to the victim might happen to the self. It may be due to feeling threatened by the victim's distress because one is highly dependent on the victim, as when one is a child and the victim is one's parent. Still another possibility, as noted in discussing empathic overarousal, is that the observer's empathic distress may be so aversive that his or her attention is redirected toward one's own discomfort rather than the victim's; though the observer appears distressed, his or her concern is mainly for his or her own upset state.

Finally, according to the research on attribution, there is still another influence on how people respond to victims. This is that people tend to make causal inferences about events. We may therefore expect a person who encounters someone in distress to make inferences about the cause of the victim's plight. The nature of the inference depends on the cues relevant to causality, and the inference may then serve as a cognitive input, in addition to the observer's sense of the other, that helps shape the observer's affective experience. Thus, if the cues signify that the victim is responsible for his or her own plight, this may neutralize the empathic distress, and the observer may end up feeling indifferent or even derogating the victim. If the cues indicate that a third person is to blame, observers may feel anger at that third person because they sympathize with the victim or because they empathize with the victim and therefore feel attacked themselves. It is only when the cues indicate that it was an illness or accident over which the victim had no control that the analysis of empathic distress that I outlined, including the partial transformation of empathic into sympathic distress, may apply. Culture can play a role in all of this: If the victim belongs to an outcast group, for example, his or her misery may be attributed to false causes or responded to with indifference.

People may also make causal attributions about the victim's plight for reasons not based on situational cues. For example, as noted, they may use perceptual or cognitive strategies including blaming the victim as ways of reducing the discomfort of overarousal. These tendencies may be a function of individual differences in personality, although Lerner and Simmons (1966) claim evidence for a widespread tendency to respond with a derogatory attitude toward victims. There is some evidence that their findings may be due to the instructions given the subjects (Aderman, Brehm, & Katz, 1974). If the findings do reflect a real phenomenon, however, they must somehow be reconciled with the extensive research summarized earlier indicating that people of all ages typically do respond empathically and with some attempt to help the victim. Perhaps the different findings can be explained by differences in research design. More likely, there may be no contradiction at all. For example, people may tend to derogate victims only in situations in which the victim's misfortune can readily be perceived as a threat to their "belief in a just world" or in situations in which there is little or no opportunity to help (Cialdini, Darby, & Vincent, 1973). In other, more usual situations, people may empathize. It is also entirely possible that people may have negative attitudes toward a victim, and still be empathically aroused and motivated to help the victim in the immediate situation.

Empathy is thus one component of the observer's affective response to someone's plight. It is probably, in general, a large component, given all the evidence that an affective response to another's plight typically leads to a disposition to help. Nevertheless, our analysis suggests that empathy should be treated as a component of one's response to others, and studies of empathy should be designed to rule out, control, or at least take account of the nonempathic components insofar as possible.

Thus far in my analysis, the observer is an innocent bystander. A special case of interest is that in which the cues indicate that the observer is the cause of the other's distress. It seems reasonable to assume, when one feels empathic distress, that if the cues indicate that one has caused the victim's distress one's empathic distress will be transformed by the self-blame attribution into a feeling of guilt. That is, the temporal conjunction of empathy for someone in distress and the attribution of one's own responsibility for that distress will produce guilt.

GUILT

Let us examine this guilt response more closely. First, it should be clear that this type of guilt differs from the early conception of guilt in the literature as a conditioned anxiety response to anticipated punishment. Nor is it the same as the Freudian guilt, which is a remnant of earlier fears of punishment or retaliation that resulted in repression of hostile and other impulses, and which is triggered by the return of the repressed impulses to consciousness. (I suspect that these quasi-pathological conceptions account for the negative reputation guilt has acquired among psychologists.) What I am striving for is a concept of true, interpersonal guilt, which may be defined simply as the bad feeling one has about oneself because one is aware of actually doing harm to someone. Freud was aware of the necessity of this type of guilt, but neither he nor his followers have succeeded in integrating it into the main body of psychoanalytic theory.

Guilt and Reparative Altruism

It is intuitively obvious and there is considerable evidence that most people from an early age feel guilt after harming someone (see review by Hoffman, in press, a). The positive social value of guilt is also indicated by the research showing that guilt arousal usually includes a disposition to help the victim. For example, in Murphy's (1937) nursery school observations there were several instances of one child's harming another. Usually they occurred in the context of a fight or argument, and the victim typically was helped by a bystander rather than by the aggressor. In the few instances of accidental harm, however, the responsible child typically did make a spontaneous attempt at reparation, although the act was sometimes delayed. Another example of the relation between guilt and prosocial action can be found in the research using projective story completion items involving moral transgressions by story characters the same age as the subjects (fifth graders, seventh graders, and adults). In this research, the guilt feelings attributed to the story characters were almost always followed by some sort of reparative behavior (Hoffman, 1975b; in press-a). In many instances the reparative act was followed by a reduction in guilt intensity. When reparation was precluded by the story conditions (it was too late for anything to be done), the guilt response was typically prolonged.

There is also evidence that guilt arousal may serve as a generalized motive for altruistic action beyond reparation to the victim. In numerous laboratory studies, done mainly in the late 1960s and early 1970s, (e.g., Regan, 1971), adults who were led to believe that they had harmed someone showed a heightened willingness to help other people as well as the victim. These studies are limited, since they did not include a direct measure of guilt arousal, they showed only short-run effects (the altruistic deed immediately followed the guilt manipulation), and the subjects were all college students. In the story completion research, however, the evidence for guilt was explicit, and there was a suggestion of long-term effects: In some of the completions by children as well as adults, guilt appears to trigger a process of self-examination (e.g., "How could I have been so selfish?") and a reordering of one's value priorities, along with a resolution to act less selfishly in the future. Although by no means conclusive, the findings as a whole suggest, somewhat paradoxically, that guilt, which is usually the result of immoral or at least egoistic action, may subsequently operate as an altruistic motive.

If guilt over harming others is prevalent and socially beneficial, it seems unlikely that its motive base is typically as irrational as previous conceptions would suggest. The question is, what alternative, more realistic motive base is there? I have already suggested empathic distress, and my hypothesis is that true interpersonal guilt may be due to the conjunction of an empathic response to someone's distress and the awareness of being the cause of that distress.

Development of Guilt

It is too soon to advance a coherent theory, but I would like to discuss the cognitive prerequisites of guilt, to offer some preliminary speculations about the development of guilt and its parallels with empathy, and finally, to say something about a type of guilt that is neither Freudian nor based on the actual harm one has done to another. The aim of all this is to stimulate further research and theoretical discussion about this important, though neglected, concept.

First it must be noted that, like empathic distress, guilt has three components: affective, cognitive, and motivational. The affective dimension pertains to the painful feeling of disesteem for the self because of the harmful consequences of one's action; in the extreme, a sense of being a worthless person. The motivational dimension pertains to the fact that when one feels guilty, one also feels the urge to undo the damage or to make some form of reparation. The cognitive dimension, although having a lot in common with empathy, is far more complex and requires further discussion.

Cognitive Dimension of Guilt

For a person to feel guilty requires an awareness of the harmful effects that one's behavior might have on others. One dimension of this awareness is the cognitive sense of others that is also important for empathy. For example, a child who does not know that others have independent inner states may not feel guilty over hurting their feelings. And, a child who is not yet aware of the self and the other as separate entities may even be uncertain as to who committed the harmful act—the victim or the self.

The cognitive dimension of guilt also includes the awareness that one has been the agent of the harm. This requires the ability to make causal inferences involving one's own actions—for example, the ability to infer from the temporal relation between one's act and a change in the other's state—that one's act was the cause of that change in state. Although research has been done on children's awareness of cause-effect relations in both the social and physical domains, there is very little research on cause-effect relations involving the child's own actions. What little research there is (for review see Hoffman, in press-b) suggests that children may begin to be aware that their actions can have simple physical effects on the external world before 1 year of age. Keeping both this and the social-cognitive levels discussed earlier in mind, we can make some reasonable speculations about the kinds of behaviors that might make the child feel guilty. The simplest case is when the child commits a physically harmful act. This is minimally demanding cognitively, because the consequences of the act are immediate and observable. Guilt over inaction, or omission, is more demanding cognitively because it requires the ability to imagine something that might have happened but did not, and to be aware of the consequences of that omission. That is, observers witness victims' distresses, imagine what they might have done to prevent or alleviate them, and realize that although they did not cause a distress, their inaction contributed to its continuation. Guilt over inaction must therefore be a later developmental acquisition. Perhaps even more demanding cognitively is guilt over contemplating a harmful act, or anticipatory guilt. Anticipatory guilt requires that one can not only establish connections between thoughts, intentions, and actions, but also that one can imagine both an act and its harmful social consequences when neither of these has yet occurred.

Another important cognitive dimension of guilt is the awareness that one has choice and control over one's behavior. Without this awareness there would be no grounds for feeling guilty. Here, too, there is very little research. The recent moral judgment research does show that children as young as 3 or 4 years will judge another child as being naughtier if what he or she did was intentional rather than accidental (e.g., Imamoglu, 1975). Although the actions judged were not the child's own, the findings do suggest that 4-year-olds may be sensitive to choice and control. What about younger children? Psychoanalytic writers have long suggested that there is a period of "omnipotence" in early infancy, before the differentiation of self and others, before "person permanence" (See Mahler, Pine, & Bergman, 1975). This makes sense when we consider that at that age the infant's utterances of distress are typically acted upon fairly quickly by the mother. If the infants, as a result, feel that they control the world, then they may also have a rudimentary sense of controlling themselves since they are a part of the world. There is no evidence, however, that infants have any awareness of *choice*. The cry that controls the mother's behavior is very likely a natural response to discomfort, rather than an instrumental act of choice. It may not be until much later that children are aware of choice, and act on the basis of choice.

If there is an early period of omnipotence that is linked to a nondifferentiated state, then it seems likely that as one becomes aware of one's own separateness, one also becomes aware of the new and disturbing reality not only that other people's actions are mediated by *their* desires, not one's own, but also that one's actions are to some extent subject to control by others. With this insight, the delusion of omnipotence can no longer be maintained, and it may give way to a sense of helplessness and loss of control of one's own behavior. This, in time, is presumably followed by a more realistic awareness of having partial control and choice. Until the necessary research is done, it seems plausible tentatively to assume that there is an early developmental progression from a sense of omnipotence, to a sense of helplessness, and finally to an awareness of having some but not total control over one's actions.

A final cognitive dimension of guilt may appear sometime later in development, at least in most societies. This includes the awareness that there exists a moral norm against harming others and that one's act, or contemplated act, is discrepant from that norm. To the extent that one has been socialized to view oneself as an upholder of the norm, this discrepancy may be a threat to one's self-image, and the resulting negative affect may add to the intensity of the empathically based guilt. The awareness of a norm against harming others may thus contribute affectively as well as cognitively to the guilt response.

Developmental Levels of Guilt

I will not present a complete developmental model for guilt, as I did for empathy, but rather a brief preliminary scheme that utilizes the points made in the foregoing discussion. In this scheme the capacity for guilt develops in parallel with the levels of empathic distress described earlier.

First, a minimal requirement for feeling guilty over harming others is that one is psychologically separate from them. We may therefore not expect any signs of guilt until children have the faint beginnings of awareness of others as separate physical entities from themselves, which is around the end of the first year. Furthermore, in the earliest instances of guilt we may expect to see the most primitive kind of causal schema, which according to Heider (1958) is based on the simple contiguity of events. That is, children may feel that they are to blame just because of the temporal or geographical association of their actions with another person's signs of distress. Whether or not they actually caused the distress is irrelevant. Though they may be confused about who is the causal agent, they may nevertheless feel something like guilt, even if they are totally innocent. The guiltlike responses observed in a third of Zahn-Waxler et al.'s (1979) sample of 15–18-month-old infants may be illustrative of this level of guilt. For example, a child is playing with her mother. The mother looks sad for some reason. The child, who has done nothing wrong, looks sad and says, "I sorry, did I hurt your Mommy?" In another example, a child is arguing with a sibling. The sibling is accidentally hurt. The child then alternates between continuing his aggressive behavior and comforting the sibling. He says he is sorry, kisses the sibling's hand, and then hits his own head. These examples illustrate the young child's empathic distress and his or her confusion about causality. Perhaps more importantly, they also suggest a rudimentary sense of being responsible for an act, which predates some of the cognitive requisites of guilt mentioned earlier—for example, a sense of having choices. Why should children feel that they are to blame? I suggest that they feel culpable because of their sense of omnipotence, which, together with their cognitive limitations, lead them to view all things associated with their actions as caused by them. To summarize, an early, nonveridical sense of being the causal agent may combine with empathic distress to produce a rudimentary feeling of guilt.

A note of caution before we proceed. The examples just cited may reflect a primitive guilt feeling in the child, as suggested. It is also possible, however, that the child feels empathic distress and says "I'm sorry" and yet the words do not reflect a feeling of culpability, but rather a simple parroting of what others have said in similar situations. A careful examination of the child's words, along with accompanying changes in his or her facial expression and any other behavioral indexes of guilt, may be necessary to resolve this issue. The child's hitting him- or herself on the head may be more convincing evidence for guilt feelings than conventional expressions like "I'm sorry," although it is possible that the child has seen others engage in this behavior.

In any case, sometime later in development when children are aware of the impact of their actions, the stage may be set for the development of true interpersonal guilt. This development should proceed along lines corresponding roughly to the levels of social-cognitive development discussed earlier. Thus the earlier true guilt should occur when the child has engaged in some simple physical action that has harmed someone such as knocking another child down, hitting that child, or breaking the child's toy. The cues from the victim indicating he or she is hurt, usually a cry or a pained look, will elicit a guilt feeling, though it may be fleeting. Instances of this abound in the nursery school. For example, a boy takes a toy from another, who cries. The child who took the toy responds with a seemingly genuinely sad look on his face and returns the toy, sometimes with a comforting gesture. We do not know why he responds that way. It might be to avoid a scolding by the teacher, but the child's manner is often that of a contrite and sympathetic, not fearful, child, and it seems plausible that he might feel guilty. Interesting instances of delayed reparation can also be found, which suggest guilt. An example is the girl who offered to give a ride on a swing to someone she accidentally knocked down 15 minutes earlier.

Once the child begins to be aware that others have their own inner states—by 2 or 3 years, as noted earlier—guilt over hurting people's feelings should become a possibility. At about the same time, the child may also begin to show evidence of having the cognitive requisites of guilt over inaction. Finally, when the child becomes aware that other people have their own existence and personal identity—in late childhood or early adolescence—he or she can begin to feel guilty over the harmful effects of his or her action or inaction beyond the immediate situation. In its earliest manifestation, such guilt may be felt when one imagines discrete instances of distress in the victim, although eventually it may also be felt when one is aware of the harmful effects that one's actions may have on the victim over time.

"Existential Guilt"

There is another type of guilt that I have discussed at length elsewhere (Hoffman, 1976b; 1980; in press-a) and should be mentioned at least briefly in any work on altruism: Namely, people may at times feel culpable because of the vast differences in well-being between themselves and others. The most obvious example is survivor guilt. More important for present purposes because of its possible developmental implications is the feeling reported by some of the affluent 1960s social activists who were guilty over how privileged they were in life as compared to others. I call this existential guilt, to distinguish it from true guilt, since the person has done nothing wrong but feels culpable because of circumstances beyond his or her control. It obviously has something of the quality of guilt over inaction, however, as illustrated by some of the activists in Keniston's (1968) sample who felt that because of their privileged position they should be able to do something to alleviate the condition of less fortunate people; and if they did nothing they were therefore responsible for perpetuating this condition. For some, who believed that actions by their relatives or members of their social class contributed to the plight of the less advantaged, existential guilt appeared to shade into an actual feeling of guilt over commission, a sort of guilt by association.

Existential guilt may be heavily influenced by cultural and situational factors, since it requires not only the perception that one is relatively advantaged but also the belief that there is no justification for this. Privilege in the past was often justified by religious doctrine or ideas about racial superiority. These have lost much of their force in our society, and even the idea that one deserves what one earns is no longer tenable for the increasing number of young people who live on loans or gifts from relatives. Thus, although existential guilt may be the most advanced developmentally because of its cognitive complexity, it may be confined to one's culture, social status, and historical period.

Relation between Guilt and Empathic Distress

I will now summarize this highly speculative developmental scheme for guilt, highlighting its parallels with empathic distress. First, before becoming aware of others as separate physical entities, children respond to simple expressions of pain by others with empathic distress and also at times with a rudimentary guilt feeling, even though they may lack a keen sense of being the causal agent. Once they know that others are separate entities, they experience empathic distress when observing someone who is physically hurt, and their empathic distress may be transformed into guilt if their own actions were responsible for the hurt. Similarly, once aware that others have inner states, the empathic distress one experiences in the presence of someone having painful or unhappy feelings may be transformed into guilt if one's actions were responsible for those feelings. Finally, once aware of the identity of others beyond the immediate situation, one's empathic response to their general plight may be transformed into guilt if one feels responsible for their plight, or if one's attention shifts from their plight to the contrast between it and one's own relatively advantaged position.

Although empathic distress is here viewed as a prerequisite for the development of guilt, it seems likely that guilt may eventually become largely independent of its empathic origin. In some situations—for example, those in which the victim is visibly sad or hurt—guilt may continue to be accompanied by empathic distress. In other situations, however, the victim and his or her hurt may be less salient than other things—for example, the actor's behavior or motivation. In these cases, the actor may feel guilt without empathy. And, in most instances of anticipatory guilt, there may rarely be empathic arousal except in the unusual case in which one imagines the other's response to one's planned action especially vividly. In general, then, at some point in development, the awareness of being the causal agent of another's misfortune may be enough to trigger guilt feelings without empathy. Thus, although empathic distress may be a necessary factor in the *development* of guilt, it may not, subsequently, be an inevitable accompaniment of guilt.

It seems likely, moreover, that once the capacity for guilt is attained, especially guilt over omission or inaction, the weight of influence may be the other way around. That is, guilt may become a part of all subsequent responses to another's distress, at least in situations in which one might have helped but did not. From then on, even as an innocent bystander, one may rarely experience empathic distress without some guilt. The line between empathic distress and guilt thus becomes very fine, and being an innocent bystander is a matter of degree. To the degree that one realizes that one could have acted to help but did not, one may never feel totally innocent. Empathy and guilt may thus be the quintessential prosocial motives, since they may transform another's pain into one's own discomfort and make one feel partly responsible for the other's plight whether or not one has actually done anything to cause it.

Evidence for the connection between empathy and guilt is scanty and largely circumstantial. It includes the fact that children typically respond empathically to others in distress, taken together with the finding (to be discussed later) that discipline techniques that point up the victim's distress and the child's role in causing it appear to contribute to guilt development. There is also some experimental evidence (Thompson & Hoffman, 1980). The subjects—first, third, and fifth grade children—were shown stories on slides, which were also narrated by the experimenter, in which a story character does harm to another person. For example, a boy who accidentally bumps into another boy, scattering his newspapers, does not stop to help because he is in a hurry. After each story, two guilt measures were administered. One is simple: The subject is asked how he or she would feel if he or she were the story character who committed the transgression. The other is a projective item: The subject completes the story, and guilt scores are derived from the amount of guilt attributed to the culprit. Before administering the guilt measures, half the subjects were asked to tell how they think the *victim* in each story felt. The subjects in this empathy arousal condition produced higher guilt scores than a control group who were not asked to think about the victim. These results do not bear directly on the origin of guilt, but they suggest that guilt may at least be intensified by arousal of empathy for the victim of one's actions.

THE ROLE OF SOCIALIZATION

The discussion so far has dealt with the natural processes of empathy and guilt development assumed to occur under ordinary conditions in most cultures because of the tendency of humans to respond vicariously to others. People also have egoistic needs, however, which must not be overlooked, and socialization, which in part reflects the larger themes in society, may build upon the child's empathic or egoistic proclivities in varying degrees. I have suggested elsewhere (Hoffman, 1970b) that there may be little conflict between empathic and egoistic socialization in early childhood, even in individualistic societies like ours. At some point in life the two may begin to clash, however, sometimes dramatically, as one becomes aware that the society's resources are limited and that one's access to them is largely contingent on how well one competes with others. Parents know this, and it may affect their child-rearing goals. For this and other reasons (e.g., their patience with the child, their own personal needs, and the stresses under which they operate), wide variations in child-rearing practices, hence in children's capacity for empathy and guilt, can be expected. What follows are speculations about these socialization effects.

Empathy

There is little research on socialization and empathy, but if we assume that helping another in distress reflects on empathic response—which seems reasonable in view of the findings relating empathy to helping—then we can find modest support for speculations based on our theoretical model.

First, we would expect people to be more likely to empathize with someone else's emotion if they have had direct experience with that emotion themselves. It follows that socialization that allows children to experience a variety of emotions, rather than protecting them from these emotions, will increase the likelihood of their being able to empathize with different emotions. That is, it will expand their empathic range. The only evidence to date for this hypothesis is that preschool children who cry a lot themselves appear to be more empathic than children who do not often cry (Lenrow, 1965). There is a theoretical limitation to this hypothesis: Certain extremely painful situations might be repressed, resulting in an inability to empathize with the emotions involved.

A second expectation can be derived from the idea that empathy is a largely involuntary response. By involuntary we mean that if a person pays attention to the victim, he or she usually will have an empathic response. It follows that socialization experiences that direct the child's attention to the inner states of other people should contribute to the development of empathy. We should therefore expect that in situations in which the child has harmed others, the parent's use of discipline techniques that call attention to the victim's pain or injury or encourage the child to imagine him- or herself in the victim's place—inductive techniques—should help put the feelings of others into the child's consciousness and thus enhance the child's empathic potential. The positive correlation between inductive techniques and helping in older children has long been known (see review by Hoffman, 1970a), and the same thing has recently been reported in children under 2 years (Zahn-Waxler et al., 1979).

We would expect role-taking opportunities to help sharpen the child's cognitive sense of others and increase the likelihood that he or she will pay attention to others, thus extending the child's empathic capability. We must remember, however, that role taking is an ego skill potentially useful in manipulating as well as helping others. Role-taking opportunities in positive social contexts should therefore be a more reliable contributor to empathy and helping than role-taking opportunities in competitive contexts. The research thus far seems to provide modest support for this expectation: Role-taking training in prosocial contexts has been found to increase helping behavior in children and adults; the research on role taking in competitive contexts, all of it correlational, unfortunately, appears to show a lack of relation between role taking and helping (see review by Hoffman, in press-a).

Finally, we would expect that giving children a lot of affection would help keep them open to the needs of others and empathic, rather than absorbed in their own needs. And, we would also expect that exposing the child to models who act altruistically and express their sympathetic feelings would contribute to the child's acting empathically rather than making counterempathic attributions about the cause of people's distress. Both these expectations have been borne out by the research (see review by Hoffman, in press-a).

It thus appears that empathy and helping may be fostered by relatively benign, nonpunitive socialization experiences. These experiences may be effective because empathy develops naturally, as I suggested, and is to some extent present at an early age. Empathy may thus serve as a potential ally to parents and others with prosocial child-rearing goals for the child— something to be encouraged and nurtured, rather than punished as egoistic motives must sometimes be. And, besides benefiting from the child's existing empathic tendencies, these same socialization experiences may also help enhance those empathic tendencies. In other words, there may be a mutually supportive interaction between naturally developing empathy and these socialization experiences.

Guilt

Socialization should be especially important in guilt development for the following reason. Guilt feelings are not only aversive, as is empathic distress, but they are also highly deprecatory and threatening to the child's emerging self-image. We may therefore expect children to be motivated to avoid guilt. And they can often succeed in this, because most situations in which children harm others are ambiguous in one way or another as regards who, if anyone, is to blame. That is, children rarely harm others intentionally and without provocation, in which case it would be easy to assign blame. The ambiguity is most apparent when one has harmed another accidentally—whether in rough play or in independent pursuit of one's own interests. But ambiguity also exists in fights and arguments, where it may seem as reasonable to assign blame to the other as to blame the self. In competitive situations one might conceivably feel guilt about wanting to be victorious over the other, about wanting the other to lose, but then one knows that the other is similarly motivated, and so there may be no grounds for guilt. Besides blaming others, or blaming no one, children can use perceptual guilt-avoiding strategies such as turning away from the victim. It seems to follow that even when children have the necessary cognitive and affective attributes for guilt, they often will not experience it unless an external agent is present who somehow compels them to attend to the harm done to the victim and to their own role in the victim's plight. This is exactly what parents often do when the child does harm to someone, and it seems reasonable to expect that the type of discipline used in these situations will have an effect on the development of a guilt disposition in children.

Indeed, the discipline research does show, fairly consistently, that parents who frequently use discipline techniques in which the salient component is induction, that is, techniques in which the parent points up the harmful effects of the child's behavior on others—combined with a lot of affection outside the discipline encounter—have children who tend to experience guilt feelings when they have harmed others (Hoffman, 1970a). Parents who frequently use power assertion—which includes force, deprivation of material objects or privileges, or the threat of these—are apt to have children who tend to respond with fear of retaliation or punishment, rather than guilt. (The frequent use of love withdrawal, in which the parent simply gives direct but nonphysical expression to his anger or disapproval of the child for engaging in undesirable behavior, does not seem to relate to guilt, although such a relationship might be expected from a psychoanalytic perspective.)

My theoretical explanation of these findings, presented elsewhere (see especially Hoffman, in press-b), will be summarized briefly. First, although the research describes discipline techniques as fitting one or another category, when examined empirically most discipline techniques have power-assertive and love withdrawing properties, and some also contain elements of induction. The first two comprise the motive-arousal component of discipline techniques that may be necessary to get the child to stop what he or she is doing and attend. Having attended, the child will often be influenced cognitively and affectively by the information contained in the inductive component, when it is present. Second, if there is too little arousal the child may ignore the parent; too much arousal, and the resulting fear, anxiety, or resentment may prevent effective processing of the inductive content, as well as direct the child's attention to the consequences of his or her action for the self. Techniques having a salient inductive component ordinarily achieve the best balance, and direct the child's attention to the consequences of his or her action for the victim. Third, the child may process the information in the inductive component; and the cognitive products of this processing constitute knowledge about the moral norm against harming others. Processing this information should also often enlist the capacity for empathy that the child brings to the discipline encounter. The child thus may feel badly due to the other's distress rather than, or, in addition to, anticipated punishment to the self. Fourth, since inductions also point up the fact that the child caused the victim's distress, these techniques may often result in the temporal conjunction of empathic distress and the attribution of personal responsibility for the other's distress that may be needed to transform empathic distress into guilt. (This analysis is most applicable to those instances in which the victim of the child's act exhibits clear signs of being sad and downcast, hurt, or otherwise distressed. If the victim is angry and retaliates, the child may feel anger or fear rather than empathic distress and guilt.)

Fifth, the cognitive products of the information processing that occurs in discipline encounters are hypothesized as being semantically organized and encoded in memory. They are then activated in future discipline encounters, modified, and cumulatively integrated with similar information from other inductions over time. The associated guilt feelings are also activated in these future situations. The source of the information—the discipline encounter settings—is organized separately in a shallower, nonsemantic mode (Craik & Lockhart, 1972) or encoded in "episodic" memory (Tulving, 1972). Consequently, it interferes minimally with the semantic organization, and may be soon forgotten. Sixth, owing to the child's active role in processing the information in inductions, as well as the differential memory for idea content and setting, the child may eventually experience the moral cognitions and guilt feelings generated in discipline encounters as deriving from the self.

I also suggested that once guilty feelings are aroused in discipline encounters, the ideas about the harmful consequences of one's actions that gave rise to them may be suffused with guilty affect and become "hot cognitions" whose affective and cognitive features are inseparable. These hot cognitions may then be encoded in memory and eventually experienced in temptation situations or moral encounters as an affective–cognitive unity. Another interesting possibility is that although the guilty feelings derive from the ideas about harmful consequences, they may be encoded separately, through a special process or channel reserved for affects. If so, then in later temptation situations the guilty feelings may be evoked without any conscious awareness of the ideas about consequences that gave rise to them. (This may sound like the Freudian notion of guilt, but it is different because it is not based on repression.) Stated most generally, this theory suggests that it is (a) the appropriate mix of parental power, love, and information; (b) the child's processing of the information in discipline encounters and afterwards; and (c) the cognitive and affective products of that processing that determine the extent to which the child feels guilty when he or she has harmed another, contemplates acting in a way that might harm another, or does not help another when it is appropriate to do so. Thus the child's empathic and cognitive capabilities that I described earlier may be mobilized for the first time in discipline encounters, with guilt feelings as the result, and the resulting guilt capability may then be generalized to other situations.

CONCLUDING REMARKS

A theoretical model of empathic arousal, its developmental course, its transformation into guilt, and its implications for altruistic motivation has been presented. The model differs from others in the prosocial area in its stress both on emotion and on the interaction between affective and cognitive processes within a developmental framework. It may be useful to point up in general outline the main characteristics of the model. First, the emotion in question, whether empathic distress or guilt, has a cognitive as well as an affective component. The affective component pertains to the arousal and motivational properties of the emotion. The cognitive component pertains to the shaping and transformation of the affective experience that results from the actor's awareness that the event is happening to someone else, and the actor's causal attributions about the event and its impact on the other person. Second, the affective and cognitive components are seen as developing largely through distinctly different processes. Third, the two components are constantly interacting, and, furthermore, despite the differences in the processes underlying their development, they tend to be experienced not so much as separate states but as a fusion. That is, empathic distress and guilt are what may be called "hot cognitions." Fourth, at all four developmental levels, the experience of these emotions is assumed to include a motivational disposition toward prosocial action.

Although as yet loose and tentative, the model appears to provide a broad integrative framework for ordering existing developmental knowledge about the motivation to consider others. A true assessment of the model, however, awaits the test of hypotheses derived specifically from it. It should also be noted that the model has certain limitations. Although empathy and guilt may explain why people act morally and feel bad when they harm someone, no affect theory by itself can explain how children learn to negotiate and achieve a balance between this moral motive and the egoistic motives that may also be aroused in situations. And as I suggested, although one's empathic proclivities may make one more receptive to certain moral values, empathy alone cannot explain how people formulate complex moral ideologies and apply them in situations.

Another limitation of an empathy-based morality may be revealed in situations in which moral judgments must be made, especially when several behaviors are to be compared or competing claims evaluated. Although the model predicts that a mature empathizer responds in terms of a complex network of information including knowledge of the other's life condition, and is thus sensitive to subtle differences in the severity and quality of the consequences that different actions might have for different people, mature empathizers may still show a bias in favor of certain persons, for example, those perceived as similar to themselves. It may be impossible to make objective moral judgments in such complex situations without recourse to moral principles that transcend particular individuals and that may be reduced to one universally accepted principle. Unfortunately, there is no universally accepted principle and as a result competing principles may apply in a given situation (e.g., fairness requires allocating resources according to need *versus* fairness requires allocating according to effort or productivity). The principle one chooses may then simply reflect one's personal values, and judging on the basis of principle may be as vulnerable to bias as relying on empathy.

Without a universal moral principle, it may be beneficial to look for connections between empathy and principles having some consensus in our society. Since empathy is a response to another's state, it may be reasonable to expect empathy to develop into a motive to act in accord with the welfare of others, and, furthermore, to expect this motive to acquire an obligatory quality and be transformed into a verbalized principle for judging the behavior of others as well as guiding one's own actions. The link between empathy and other principles like fairness or justice may be less direct because they often involve competing claims. Even these principles have a welfare-of-others component, and so it may seem reasonable to hypothesize that when empathic children are exposed to these principles they are more likely to adopt them and express them in behavior than are nonempathic children.

The simple moral motives discussed here, then, may link up developmentally with the complex cognitive processes involved in building prosocial moral ideologies and establishing moral priorities. The investigation of this link would seem to be a worthy topic for developmental research.

REFERENCE NOTES

1. Aronfeed, J., & Paskal, V. Altruism, empathy, and the conditioning of positive affect. Unpublished manuscript, University of Pennsylvania, 1965.
2. Radke-Yarrow, M., & Zahn-Waxler, C. Roots, motives and patterning in children's prosocial behavior. Presented at the International Conference on the development and maintenance of prosocial behavior, Jablonna, Poland, June 1980.
3. Strayer, J. Empathy, emotions, and egocentrism. Presented at meetings of the International Congress of Psychology, Leipzig, Germany, July 1980.
4. Main, M., Weston, D. R., & Wakeling, S. "Concerned attention" to the crying of an adult actor in infancy. Presented at meetings of the Society for Research in Child Development, San Francisco, March 1979.
5. Sawin, D. B. Assessing empathy in children: A search for an elusive construct. Presented at meetings of the Society for Research in Child Development, San Francisco, March 1979.
6. Lieman, B. Affective empathy and subsequent altruism in kindergartners and first graders. Presented at meetings of the American Psychological Association, Toronto, September 1978.

REFERENCES

Aderman, D., Brehm, S. S., & Katz, L. B. Empathic observation of an innocent victim: The just world revisited. *Journal of Personality and Social Psychology,* 1974, *29,* 342-347.
Bandura, H., & Rosenthal, L. Vicarious classical conditioning as a function of arousal level. *Journal of Personality and Social Psychology,* 1966, *3,* 54-62.
Barnett, M. A., King, L. M., Howard, J. A., & Dino, G. Empathy in young children. *Developmental Psychology,* 1980, *16,* 243-244.
Borke, H. Interpersonal perception of young children: Ego-centrism or empathy? *Developmental Psychology,* 1971, *5,* 263-269.

Cialdini, R. B., Darby, B. L., & Vincent, J. E. Transgression and altruism: A case for hedonism. *Journal of Experimental Social Psychology,* 1973, *9,* 502–516.

Craik, F. I. M., & Lockhart, R. S. Levels of processing: A framework for memory research. *Journal of Verbal Learning and Verbal Behavior.* 1972, *11,* 671–684.

Feshbach, N. D., & Feshbach, S. The relationship between empathy and agression in two age groups. *Developmental Psychology,* 1969, *1,* 102–107.

Feshbach, N. D., & Roe, K. Empathy in six- and seven-year-olds. *Child Development,* 1968, *39,* 133–145.

Heider, F. *The Psychology of interpersonal relations.* New York: Wiley, 1958.

Hoffman, M. L. Parent discipline and the child's consideration for others. *Child Development.* 1963, *34,* 573–588.

Hoffman, M. L. Moral development. In P. Mussen (Ed.), *Handbook of child psychology.* New York: Wiley, 1970. (a)

Hoffman, M. L. Conscience, personality, and socialization techniques. *Human Development,* 1970, *13,* 90–126. (b)

Hoffman, M. L. Developmental synthesis of affect and cognition and its implications for altruistic motivation. *Developmental Psychology,* 1975, *11,* 607–622. (a)

Hoffman, M. L. Sex differences in moral internalization. *Journal of Personality and Social Psychology,* 1975, *32,* 720–729. (b)

Hoffman, M. L. Empathy, role-taking, guilt and development of altruistic motives. In T. Lickona (Ed.), *Moral development and behavior: Theory, research and social issues.* New York: Holt, Rinehart & Winston, 1976.

Hoffman, M. L. Moral internalization: Current theory and research. In L. Berkowitz (Ed.), *Advances in experimental social psychology,* Vol. 10. New York: Academic Press, 1977, pp. 86–135. (a)

Hoffman, M. L. Empathy, its development and prosocial implications. In C. B. Keasey (Ed.), *Nebraska Symposium on Motivation,* (Vol. 25). Lincoln: University of Nebraska Press, 1977, pp. 169–218. (b)

Hoffman, M. L. Adolescent morality in development perspective. In J. Adelson (Ed.), *Handbook of adolescent psychology,* New York: Wiley, 1980, pp. 295–344.

Hoffman, M. L. Is altruism part of human nature? *Journal of Personality and Social Psychology,* 1981, *40,* 121–137.

Hoffman, M. L. Empathy, guilt, and social cognition. In W. F. Overton (Ed.), *Knowledge and development.* Hillsdale, N.J.: Erlbaum, in press. (a)

Hoffman, M. L. Affective and cognitive processes in moral internalization: An information processing approach. In E. T. Higgins, D. Ruble, & S. W. Hartup (Eds.), *Developmental social cognition: A socio-cultural perspective.* New York: Cambridge University Press, in press. (b)

Hoffman, M. L. Measurement of empathy. In C. Izard (Ed.), *Measurement of emotions in infants and children.* New York: Cambridge University Press, in press. (c)

Hoffman, M. L. Affect and moral development. In D. Cicchetti (Ed.), *New directions in child development.* San Francisco: Jossey-Bass, in press, (d).

Humphrey, G. The conditioned reflex and the elementary social reaction. *Journal of Abnormal and Social Psychology,* 1922, *17,* 113–119.

Imamoglu, E. O. Children's awareness and usage of intention cues. *Child Development,* 1975, *46,* 39–45.

Kagan, S., & Madsen, M. Cooperation and competition of Mexican, Mexican-American, and Anglo-American children of two ages under four instructional sets. *Developmental Psychology,* 1971, *5,* 32–39.

Kameya, L. I. *The effect of empathy level and role-taking training upon prosocial behavior.* Unpublished doctoral dissertation, University of Michigan, 1976.

Kaplan, L. J. The basic dialogue and the capacity for empathy. In N. Freedman & S. Grand (Eds.), *Communicative structures and psychic structures.* New York: Plenum, 1977.

Keniston, K. *Young radicals.* New York: Harcourt, 1968.

Klein, R. Some factors influencing empathy in six and seven year old children varying in ethnic background (Doctoral dissertation, University of California, Los Angeles, School of Education, 1970). *Dissertation Abstracts International,* 1971, *31,* 396A. (University Microfilms No. 71-3862)

Krebs, D. L. Empathy and altruism. *Journal of Personality and Social Psychology,* 1975, *32,* 1124-1146.

Lenrow, P. B. Studies in sympathy. In S. S. Tomkins & C. E. Izard (Eds.), *Affect, cognition and personality.* New York: Springer, 1965.

Lerner, M. J., & Simmons, C. Observer's reaction to the innocent victim: Compassion or rejection? *Journal of Personality and Social Psychology,* 1966, *4,* 203-210.

Levine, L. E., & Hoffman, M. L. Empathy and cooperation in 4-year-olds. *Developmental Psychology,* 1975, *11,* 533-534.

Lipps, T. Das Wissen von fremden Ichen. *Psychologische Untersuchungen,* 1906, *1,* 694-722.

Mahler, M. S., Pine, F., & Bergman, A. *The psychological birth of the human infant.* New York: Basic Books, 1975.

Marcus, R. F., Telleen, S., & Roke, E. J. Relation between cooperation and empathy in young children. *Developmental Psychology,* 1979, *15,* 346-347.

Murphy, L. B. *Social behavior and child personality.* New York: Columbia University Press, 1937.

Regan, J. W. Guilt, perceived injustice and altruistic behavior. *Journal of Personality and Social Psychology,* 1971, *18,* 124-132.

Sagi, A., & Hoffman, M. L. Empathic distress in newborns. *Developmental Psychology,* 1976, *12,* 175-176.

Schacter, S., & Singer, J. E. Cognitive, social and physiological determinants of emotional state. *Psychological Review,* 1962, *69,* 379-399.

Simner, M. L. Newborn's response to the cry of another infant. *Developmental Psychology,* 1971, *5,* 136-150.

Stotland, E. Exploratory investigations of empathy. In L. Berkowitz (Ed.), *Advances in experimental social psychology,* (Vol. 4). New York: Academic Press, 1969.

Stotland, E., Mathews, K. E., Sherman, S. E., Hansson, R., & Richardson, B. Z. *Empathy, fantasy and helping.* Beverly Hills, Calif.: Sage, 1979.

Thompson, R., & Hoffman, M. L. Empathy and the arousal of guilt in children. *Developmental Psychology,* 1980, *15,* 155-156.

Tulving, E. Episodic and semantic memory. In E. Tulving & W. Donaldson (Eds.), *Organization of memory,* New York: Academic Press, 1972, pp. 381-403.

Zahn-Waxler, C., Radke-Yarrow, M., & King, R. A. Childrearing and children's prosocial initiations towards victims of distress. *Child Development,* 1979, *50,* 319-330.

NORMA DEITCH FESHBACH

Sex Differences in Empathy and Social Behavior in Children [1]

INTRODUCTION

The content of this chapter is addressed to empathy in children and its relationship to social behavior. Central to this discussion will be the role of sex differences. Data drawn from a recent field training study will be presented in an effort to help illuminate the complex relationship between empathy and other personal and social attributes in boys and in girls. A new empathy measure, developed in conjunction with the field training project, and the basis for the empathy-related data to be reported, will be described.

Empathy processes and responses are ascribed a major role in social understanding and interpersonal processes. Empathy is also awarded a special place in the emergence and expression of prosocial behavior. However, theoretical and empirical consistency in the relationship between empathy and positive social behavior, especially in children, is hardly uniform (Feshbach, 1978; Feshbach & Feshbach, 1969, 1979, Note 4; Hoffman, 1977). This is not surprising given the matrix of possible factors that can be implicated in the relationship between empathy and prosocial behavior. In attempting to decipher the reported waxing and waning association between

1. The collection of the data reported in this chapter was partially supported by grants from the National Science Foundation (Grant no. BN 376 01261) and the Bush Foundation Training Program in Child Development and Social Policy at the University of California, Los Angeles. The chapter was written while the author was on sabbatical leave in the Department of Experimental Psychology at the University of Oxford and a recipient of a James McKeen Cattell Sabbatical Award.

315

empathy and prosocial behavior, one can look both to conceptual and to methodological measurement issues as the source of variations in outcome.

Empathy is a highly complex process thought to involve the cognitive, affective, and social domains of the individual. The complexity and multidimensionality of the construct has contributed, in part, to diverse conceptions to empathy, to varying behaviors considered to be empathic and to diverse measurement indices that reflect and are compatible with the theoretical approach to its study (Borke, 1971; Chandler, Greenspan, & Barenboim, 1974; Deutsch, 1971; Feshbach, 1975(a), 1978; Feshbach and Roe, 1968; Rothenberg, 1970). The conceptual issue of whether empathy is predominantly cognitive or affective or both cognitive and affective, a major controversy that dominated the 1970s, has been more recently replaced by such theoretical questions as whether dysphoric and euphoric affects are functionally equivalent in invoking empathy and whether empathy mediates prosocial behavior or merely accompanies it (Feshbach, 1978, Note 3; Feshbach & Feshbach, Note 4; Hoffman, 1975, 1977).

The age stage of the child being studied is probably an important determinant of the observed relationship between empathy and other behaviors, and for a number of reasons. Developmental age changes can occur in the structure and meaning of empathy as well as in the correlated behaviors. Moreover, these age changes can reflect decrements as well as age increments. Affective manifestations of empathy probably sharply change with development. The almost automatic mirroring of a felt emotion in a young child's face is generally replaced by more subtle and elusive cues of an emotional experience in the older child and adult. In fact, in older children gross or strong facial and postural affective responsiveness when observing strong affective stimuli may be a sign of emotional lability and indicate weak ego controls, egocentricity and low empathy. Thus, to observe empathy in a more mature population frequently requires dependence on more inferential information such as that provided by tests and rating scales, measures that involve verbal fluency in the response or receptive comprehension of the requirements of the task.

THE FESHBACH AND ROE AFFECTIVE SITUATION TEST FOR EMPATHY

The difficulties inherent in the conceptualization of empathy are reflected in the problems entailed in its assessment. In the mid-sixties there were few available measures for the assessment of empathy in children. Guided by an interactive cognitive–affective conception of empathy, Feshbach and Roe (1968) developed a series of slide sequences depicting 6–7-year-old children in a variety of different affective situations.

In order to facilitate the evocation of affect, cognitive cues denoting affect were presented in as articulated and explicit a form as possible. Thus, pictures of real children were used instead of stick figures, cartoons, or caricatures (Chandler et al., 1974; Gordon, 1934; Hobart & Fahlberg, 1964–1965); a sequence of pictures (slides) resembling a vignette was employed instead of single pictures or situations (Borke, 1971); and both visual and auditory information were provided rather than visual or auditory alone (Deutsch, 1974; Izard, 1971; Mood, Johnson, & Shantz, 1978). These procedures were selected to enhance the affective involvement of the observer. Maximizing the clarity of the affective cues by including both situation and child in the stimulus presentation was an attempt to minimize variability in empathy arising from differences in social comprehension, thus allowing for the analysis of other experimental effects.

This Affective Situation Test could be used as a social comprehension measure. In this case the child would be asked, "How does the child on the screen feel?" If the intention was to assess empathy, however, the child was asked to state how he or she felt. Each child's direct verbal report was recorded verbatim and constituted the primary index of empathy. Two different empathy indexes could be derived from this procedure, a specific empathy index and a broader empathy index. The specific empathy index required a specific match between the response and the observed situation. For the broader empathy index, a precise verbal match was not required. A major finding of the initial study was the observation that the empathy measure was distinct from the social comprehension measure and that variations in empathy could not be accounted for solely by the ability to recognize the affective experience of others (Feshbach & Roe, 1968).

A number of investigations using the Feshbach and Roe Affective Situation Test for Empathy (FASTE), exploring its different facets and its antecedents and correlates, were subsequently carried out at UCLA and in other laboratories. One of the early studies focused on the relationship between empathy and the converse of prosocial behavior—aggression (Feshbach & Feshbach, 1969). The inverse relationship between empathy and aggression obtained for 6- and 7-year-olds in this study has subsequently been confirmed by a number of other researchers sometimes using the Feshbach and Roe measure or a variation of it, and other times using a different procedure and a different age population (Huckabay, 1972; Mehrabian & Epstein, 1972).

THE EMPATHY TRAINING STUDY

The significance and consistency of the inverse relationship between empathy and aggression was one factor in the underlying rationale of the

Empathy Training Study (Feshbach, 1979). This study is one in a series of investigations in which training procedures and curricula were developed for use with children in the middle elementary grades (Feshbach & Feshbach, Note 5). There were two major overall objectives of the broader experimental program: (a) to develop empathy and fantasy training procedures and curricula to be used with middle elementary children in a variety of settings for the purpose of reducing aggression and antisocial behaviors and fostering prosocial values and behaviors; and (b) to further our theoretical understanding of the psychological properties of empathy and fantasy, particularly in regard to their role in the regulation of aggressive behaviors and the mediation of prosocial behavior.

Whereas the multiple roots of aggressive behavior are acknowledged, a major underlying assumption of this approach is that aggressive and acting-out youngsters in this age range have limited empathic skills or do not make use of these skills in pertinent social situations. A further assumption is the belief that these cognitive and cognitive–affective behaviors can be trained through prescribed intervention procedures, procedures that have evolved from a conceptual model of empathy and social understanding. One consequence of these assumptions is the implication that aggressive and prosocial behavior can be modified without direct efforts to modify the social behaviors themselves, but can be brought about by enhancing mediating processes such as empathy.

The empathy training program was carried out over a 10-week period, in which groups of six children in the third and fourth grades met with a trainer for a 1-hour session three times a week. The population of children was diverse, and included both high and low aggressive boys and girls and a range of ethnic and socioeconomic backgrounds. A variety of assessment approaches entailing different sets of procedures were used. One set was designed to assess the dynamics of the training process itself, and involved the continuous monitoring of each child at each training and control session on a variety of aggressive, prosocial, and attentional scales by highly trained observers. Another set of measures was included to assess the effects or outcome of the training program on the children's level of aggression, prosocial behavior, and achievement skills. Thus, numerous individual difference measures were administered before and after the training intervention to evaluate behavioral changes. The set of measures addressed to children's social behaviors included ratings by teachers, peers, and the subjects themselves of aggressive and of prosocial behaviors. Other measures assessing various cognitive competencies such as perspective taking and role taking, reading achievement, vocabulary, and social comprehension were also included. A third set of empathy-related measures was administered to evaluate intervention effects and to provide information on the mediating processes of empathy and social understanding. But, before these empathy-related measures could be administered, they first had to be developed.

The task of assessment highlights the complexity of the empathy construct and the inevitable discrepancy that exists between psychological processes and their operational representations. A subtle, internal multidimensional process, such as empathy, is especially difficult to catalog through direct observation or standard objective measurement procedures. Studying the phenomenon in children exaggerates the problem of assessment, since verbal reports in young people can be confounded by linguistic competencies. These obstacles notwithstanding, efforts to measure empathy must continue in order to pursue the more central goal of determining its antecedents, its role in development, its behavioral properties, its amenability to change, and its potential as an antidote to the narcissistic and aggressive forces in personality and society (Feshbach, Note 3; Lasch, 1978).

THE THREE-COMPONENT MODEL OF EMPATHY

As suggested earlier, empathy is an elusive concept that has been afforded a diversity of meanings. In essence, empathy is the vicarious sharing of another person's experience. Every empathy situation involves an observer and a stimulus object, who is the person or group of persons perceived by the observer. Through the process of empathy, the observer vicariously shares in some manner and to some degree the experience of the stimulus object. Thus, empathy entails an internal representation in one person of a psychological experience taking place in another person. The potential for empathy exists in any interpersonal context: between parent and child, friend and peer, captor and captive, or worker and co-worker. The realization of this potential, however, depends upon a number of factors concerning the persons involved, such as the nature of the relationship, the level of developmental maturity, the degree of interpersonal sensitivity and similarity, and many situational and dispositional variables that are only beginning to be specified and systematically studied.

It should be noted that the breadth of the construct (and the concomitant problems in definition) frequently leads to the overuse of the word "empathy" so that it explains too much or takes on the property of an all-embracing "good." For example, in recent years empathy has received major attention in the writings of Heintz Kohut (1977). According to Kohut, parental failure to respond empathically to the child's quest for affirmation can lead to the development of a fragmented self-concept and other forms of psychopathology in the child. Kohut's exploration of empathy and its place in the socialization process conveys its theoretical and clinical possibilities.

At the same time, it reflects a problem that commonly arises in the theoretical application of the empathy construct. The construct is weakened when "empathy" becomes synonymous with love, good parenting, emotion, and morality. But empathy can be implicated in many different situations, and therefore the potential for behavior consequences is great.

An analysis of the functions of empathy, especially in children, suggests a broad network of possible effects mediated by empathy. These include social understanding; greater emotional competence; heightened compassion, caring, and related behaviors; regulation of aggression and other antisocial behaviors; increased self-awareness; enhanced communication skills; and greater cohesion between the cognitive, affective, and interpersonal aspects of the child's behaviors (Feshbach, Note 2). Empathy is not equivalent to these personal and interpersonal competencies, nor is it a magic elixir that automatically produces social competence and prosocial behavior. It is but one factor in a matrix of developmental variables that mediates cognitive and affective behaviors.

The three-component conceptual model of empathy that has evolved from my own research with children takes both cognitive and affective factors into account (Feshbach, Note 1; 1975a). The first component of the model—the ability to discriminate affective states of others—derives from the notion that rudimentary manifestations of empathy are dependent upon a cognitive skill. For example, for a child to react empathically to sadness or joy displayed by another person, the child must be able to identify the relevant affective cues that discriminate these emotional states from each other and from a neutral affective state. This discriminatory ability reflects an elementary form of social comprehension. A second cognitive factor influencing empathy that reflects a more advanced level of cognitive competence is the ability to assume the perspective and role of another person. The observing child must be able cognitively to understand the situation from the point of view of the child who is actually experiencing the situation.

Emotional responsiveness is posited as a third component. That is, the observing child must be able to experience the emotion that is being witnessed in order to be able to share that emotion. Emotional responsiveness or readiness represents the affective component of this three-part model of empathy. Each of these three factors—discrimination of affective cues, other-person role perspective, and affective responsiveness-provides the conceptual basis and rationale for our understanding of the functions and consequences of empathy. This conceptual model has proved useful in our Empathy Training Project (Feshbach & Feshbach, Note 5; Feshbach, 1979). Each of these components of empathy provided us with the conceptual basis and rationale for the design and development of the empathy curriculum strategies and the new empathy-related measures.

A question may arise as to why we developed a new empathy measure instead of using the Feshbach and Roe Affective Situation Test (Feshbach & Roe, 1968). There were a number of factors that influenced this decision. Our sample, predominantly 8½–9½-year-olds, was too mature for the original measure. The Feshbach and Roe test appears to be most appropriate for children in the 4–7-year-old age range. Second, we wanted to expand the range of emotions and, particularly, to include another positive affect, the Feshbach and Roe measure including themes for three dysphoric affects—fear, anger, and sadness—and one euphoric affect—happiness. Third, we wanted to include affective stimuli that represented children's perceptions of emotional situations. The stimuli used in the original Feshbach and Roe procedure had been based upon the authors' observations and clinical intuitions (to a large extent validated by our current data). Finally, we wanted to improve the stimuli. Even with young children, changes in fashion affect children's hair styles and clothing. The Feshbach and Roe slides were developed more than 15 years ago, and children's appearances have changed in the intervening period.

THE EMOTIONAL REPORT STUDY

In order to provide appropriate affective stimuli for the new measures, stimuli that would be appropriate to age, sex, and ethnic group, we carried out a study in which we attempted to determine situations that have emotional impact for children. Two hundred forty children ranging in age from 5 to 11, and drawn from five schools varying in socioeconomic status and ethnicity were interviewed. The sample consisted of equal numbers of boys and girls from kindergarten and second, third, fourth, and sixth grades. The children were questioned about situations that respectively aroused each of the following eight emotions: sadness, anger, fear, happiness, pride, embarrassment, surprise, disgust. Responses for the first five of these emotions—sadness, anger, fear, happiness, and pride—that were normative across sex, ethnicity, and the ages we were working with were then used in developing the Empathy-Related Measures (Feshbach & Hoffman, Note 6; Hoffman and Feshbach, Note 7).

A TRIO OF EMPATHY-RELATED MEASURES

Three new instruments were developed: an Affective Matching Measure designed to assess affect discrimination and comprehension, an Emotional Responsiveness Measure designed to tap affective reactivity, and an overall Empathy Measure. In the case of role taking, our efforts to improve upon available measures were unsuccessful. Although the three new measures will be described, the subsequent presentation of data and discussion will be primarily restricted to the Empathy Measure. However, the measures will be reviewed in detail since they are newly developed and unfamiliar in the literature.

The Affective Matching Measure

The Affective Matching Measure is an instrument designed to tap third and fourth grade children's comprehension of affective social events.

The measure is composed of 20 separate 8 × 11 black and white drawings—one set of 10 pictures comprises the male version, and the other set of 10 pictures comprises the female version. Each set contains two drawings illustrating affect-laden events in childhood connected to each of the five emotions: happiness, pride, anger, sadness, and fear. These situations typically involve a main child character in interaction with other children or adults. For example, a happiness situation depicts a child receiving presents at a birthday party. A sadness situation drawing displays the main character at the bedside of a sick grandparent. On each picture the affective facial cues of the central (main) character (child) have been deleted. The subject child is asked to select the appropriate facial stimulus from five different emotional expressions to match each pictorial situation.

As indicated previously, the situational themes represented in the drawings were based on the self-reports of third and fourth grade children about circumstances eliciting emotions in their daily lives. The high frequency responses from intensive interviews with 96 children were incorporated into each drawing.

In order to capture the information represented in such cues as expression and posture, drawings were copied from photographs taken of actual enactments of each situation. Artistic control was used to minimize racial features of the characters. In order to reduce possible sex bias, the two sets of drawings were created using similar sex characters for the boy and girl versions. An essential feature of each drawing is that the face of the main character has been shaded in order not to give informational cues regarding emotional expression or feeling.

The measure is intended for individual administration. The tester tells the subject child that he or she will be viewing pictures of similarly aged children and will be asked to select a face that shows how the story character feels. The child is then shown the response sheet containing five faces, each face displaying characteristic emotional expressions of either anger, fear, happiness, pride, or sadness. The set of 10 pictures is then administered to the child in a prearranged sequence, and in each case the child is asked to pick the appropriate face for the main character for each situation. The order of pictures is controlled to balance emotional valence of the set. The drawings of the emotional situations are shown in the following order: pride, sadness, anger, happiness, fear, sadness, pride, anger, fear, happiness.

Identification of the face displaying the emotional expression that exactly matches the expected emotion receives a score of 1. All other responses were scored 0. The final outcome measure of affective comprehension is the sum score across all 10 drawings.

The Emotional Responsiveness Measure

This empathy and emotional responsiveness measure is designed to tap third and fourth grade children's level of emotional responsiveness to affect laden situations. It consists of a series of taped stories about common childhood experiences that arouse a directed emotional response. In each audio story the child experiences the role of the main character. At the end of each story, the child reports his or her self-perceived level of immediate emotional arousal on a nonverbal response scale.

The measure is comprised of five 1½-minute tape vignettes, each designed to elicit a different emotion: pride, happiness, anger, fear, or sadness. These five emotions were selected for their ease of child identification and their internal balance of positive and negative valence. In addition, a semineutral practice tape for pretest purposes complements the set of stimuli proper.

As indicated previously, the situations for each vignette were based on the self-reports of third and fourth grade children about circumstances eliciting emotions in their daily lives. The high frequency responses from intensive interviews with 96 children were incorporated into each vignette.

Each vignette resembles the style of early radio shows in which a child goes through an emotionally arousing experience. (A representative example for happiness is a family trip to Disneyland at which the child wins a contest.) An adult male narrator outlines the story while background dialogue and sound effects enhance its realism. The story is related in the second person, "you," to allow the subject to enter the central child's role. Since the background material includes some reference to the sex of the central character, two identical, sex-appropriate tapes were created for each vignette.

In order to ensure design similarity, the five vignettes were balanced on a number of critical dimensions. Formally, tapes were matched for number of nouns, verbs, and total quantity of dialogue and narration. Subjectively, tapes were matched on format, style of presentation, and progression of emotional stimulation. A high level of consistency was maintained throughout the stimuli.

In order to increase the verisimilitude of presentation, a number of techniques were employed in the production of taped vignettes. Each story was recorded binaurally to give the listener an impression of actual movement and sound depth. Professional engineering staff and actors were employed to attain the maximum degree of realism in the production and technical quality in the taped product.

The level of children's emotional responsiveness is assessed through children's self-reports of arousal on a 9-point Likert scale. Children are asked to point to the number between 1 (very little) and 9 (very much) that reflects their level of emotional arousal. To ensure children's comprehension of the scale, extensive verbal instructions are used to anchor terminal points. The actual indicated level of response is the outcome measure for each tape. With five vignette presentations, total scores may range between 5 and 45.

The measure is intended for individual administration using a stereo tape recorder. The tester first introduces the child subject to the tape recorder and adjusts the sound level with a prerecorded music tape. The tester informs the subject that he or she will be listening to tapes in which he or she is like the main character. The tester plays the practice tape. The tester introduces the response scale and instructs the child in its use. The tester then asks the child to indicate his or her level of emotional response to the tape. (This response is *not* recorded.)

After each tape presentation, the tester identifies the emotional theme of the story and the child is asked to indicate his or her level of response. In order to ensure minimal overlap between responses, the tapes are presented in a balanced order of emotional valence (negative, positive, negative, negative, positive). Similarly, a nonsense task is inserted between each response and the presentation of the next tape.

The Feshbach and Powell Audiovisual Test for Empathy

The Empathy and Emotional Responsiveness Measure, the main focus of our discussion, was developed to be used with third and fourth grade children for the purpose of assessing emotional responses to the perception of another child experiencing strong emotion. It consists of a series of brief videotapes showing real children involved in common childhood situations related to the experience of different emotions. In each videotape, the subject child sees a story character within an affect-laden situational context, and the story character's immediate facial, postural, behavioral, and verbal emotional reactions. At the end of each tape, the subject child reports his or her self-perceived level of immediate emotional arousal either verbally or on a nonverbal response scale.

The measure is made up of 20 audiovisual tapes, each of approximately 2 minutes' duration. There are two separate stories, each designed to illustrate children experiencing one of five emotions: pride, happiness, anger, fear, or sadness. There is a separate set of 10 videotapes to be used with boys and a similar set to be used for girls. These five emotions were selected for their ease in child identification, and their internal balance of positive and negative valence as a set.

The affect-laden situations contained in each videotaped story were based on the self-reports of third and fourth grade children about circumstances eliciting emotions in their daily lives. High frequency response themes from these intensive interviews with 96 children were incorporated into each story.

The situational contexts of each story are related through the use of dialogue between actors, the use of narration, and the visual elements themselves. Initial narration serves to identify the main character and set the scene for the following story. (Example: It is Saturday afternoon and David or Jane is preparing to fly his or her kite at the park.) The opening shot of each story also visually targets the main character. Narration is used to supplement dialogue and the excitement of the event itself. The final shots in the story end with closeups on the main character to capture more effectively his or her affective response to the situation. In general, each videotaped story builds to an emotionally intense climax. For instance, in one anger story, the main character is repeatedly interrupted by another child while playing. Interference becomes increasingly greater until finally the second child completely destroys the main character's counting game.

The measure was videotaped in color to provide a heightened sense of realism for the viewer. Whenever possible, taping was done outside; the interior scenes were taped in homes. Real settings were employed. All production areas (direction, camera, lighting, sound recording and mixing, editing, and narration) were handled professionally so that the tapes resemble a commercial television product. Whenever possible, children and adults with acting experience were utilized.

Two alternate sets of tapes were filmed to control for sex bias. These sets used the same stories, but were filmed with boy actors in the male version and girl actors in the female version. In order to control ethnic variance, children in the stories represented a variety of ethnic backgrounds (Asians, Caucasians, Hispanics, and Negroes). However, the main child actor in each episode is Caucasian.

The measure using color videoplayback equipment can be administered individually or in small groups. Children are told that they will be seeing short films about children their age, after which they will be asked questions about the films. For the individual administrations each child is individually shown the practice tape and then is asked how he or she feels.

The child's emotional label is recorded verbatim. The child is then asked how much he or she feels: a little, some, or very much. This is also recorded. Following the practice session, the 10 experimental tapes are played. After each tape is viewed, the child is asked to state verbally how he or she feels and how much. In between tape presentations a short word task is inserted to minimize emotional overlap between taped presentations. In the group administration, children in groups of four to six are shown the practice tape. They then receive a packet of response sheets that lists eight different emotions (jealous, embarrassed, proud, afraid, happy, nothing, sad, angry). Alongside each emotion word is a 10-point scale. Children are first asked to circle the emotion label that best describes what they feel, and they are then asked to indicate on the scale how much they feel. Extensive instructions are given to insure children's comprehension of intensity levels on the Likert scales. Children are then shown the 10 experimental videotaped stories in sequence and asked after each tape to indicate on paper what they feel and how much they feel on these nonverbal response scales. In order to eliminate emotional overlap, a short task requiring children to choose appropriate endings for the stories is inserted between tapes. In both administrations, tapes are presented in a balanced order of emotional valence (happy, sad, fear, pride, sad, anger, happy, fear, anger, pride). The emotions of pride and happiness were designated as euphoric empathy; the emotions of anger, fear, and sadness as dysphoric.

The empathy score is a statistic based on the degree to which the subject child's emotional response to each of the 10 videotapes corresponds to the affect experienced by the stimulus child. There were two ways in which this statistic, providing an index of empathy, could be calculated. It is important that we pursued two alternative scoring procedures, since we found that a child's empathy profile looks different according to which factors are considered in measuring empathy. The first procedure relied on a factor analytic model of emotions developed by Davitz (1966). In this case, the empathy score is a function of the extent to which the emotion reported by the child approaches that for the emotion depicted in the videotape. This method is essentially a matching procedure, comparable to that used in earlier studies with the additional property of providing an empirical base for determining the degree of affective match. Also, less information is lost in using this scoring procedure. Whereas the previous scoring method is based essentially upon a "correct–incorrect" match, the factorially based method takes into account the *degree* of similarity between the affect depicted in the videotape and the subject's response. The latter empathy score is an index of the distance, spatially represented, between the depicted affect and the subject's affective label. This distance is based upon the position of each affect in a two-dimensional space formed by the two orthogonal factors, hedonic tone or valence, and physiological activity level, yielded by Davitz's factorial study. The degree of correspondence between the depicted affect and the subject's report of his or her own affect was determined by a geometric averaging of the difference or distance between these respective affects on each of the two factors. When distances between affects are calculated by this method, we find, as we would expect, that affects such as happiness and pride share similar locations, whereas the affects of happiness and depression are quite distant from each other. A less expected and theoretically interesting finding is the relative closeness of fear and anger.

The second procedure for determining an empathy score was based on a different, although related, method for ascertaining the affective match. However, the unique feature of this second scoring procedure was the weight given to the intensity of the subject's affective response, intensity being a multiplicative factor. As in the first procedure, the determination of affect correspondence or matching was empirically based. The Audiovisual Test of Empathy was administered to another sample of children resembling in age and socioeconomic background the subjects in the experimental field training study. These children were asked to describe the emotion experienced by the central figure in each taped vignette. The proportion of children stating a particular affect label for each vignette was determined. These proportions were in close accord with the a priori label of the affect depicted. However, this method allows for the variations in the interpretation of the affect experienced by the central character in the vignette. These affect proportions were then assigned as weights to the affect labels reported by the subjects in the field study in describing their feelings after viewing a vignette. These proportions were then multiplied by the intensity of the subject's affective self-description as indicated on an affect self-rating scale varying from 1 to 9. Intensity of the subject's affective response assumes a major role in this method of scoring empathy.

It should be noted that the potential influence of the sex of the tester (or interviewer) was controlled by the presence and continuous involvement of both a male and female tester during the administration of the empathy related measures. Counterbalancing the sex of the tester was another procedure that could have been followed.

SEX DIFFERENCES IN EMPATHY AND ITS CORRELATES

As indicated earlier, these two alternative scoring methods strongly influence the empathy data obtained in the training study, especially in the reflected relationships between empathy and other dimensions of personality. Whereas the data yielded by the different indexes illuminate some of the theoretical properties of empathy, including its relationship to some aspects of prosocial behavior, the finding of even greater significance is the striking difference in the pattern of relationships obtained for boys and girls. A major finding of these studies is the consistency of sex differences in the personality correlates of empathy. The factors that mediate empathy in boys appear to be quite different from those associated with empathy in girls. These findings have substantial theoretical import and merit more specific review.

Overall, girls respond more empathically than boys. This difference is quite modest, and holds primarily for the euphoric affective stimuli of happiness and pride. However, the correlations between empathy and the various cognitive and social behavior measures were strikingly different for the two sexes.

In examining the results derived from the first affective match measure, which recorded how closely the subject child's emotional state matched that of the story character child, we found that for boys, the correlations between empathy and the various cognitive and social behavior measures were strongly cognitive in nature. Empathy in boys is positively associated with competencies in vocabulary, reading skills, comprehension, spatial perspective taking, fantasy elaboration, and the recognition of changes in feelings of others as assessed by the Rothenberg measure (1970). Less pronounced are positive associations with anxiety over aggression and negative associations with teacher and peer ratings of aggression.

In contrast, empathy in girls is associated with a positive self-concept with teacher, peer, and self ratings of prosocial behavior, and is negatively associated with teacher, peer, and self ratings of antisocial behavior. This sex difference obtains regardless of the particular affect experienced.

These findings showing sex differences in correlations between empathy and personal attributes—namely, association for boys with cognitive competence and low aggression and for girls with positive self-concept and prosocial behavior—are based upon the first index of empathy, the index in which the intensity of the child's affective response was not considered.

When empathy is scored so that the intensity of the child's feeling is given substantial weight, a different picture emerges. This picture varies substantially with the sex of the child and also with the euphoric or dysphoric nature of the affect. That is, the correlates of empathy are influenced by three interacting factors—the sex of the child, the euphoric or dysphoric nature of the vicariously experienced affect (whether happiness and pride or sadness, fear, and anger), and the intensity of the child's affective experience—as to whether the degree of happiness or sadness or other reported affect is taken into account, as well as the affective match. To explicate this interaction, it is helpful to examine the findings separately for each sex.

As Table 12.1 indicates, for boys the interaction of these factors is quite

Table 12.1

Correlates of Empathy in Boys as Related to Scoring Index and Valence of Affect

	Euphoric empathy		Dysphoric empathy	
Affective match	Affective match × intensity	Affective match	Affective match × intensity
Vocabulary		Vocabulary	
		Reading competence	
		Social comprehension	
		Spatial-perspective	
Role-taking skills		Role-taking skills	
			Social sensitivity
Field independent			
	Low prosocial behavior	Prosocial behavior	
			Helping (Exp. Task)
	Antisocial		
	Aggressive		Low aggressive
	Aggression anxiety		Aggression anxiety
	Poor self-concept		

dramatic. With the introduction of the intensity of the child's affective report as a major component of the empathy score, the personality and social behavior correlates of euphoric and dysphoric empathy change, but in very different ways for boys and girls. Boys who report intense dysphoric feelings when viewing children in dysphoric situations of sadness, fear, or anger are more likely to display helping behaviors in experimental situations, to perceive themselves as helpful, to be low in aggression as assessed by peers and teachers, to be anxious over aggression, and to be sensitive to the feelings and motives of others (Rothenberg, 1970). On the other hand, the correlations obtained for boys who report intense euphoric feelings when viewing children in euphoric situations of happiness and pride convey a sharply different image. Boys who report strong euphoric empathic feeling are rated by their teachers as antisocial and by their peers and themselves as aggressive. In addition, these children are rated low in prosocial behaviors, and they tend to have a poor self-concept and to experience considerable anxiety in regard to aggression. It is clear that those boys who empathize strongly in dysphoric situations are different individuals from those who empathize strongly in euphoric situations.

What has happened? The introduction of an affect intensity dimension seems to produce a qualitative change in the meaning of the empathic response. When the first empathy index was used, an index that is essentially a match between the particular affect experienced by the child and that of the stimulus observed without regard to the intensity of the reported affect, empathy in boys is related to a wide range of cognitive skills. This configuration is not dissimilar for euphoric and dysphoric empathy. With the introduction of an intensity factor, social behaviors are now correlated with empathy. Furthermore, the correlations differ for euphoric and dysphoric empathy. (It is of note that the two methods of scoring empathy are uncorrelated.)

These data suggest that empathy in boys does not have a singular meaning. Its meaning depends upon the intensity of the empathic response and whether the boy is empathizing with a euphoric or dysphoric affective situation. *Empathy*, a term that generally carries positive connotations, is found to be associated with negative attributes for boys who respond with intense empathy when seeing others in situations of happiness and pride.

To summarize, then, the correlates of empathy are influenced by three interacting factors: (a) the sex of the child; (b) the euphoric or dysphoric nature of the vicariously experienced affect (happiness and pride versus sadness, fear, and anger); and (c) the intensity of the child's affective experience—that is, whether the reported intensity of affect is weighted heavily, as well as the affective match itself.

Why should this be so? It may be that the critical factors have to do with control and with boundaries—control over emotional responses and boundaries between self and environment. Empathy, to have constructive consequences, demands separation between self and object. The vicarious experience of affect should not reflect the merging of observer and object, but should derive from the observer's ability to assume the perspective and share the feeling of the object. Intense empathic responsiveness may indicate a blurring of the bounds between the self and others. Moreover, the experience of strong affect may override cognitive controls and lead to impulsive behaviors. In the case of boys reacting to an intense emotion, aggression may represent an accessible outlet. This interpretation does not entirely account for the correlational differences found between euphoric and dysphoric empathy.

In general, the capacity to empathize with individuals who are experiencing sadness, anger, or fear (intensely or not) is generally predictive of boys' positive personal and interpersonal attributes. Apparently, the psychological consequences ensuing from sharing another's distress are different from those experienced in sharing another's pleasure. Experiencing another's pain may be very uncomfortable and may motivate one to reduce that discomfort by being helpful and mitigating the other's distress. This motivational sequence may function to control the possible flood of distress feelings. In contrast, for boys, experiencing the other's pleasure would not seem to have these motivational consequences and therefore may not provide restraints against excessive emotional release. A lack of emotional control could well be manifested in boisterousness, hyperactivity, aggressiveness, and other egocentric behaviors. Thus, paradoxically, whereas ordinarily empathy implies an other-centered orientation, associated, for example, with altruism, intense euphoric empathy can foster an egocentric antisocial orientation. Although the disruptive effects of affect intensity appear restricted to euphoric empathy, there are situations in which intense dysphoric empathy can be dysfunctional as well.

This intricate pattern of the meaning of empathy in boys does not hold true for girls. Empathy in girls is associated with a positive self-concept, with teacher and peer ratings of prosocial behavior, with social understanding, and is inversely related to aggression and antisocial behaviors. Girls' personal and social correlates of empathy are fairly consistent for both euphoric and dysphoric empathy regardless of whether affective intensity is measured.

Thus, the factors that appear to contribute to empathy and the relationship of empathy to other personality components seem to be quite different in girls than in boys. Two principal sex differences warrant special comment: the role of cognitive factors and the influence of the intensity of the empathic affect. In the absence of data directly bearing on these differences, one must rely on related studies, conjecture, and ad hoc hypotheses.

In exploring the findings that girls tend to be more empathic than boys, it seems reasonable to infer that girls tend to be interpersonally responsive and sensitive to affective cues in others and in themselves as a consequence of socialization. Some attribute this to the fact that women are usually the primary care givers (Dinnerstein, 1977; Chodorow, 1978). The accuracy of this insight notwithstanding, the data we have collected indicate that empathy is a less convoluted process for girls than for boys. The data also suggest that it takes greater stimulation to induce empathy in boys than in girls. For boys to be empathic to the same degree as girls, greater cognitive sophistication or more intense dysphoric affect is apparently required. The data also suggest that girls assimilate affective experiences more easily than boys. It is likely that the antecedents of empathy and the portrayed emergence of empathy differ for boys and girls.

SEX DIFFERENCES AND THE ROOTS OF EMPATHY

The findings of an earlier study conducted with 6–8-year-old children and their parents bear on the question of sex differences in the developmental antecedents of empathy (Feshbach, 1975b). Using the Feshbach and Roe Affective Situation Test as a measure of empathy, striking sex differences in parental antecedents of empathy were found. The most extensive and reveal-ing set of relationships was obtained for maternal antecedents of empathy in girls. For girls, empathy appears to be related to maternal behaviors reflecting a positive and nonrestrictive relationship with their daughters. Thus, empathy in girls is positively correlated with maternal tolerance and permissiveness and negatively correlated with maternal conflict, rejection, punitiveness, and excessive control.

No significant relationships were obtained between fathers' child-rearing ideas and practices and their daughters' empathic responsiveness. It appears that empathy in girls is linked to mothers and to positive socializa-tion experiences. For boys, the only significant correlation obtained was an inverse relationship between empathy and fathers' fostering of competitive behavior: A paternal emphasis on competition was associated with low empathy in their sons.

The finding that mothers contribute significantly to the development of empathy in their daughters and not in their sons is consistent with the psychodynamic description of the close and unique relationship noted be-tween mothers and daughters. It is of interest that empathy in girls is as-sociated with those maternal antecedents that are likely to foster prosocial behavior and a positive self-image. The finding that empathy in boys is only weakly associated with socialization antecedents is consonant with the link-age in some boys between empathy and various cognitive skills. It is as though empathy in girls develops through identification, normative role adaptations, and positive child-rearing experiences, whereas the routes to empathy in boys are as numerous as the diverse manifestations of empathy for this sex. Another way of phrasing this sex difference is that empathy is ego- or role-syntonic for girls and less so for boys.

What, then, are the roots of empathy in boys? Extant data do not answer this question directly. However, indirect inferences can be drawn. Possible antecedents for boys might include experiences that foster cognitive com-petencies, especially those allied to social understanding. Perceptiveness and social competence, however, do not necessarily imply altruism. In con-trast, boys who have had a dysphoric experience (a serious familial illness or a loss, for example) are, in my opinion, more motivated to be helpful be-cause of their dysphoric empathic responsiveness. Some boys would also appear to be vulnerable to socialization experiences that foster excessive empathic reactions to euphoric situations. One might surmise that this kind of empathic response derives from a child rearing that fosters egocentric concerns and poor emotional controls. It may be more accurate to conceive of the empathy-like behavior of these boys in terms of projection and be-havioral contagion rather than identification and a genuine vicarious emo-tional experience.

These considerations regarding the antecedents of empathy have implications for the development and fostering of empathy through systematic training. The three-component model of empathy described earlier has been refined and embellished. The three components—the ability to identify and discriminate affective cues, the ability to assume the perspective and role of another person, and the capacity to have affective experiences—remain critical components of the empathy process and response. The salience and significance of these components, however, differ according to sex, euphoric and dysphoric empathy, and the affect experienced.

EMPATHY TRAINING AND PROSOCIAL BEHAVIOR

It is useful now to review briefly the findings from the Empathy Training Program. As indicated, the overriding goals of the Empathy project were the regulation of aggression and the promotion of positive social behaviors. The findings were generally consistent with these objectives, particularly in the facilitation of prosocial behavior. Children in the empathy training condition significantly differed from both control conditions in the increment displayed in prosocial behavior. This change is most graphically reflected in the daily behavior ratings made by the children's classroom teachers who had no information regarding the difference between the experimental and control training conditions. Figure 12.1 illustrates that difference in prosocial behavior between the empathy training group and the two control groups became increasingly greater during the course of the training period. The findings for aggression were less clear. Although children in the empathy training groups declined in aggression relative to the nonparticipating controls, the problem solving controls also displayed a decline in aggressive behavior.

We believe the Empathy Training Program could be strengthened by incorporating procedures sensitive to individual and sex differences in the antecedents of empathy. For example, our role-taking activities should take on a stronger emotional note with special attention to dysphoric emotions in addition to the cognitive training component. Perhaps a more fundamental question to raise is whether empathy training itself is the path to prosocial behavior and management of aggression in boys. Boys, particularly, would seem to benefit from training sequences that directly link empathy to such prosocial behaviors as helping, altruism, and nonaggressive methods of conflict resolution. The linkage to empathy would strengthen these prosocial behaviors by integrating the responses with affective and cognitive mediators. Just as it is often insufficient to train merely the behaviors, it may often be insufficient to focus solely on the mediating process.

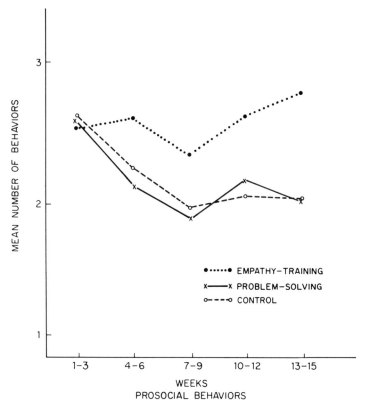

Figure 12.1. **Mean number of prosocial behaviors manifested by the children in the experimental and control groups.**

The observed sex differences, in addition to their implications for training, may also help clarify some unresolved issues and theoretical concerns in the study of empathy, for example, the historical and recurrent question of whether empathy is predominantly a cognitive or an affective process (Chandler, 1973; Chandler, Greenspan, & Barenboim, 1973), the bases for empirical inconsistencies found between empathy and prosocial behavior (Feshbach, 1979), and the nature of the differences between behavioral contagion and empathy. The data suggest that empathy can be predominantly cognitive some of the time. Empathy is more likely to lead to prosocial behavior when the empathic response has a strong affective component, and behavior contagion can predominate over vicarious emotional sharing when emotions are strong and boundaries of self are weak. It follows, then, that empathy and social behavior are not likely to be related in a one-to-one manner.

SOME CONCLUDING COMMENTS

The relationship between empathy and prosocial behavior reflects the complex structure of empathy. The emotional component, in particular, appears to be a source of the variability that is frequently observed in this relationship. If the person is emotionally constricted, the empathic response is likely to be flat and devoid of such motivating properties as aggression inhibition (Feshbach & Feshbach, 1969) and impetus to generosity (Feshbach, Note 2). On the other hand, if the person lacks emotional control and differentiation, the empathic response is likely to be excessive and egocentric, obscuring the cognitive aspects of the social interaction and facilitating inappropriate social behavior. Thus, the cognitive component of empathy, a necessary prerequisite, may be rendered ineffective by the intensity of the stimulated affect.

Still another factor complicating the association between empathy and prosocial behavior is the general issue of the circumstances under which empathy is likely to be evoked. Even highly empathic individuals are not empathic in all situations. Some situations are ambiguous and the affects experienced by the protagonists may be unclear. Or again, there may be conflicting affective and social cues. Still other factors may reduce empathic responsiveness through interference with role and perspective taking. For example, it may be difficult to assume the perspective and adopt the framework of an individual whom one intensely dislikes or with whom one is in sharp disagreement or with whom one has very little in common. Yet other situational factors may have such affective-laden significance that they may overstimulate or, conversely, even block affective responses. All of these situational contingencies reduce the likelihood of an empathic response and of prosocial behaviors that might be mediated by empathy. Thus, the three-component model of empathy—affective discrimination, perspective taking, and affective responsiveness—that provided a basis for examining individual differences in empathy may also provide a basis for analyzing situational sources of variation in empathic responsiveness. Parenthetically, sources of variation suggested by this model can be directly incorporated into the measurement of empathy, and the model can be used as a basis for comparing and analyzing different measures.

The study of sex differences in correlations between empathy and social behaviors provided an opportunity for the indirect assessment of the role of several of these sources of variance. Thus, the nature of the affect displayed by the stimulus person and the emotional responsiveness of the observer proved to influence significantly the empathy reaction and its relationship to social behavior.

The sex difference findings also suggest the importance of factors directly affecting the linkages between empathy and social behavior. Whereas the evocation of empathy may increase the probability of generosity, sharing, helping, and other prosocial responses, it does not automatically elicit these behaviors. Empathy and prosocial behavior, although compatible and synchronous, are not automatically or inevitably tied to each other. There are a number of factors that influence the strength of this linkage. For one, prosocial responses must be available in the child's or adult's repertoire. Some history of specific behaviors and general values concerning prosocial acts is probably a necessary prerequisite, and girls may get more training here. Similarly, some first-hand experience in which empathy has been linked to an effective prosocial action may also be a necessary condition. Second, and perhaps more importantly, it is critical to take into account other motives and values that may be influencing the social behavior of an individual who is experiencing empathy. Thus, parents in the course of child rearing may have to sustain some of the child's frustration and distress; the teacher, to promote a child's independence in problem solving, may have to deny requests for help; and a peer may want to be the winner in spite of the pain resulting from the friend's loss.

In summary, the presence of prosocial behavior cannot be taken as the criterion for empathy. Whereas we expect empathy to contribute to and facilitate prosocial behaviors, the relationship will inevitably be attenuated and complex. Nevertheless, empathy can be one important ingredient of prosocial development. It is the substance that interrelates and sustains positive social orientation and responses in a wide variety of conditions and contexts. Further research will help us specify those conditions and contexts.

REFERENCE NOTES

1. Feshbach, N. D. Empathy: An interpersonal process. In W. Hartup (Chair), *Social understanding in children and adults: Perspectives on social cognition.* Symposium presented at the meeting of the American Psychological Association, Montreal, August 1973.
2. Feshbach, N. D. Empathy in children: A special ingredient of social development. Invited address, Western Psychological Association Meetings, Los Angeles, April 1976.
3. Feshbach, N. D. *The psychology of empathy and the empathy of psychology.* Presidential Address, presented at the 60th Annual Meeting of the Western Psychological Association, Honolulu, May 5–9, 1980.
4. Feshbach, N., & Feshbach, S. Modification of social behavior through empathy training: Conceptual, methodological and ethical issues. Paper presented in D. B. Sawin (Chair), *Empathy in children: Conceptual and methodological issues in current research.* Symposium presented at the meetings of the Society for Research in Child Development, San Francisco, 1979.
5. Feshbach, S., & Feshbach, N. D. *Effects of fantasy and empathy training on aggression.* National Science Foundation Grant no. BN 376 01261 (University of California, Los Angeles), 1975.

6. Feshbach, N. D., & Hoffman, M. Sex differences in children's reports of emotion-arousing situations. Paper presented in D. McGuiness (Chair), *Sex differences: Commotion, motion, or emotion: Psychological gender differences.* Symposium presented at Western Psychological Association Meetings, San Francisco, April 19–22, 1978.
7. Hoffman, M., & Feshbach, N. D. *The ontogeny of sadness in elementary school children.* Paper presented at the 59th Annual Meeting of the Western Psychological Association, San Diego, April 5–8, 1979.

REFERENCES

Borke, H. Interpersonal perception of young children: Egocentrism or empathy. *Developmental Psychology,* 1971, *5*(2), 263–269.
Chandler, M. J. Egocentrism and antisocial behavior: The assessment and training of social perspective-taking skills. *Developmental Psychology,* 1973, *9*(3), 326–332.
Chandler, M. J., Greenspan, S., & Barenboim, C. Judgments of intentionality in response to videotaped and verbally presented moral dilemmas: The medium is the message. *Child Development,* 1973, *44,* 315–320.
Chandler, M. J., Greenspan, S., & Barenboim, C. The assessment and training of role-taking and referential communication skills in institutionalized emotionally disturbed children. *Developmental Psychology,* 1974, *10*(4), 546–553.
Chodorow, N. *The reproduction of mothering: Psychoanalysis and sociology of gender.* Berkeley: University of California Press, 1978.
Davitz, J. R. *The language of emotion.* New York: Academic Press, 1969.
Deutsch, F. Female preschooler's perceptions of affective responses and interpersonal behavior in videotaped episodes. *Developmental Psychology,* 1971, *10*(5), 733–740.
Deutsch, F. Observational and sociometric measures of peer popularity and their relationship to egocentric communication in female preschoolers. *Developmental Psychology,* 1974, *60,* 745–747.
Dinnerstein, D. *The mermaid and the minotaur: Sexual arrangements and human malaise.* New York: Harper & Row, 1977.
Feshbach, N. D. Empathy in children: Some theoretical and empirical considerations. *The Counseling Psychologist,* 1975, *4*(2). (a)
Feshbach, N. D. The relationship of child-rearing factors in children's aggression, empathy and related positive and negative social behaviors. In J. DeWit & W. W. Hartup (Eds.), *Determinants and origins of aggressive behavior.* The Hague, Netherlands: Mouton Publishers, 1975. (b)
Feshbach, N. D. Studies on empathic behavior in children. In B. A. Maher (Ed.), *Progress in experimental personality research* (Vol. 8). New York: Academic Press, 1978.
Feshbach, N. D. Empathy training: A field study in affective education. In S. Feshbach & A. Fraczek (Eds.), *Aggression and behavior change: Biological and social processes.* New York: Praeger, 1979, pp. 234–249.
Feshbach, N., & Feshbach, S. The relationship between empathy and aggression in two age groups. *Developmental Psychology,* 1969, *1,* 102–107.
Feshbach, N. D., & Roe, K. Empathy in six and seven year olds. *Child Development,* 1968, *39,* 133–145.
Gordon, K. A device for demonstrating empathy. *Journal of Experimental Psychology,* 1934, *17,* 892–893.
Hobart, C. W., & Fahlberg, N. The measurement of empathy. *American Journal of Sociology,* 1964–1965, *70,* 595–603.

Hoffman, M. L. Developmental synthesis of affect and cognition and its implications for altruistic motivation. *Developmental Psychology,* 1975, *11,* 607–622.

Hoffman, M. L. Empathy, its development and prosocial implications. In C. B. Keasey (Ed.), *Nebraska Symposium on Motivation* (Vol. 25). Lincoln: University of Nebraska Press, 1977, pp. 169–218.

Huckabay, L. M. A developmental study of the relationship of negative moral–social behaviors to empathy to positive social behaviors and to cognitive moral judgment. *Science and direct patient care II,* 5th Annual Nurse Scientist Conference Proceedings, Denver, 1972.

Izard, C. E. *The face of emotion.* New York: Appleton, 1971.

Kohut, H. *The restoration of the self.* New York: International Universities Press, 1977.

Lasch, C. *The culture of narcissism.* New York: W. W. Norton, 1978.

Mehrabian, A., & Epstein, N. A measure of emotional empathy. *Journal of Personality,* 1972, *40*(4), 525–543.

Mood, D. W., Johnson, J. E., & Shantz, C. U. Social comprehension and affect matching in young children. *Merrill-Palmer Quarterly,* 1978, *24*(1), 63–66.

Rothenberg, B. B. Child's social sensitivity and the relationship to interpersonal competence, intrapersonal comfort and intellectual level. *Developmental Psychology,* 1970, *2*(3), 335–350.

ROBERT B. CIALDINI
DOUGLAS T. KENRICK
DONALD J. BAUMANN

Effects of Mood on Prosocial Behavior in Children and Adults

Acknowledging some protestations to the contrary (e.g., Wispé, 1980), it is nonetheless our argument that mood state is a powerful determinant of altruistic action. The relationship, though, does not appear simple. On its surface the body of mood–altruism findings seems fraught with complexity and qualification. Our review of the literature, however, suggests that the data can be rendered surprisingly systematic and coherent through the application of a straightforward organizing principle or two. Our review suggests, furthermore, that the effort will be worthwhile, in that the nature of the mood–altruism relationship provides an important insight into the basic character of prosocial action.

Before describing the important experimental findings of the mood–altruism area, it will be necessary to present a few simple definitions and one fundamental contention. First, by *altruism* we refer to action taken to benefit another for reasons other than extrinsic reward (e.g., payment, public approval, return favors). Internal reasons for prosocial behavior such as empathic distress, or feelings of personal satisfaction, would not disqualify an action as altruistic by this definition. Second, by *mood* we refer to a condition of labile affective tone that is subject to change through the intervention of relatively weak situational events. Thus, we do not mean to include deep or chronic affective states such as clinical depression. Finally, by *positive* and *negative mood states* we refer to temporarily elevated or depressed moods corresponding to feelings of happiness and sadness. Of course, we recognize that there are a variety of positive and negative mood states in addition to happiness and sadness, especially on the negative side (e.g.,

339

THE DEVELOPMENT OF
PROSOCIAL BEHAVIOR

anger, frustration); however, for the purposes of the present analysis, we will be referring only to happy and sad moods when discussing positive and negative states.

With those definitions behind us, we can turn to our major contention: The relationship between mood and altruism is different for children and adults in a way that reflects upon the essential nature of prosocial activity. Our review of the literature indicates that, in general, children who have the opportunity to behavior altruistically do so most when in a positive mood, to an intermediate degree when in a neutral mood, and least when in a negative mood. Thus, there is a linear relation between mood and altruism for young children. Among adults who have the opportunity for altruism, however, a U-shaped relationship exists with mood state, so that, in general, both positive and negative moods produce more benevolence than a neutral mood. Quite clearly, the crucial point of difference between the two patterns lies in the area of negative moods, which are seen to decrease altruism in children but increase it in adults. Let us begin, then, with an examination of the research investigating procedures designed to induce negative mood and their effect on helping.

NEGATIVE MOOD STATE AND HELPING

The initial finding that subjects often helped others more following an unpleasant event came from studies of harm doing. After a transgression, harm doers tended to become help givers. Initially, explanations for such findings focused upon the act of transgression itself. According to one explanation, altruism following transgression was an attempt to restore equity or social justice (Walster, Berscheid, & Walster, 1970). Another, offered by Freedman and his colleagues (Freedman, 1970; Freedman, Wallington, & Bless, 1967), suggested that such an effect was due to attempts by transgressors to alleviate guilt over their wrongdoing; a third hypothesized that altruism following a transgression was an attempt to restore self-esteem (Carlsmith & Gross, 1969; Krebs, 1970; McMillen, 1971). Several aspects of the data available at that time posed problems for each of the available theories, however. Equity-based notions could not easily explain the fact that transgressors were often found to be willing to help nonvictims as well as victims (e.g., Carlsmith & Gross, 1969; Darlington & Macker, 1966; Rawlings, 1968). Although the guilt and self-esteem theories were able to handle these findings, the fact that increased altruism was often found to occur in subjects who had merely witnessed harm to another (Konečni, 1972; Rawlings, 1968; Regan, 1971) posed problems for these later explanations.

Cialdini, Darby, and Vincent (1973) suggested a Negative State Relief model designed to encompass all the above findings more parsimoniously. In line with earlier findings by Weiss and his colleagues (Weiss, Boyer, Lombardo, & Stitch, 1973; Weiss, Buchanan, Alstatt, & Lombardo, 1971), Cialdini et al. argued that (a) altruism is one means among many that people use to make themselves feel good; and (b) the sight of a harmed other causes one to feel bad (regardless of whether one is responsible for that harm). It was assumed by Cialdini et al. that persons in a negative state strive to make themselves feel better again. The technique used to make oneself feel better need not be tied to the procedures that induced the distress. Thus, the distress caused by transgression could be reduced by altruism, but need not be. An ice cream cone or any other rewarding event would produce the same effect.

In a test of the Negative State Relief model, Cialdini et al. exposed subjects to a rigged accident in which a deck of computer cards was dumped on the floor. A confederate expressed dismay, explaining that the cards were data for a graduate student's thesis and were now hopelessly mixed up. Half the subjects were led to believe that they themselves were responsible for the accident, and the other half believed the confederate to be responsible. Some of the subjects were subsequently exposed to an event (praise or an unexpected and noncontingent sum of money) designed to offer "relief" from the thus induced negative state. The remaining subjects did not experience such a rewarding event. An additional control group was exposed to neither the harmful act nor the rewarding event. All subjects were subsequently asked if they would be willing to donate time to help a fellow student with a class project.

In line with Negative State Relief predictions, subjects exposed to a harmful event were more altruistic than controls, regardless of whether they were themselves responsible for the harm. This effect was erased, however, for subjects who had received a reinforcing event between the occurrence of harm and the request for help.

Receipt of a noncontingent monetary reinforcer could not easily be seen as relieving a sense of guilt, inequity, or lowered self-esteem resulting from harm doing. Yet, that reinforcing event eliminated the tendency to help after transgression, for both harm doers and harm witnesses. Hence, Cialdini et al. concluded that the more general Negative State Relief model best accounted for their own and earlier findings.

Results of a study by Kidd and Berkowitz (1976) also are consistent with the Negative State Relief model. These authors aroused unpleasant dissonance in subjects by asking them to advocate a counterattitudinal position (female college students were to argue *against* the notion that women should receive equal salaries for equal work). Results indicated that dissonance arousal led to significantly more help than in a control condition,

except when subjects were exposed to a humorous tape between the dissonance arousal and the helping opportunity. Again, a positive event unrelated
to self-esteem, guilt, or equity eliminated the increased tendency to help of
subjects in a negative mood state, suggesting that the crucial component of
such helping is its function as a self-gratifier that relieves negative mood.
Correlational data indicated that the mood of subjects in the crucial
dissonance–no relief condition was related to helping in a manner consistent
with the assumptions of the Negative State Relief model. Most help was
rendered by subjects who were experiencing the highest levels of discomfort.

A recent study by Cunningham et al. (1980) provides further support for
the Negative State Relief model. Cunningham et al. (1980) suggested that
since the reinforcing event in the Cialdini et al. (1973) study followed the act
of transgression, it could have been a distraction, serving to displace the
effect of the earlier negative mood inducement, rather than to neutralize it.
Cunningham found, however, that when a positive mood induction (finding
a dime) always preceded a negative mood induction (breaking a piece of
equipment) the effect was the same; the tendency for negative mood to lead
to increased helping was eliminated. Thus, even when the reinforcing event
could not have distracted subjects from their negative state, helping declined
to control levels. Consistent with our model, helping by subjects in a negative mood appeared to be an attempt to relieve their affective condition. The
combination of a positive and negative mood inducement, in either order,
seems to result in the neutralization of both, and the elimination of enhanced helping effects.

Altruism as Self-Reinforcing

Recall that a crucial assumption of the Negative State Relief model is
that altruistic behavior has self-reinforcing qualities. The research of Weiss
and his colleagues (Weiss et al., 1971, 1973) demonstrated that college
subjects would rapidly learn an instrumental response, the sole reinforcer for
which was termination of shock to a fellow student. Likewise, survey data
gathered by Harris (1977) indicate that college students believe altruistic
behaviors to have a mood-enhancing component. Also in line with the view
of altruism as a self-reinforcer is Pisarowicz's (1976) finding that altruistic
behavior canceled the tendency to self-gratify in his adult subjects. Consistent with the viewpoint being presented here, Pisarowicz's data suggest that
for adults altruism is a form of self-reward, in that altruistic action reduced
the need for other forms of self-gratification.

It should be noted that Weiss et al. (1971) indicated that their finding
that "altruism is rewarding [p. 1262]" could be seen to be compatible with

either an evolutionary view in which altruism is viewed as a *primary rein-forcer* for members of the human species, or with a social learning view in which altruism is seen as a *secondary reinforcer* acquiring its rewarding qualities through association with other rewarding events. Cialdini *et al.* (1973) assumed that the latter explanation was true. Our subsequent work was to move us from the realm of attempting to explain the limited transgression–altruism effect to an investigation of the broader issue of the socialization of altruism as a self-reinforcer.

Some Contradictory Data

Although we have discussed a variety of studies that support the direct relationship between negative mood state and helping, a number of investigations by Rosenhan and his colleagues have yielded data that do not fit such a pattern, but instead suggest the reverse. According to Rosenhan's data, negative mood leads to less helping than neutral mood.

Isen, Horn, and Rosenhan (1973), for instance, found that fourth grade children who had been led to believe they had privately failed on a bowling game donated somewhat less to charity than controls.[1] Likewise, Moore, Underwood, and Rosenhan (1973) found that second and third grade children who were instructed to reminisce about sad events were less likely to make charitable donations than were children in a neutral mood control group. This finding was replicated by Rosenhan, Underwood, and Moore (1974) who found that, relative to neutral reminiscences, sad reminiscences produced less altruism in their primary grade subjects. Similarly, Underwood, Froming, and Moore (1977) found negative mood to generate less helping than neutral mood in their elementary school subjects.

A Reconciliation

Although the results that Rosenhan and his colleagues obtained with children would seem to contradict the Negative State Relief model, Cialdini and Kenrick (1976) argued that they were quite compatible if it were assumed that altruism attains its self-gratifying properties as a function of the socialization process. In fact, Cialdini *et al.* (1973) had already argued for a view of altruism as a socialized, secondary reinforcer. As Cialdini and Kenrick (1976) elaborated, altruistic behavior is likely to be paired with a number of reinforcing events in the course of a child's socialization. Parents and teachers, they argued, tend to reinforce selfless behaviors in accordance

---

1. Isen *et al.* (1973) found that a failure experience would in some cases lead to increased helping even in children. This point will be returned to later in the chapter.

with the widely shared norm of social responsibility (Berkowitz & Daniels, 1963, 1964; Goranson & Berkowitz, 1966). Additionally, favors in our society are likely to result in reciprocated benefits (Gouldner, 1960). Finally, Aronfreed and Paskal (cf. Aronfreed, 1968) demonstrated how socialization experiences could lead to the pairing of cues for suffering in others with unpleasant affect in oneself. As a result, aid to another in need could come to produce a positive affective state not only in the recipient, but also in the helper. For young children, who have had relatively fewer experiences with such pairings, altruistic behavior would not be expected to have yet attained the status of a self-gratifier. Thus, Cialdini and Kenrick (1976) predicted that, although children in primary grades (like those studied by Rosenhan and his colleagues) would not engage in helping to relieve a negative mood, children in more advanced grades would progressively do so until they showed the complete adult pattern (i.e., greater help when in a negative mood) by high school age.

To test this hypothesis, Cialdini and Kenrick (1976) had children in three age groups (6-8, 10-12, and 15-18 years) reminisce about sad or neutral experiences. Subsequently, they were given a private opportunity to donate prize coupons to other students. In line with predictions, the youngest children donated slightly less in negative than in neutral mood. These results were reversed in 10-12-year-olds, and this trend continued in 15-18-year-olds, who shared significantly more in the negative than the neutral mood condition.

Sex, Age, and Helping under Negative Mood

Cialdini and Kenrick's results provide support for the position that altruism acquires the properties of a secondary reinforcer through the socialization process. This view implies that helping, in the absence of external reward, should occur earliest for those individuals who have had sufficient conditioning experiences to have internalized the behavior. In our culture, a helpful interpersonal orientation has traditionally been a major part of the socialization experience of females (Block, 1973), and as such they are likely to have internalized this behavior earlier than males. This conditioning could occur in a number of ways. Young females may be rewarded more frequently for helping others and may receive help more often than males (Fagot, 1978). Furthermore, the kinds of vicarious or empathic reinforcement described by Aronfreed (1970) to be a critical part of the socialization of altruism may happen more often for young females. Hoffman (1977), for example, points out that numerous studies have shown females of all ages to be more empathic than males. This affective base is likely to lead to more frequent pairings of vicarious positive and negative reinforcement associated with witnessing a helping situation. Thus, in a number of ways, females may be provided with a more intensive experience with reward and helping and would be expected to exhibit an earlier altruistic orientation.[2]

Given the developmental perspective offered by Cialdini and Kenrick (1976), it could be presumed that there is a particular age range at which altruism would be expected for females but not for males. Recall that young children in that study were the least helpful in a private helping situation when in a negative mood. Cialdini and Kenrick argued that these children (ages 6–8) had not as yet internalized the reward value of altruistic behavior and as such were unable to dispel the mood state via the self-reinforcing effects of prosocial action. Saddened children in this study who were slightly older (ages 10–12) tended to help somewhat more than did neutral subjects. This reversal became significant among the older subjects (ages 15–18) who did employ altruism in the service of mood relief. No effects for sex of subject were found. These data suggest that the males and females had not as yet internalized altruism by age 12; however, somewhere between ages 12 and 15 they had.

From the point of view we have developed thus far, we would expect females between ages 12 and 15 to have internalized altruism earlier than males of this same age group. The Negative State Relief model suggests that females of this group should, to a greater degree than males, attempt to dispel a negative mood through increased benevolence. Our own data in an unpublished study support this prediction. In that experiment, males and females between the ages of 12 and 13 were chosen as subjects and proce-dures similar to those used by Cialdini and Kenrick were employed. Subjects were administered a bogus hearing test and provided with prize coupons as a result of their participation. They were subsequently asked to reminisce about sad or neutral experiences and next were provided with an opportu-nity to donate some coupons to other students. Although subjects were randomly assigned to a public or a private opportunity to behave charitably, only the results concening private charitability need concern us here. The results (displayed in Table 13.1) indicated that female subjects donated significantly more prize coupons than males, $F(1, 30) = 23.13$, $p < .01$. The means in Table 13.1 also reveal a significant sex by mood interaction, $F(1, 30) = 7.05$, $p < .02$; male subjects in a negative mood contributed the fewest prize coupons, whereas female subjects in this condition contributed

---

2. We realize that there is a great deal of controversy surrounding reviews of this literature (Block, 1976; Maccoby & Jacklin, 1974; Whiting & Edwards, 1973). However, these reviews did not limit their consideration to only those behaviors that we would define as altruistic (i.e., helping in the absence of external reward). Therefore, we do not find those reviews directly informative for the points we wish to make.

Table 13.1
Mean Number of Prize Coupons Donated[a]

| | Sex of subject | |
Mood	Males	Females
Negative	2.22 (9)	8.80 (10)
Neutral	4.50 (6)	6.44 (9)

[a] N per cell is indicated in parentheses.

the largest number of prize coupons. Female subjects in this study behaved in a manner analogous to Cialdini and Kenrick's older group subjects, whereas males were comparable in behavior to the younger subjects. If, as we suspect, females internalize the reward value of prosocial action at an earlier age than males, these data fit our Negative State Relief perspective quite well. Young women, but not young men, of 12–13 years of age will have been socialized to find helping a self-gratifying event and will employ it to remove negative mood. Of course, the exact age at which this male– female difference occurs is likely to be affected by other factors such as socioeconomic status, race, etc.; however, in general, we would expect that girls would show increased altruism under negative mood earlier than boys.

Further Support for the Instrumental Argument

One tenet of the Negative State Relief model is that altruism is a so-cialized (i.e., conditioned) reinforcer that can be used to relieve temporary states of sadness. The logic of this view suggests that young children, who have not yet completed the socialization process, would not find altruism self-gratifying and, hence, would not normally employ it to relieve a sad mood. For them, an altruistic response normally would not be a rewarding one since it involves the giving up of resources. However, this same logic suggests that if the helping opportunity were imbued with a reward quality, young children would use this opportunity to dispel a negative affective state. A condition meeting that requirement is one in which helping while in a negative mood is associated with direct extrinsic reward. Social approval is one example of extrinsic reward commonly associated with benevolence. This form of reward, then, could also be instrumental to the relief of a negative mood state and might well be employed for that purpose, even by young children.

A recent study investigated this possibility. In that study, Kenrick, Baumann, and Cialdini (1979) contended that young children, although aware that helpfulness is highly approved of by adults (Eisenberg-Berg, 1979), have not internalized these standards (cf. Bryan & Walbek, 1970; Ugurel-Semin, 1952). In keeping with the instrumental perspective of the Negative State Relief model, Kenrick *et al.* proposed that, since young children should be aware of the normative sanctions for helping, they would show increased helping as a function of negative mood when the helping response was imbued with a reward quality in the form of adult approval.

In a test of this view, Kenrick *et al.* chose males and females aged 6–8 as subjects in the first of two experiments. External reward for charitable behavior was made available to one-half of these subjects in the form of social approval through the presence of the experimenter (the public condition). In a second condition, children were allowed to behave charitably in the absence of the experimenter (the private condition). Prior to this manipulation, the children were placed in a negative or neutral mood through a reminiscence procedure identical to that used by Cialdini and Kenrick. It was hypothesized that helping would be increased for only those subjects who were in a negative mood and in the public condition. These subjects were expected to help in order to dispel the negative mood via the approval of the experimenter. Subjects in the other three conditions were not expected to differ among themselves. Results confirmed these expectations: Subjects in a negative mood for whom a helping response might perform an instrumental function were significantly more charitable than all other subjects. Furthermore, and in line with previous literature involving children's helping in the absence of external reward, negative mood subjects were somewhat less likely to be helpful in private. Thus it seems that young children for whom altruism has not as yet become internalized will help in the service of mood relief only when it is associated with extrinsic reward. In a second experiment, Kenrick *et al.* replicated these results.

Taken in combination with earlier studies by Cialdini and his associates, the results of the study by Kenrick *et al.* can be interpreted as favoring the Negative State Relief model. In keeping with the instrumental basis of the model, it appears that if altruistic behavior is not perceived as leading to the relief of negative mood, helping will not occur. A study by Weyant (1978) with adults provides additional support for this instrumental view. Weyant suggested an interpretation of the findings of Cialdini and his associates that is entirely compatiable with the model. According to Weyant, the critical factor in determining an individual's willingness to help while in a negative mood state is the perceived reward value of the helping act. The reward value of helping is suggested to be a function of the perceived costs and benefits associated with the act. Weyant argued that only when the costs of helping are low and the benefits are high should individuals attempt to alleviate a negative mood state through helping. Conversely, when costs are high and benefits low, Weyant proposed that helping should decrease. Finally, Weyant contended that if both costs and benefits are high, or if both are low, helping in a negative mood will not differ from baseline.

In a test of the above hypotheses Weyant provided college students with positive and negative mood-inducing experiences through false feedback on a bogus aptitude test. Neutral mood subjects were not administered the test. Following the false feedback, the perceived reward value of the request for help was manipulated. Subjects were asked to help collect donations for the American Cancer Society (high benefit) or for Little League Baseball (low benefit) by going door to door (high cost) or sitting at a collection booth (low cost). The three hypotheses concerning negative mood received support. Subjects in a negative mood helped significantly more than controls only when the cost of this behavior was low and the benefit high. When requested to help in a situation in which the cost for helping was high and the benefit low, subjects tended to help less than controls. All other negative mood conditions did not differ significantly from controls. Apparently, individuals help when in a negative mood if the reward value involved in helping is sufficient to remove the mood. If there is something associated with the helping act that prevents an individual from making a response that is instrumental to the relief of negative mood, helping will not occur. In the case of Weyant's subjects, increased helping under negative mood was obviated by experimentally removing the ability of the act to serve as a self-gratifier.

Self- versus Other-Related Sadness and Helping

A study by Thompson, Cowen, and Rosenhan (1980) provides data that might be seen as inconsistent with the Negative State Relief model. These authors asked their college student subjects to imagine a powerfully distressing event—the discovery that one's closest friend is dying of cancer. Some subjects were led to concentrate on the emotional effects of the event upon the friend. Other subjects were led to attend to what their own emotional reactions to the event would be. Mood checks showed the two imaginal sets to have produced essentially similar amounts of reported sadness in subjects. Yet, when willingness to help was measured later in the experiment, the two groups were markedly different. Those subjects in the attention-to-other's-reactions condition were significantly more helpful than neutral mood controls. Such a result fits well with the prior literature showing enhanced adult benevolence under conditions of negative mood. However, subjects in the attention-to-own-reactions condition did not help significantly more than controls.

How are we to explain these findings in terms of the Negative State

Relief model? In the case of subjects who attended to the other's reactions, there is no problem. These adults imagined a friend's anguished reactions and felt consequent sorrow. When given the opportunity to dispel their personal sadness via altruism, they seized it. But why should it be that subjects asked to attend to their own reactions, who reported themselves equally sad, did not seize that opportunity? There are two possibilities. First, in imagining their own reactions, subjects were asked to experience certain emotions in addition to sorrow that they were not asked to experience if imagining a friend's reactions. For example, subjects in the attention-to-own-reactions condition were instructed to imagine themselves "angry" at the unfortunate state of affairs. Subjects in the attention-to-other's-reactions condition, on the other hand, were instructed to imagine that their friend was "angry." Thus, those in the former condition would be likely to feel actual anger, whereas those in the latter condition might be expected only to feel sorry that their friend was angry. Were this the case (regrettably, the lack of an experimental check on anger does not allow us to be sure), the data would fit nicely with the Negative State Relief model. In each of the prior statements of the model (Cialdini *et al.*, 1973; Cialdini & Kenrick, 1976; Kenrick *et al.*, 1979), anger was specified as an unpleasant mood that would not be expected to lead to helping. Because anger frequently is reduced through aggressive rather than benevolent action, helping would not be instrumental to anger relief and thus would not occur frequently.

Although such an interpretation of the Thompson *et al.* (1980) data is conceivable, we tend toward another. It is, in fact, the explanation proposed by Thompson *et al.* themselves. They suggested that an inner focus may render an individual inattentive or insensitive to the gratifying nature of external events, such as the opportunity to help others: "For people who are not focused on others, altruism may be perceived as either unrewarding or insufficiently rewarding to induce altruistic behavior [p. 298]." An interpretation of this sort also is compatible with the Negative State Relief model. Any procedure that reduces the perceived reward character of a helping act should reduce its ability to relieve depressed affect and should, consequently, weaken the negative-mood-leads-to-help effect.

Self- versus Other-Related Sadness in Children

The Thompson *et al.* study raises the question of whether the differential helping patterns observed in the adult subjects of that experiment would occur in young children as well. The question has implications for the Negative State Relief model's assumption that such children would not show increased altruism under negative mood, regardless of a self or other focus. As Thompson *et al.* state,

If children are less altruistic during negative mood because they are insufficiently socialized, as Cialdini and Kenrick suggest, focus of attention is likely to have little impact on the altruism rates of children who feel bad because they will tend not to help under any circumstances. However, we cannot rule out the possibility that children, like adults, may show increased altruism if they focus their attention on others [p. 299].

The question, then, is whether young children focusing on other-related sad events will be more altruistic than neutral mood controls (as were Thompson et al.'s adult subjects).

Fortunately, there are data from a study by Barnett, King, and Howard (1979) that help to provide an answer. These authors had second through sixth grade children think about sad events that occurred either to themselves or others.[3] Subsequently, the children were given a private opportunity for generosity. At first glance, the results seemed to indicate that other-related sadness increases altruism even in children. However, a closer examination of the data reveals that this effect holds only for older children.[4] In fact, a trend in the opposite direction appears for young children. As Table 13.2 indicates, only the more socialized, older subjects showed the adult pattern of helping witnessed in Thompson et al.'s college students. The younger subjects, regardless of sadness focus, produced the typical reduction in altruism found so often before in the negative mood conditions of studies employing children of similar age (e.g., Cialdini & Kenrick, 1976; Kenrick et al., 1979; Moore et al., 1973; Rosenhan et al., 1974). In keeping with the Negative State Relief hypothesis, it seems that neither self- nor other-related sadness leads to enhanced altruism among young children, who are not yet able to use generosity as a self-gratifier.

A Three-Step Model of the Socialization of Altruism as a Self-Reinforcer

When the findings of our own investigations of the negative mood – altruism link are integrated with those that have emerged from other recent work on the development of altruism, a three-step model of socialization of charitable behavior emerges (cf. Kenrick et al., 1979). According to such a model, altruistic behavior is initially neutral (or punishing, to the extent that it involves loss of personal resources). The next step involves cognitive awareness of the norms concerning the positive value of altruism, without

3. Although both happy and sad inductions were attempted in this manner, manipulation checks indicated that only the sad mood was successfully manipulated. Consequently, we will discuss only the negative mood treatment effects.
4. Thanks are due Mark Barnett for making his data available to us.

Table 13.2
Generosity Data from Barnett, King, and Howard (1979)

	Younger children (approximately 7–10 years) focus		Older children (approximately 10–13 years) focus	
Mood	Self	Other	Self	Other
Neutral	3.50	5.43	9.00	8.00
Sad	2.57	3.40	2.86	12.50

Note. Cell means refer to the number of prize tokens donated to other children.

internalization of those norms. At the third step the normative standards are internalized, and altruism becomes autonomous, now maintained by self-reinforcement processes. The evidence for this sequence is reviewed below:

Step I. At this stage the individual is unsocialized, and rarely performs altruistic behavior, since it involves a loss of rewards. There is a good deal of evidence that preschool-aged children help infrequently, and that when they do, it is unrelated to social approval (Eisenberg-Berg & Hand, 1979; Fisher, 1963; Ugurel-Semin, 1952). For the individual at this stage, negative mood would be expected to have only a depressing effect on altruism (which would be experienced as additional punishment).

Step II. At this step, primary grade children have adopted norms regarding the value of prosocial behavior but have not internalized them (see Rosenhan, 1970, for a discussion of normative versus autonomous helping). Several researchers have found evidence that children at this step are aware that helping can lead to reinforcement (Bryan & Walbek, 1970; Eisenberg-Berg, 1979; Ugurel-Semin, 1952), and Kenrick et al. (1979) found that primary grade children would employ a public helping opportunity to obtain external rewards when they were in a negative mood, just as they would engage in other forms of self-gratification under such circumstances (Rosenhan et al., 1974). However, an anonymous helping opportunity is not used in such a manner at this stage. The findings from studies that have used private donations as dependent variables find either no effect of negative mood on helping among primary grade children, or a decrease in helping under such circumstances (Cialdini & Kenrick, 1976; Kenrick et al., 1979; Moore et al., 1973; Rosenhan et al., 1974; Underwood et al., 1977).

Step III. After sufficient experience with external reward for charitable action, such behavior itself becomes a secondary reinforcer. As discussed above, adults will learn an operant response solely to alleviate suffering to a fellow human being (Weiss et al., 1971, 1972). Adults perceive altruistic behavior to have mood-elevating properties (Harris, 1977), and seem to use helping opportunities in much the same way as they use opportunities to self-gratify (Cialdini *et al.*, 1973; Baumann, Cialdini, & Kenrick, 1981).

This model, and the research that supports it, are directly in keeping with earlier social learning conceptions of the development of altruism (Aronfreed, 1968; Rosenhan, 1970). According to the current social learning framework, the cognitive, behavioral, and affective domains are not independent systems, but are interdependent and mutually essential aspects of an internalized prosocial scheme. Approaches that consider only the cognitive domain or only the affective domain can only give us an incomplete understanding of altruistic behavior.

POSITIVE MOOD STATE AND HELPING

Despite the existence of the to-be-expected occasional failure to replicate (e.g., Donnerstein, Donnerstein, & Munger, 1975; Weyant & Clark, 1977), procedures designed to produce positive mood have been remarkably consistent in their effect on helping. Recalling happy events (Moore *et al.*, 1973; Rosenhan *et al.*, 1974), receipt of unexpected money (Isen & Levin, 1972) or gifts (Isen, Clark, & Schwartz, 1976), humor (Kidd & Berkowitz, 1976), empathy leading to positive mood (Aderman & Berkowitz, 1970), task success (Kazdin & Bryan, 1971), even exposure to pleasant weather (Cunningham, 1979), all have produced increased altruism. Moreover, the promotive effect of good mood on benevolence appears for both children and adults over a variety of helping measures, ranging from the sharing of experimental winnings with classmates (Rosenhan *et al.*, 1974) to volunteering for blood donations (Kazdin & Bryan, 1971).

Ironically, in the face of the mountain of data confirming the effect of happy mood on altruism, there is little understanding of why the relationship exists. The situation is almost the reverse of that on the negative mood side, where an analysis of the circumstances under which the negative mood-helping effect does and does not appear has produced a developing understanding of its mediation. The robustness of the positive mood-helping effect over operations, measures, and subject populations, however, has made it difficult for workers in the area to home in on basic mediational processes. A phenomenon that occurs over a wide range of differing situations generates evidence for its generality but not its causation. Nonetheless, there are a number of explanations for the positive effect of good mood on altruism that seem possible. These explanations can be broken down into two general categories.

Instrumental Explanations

An instrumental view of the good mood–altruism relationship would hold that increased helping occurs as a direct response to a positive mood. One such explanation would involve a mood maintenance motive (e.g., Levin & Isen, 1975). By this account, enhanced benevolence represents an attempt to maintain elevated affective tone. Using the same logic that was employed in the interpretation of the negative mood–altruism effect, one could argue that a happy individual wants to prevent the loss of positive mood and so engages in the self-gratifying act of altruism more willingly. Certain studies have produced results that are compatible with the mood maintenance notion (Isen & Levin, 1972; Isen & Simmons, 1979). However, these findings are susceptible to other, noninstrumental interpretations as well.

Furthermore, data from the experiment by Weyant (1978) argue against mood maintenance as the primary mediator of helping under positive mood. Recall in our earlier discussion of Weyant's data that we saw that the helping tendency of subjects in a negative mood was greatly affected by the rewards and costs associated with the act; increased aid was offered only when its costs were low and benefits high. However, when Weyant put subjects in a good mood, they helped to an enlarged extent regardless of the costs and benefits associated with the act. Thus, the self-gratifying nature of the aid had little effect on the helping decisions of subjects in a positive mood. Of course, we would not expect good mood to render subjects wholly impervious to reward–cost considerations; for example, a helping act involving certain death is unlikely to be performed to any greater degree by happy than neutral mood individuals. However, the Weyant data are consistent with the conclusion that mood maintenance via self-reward is not the predominant motive underlying positive mood-based benevolence.

A similar conclusion can be reached from a consideration of research on young children. Even though altruism has not acquired reward status in such children, they become significantly more generous when happy (Moore et al., 1973; Rosenhan et al., 1974). Once again the pattern stands in counterpoint to that appearing under conditions of negative mood, where young children help less (Cialdini & Kenrick, 1976; Moore et al., 1973; Rosenhan et al., 1974). Although rewards and costs influence the likelihood of virtually all acts to some degree, it seems that they play a far more primary role in the determination of prosocial action among sad than among happy individuals. In general, then, we would suggest that altruistic action will be undertaken as an instrumental attempt to influence mood only when the mood is a sad one.

Concomitance Explanations

If altruism does not occur in the service of positive mood maintenance, then why does it occur to such an enhanced degree in happy subjects? One category of explanation would suggest that a happy mood creates a state of affairs from which altruism flows as a by-product. That is, helping does not occur as a direct reaction to positive affect but as a simple concomitant of some other consequence of good mood.

Optimism concerning Future Resources

One such explanation can be derived from a study by Masters and Furman (1976). They found that children induced to feel happy were more optimistic that good things would come to them in the future. Thus, it is possible that positive mood generates a feeling that one's future outcomes will be good and, consequently, leads to generosity in the sharing, giving away, or risking of one's current resources. It may be the optimism about future outcomes accompanying positive mood, rather than the mood itself, that mediates increased altruism among happy individuals. Interestingly, Masters and Furman found no corresponding pessimism in children who had been put in a negative mood.

Accessibility of Positive Memories

A second concomitance explanation comes from the work of Isen, Shalker, Clark, and Karp (1978), who found that when their adult subjects were in a good mood they were better able to retrieve positive memories than either neutral or negative memories. It is conceivable, then, that happy mood subjects confronted by a helping opportunity will recall more positive than negative memories of past helping instances and will, accordingly, be more willing to render aid. Once again, there was no symmetrical effect for negative mood; Isen et al. (1978) found no tendency to recall more bad memories among their sad mood subjects.

Liking for Others

A third concomitance explanation suggests that positive mood inductions cause subjects to like others more. Evidence in this regard is quite strong in documenting that such inductions increase the attractiveness of strángers (cf. Clore, 1975). A consequence of this greater attraction for others may be an increased willingness to aid them. As with the other concomitance accounts, the liking interpretation proposes that it is not positive mood but a consequence of it that promotes altruism.

Currently, there is little in the literature to favor one form of concomitance explanation over another. It is our feeling, however, that a concomitance approach (or a combination of them) will eventually be demonstrated to mediate the oft-found relationship between happy mood and increased helping. But, whether a primarily instrumental or concomitant meditor proves best, the question of why good mood leads to altruism strikes us as the most interesting one in the mood–altruism area at present. We would urge researchers in the area to turn their attention to its resolution.

CONCLUSION

At the outset of this chapter, we suggested that the relationship between mood and altruism is more systematic than might appear at first glance. One organizing principle that renders the relationship much more understandable involves the functional significance of the helping act for the altruist. Altered levels of benevolence can be said to occur as an *instrumental response* to a given mood state (i.e., as an active attempt to change or preserve the mood) or as a *passive concomitant* of the mood state (i.e., as a simple by-product of the psychological consequences of mood).

Our view is that, under conditions of negative mood, the motivation for altruism is principally instrumental in character. It occurs primarily in the service of negative mood relief. Thus, the decision of whether or not to help is heavily influenced by the reward properties of the prosocial act. On the positive mood side, however, helping does not occur in reaction to the pleasant affect (i.e., as an attempt to maintain the mood). Rather, it mostly occurs through the action of certain psychological consequences of elevated mood (optimism for future outcomes, accessibility of positive memories, liking for others, etc.).

It was contended at the start of this chapter that the difference in the mood–altruism pattern for children and adults is importantly instructive as to the fundamental character of prosocial action. The crucial difference between those patterns lies in the area of negative mood, where young children have reliably been found to be less altruistic and where adults have been mostly more altruistic. It has been our argument that these opposing trends are due to the differential reward value that altruism holds for socialized versus unsocialized individuals. For young children, helping in the absence of external rewards is a losing proposition, involving the expenditure of resources without corresponding personal benefit. Under conditions of negative mood, which dispose an individual to consider the instrumental properties of helping action, young children will be unlikely to render such aid. The enculturation process, however, changes the basic nature of altruism by infusing it with a self-gratifying quality. For the normally socialized adult, then, altruism can dispel a negative mood, and, under appropriate circumstances, will be employed for that purpose by individuals whose usual affective state has been temporarily depressed.

An implication of our position is to place us squarely on the side of Campbell (1975) in his recent debate with sociobiologists (cf. Wispé & Thompson, 1976) concerning the biological versus social evolution of altruism. Campbell disputes the assertion that self-sacrifice in humans is genetically selected for, and argues that altruistic dispositions are primarily products of social indoctrination. Such an argument aligns well with our view that altruism is originally a nonpreferred response that acquires a more preferred status only through the socialization experience. Of course, it is possible that altruism becomes a more frequently emitted behavior with increasing age (cf. Bryan & London, 1970), especially among individuals in a negative mood, through a process of biological maturation. From our perspective, however, the social evolution of altruism seems the more likely possibility.

REFERENCES

Aderman, D., & Berkowitz, L. Observational set, empathy and helping. *Journal of Personality and Social Psychology,* 1970, *14,* 141-148.

Aronfreed, J. *Conduct and conscience: The socialization of internalized control over behavior.* New York: Academic Press, 1968.

Aronfreed, J. The socialization of altruistic and sympathetic behavior: Some theoretical and experimental analyses. In J. R. Macaulay & L. Berkowitz (Eds.), *Altruism and helping behavior.* New York: Academic Press, 1970, pp. 103-126.

Barnett, M. A., King, L. M., & Howard, J. A. Inducing affect about self or other: Effects on generosity in children. *Developmental Psychology,* 1979, *15,* 164-167.

Baumann, D. J., Cialdini, R. B., & Kenrick, D. L. Altruism as hedonism: Helping and self-gratification as equivalent responses. *Journal of Personality and Social Psychology,* 1981, *40,* 1039-1046.

Berkowitz, L., & Daniels, L. Responsibility and dependency. *Journal of Abnormal and Social Psychology,* 1963, *65,* 429-436.

Berkowitz, L., & Daniels, L. Affecting the salience of the social responsibility norm: Effects of past help on the response to dependency relationships. *Journal of Abnormal and Social Psychology,* 1964, *68,* 275-281.

Block, J. H. Conceptions of sex role: Some cross-cultural and longitudinal perspectives. *American Psychologist,* 1973, *28,* 512-526.

Block, J. H. Assessing sex differences: Issues, problems and pitfalls. *Merrill-Palmer Quarterly,* 1976, *22,* 283-308.

Bryan, J. H., & London, P. Altruistic behavior by children. *Psychological Bulletin,* 1970, *13,* 200-211.

Bryan, J. H., & Walbek, N. H. Preaching and practicing generosity: Children's actions and reactions. *Child Development,* 1970, *41,* 329-353.

Campbell, D. T. On the conflicts between biological and social evolution and between psychology and moral tradition. *American Psychologist,* 1975, *30,* 1103-1126.

Carlsmith, J. M., & Gross, A. Some effects of guilt on compliance. *Journal of Personality and Social Psychology*, 1969, *11*, 240-244.

Cialdini, R. B., Darby, B. L., & Vincent, J. E. Transgression and altruism: A case for hedonism. *Journal of Experimental Social Psychology*, 1973, *9*, 502-516.

Cialdini, R. B., & Kenrick, D. T. Altruism as hedonism: A social development perspective on the relationship of negative mood state and helping. *Journal of Personality and Social Psychology*, 1976, *34*, 907-914.

Clore, G. L. *Interpersonal attraction: An overview.* Morristown, N.J.: General Learning Press, 1975.

Cunningham, M. R. Weather, mood, and helping behavior: The sunshine Samaritan. *Journal of Personality and Social Psychology*, 1979, *37*, 1947-1956.

Cunningham, M. R., Steinberg, J., & Grev, R. Wanting to and having to help: Separate motivations for positive mood and guilt-induced helping. *Journal of Personality and Social Psychology*, 1980, *38*, 181-192.

Darlington, R. B., & Macker, C. E. Displacement of guilt produced altruistic behavior. *Journal of Personality and Social Psychology*, 1966, *4*, 442-443.

Donnerstein, E., Donnerstein, M., & Munger, G. Helping behaviors as a function of pictorially induced moods. *Journal of Social Psychology*, 1975, *97*, 299-300.

Eisenberg-Berg, N. The development of prosocial moral judgment. *Developmental Psychology*, 1979, *15*, 128-137.

Eisenberg-Berg, N., & Hand, M. The relationship of preschoolers' reasoning about prosocial moral conflicts to prosocial behavior. *Child Development*, 1979, *50*, 356-363.

Fagot, B. I. The influence of sex of child on parental reactions to toddler children. *Child Development*, 1978, *49*, 459-465.

Fisher, W. F. Sharing in preschool children as a function of amount and type of reinforcement. *Genetic Psychology Monographs*, 1963, *68*, 215-245.

Freedman, J. L. Transgression, compliance and guilt. In J. R. Macaulay & L. Berkowitz (Eds.), *Altruism and helping behavior.* New York: Academic Press, 1970, pp. 155-161.

Freedman, J. L., Wallington, S. A., & Bless, E. Compliance without pressure: The effects of guilt. *Journal of Personality and Social Psychology*, 1967, *7*, 117-124.

Goranson, R. E., & Berkowitz, L. Reciprocity and responsibility reactions to prior help. *Journal of Personality and Social Psychology*, 1966, *3*, 227-232.

Gouldner, A. W. The norm of reciprocity: A preliminary statement. *American Sociological Review*, 1960, *25*, 161-178.

Harris, M. D. The effects of altruism on mood. *Journal of Social Psychology*, 1977, *102*, 197-208.

Hoffman, M. L. Sex differences in empathy and related behaviors. *Psychological Bulletin*, 1977, *84*, 712-722.

Isen, A. M., Clark, M., & Schwartz, M. The duration of the effect of good mood on helping: "Footprints in the sands of time." *Journal of Personality and Social Psychology*, 1976, *34*, 385-393.

Isen, A. M., Horn, N., & Rosenhan, D. L. Effects of success and failure on children's generosity. *Journal of Personality and Social Psychology*, 1973, *27*, 239-247.

Isen, A. M., & Levin, P. F. Effect of feeling good on helping: Cookies and kindness. *Journal of Personality and Social Psychology*, 1972, *21*, 354-358.

Isen, A. M., Shalker, T. E., Clark, M., & Karp, L. Affect, accessibility of material in memory, and behavior: A cognitive loop? *Journal of Personality and Social Psychology*, 1978, *36*, 1-12.

Isen, A. M., & Simmons, S. The effect of feeling good on a helping task that is incompatible with good mood. *Social Psychology*, 1978, *41*, 346-349.

Kazdin, A. E., & Bryan, J. H. Competence and volunteering. *Journal of Experimental Social Psychology,* 1971, *7,* 87-96.

Kenrick, D. T., Baumann, D. J., & Cialdini, R. B. A step in the socialization of altruism ad hedonism: Effects of negative mood on childrens generosity under public and private conditions. *Journal of Personality and Social Psychology,* 1979, *37,* 747-755.

Kidd, R. F., & Berkowitz, L. Dissonance, self-concept, and helpfulness. *Journal of Personality and Social Psychology,* 1976, *33,* 613-622.

Konečni, V. J. Some effects of guilt on compliance: A field replication. *Journal of Personality and Social Psychology,* 1972, *23,* 30-32.

Krebs, D. L. Altruism: An examination of the concept and a review of the literature. *Psychological Bulletin,* 1970, *73,* 258-302.

Levin, P., & Isen, A. M. Further studies on the effect of feeling good on helping. *Sociometry,* 1975, *38,* 141-147.

Maccoby, E. E., & Jacklin, C. N. *The psychology of sex differences.* Stanford, Calif.: Stanford University Press, 1974.

McMillen, D. L. Transgression, self-image, and compliant behavior. *Journal of Personality and Social Psychology,* 1971, *20,* 176-179.

Masters, J. C., & Furman, W. Effects of affect induction on expectancies for serendipitous positive events success on task performance, and beliefs in internal or external control of reinforcement. *Developmental Psychology,* 1976, *12,* 481-482.

Moore, B., Underwood, B., & Rosenhan, D. L. Affect and altruism. *Developmental Psychology,* 1973, *8,* 99-104.

Pisarowicz, J. A. *Self-reinforcement following altruistic behavior.* Paper presented at the meeting of the Rocky Mountain Psychological Association, Phoenix, Ariz., May 1976.

Rawlings, E. I. Witnessing harm to others: A reassessment of the role of guilt in altruistic behavior. *Journal of Personality and Social Psychology,* 1968, *10,* 377-380.

Regan, J. W. Guilt, perceived injustice, and altruistic behavior. *Journal of Personality and Social Psychology,* 1971, *18,* 124-132.

Rosenhan, D. Some origins of concern for others. In P. Mussen, J. Langer, & M. Covington (Eds.), *Trends and issues in developmental psychology.* New York: Holt, Rinehart & Winston, 1970.

Rosenhan, D. L., Underwood, B., & Moore, B. Affect moderates self-gratification and altruism. *Journal of Personality and Social Psychology,* 1974, *30,* 546-552.

Thompson, W. C., Cowan, C. L., & Rosenhan, D. L. Focus of attention mediates the impact of negative affect on altruism. *Journal of Personality and Social Psychology,* 1980, *38,* 291-300.

Ugurel-Semin, R. Moral behavior and moral judgment of children. *Journal of Abnormal and Social Psychology,* 1952, *47,* 463-474.

Underwood, B., Froming, W. J., & Moore, B. S. Mood, attention, and altruism: A search for mediating variables. *Developmental Psychology,* 1977, *8,* 209-214.

Walster, E., Berscheid, E., & Walster, G. W. The exploited: Justice or justification? In J. R. Macaulay & L. Berkowitz (Eds.), *Altruism and helping behavior.* New York: Academic Press, 1970, pp. 179-204.

Weiss, R. F., Boyer, J. L., Lombardo, J. P., & Stitch, M. H. Altruistic drive and altruistic reinforcement. *Journal of Personality and Social Psychology,* 1973, *25,* 390-400.

Weiss, R. F., Buchanan, W., Alstatt, L., & Lombardo, J. P. Altruism is rewarding. *Science,* 1971, *171,* 1262-1263.

Weyant, J. M. Effects of mood states, costs, and benefits on helping. *Journal of Personality and Social Psychology,* 1978, *36,* 1169-1167.

Weyant, J. M., & Clark, R. D., III. Dimes and helping: The other side of the coin. *Personality and Social Psychology Bulletin,* 1977, *3,* 107-110.

Whiting, B., & Edwards, C. P. A cross-cultural analysis of sex differences in the behavior of children aged 3 through 11. *Journal of Social Psychology,* 1973, *91,* 171-188.

Wispé, L. The role of moods in helping behavior. *Representative Research in Social Psychology,* 1980, *11,* 2-15.

Wispé, L. G., & Thompson, J. N. The war between words: Biological versus social evolution and some related issues. *American Psychologist,* 1976, *31,* 341-384.

V

PERSONALITY AND PROSOCIAL DEVELOPMENT

PAUL MUSSEN

Personality Development and Liberal Sociopolitical Attitudes

Altruism, generosity, and consideration for others are not manifested exclusively in intimate interpersonal relationships. Rather, prosocial attitudes and actions can be extended and generalized to individuals or groups with whom we have no direct contacts. Donating money to provide food, shelter, and medical care for impoverished children in faraway lands is obviously a prosocial act. Advocacy of social and political changes that improve the welfare of others and, at the same time, entail some significant costs to the advocates, may also be regarded as prosocial behavior. By definition, sociopolitical liberalism—that is, maintaining liberal attitudes and orientations—involves consideration of others and giving higher priority to the welfare of others, or of society at large, than to one's own interests. Hence, sociopolitical liberalism may be regarded as conceptually linked with proclivities to prosocial behavior. Suppose, for example, that a wealthy businesswoman devotes time, money, and energy to campaigning for candidates who promise improved education and greater welfare benefits for the poor as well as higher minimum wage levels. If the businesswomen's actions are successful and those candidates are elected to office, she will have to make some substantial sacrifices, probably paying higher taxes and raising her employees' wages.

The thesis of this chapter is that political liberalism is, in fact, generally prosocial and, furthermore, liberalism has, to a great extent, the same antecedents that prosocial behavior has. The contents of the chapter are primarily accounts of two studies of the personalities and backgrounds of political liberals and conservatives, and an attempt is made to delineate clearly the

363

THE DEVELOPMENT OF
PROSOCIAL BEHAVIOR

parallels between these and the personal and socialization factors associated with strong proclivities toward prosocial behavior.

Except for the now classic study of *The Authoritarian Personality* (Adorno, Frenkel-Brunswick, Levinson, & Sanford, 1950), we have little information about how personality structure and dynamics affect sociopolitical beliefs and activities. There has been relatively little research related to this issue in recent years, perhaps because many social scientists have become disillusioned with the notion that personality variables play a significant role in shaping social behavior. Some researchers in the area of social development maintain that personality structure accounts for relatively little of the variance in prosocial behavior (see, for example, Gergen, Gergen, & Meter, 1972); analogously, some students of political socialization are convinced that political behavior cannot be explained in terms of personality variables (Greenstein, 1965; Rossi, 1966; Sears, 1975).

To scholars concerned with personality development, such conclusions seem counterintuitive and premature. In their view, personality structure mediates the individual's perceptions and his or her conceptualization of other people and of society, and, thus, influences a broad range of social attitudes and behavior. Political orientations and dispositions toward prosocial actions are therefore regarded as linked in important ways with the individual's personality structure and this structure, in turn, develops from, and is continuous with, early established, deep-seated characteristics and self-concepts.

There is already substantial evidence that strong tendencies to behave prosocially are associated with a number of basic traits of personality. Summarizing the relevant literature on this issue, Rushton concludes that "there appears to be a general prosocial, moral person characterized by what has often been labelled ... 'ego strength' [Rushton, 1980, p. 83]." "Furthermore, the consistently altruistic person is likely to have an integrated personality, strong feelings of personal efficacy and well-being, and what generally might be called 'integrity' [Rushton, 1980, p. 85]." The findings of two studies reported in this chapter suggest that these kinds of personal characteristics are also descriptive of many political liberals.

ANTECEDENTS OF LIBERALISM AND CONSERVATISM IN ADULTS

The data of the first study were collected between 1968 and 1970 when the participants, members of the longitudinal studies conducted at the University of California, Berkeley, were between 40 and 50 years of age (Mussen & Haan, 1982). At that time, they were asked their opinions about two issues that were polarizing the nation, black demands and the Vietnam war. In addition, each participant rated himself or herself on a scale from "very conservative" to "radical."

Participants were classified as liberals, conservatives, or middle-of-the-roaders only if their responses to questions about the war and black demands, and their self-rating on political position, were self-consistent. That is, only those who rated themselves as liberal or liberal-radical felt the war was wrong from the beginning, favored rapid withdrawal from Vietnam, supported black demands, and felt black militancy was justified were classified as liberals. The conservatives were those who rated themselves as strongly or moderately conservative, believed the United States must win the war, and were unsympathetic with black demands, believing that the socioeconomic position of most blacks was "their own fault." Middle-of-the-roaders were those who rated themselves as "middle-of-the-road," said they "didn't know what to think" about ending the war although they had approved of it in the beginning, and claimed they were not prejudiced against blacks but disapproved of black militancy.

Using these criteria, we were able to classify 73% of the total group: 31 (21 females and 10 males) were liberals, and 71 (33 females and 38 males) were conservatives, and 43 (18 males and 25 females) were middle-of-the-roaders. Of the 26% who were unclassifiable, 7% had given insufficient information; the other 19% were inconsistent in their ideological positions.

Since the participants included in the present investigation were members of comprehensive longitudinal studies, all of them have been studied intensively—by means of periodic tests, observations, and interviews—for approximately 40 years. Half of them have been studied since birth, and the other half since they were 10 or 11 years of age. The vast amount of accumulated data on these individuals permits tests of a number of hypotheses about the associations between personality variables and sociopolitical views in middle adulthood. Furthermore, because the personalities of the participants had been studied longitudinally, we could investigate these relationships developmentally. Specifically, the longitudinal data could be used to determine whether personality characteristics that distinguish adults of different political orientations emerge early and differentiate liberals and conservatives consistently over long periods of time.

The investigation focused on personality characteristics in four time periods: early adolescence (ages 13 and 14), late adolescence (17 or 18), early adulthood (the early 30s), and middle adulthood (the ages between 40 and 50). A Q-sort technique was used to objectify and quantify the rich qualitative personality data and to provide assessments of 90 personality variables at all four time periods (Block, 1961). In making the Q-sort ratings, each of the raters, a well-trained clinician, had a set of 90 cards, each with an adjective or statement, such as *rebellious, values intellectual matters, is self-dramatizing, seeks reassurance.* The Q-sort rater read through all the relevant interview protocols for a particular participant for one period—late adolescence, for example—and then sorted the 90 cards into seven piles according to the degree to which they described the participants. The items most characteristic of him or her were placed in Pile 7, and the least descriptive adjectives or phrases in Pile 1. The ratings were made for each participant for each time period separately and independently, that is, the clinician rating a participant's characteristics in late adolescence had no information about his or her personality in early adolescence or early adulthood; the clinician making the early adulthood rating had no information about the subject's personality characteristics at other periods.

We were particularly interested in 32 of the 90 personality and social variables on which the participants had been assigned Q-sort ratings at all four time periods. Specific hypotheses were formulated about the differences between liberals and conservatives in these variables. These hypotheses were derived from the findings (and interpretations of findings) of *The Authoritarian Personality* study (Adorno et al., 1950). Although the population studied included very few real authoritarians, it was assumed that liberals would be relatively more similar to nonauthoritarians than to authoritarians, whereas conservatives were more likely to resemble authoritarians more closely.

Therefore, it was hypothesized that liberals would have higher mean ratings than conservatives on these 15 Q-sort items: *introspective; unconventional in thinking; expressive; values intellectual matters; insightful; socially perceptive; fantasizing; aesthetically reactive; sensuous; philosophically concerned; values independence; evaluates situations in motivational terms; rebellious; wide interests; prides self on objectivity.*

Conservatives, according to our hypotheses, would be rated higher on the average than liberals on the following 17 variables: *uncomfortable with uncertainty; skeptical; somatizes; self-defensive; fastidious; submissive; reassurance-seeking; repressive; extrapunitive; overcontrolled; condescendings; basic hostility; moralistic; conventional; power-oriented; distrustful;* and for males, *masculine sex-typed behavior,* and for females, *feminine.*

To test the relationships between political orientation and each of the 32 Q-sort items, the technique of multivariate analyses of repeated measures was used. This procedure enabled us to examine all the relationships of interest. Specifically, we could determine whether each of the 32 characteristics differentiated the three political groups (liberal, middle-of-the-road, and conservative) when all four periods of measurement were considered as one (that is, with sex and period of testing controlled) or whether the three political groups had different developmental trends (that is, significant period of testing × political orientation interaction with sex-controlled). The same analyses showed that there were no significant differences between men and women on any of these variables.

Results

The statistical analyses demonstrated that liberals and conservatives were significantly differentiated, as predicted by the hypotheses, persistently—that is, in at least three of the four time periods—in 9 of the 32 variables. Throughout the prolonged period extending from early adolescence through middle adulthood (*all four* time periods, covering approximately 35 years) the liberals were, according to the Q-sort ratings, significantly more *philosophically concerned* and *rebellious* than conservatives, *valued independence more,* and *prided themselves more on objectivity.* On the other hand, for these same long periods, conservatives were consistently rated higher than liberals in *submissiveness* and *seeks reassurance.*

In addition, as predicted by the hypotheses, liberals and conservatives were significantly different from each other, in the predicted directions, in their tendencies to be *moralistic, conventional,* and *uncomfortable with uncertainty* (intolerant of ambiguity) during early adolescence and adulthood, but not during late adolescence, that is, at three of the four time periods. Specifically, the liberals were more *moralistic* than the conservatives in late adolescence, and the two groups did not differ in *conventionality* or *uncomfortable with uncertainty* at that time. However, later on, according to the Q ratings, the liberals became less *moralistic, conventional,* and *uncomfortable with uncertainty,* whereas conservatives maintained consistently high ratings in these variables over the years.

It may be concluded that from early adolescence to middle adulthood, liberals are more concerned with subjective matters and philosophical issues, show relatively little adherence to conventional values, value their independence highly, and are rebellious. These qualities, together with their willingness to acknowledge their own feelings and to regard their own and others' problems with detachment (high ratings in *prides self on objectivity*), reflect high levels of ego strength. In contrast, from early adolescence onward, conservatives are relatively insecure and submissive to authority, feeling that they are controlled by external forces or conditions (external locus of control); hence they have strong needs for reassurance.

Perhaps the liberals' relatively high *moralistic* rating during later adolescence represents an aspect of their philosophical concerns. Philosophically concerned adolescents are likely to hold strong, and perhaps absolute, moral values and hence are likely to be regarded as highly moralistic. However, with increasing maturity, the liberals apparently become more aware of the relativity of moral values. For many reasons, adolescents commonly have powerful needs to be "one of the group" and to structure their lives and activities. Consequently, it may be difficult to detect group differences in conventionality and comfort with uncertainty, even among groups that differ in other significant respects.

Hypotheses about liberal–conservative differences in *tendencies to fantasize, sensuousness,* and *extrapunitiveness* were also partially confirmed. That is, the predicted differences in these characteristics were found at some, but not all, phases of the long period of development studied. Thus, in adolescence, liberals were not markedly different from conservatives in amount of *fantasizing,* or in *sensuousness* but, according to the Q-sort ratings, the former became strikingly more prone to fantasizing and more sensuous than the conservatives in early and middle adulthood, as the hypotheses predicted. The mean rating of liberals on *extrapunitive* was lower than that of conservatives in late adolescence and early adulthood, partially confirming another hypothesis, but the two political groups did not differ with respect to this variable either in early adolescence or in middle adulthood.

Independent corroboration for some of these Q-sort findings was found in the scores on the California Personality Inventory, a personality test administered to the participants during the two adult periods. Although none of these CPI subscales differentiated among the men of different political orientations in early adulthood, liberal women scored highest of the three political groups on a number of scales that measure adaptability, ego strength, independence of thought, responsibility, and intellectuality. Specifically, they received relatively high scores in the following subscales: *flexibility, psychological mindedness* ("interest in, and responsiveness to, the inner needs, motives, and experience of others [Gough, 1957, p. 11]"); *intellectuality* (capable of detachment in situations requiring impartial analysis and awareness); *logical analysis* ("analyzing thoughtfully, carefully, and cogently the aspects of situations personal and otherwise [Gough, 1957, p. 11]"); *concentration* (ability to set aside disturbing or attractive feelings or thoughts in order to concentrate on the task at hand); *suppression* ("holding infeasible and inappropriate impulses in abeyance and restraining such expression until an appropriate time or place presents itself [Haan, 1965, p. 374]"); and *total coping* (general use of coping mechanisms to handle problems). Consistent with their characteristically conventional thinking noted in the Q-sort assessments, conservative women scored highest of the three groups in the *communality* scale, which indicates that "their reactions and responses correspond to the modal (common) pattern of this inventory [Gough, 1957, p. 11]."

The tests administered in middle adulthood revealed these same kinds of group differences, and, in addition, at this time the liberal women scored highest of the three groups in the subscale *regression in the service of the ego*. This last measures their willingness and ability to "utilize past feelings and ideas . . . in an imaginative way in order to enrich the solution of problems, the handling of situations and the enjoyment of life [Haan, 1965, p. 5]." In middle adulthood, the conservative men, like their female counterparts, scored highest of the three groups in the *communality* scale, whereas the liberals scored highest in *flexibility*.

What emerge from all these findings, taken together, are two distinct personality constellations, each reasonable, coherent, internally consistent, and to a large extent stable over time. The first, the liberal personality constellation, reflects fundamental ego strength, emotional security, a strong sense of self, flexibility, realization of one's own and others' psychological makeup—characteristics associated with proclivities to prosocial behavior (Mussen & Eisenberg-Berg, 1977; Rushton, 1980; Staub, 1978). The particular traits that make up this constellation include independence, rebelliousness, unconventional thinking, orientation toward philosophical and intellectual matters, pride in objectivity, and flexibility, as well as a sense of responsibility for one's own actions and ability to cope with problems. The conservative personality constellation, which contrasts sharply with the liberals', is characterized by relatively low ego strength, lack of self-confidence, belief that one cannot control important events, and dependence upon others for guidance and reassurance. Specifically, the conservatives were found to be lacking in independence, submissive, conventional in their thinking, high in needs for reassurance from others, moralistic, disinclined toward introspection, and uncomfortable with uncertainty (that is, intolerant of ambiguity).

Most of the characteristics, or constellations of characteristics, associated with liberal and conservative orientations develop early, are clearly discernible by early adolescence, and remain relatively stable (continuous) over prolonged periods of time. For these reasons it may be concluded that sociopolitical ideologies, like tendencies to behave in prosocial ways, are linked to fundamental, early established personality structures, and cognitive styles.

Unfortunately, we have only limited understanding of the processes involved in the acquisition of these characteristics or in their expression in attitudes and actions. However, it seems reasonable to hypothesize that individuals who possess high degrees of ego strength, self-confidence, and a sense of security also have an *active* orientation to the world, the ability to evaluate situations objectively, and a willingness to take risks and make personal sacrifices. Consequently, they are more likely to help people in need or distress, to cooperate with others and share what they have, and to act altruistically. At the same time, these personal characteristics may be the bases of proneness to examine, and to challenge, the sociopolitical and economic status quo, and to advocate changes in existing institutions—that is, the bases of liberal political views and actions consistent with these views.

In contrast, those who are submissive, conventional, intolerant of ambiguity, and strongly in need of reassurance feel that they are controlled by external forces, unable to determine what happens to them. Accepting the notion of helplessness, they are likely to be constricted in their approaches toward social problems and events, more threatened by personal sacrifice, less willing or able to assess the degree of another's distress or to respond to it, and thus less apt to act altruistically. Such individuals also tend to accept the status quo without question or challenge, to advocate maintaining the existing sociopolitical system, and to oppose social change—in short, they adhere to a conservative sociopolitical philosophy and behave accordingly.

PERSONALITY AND SOCIALIZATION IN RELATION TO ADOLESCENTS' POLITICAL ORIENTATIONS

Although the data of the longitudinal study demonstrate that liberal and conservative orientations are embedded in personality structure, they tell us nothing about the socialization experiences or other factors that shape these characteristics and attitudes.

To investigate these dynamics, Nancy Eisenberg-Berg and I (1980) studied a group of 13 –18-year-old high school students because early adolescence is the period during which political attitudes begin to be formed, "a watershed era in the emergence of political thought [Adelson, 1971, p. 1013]." The findings of an earlier study revealed that, during the high school years, many boys and girls become more clear and consistent in their sociopolitical attitudes, liberal or conservative (Mussen, Sullivan, & Eisenberg-Berg, 1977).

Two major hypotheses were the foci of this study. The first states that adolescents, like adults, formulate sociopolitical ideologies that are consistent with their underlying personality structures and motivations; liberal adolescents are significantly more independent, nonconventional, flexible in their thinking, introspective, and philosophically oriented than their conservative peers. The latter are expected to be more conforming and conventional, less tolerant of ambiguity, and less concerned with intellectual matters.

The second hypothesis is based on the assumption that personality structure is, to a great extent, shaped by socialization experiences, particularly early experiences in the family. It was therefore hypothesized that, in their interactions with their children, parents of liberal adolescents foster the development of characteristics such as flexibility, tolerance, examination of one's own and others' motives, autonomy, and independence. In contrast, parents of conservative adolescents promote the acquisition of a configuration of traits that includes rigidity, intolerance of ambiguity, conformity, extrapunitiveness, anti-intraceptiveness, and adherence to traditional ways of thinking and behaving.

A test of sociopolitical liberalism consisting of 32 agree–disagree items (for example, "Whether you are rich or poor you can get the same good education in this country"; "Communists who disagree with the American system should not be allowed to make speeches against our government") was administered to 209 students in the ninth, eleventh, and twelfth grades of a high school in an upper middle-class, white, conservative suburban community. The 37 students (19 boys and 18 girls) who scored highest in liberalism and the 35 most conservative (16 boys and 19 girls) became participants in a more intensive personality study. Included were the following measures: a 49-item self-concept Q sort with adjectives or phrases such as "successful . . . really tops," "sympathetic," "conventional"; a 91 child-rearing practices Q sort with parallel items applying to mother and father (examples: "my mother [father] wanted me to make good impression on others"; "my mother [father] encouraged me to control my feelings at all times"); a questionnaire about parent–child agreement on attitudes, political issues, religion, friends, and vocational choice; and an empathy scale. In responding to the Q sorts, participants sorted the deck of cards into seven equal piles according to the degree to which they were descriptive of themselves or their parents. Thus, in taking the self-concept Q sort, they placed adjectives or phrases that were regarded as most characteristic in Pile 7, and the least descriptive items were placed in Pile 1. Analogously, in sorting the 91 child-rearing Q-sort cards, participants placed the 13 items most descriptive of the parent in Pile 7, the 13 least descriptive in Pile 1.

In responding to the questionnaire on parent–child agreement in attitudes, participants rated the degree of perceived similarity between their own attitudes and those of their mothers and fathers (from 1 for "no agreement" to 4 for "complete agreement") on religion, political party preference, student demonstrations, civil rights, occupational choice, and choice of friends. The Mehrabian–Epstein questionnaire (Mehrabian & Epstein, 1972), which contains 33 items—for example, "I often remain cool in spite of the excitement around me," and "Some songs make me happy"—was administered to assess each participant's empathic tendencies. Respondents indicated the degree of agreement with each statement on a scale of 1 to 4.

The hypotheses underlying the study were tested by comparing the responses of the liberal and conservative adolescents to the items of the Q-sort decks and the questionnaires. The two groups differed significantly, or nearly significantly, in 12 of the 49 self-concept variables, and, what is most important, the differences were consistent with predictions derived from the first hypothesis, and also with the findings of the study of middle-aged liberals and conservatives reported earlier. Like liberal adults, liberal adolescents gave evidence of greater ego strength, self-esteem, independence, and more inner locus of control than the conservatives did. The latter proved to be less inner-directed, more conventional, more concerned with adherence to traditionally approved values, and governed by external authority.

Specifically, analysis of the self-concept Q-sort ratings showed that conservatives regarded themsleves as significantly, or nearly significantly, more *conventional* or *square* than liberals; more *responsible, more dependable;* more *ambitious,* eager to *make something of themselves;* more likely to *worry about doing something bad* (that is, disapproved). Their needs for order and intolerance of ambiguity were evident in their relatively high self-ratings on the two items *orderly, neat,* and *organized, plan ahead.* In addition, their mean self-rating on *successful, really tops*—significantly higher than that of the liberals—seems entirely consistent with the prediction that they are not inclined toward self-examination or self-criticism, that is, they tend to be antiintraceptive.

In contrast to their conservative peers, the liberal adolescents regarded themselves as more *rebellious* and as *independent thinkers,* and they disagreed more strongly with their parents' attitudes on religion, political party preference, student demonstration, and civil rights. (However, the two groups did not differ in degree of agreement with parents' attitudes about nonpolitical or nonideological issues, such as attitudes about vocational choice and choice of friends.)

The liberals also exhibit more inner-directedness than conservatives, and closely connected with this, more marked tendencies toward introspection. According to their self-ratings, they regarded themselves as more *self-pitying* and more *sympathetic,* more accepting of others' feelings and emotions. Liberal boys also rated themsleves as more *loving, tender,* and *mellow* than their conservative peers. These self-ratings may be interpreted as indicating that great capacity for empathy, believed to be a fundamental motive for altruism, is also an important determinant of political liberalism. Independent support for this interpretation is found in the participants' responses to the empathy questionnaire. Liberals of both sexes scored higher in empathy than their counterparts among the conservatives.

From these findings it may be reasonably inferred that the liberal adolescents regard their locus of control as internal, and they possess a strong sense of personal control. A number of investigators suggested that these characteristics are critical antecedents of propensities toward helping and behaving altruistically (Rushton, 1980; Staub, 1978). Again, we find that the same personal qualities are associated with both high levels of prosocial behavior and liberal sociopolitical attitudes. Apparently, both of these aspects of social interaction are related, for they reflect, or are mediated by, the same basic, underlying personality–motivational patterns.

To test the second major hypothesis concerning parent–child interactions that foster liberal or conservative thinking, we examined the ratings assigned to the maternal and paternal child-rearing Q-sort items by the two groups of adolescents. Analysis of the significant differences in ratings makes it clear that liberals' and conservatives' relationships with their parents were very different and that the two groups perceived their parents as stressing different values and orientations.

According to their Q-sort responses, the parents of the liberal adolescents maintained high standards for their children, encouraging them to develop independence, personal responsibility, and inner controls. This is indicated by the liberal girls' endorsements—much stronger than those of their conservative peers—of statements about their mothers' expectation that they would "handle problems themselves when [they] got into trouble" and teaching them that they were "responsible for what happens" to them. The findings for the boys were comparable. Compared with their conservative peers, liberal boys assigned higher ratings to statements about their fathers' high expectations and encouragement of independence and about their mothers' permitting them to make their own decisions about many matters.

In addition, liberals of both sexes more frequently reported that they were trained to control their feelings. Liberal boys reported that their mothers did not permit them to express anger at them, and that their fathers punished them for showing jealousy toward siblings. This parental emphasis on emotional self-control may reflect the parents' attempts to inculcate in their children maturity, independence, and a sense of personal responsibility.

Conservative adolescents reported that, in their training, their parents stressed conformity with authority, making a good impression on others, and the acquisition of "good"—that is, conventional, traditionally approved—behavior. For example, conservative girls reported that their mothers wanted them to make good impressions on others, and neither parent permitted them to say "bad" things to teachers. Their mothers were also more likely than the mothers of liberal girls to reward them with extra privileges when they were "good" and their fathers thought it was "good practice for me to perform in front of others." Such emphases in child rearing are likely to promote powerful motives to seek approval and reassurance from others as well as the belief that external forces—rather than one's own desires and decisions—control behavior.

In brief, as predicted from the second hypothesis, parents of conservatives trained their children for an "external" orientation, that is, an orientation toward conformity and compliance with authority, making a good impression on others, and seeking reassurance from others. The liberals' parents, in contrast, have socialized their children in ways that foster greater internalization, reflected in acceptance of responsibility for one's own actions, independence of thought and behavior, and self-control of feelings and emotions.

Several of these antecedents of political liberalism resemble the socialization experiences that produce prosocial behavior in children. For example, the parents of the politically liberal adolescents, like the parents of prosocial children, maintain high standards for their children and expect them to behave in mature ways. These parental practices and attitudes form an integral part of what Baumrind (1971) describes as authoritative parenting.

Although parental modeling of prosocial behavior is considered to be a major factor in stimulating children's prosocial behavior (Mussen & Eisenberg-Berg, 1977), we find no evidence that among participants in this study, political liberalism is the outcome of identification with parents or observation of parental liberalism. On the contrary, compared to the conservative adolescents, liberals regard themsleves as less closely attached to their parents, more rebellious against them, and more independent of their authority, ideas, and opinions. This is, perhaps, a function of the demographic characteristics of the population studied, children of middle-class parents living in a predominantly conservative community. Although we do not have any direct assessments of the parents' political beliefs, it seems safe to assume that few of the parents were politically liberal or active in behalf of liberal causes. It may be more appropriate to explore the role of modeling or identification with parents in the formation of politically liberal attitudes in a population of adolescents that includes a substantial number whose parents are politically liberal. Further research needs to be addressed directly to this problem as well as to the more general issue of the specific techniques used by parents in attempting to inculcate political values in their children.

Comparisons between the factors found to be associated with political liberalism and the antecedents of prosocial behavior reveal many similarities and parallels, thus providing convincing support for the notion that liberalism and prosocial behavior are indeed conceptually linked. Both kinds of social responses—attitudes that play a major role in voting, and actions exhibited in interactions with others—are based on willingness to make sacrifices and to put the welfare of others, or of society at large, ahead of one's own special interests.

Speculation about the conceptual links between prosocial behavior and liberalism—and weak prosocial tendencies and conservatism—must, of course, be checked by empirical research. Are they, in fact, highly correlated? Certainly, some conservatives act in highly prosocial ways and some liberals do not. There are also prosocial individuals who are basically conservative in political orientation. Is it possible to specify personality characteristics and socialization experiences that differentiate these groups from liberals with strong prosocial tendencies? Does the latter group manifest distinct personality configurations, and, if so, how do these differ from the personality strucutres of liberals who do not ordinarily behave in highly prosocial ways? All of these problems must be the foci of empirical investigation if we are to achieve a deeper understanding of the dynamics underlying liberal and conservative sociopolitical orientations, strong and weak tendencies toward prosocial behavior, and the relationships among these.

REFERENCES

Adelson, J. The political imagination of the young adolescent. *Daedalus* 1971 (Fall), 1013–1049.

Adorno, T. W., Frenkel-Brunswik, E., Levinson, D. J., & Sanford, R. N. *The authoritarian personality.* New York: Harper, 1950.

Baumrind, D. Current patterns of parental authority. *Developmental Psychology Monographs,* 1971, *1,* 1–103.

Block, J. *The Q-sort method in personality assessment and psychiatric research.* Springfield, Ill.: Charles C Thomas, 1961.

Eisenberg-Berg, N., & Mussen, P. Personality correlates of sociopolitical liberalism and conservatism in adolescents. *Journal of Genetic Psychology,* 1980, *137,* 165–177.

Gergen, K. J., Gergen, J. M., & Meter, K. Individual orientations to prosocial behavior. *Journal of Social Issues,* 1972, *28* (3), 105–130.

Gough, H. *Manual for the California Psychological Inventory.* Palo Alto, Calif.: Consulting Psychologists' Press, 1957.

Greenstein, F. I. Personality and political socialization: The theories of authoritarian and democratic character. *The Annals of the American Academy of Political and Social Science,* 1965, *361,* 81–95.

Haan, N. Coping and defense mechanisms related to personality inventories. *Journal of Consulting Psychology,* 1965, *29*(4), 373–378.

Mehrabian, A., & Epstein, N. A. A measure of emotional empathy. *Journal of Personality,* 1972, *40,* 523–543.

Mussen, P., & Eisenberg-Berg, N. *Roots of caring, sharing, and helping: The development of prosocial behavior in children.* San Francisco: W. H. Freeman, 1977.

Mussen, P., & Haan, N. A longitudinal study of patterns of personality and political ideologies. In D. H. Eichorn, J. A. Clausen, N. Haan, M. P. Honzik, & P. Mussen (Eds.), *Present and past in middle life.* New York: Academic Press, 1982.

Mussen, P., Sullivan, L. B., & Eisenberg-Berg, N. Changes in political–economic attitudes during adolescence. *Journal of Genetic Psychology,* 1977, *130,* 69–76.

Rossi, P. H. Trends in voting behavior research: 1933–1963. In E. C. Dreyer & W. H. Rosenbaum (Eds.), *Political opinion and electoral behavior.* Belmont, Calif.: Wadsworth, 1966, pp. 67–78.

Rushton, J. P. *Altruism, socialization, and society.* Englewood Cliffs, N.J.: Prentice-Hall, 1980.

Sears, D. O. Political socialization. In F. I. Greenstein & N. W. Polsby (Eds.), *The handbook of political science* (Vol. 2). *Micropolitical theory.* Reading, Mass.: Addison-Wesley, 1975.

Staub, E. *Positive social behavior and morality.* (Vol. 1). *Social and personal influences.* New York: Academic Press, 1978.

JANUSZ REYKOWSKI

Development of Prosocial Motivation: A Dialectic Process[1]

What we are talking about when we say that we are interested in the development of personality? The answers that we meet in textbooks and monographs are enormously divergent. Personality development is described in terms of general social skill, general attitudes, motivational dispositions, complex behavioral patterns, emotional functioning, cognitive organization, and so on. But whatever conceptualization of development is chosen, the description of development and a search for its preconditions are typically based upon assumptions that (a) the given category of behavior—for example, aggression, dependency, achievement seeking—is a manifestation of a relatively homogeneous disposition; and (b) it is possible to identify a set of crucial factors, internal and external, that are "responsible" for the development of a given disposition.

These assumptions can be found in various popular textbooks that deal with the development of personality variables, for example, development of aggression (Ziegler & Child, 1973), dependency (Schaffer, 1979), achievement motivation (Ziegler & Child, 1973), and emotional control (Maccoby,

1. This is an enlarged version of a chapter entitled "Origin of Prosocial Motivation: Heterogeneity of Personality Development" which originally appeared in R. K. Silbereisen (Ed.), Bericht über die 4. Tagung Entwicklungspsychologie, Berlin 30.9.-3.10.1979. Berlin: Technische Universität Berlin Dokumentation Kongresse und Tagungen, 1980, 4. It is based upon studies sponsored by the Polish Academy of Science, Project 11.8. The present version was prepared while the author was visiting at the Department of Psychology and the Center for Human Growth and Development, University of Michigan.

THE DEVELOPMENT OF
PROSOCIAL BEHAVIOR

1980). In all those cases and many others, we are dealing with the two above-mentioned assumptions—let me call them assumptions of homogeneity.

The assumptions of homogeneity are very convenient ones. They enable the formulation of some relatively simple recommendations as to how the particular personality disposition should be formed and these recommendations can be taught to parents and teachers. The only task that educators face if they want to avoid some behaviors (e.g., aggressiveness) in children or if they wish to foster some others is to follow the recommendations.

To characterize the model described earlier, we may use a botanic analogy; personality can be viewed as a garden, and personality dispositions are like flowers. One can learn what conditions are optimal for rearing a specific kind of flower (as well as conditions for growing plants that one does not like in the garden and wants to get rid of).

However, the model seems questionable. To begin with, it is doubtful if we can deal with each kind of flower separately, not taking into account that in the garden there are a multitude of flowers and they might require conditions incompatible with one another.

But, even more so, it is rather doubtful if there are flowers in the "garden" at all. In other words, the very existence of personality dispositions as "real entities" is questionable. To clarify this point, I will turn to the analysis of one specific behavioral domain—prosocial behavior. The reason for the choice is somewhat accidental. I am not presupposing that prosocial behavior is exceptionally convenient for this analysis. I am simply choosing it because I had the opportunity to study the topic together with my collaborators for more than a decade. During those studies, it occurred to us that widespread ideas about personality development may have some important limitations.

PROSOCIAL BEHAVIOR AND ITS ANTECEDENTS

The term *prosocial behavior* covers a wide range of phenomena such as helping, sharing, self-sacrifice, and norm observing. All those phenomena have one common characteristic—namely, that an individual's action is oriented toward protection, maintenance, or enhancement of well-being of an external social object: a specific person, a group, a society as a whole, a social institution, or a symbolic being, for example, an ideology or system or morality.

It should be stressed that the concept of "prosocial behavior" as defined here does not include assumptions concerning motivation of the act. An act is classified as prosocial according to its social meaning, that is, if its phenomenological characteristics show that it has valuable consequences for someone else (or such consequences are likely to occur) and the consequences have been reached deliberately and not by chance only. The act may require a high degree of self-sacrifice as in the case of altruism, or nothing more than natural costs of action, that is, time and effort, that are necessary to realize any activity. In many instances, the act may simply involve a certain level of coordination between own interest and interest of a social object, as in case of cooperative behavior or considerateness.

Now the question arises: How do the ability and readiness for prosocial action develop? These are quite a few answers to this question present in psychological literature:

1. Psychoanalysis would explain the origin of prosocial behavior as a consequence of superego formation, which depends in turn upon the resolution of the Oedipal complex.
2. Social learning theory would stress the role of modeling and reinforcement of prosocial acts.
3. Maslow assumed that gratification of basic needs facilitates an unfolding of prosocial tendencies inherent to most human beings.
4. Miasishchev, a well-known Soviet psychologist, emphasizes the role of consistency of moral demands formulated and executed by various socializing agencies.

In recent years, a more elaborate approach has been offered by E. S. Staub, one of the leading specialists in the field. Staub has described some factors that foster prosocial behavior. He presented the following major factors: (a) parental affection and nurturance; (b) parental control; (c) induction (i.e., the procedure originally described by M. Hoffman consisting of the use of reasoning in disciplinary encounters); (d) modeling; and (e) responsibility assignment (Staub, 1975).

The subject has been studied extensively by many psychologists. Some years ago we asked similar questions. T. Szustrowa selected from among high school students by means of a specially designed peer-rating technique (so-called "guess who" technique) three groups of youngsters: one group perceived by peers as prosocial and two egocentric groups, active egocentrics who energetically pursued their personal goals, and passive egocentrics who were timid, anxious, and withdrawing. All subjects filled out a biographical questionnaire. On the basis of the answers to this questionnaire it was possible to identify some possible conditions differentiating among groups. There were some clear-cut differences related:

1. To the emotional atmosphere at home: In the prosocial group the atmosphere was more positive and approving than in both egocentric groups.

2. To the amount of parental control: The prosocial group perceived control as moderate, whereas egocentrics believed it either as rather high or very low.

3. To the techniques of control: In the prosocial group psychological techniques predominated over the physical, and positive reinforcement predominated over negative reinforcement.

4. To the clarity of parental demands: Demands were not very high but were consistent for the prosocial group, whereas in egocentric groups, they were more extreme (high or low) and very often less consistent. All described differences were statistically significant (Szustrowa, 1972).

Szustrowa's findings are consistent with generalizations made by others, for example, with the conclusions of Staub. But our subsequent research threw some doubts on the value of this approach. First of all, it occurred to us that the basic assumption of this study, namely, the idea of classification of people into prosocial and nonprosocial, has some inherent fallacy.

As a matter of fact, we overlooked something that should have been obvious right from the beginning—that behavioral patterns classified in the same category based on their social meaning may have different motivational mechanisms and different concomitant characteristics.

Not taking this into account leads to serious ambiguities. The problem that can arise may be illustrated by one of our studies. Its author, a postgraduate student from Bulgaria, H. Paspalanowa, investigated reactions of students from colleges in Sofia to a request for help from an unknown person (Paspalanowa, 1979).[2]

She found that subjects who were classified on the basis of a peer-nomination technique as prosocial were in fact deferent to social expectations. They did what their group wanted them to do. We may wonder, therefore, what kind of people are called prosocial in everyday situations since people classified here as prosocial turned out to be the rather conformity-oriented. Such people can be very helpful to their classmates, or more generally, to members of their own reference group, but not necessarily to strangers. Paspalanowa's findings indicate that persons' attitudes toward strangers depend upon group norms. They might be quite helpful if this is expected by the group and very unhelpful if the group is indifferent or unsympathetic toward strangers.

It is hardly surprising, of course, that many prosocial acts are performed out of conformity. But since it is so, one may ask: What does it mean to rear a helpful (prosocial) child? Does it mean to rear a conformist? Should we come to the conclusion, therefore, that factors allegedly fostering prosocial

2. Some details of the study are described in Reykowski, 1982.

behavior are, in fact, facilitating the development of dependency on peer-group normative demands? This would be a rather extreme statement. On the basis of the data, we can say only that in *some* cases people's prosocial behavior can be explained as a result of dependency on group normative expectations; that we, in studying antecedents of such a behavior, in fact are dealing with antecedents of conformism. To avoid such confusion, we must take into consideration that prosocial behavior can have various motivational mechanisms. If we want to study the origin of prosocial behavior, we should deal primarily with those mechanisms.

MOTIVATIONAL MECHANISMS OF PROSOCIAL ACTS

It has been recognized for some time that apparently identical forms of behavior may be brought about by different motives. In the area of prosocial behavior there are a few studies that deal with this problem directly.

In the early 1960s, two Polish psychologists, H. Malewska and H. Muszynski, while studying children's attitudes to telling the truth, found that the same behavioral act, namely, endorsing the truth-telling principle, had a different underlying motivation in different children. The authors classified children's motives into three groups describing three types of orientation: conformism to authority (conformist orientation), yielding to moral norms due to an internal compulsion (ritualistic orientation), and caring about the possible consequences for others (altruistic orientation) (Malewska & Muszynski, 1962).

This classification has a clear resemblance to the theory of moral development proposed by Martin Hoffman (1970).[3] He suggested that moral behavior can be regulated by anticipation of consequences for oneself—external moral orientation, or by two kinds of internal moral orientation: either strong adherence to social norms (conventional rigid orientation) or interest in the well-being of someone else (flexible humanistic orientation).

The description of the three orientations made by Meleswka and Muszynski, as well as by Hoffman, refers not so much to a behavior but to its internal sources or mechanisms. In fact, we are dealing here with phenomenologically the same forms of behavior, that is, with moral acts of certain kinds (e.g., helping, telling the truth), but these acts are being controlled by different motives.

Very similar mechanisms have emerged in our studies on prosocial behavior. The theoretical framework of this research is based upon a cognitive approach (Zajonc, 1968a). We are assuming that regulation of human

---

3. The theory was developed over a certain period of time. See Hoffman (1970).

behavior is realized by cognitive organizations that are formed as a product of interactions between a developing person and his or her social environment. The cognitive organizations are conceived here as a system representing physical and social objects and their interrelationships. The objects are encoded in the system as cognitive structures. Although the cognitive system is formed as a representation of objects, events, and relations, it also has generative capabilities. The material that is included in the system undergoes transformation, and the structures that emerge are not a direct replication of experience but have some new qualities that originally were not here.[4] The cognitive system can operate, therefore, not only as an internal map reproducing past and existing orders of objects and events, but also, at the same time, has productive capabilities since it can generate new symbolic organizations (plans, ideas, creative images, etc.) Transformations that are going on in the system are due to the process of internalization of practical operations (Piaget, 1967; Vygotsky, 1966).

But in contrast to the traditional view, the cognitive system is regarded here as more than a mere instrument of orientation. It is assumed that cognitive organizations have a motivational potential originating in their tendency to preserve a state of equilibrium (Abelson & Rosenberg, 1958; Heider, 1946; Piaget, 1967). Actually, many authors have pointed out that cognitive organizations do have motivational potential. This view has been developed in the early studies of Lewin (1938) and in more recent writings of other authors (e.g., Festinger, 1958; Hunt, 1963; Lukaszewski, 1974; Zajonc, 1968a). Motivation originating in the cognitive systems may have two different forms (Kochanska, 1980). One is purely cognitive and controls orientation processes (e.g., curiosity). But the cognitive system can generate motivational processes that regulate behavior aimed at the modification of physical or social states of affairs, as well. Motivation of this kind is raised whenever information about the real or possible state of an object represented in the system is discrepant from standards embedded in the cognitive organizations.

We are assuming that physical and social objects are represented in the system as relatively independent cognitive structures. Embedded in the given structures are some standards of a normal (typical) state of an object (its normal functioning, location, construction, color, size, etc.). The standards function as the criteria of equilibrium of the cognitive structure since a

---

4. It is worthwhile to observe that this constructivistic characteristic of cognitive organizations is recognized by authors of different methodological orientations; for example, neopositivists were saying that theoretical constructs have "surplus meaning," and Marxist authors are emphasizing that concepts are not reducible to the perceptual material on basis of which they were built.

deviation from them produces an equilibration process: Discrepancy between standards and incoming information results in a state of tension and tendency to restore "a normal state of affairs." This tension seems to be "a core" of the motivational process.

The strength and direction of the motivation depends upon the characteristics of the cognitive structure in which it originated, that is, upon the content of its standards, upon its position in a system, and upon its affective value.[5] It also depends upon the degree of involvement of the given structure (related to the amount of discrepancy between information and standards embedded in a given structure).

Our analysis implies that highly elaborated structures that have a high position in a system consisting of well-established standards[6] should have high motivational potential. For many (or most) people living in contemporary culture, the representation of one's own person—the self structure— seems to be a highly developed organization having a position of importance in a cognitive system. It consists of standards of different kinds. For the purpose of the present argument two kinds of standards can be distinguished: *standards of personal well-being* concerning, for example, a person's status, level of need gratification, degree of control of outside world, etc., and *standards of social behavior* (moral standards) that define "proper way of conduct" in social situations. Realization of these standards (of both kinds) is a source of positive affective states, whereas a negative discrepancy[7] with these standards produces negative affect.

Prosocial behavior may come about owing to the operation of both kinds of standards. With respect to the standards of personal well-being, a prosocial behavior may have (in many situations) an instrumental value; that is, doing good to others may bring profit for oneself (may protect or enhance one's own interests as defined by personal standards of well-being).

The relationship between standards of social behavior (moral standards) and prosocial behavior is an inherent one, that is, to meet one's standards a person has no other way than to perform a prosocial act. It should be borne in mind that in the case of standards of personal well-being and in the case of moral standards, self-satisfaction plays an important mediating role. But

---

5. The cognitive structures have not only descriptive but affective characteristics as well. See Zajonc (1980).

6. Not all standards represent the normal state of an object. Some of them are produced by the system (or acquired from other people), and describe the ideal state, that is, a state that has never been achieved before and has a higher affective value than the normal state. Owing to ideal standards, human motivation can have not only "conservative" but also "progressive" characteristics.

7. A positive discrepancy may occur when the situation differs from normal state in the direction of ideal standards.

whereas the former standards can be met by various forms of behavior (prosocial and nonprosocial), the latter can be achieved only by prosocial ones.

It can be said that we are dealing here with two different motivational mechanisms of prosocial behavior; both are located in the self but in different ways. Whereas in the first case prosocial behavior is controlled by anticipation of personal gain (or avoidance of personal loss) and both—gain and loss—are only incidentally related to this behavior, in the second case, prosocial behavior is controlled by anticipation of changes in self-esteem depending upon realization of socially established norms of proper conduct.

We will call the first one *ipsocentric motivation* (cf. Hoffman's external moral orientation) and the second *endocentric motivation*[8] (cf. Hoffman's conventional rigid moral orientation).

But the self-structure is not the only structure in the cognitive system that has a position of importance. There are structures representing external social objects that can have a more or less significant role in the system. Standards embedded in these structures can be a source of strong motivation. Since this motivation is directed toward retainment of a normal state for External Social Objects (or attainment of ideal ones), we might call it *intrinsic prosocial motivation* (cf. Hoffman's flexible moral orientation). According to Karylowski, it is one of the forms of so-called egzocentric mechanisms of prosocial behavior. He uses the term *egzocentric* for all those forms of behavior that are controlled by changes in conditions of another person (or any other social object). He makes a differentiation between *endocentric* prosocial behavior motivated by a desire for bringing about the positive changes in self-esteem and *egzocentric* prosocial behavior motivated by a desire for improving someone else's conditions (Karylowski, 1977, 1982).

By stating that a prosocial act can be controlled by any of the previously mentioned motivational mechanisms, we are assuming that there are substantial differences in the processes of regulation of those acts.

The differences amount to (a) differences in the *conditions of initiation* of a given act; (b) differences in *characteristics of the end state* of a given act, that is, those anticipatory characteristics of outcome that control the act; (c) differences in *conditions that facilitate occurrence* of a given act; (d) differences in *conditions that exert an inhibitory* effect upon a given act; and (e) differences in *qualitative characteristics* of a given act. Now let us compare the above described mechanisms from the point of view of the five mentioned criteria (see Table 15.1).

The description of differences presented in Table 15.1 is, to be sure, not

8. This term has been coined by J. Karylowski who presented an extended model of prosocial behavior (Karylowski, 1977).

Table 15.1
Comparison of Three Motivational Mechanisms of Prosocial Behavior

Condition of initiation	I[a]:	Expectation that in a given situation a prosocial act will lead to some social reward (praise, material gain, fame, etc.) or will prevent social punishment.
	En:	Actualization of relevant norm.
	In:	Perception of social need
Anticipatory outcome	I:	Personal gain (protection of own interest)
	En:	Increment of self-esteem or avoidance of its decrement
	In:	Information that social interest is taken care of (interests as defined by standards embedded in the object's representation)
Facilitating conditions	I:	Increased demand for rewards mediated by prosocial behavior or increased fear of loss of reward if prosocial act is not performed
	En:	Concentration on a moral aspect of own behavior and moral aspects of the self
	In:	Concentration on the state of a social object
Inhibitory conditions	I:	Possibility of personal loss or harm due to involvement in prosocial action. Possibility of obtaining higher rewards for nonprosocial activity.
	En:	Concentration on those aspects of self that are not related to prosocial norms (as a result of stress, deprivation, striving for achievement, etc.)
	In:	Self-concentration
		Realizing that a social object is able to satisfy its needs by other means.
		High disproportion between possible gain of social object and possible personal loss (low partner's profit—high personal costs)
Qualitative characteristics of an act	I:	Low level of interest in the real needs of a social object. Low degree of accuracy of offered help.
	En:	The same as I
	In:	High level of interest in the real needs of a social object. High degree of accuracy of offered help

[a] I = ipsocentric; En = endocentric; In = intrinsic.

complete, but it seems to indicate that the three motivational mechanisms are, in fact, different. We are not going to say, however, that those are the only sources of prosocial behavior. It is possible to present a theoretical argument to the point that there are still other possible mechanisms (Reykowski, 1982), but for the present purposes we will concentrate on those three.

If we accept the proposition that prosocial acts can be controlled by different mechanisms, we must also acknowledge as probable the supposition that the development of each of the mechanisms is promoted by different factors. In other words, we can expect that prosocial tendencies having different motivational bases might have different natural histories.

As a matter of fact, two previously mentioned approaches—that of Malewska and Muszynski, as well as Hoffman's—are consistent with the preceding proposition. In both cases, the authors presented arguments that each kind of moral orientation, as described by them, develops under different conditions.

Now the question arises: How do these conditions relate to each other? Are they additive? Can we expect that a child exposed to the wide range of conditions promoting formation of each of the mechanisms has the best possibility of full development? Should we recommend to parents and teachers socializing procedures that are directed simultaneously to all mechanisms? This problem also can be expressed in more concrete terms using as an example the Malewska and Muszynski model: The authors present arguments that altruistic motivation develops when parents use, primarily, the method of reasoning and persuasion, whereas a ritualistic orientation is fostered by punitive techniques. If we want to bring up a child who is altruistic and norm-observing, should we use both persuasion *and* punishment?

There are reasons to believe that contrary to the popular view, the answer to this question seems to be a negative one. Let us consider some of them.

DIALECTICS OF DEVELOPMENT

Not so long ago, P. Mussen and a group of California psychologists conducted extensive research on the relationship between child-rearing practices on the one hand, and honesty and altruism manifested in behavior on the other. They were expecting that a high level of moral conduct, that is, a high degree of honesty and altruism, would be related to parental warmth, and use of explanation and reasoning (the procedure that Hoffman calls "induction" and, according to Hoffman, promotes flexible, humanistic moral orientation). Subjects, 12-year-old boys and girls, were studied by means of both peer-rating techniques and experimental procedures. Child-rearing practices were evaluated via special interviews with mothers and questionnaires with children. The results were rather surprising; namely, honesty and altruism seemed to develop under conditions that were almost mutually exclusive. The authors summarized their findings as follows:

> According to these data, for boys, both honesty in the situational . . . test and relatively good reputation for honesty among peers were found to be inversely

correlated with measures of maternal nurturance, permissiveness, and the tendency to use positive rewards; that is, the findings were opposite of what was predicted. . . . In marked contrast, altruism in a competitive game with an unseen, unknown rival was associated with positive, identification enhancing maternal behavior (nurturance, affection, and easygoing relaxed attitudes toward child rearing) . . . [p. 188].

It should be added that for girls there was a different pattern of results.

If we take into consideration such conditions as "parental nurturance," "demands," "permissiveness," the data suggest that their role in the process of formation of altruism and honesty is different; the same factor that facilitates honesty may inhibit the development of altruism and vice versa. We are facing here, therefore, the *phenomenon of interference* among socializing factors.

The authors of the previously described research would not go along with this interpretation. They have argued that their original hypothesis, if somewhat modified, has been supported. Their arguments would require more extensive discussion than is possible here.

But it is possible to look at those data differently. As it was observed by anthropologist, Ronald Cohen: "To become emotionally involved with people is . . . to weaken or lessen one's capacity to cathect roles, norms or rules [Cohen, 1972, p. 50]." According to his argument, developmental conditions favorable for "value cathection" are opposite to conditions of "emotional involvement." In other words, socializing procedures fostering one mechanism may have an inhibitory effect on the other.

It should be noted that altruism and honesty as described by Mussen, Harris, Rutherford, and Keasey (1970) cannot be identified with the mechanisms described above. We may say only that both forms of moral behavior seem to develop under different conditions, and the conditions are apparently contradictory ones. It suggests that moral development may not be looked upon as a gradual harmonious increase of all potentials for moral behavior.

We have, however, some data from our laboratory that pertain rather directly to the issue of the development of mechanisms of prosocial behavior as they are conceptualized here.

Kochanska (1980), studying 9-year-old pupils, used two different procedures for enhancement of a prosocial behavior (sharing). In one group (extrinsically rewarded), pupils received a material reward (a chocolate bar) for doing something on behalf of children in an orphanage (drawing pictures for them). The second group of pupils (intrinsically rewarded) performed the same task under different conditions: While the subjects were drawing the pictures they had an opportunity to see photographs of sad faces of children that were pinned up on the blackboard; on the second day another set of photographs, this time the happy faces of the same children, were shown. In addition, they listened to a tape-recorded conversation with children in the orphanage talking about their pleasure with getting the pictures. The subjects were neither promised nor given a material reward.

In the second phase the pupils had an opportunity to share attractive stickers with other children. The number of stickers offered (apparently anonymously) was a measure of prosocial behavior.

The means for three groups were, respectively: control group, 1.53; extrinsically rewarded, 2.40; intrinsically rewarded, 3.53. (The difference between control and intrinsically rewarded groups was significant below the .05 level.)[9] Both groups acted more prosocially than the control group not involved in any task for children from the orphanage (although the difference between control and extrinsically rewarded groups only approached significance); in other words, both procedures were effective as a means of boosting prosocial behavior, although to different degrees. Apparently, the second procedure (information about effects) produced more impact than the first one (material rewards). But there were also differences between the groups in some other characteristics of their behavior that were measured in the study, that is, in their interest in other children and in accuracy of perception of others' needs. These variables were measured in the following way: Subjects from all groups were asked by a person who presented herself as a representative of a children's magazine to evaluate how much they liked various stories about children; each subject received some pages of the magazine. On each page there were a few lines from the initial part of a story (about a child from a hospital). If the subject wanted to learn more about the hero, he or she could buy new pages from the experimenter by paying with special coupons. Coupons that were not used for buying pages of the stories could be spent for buying sweets or toys for themselves. Therefore, the number of coupons the subject spent for "buying pages" was a measure of his or her motivation for getting information about other children.

Subjects were also asked to help the experimenter to select toys for children in the hospital. Children in the hospital were described by name, age, sex, and health status. Thus, subjects' choices could be evaluated as to the degree of accuracy (for instance, an inaccurate choice was scored if the subject suggested a ball for a child who cannot move)—a special index of accuracy had been constructed. The obtained data are presented in Table 15.2.

9. The original study included more variables not mentioned here. Two × two ANOVA and contrast tests have been applied.

Table 15.2

Amount of Interest in Other Children's Fates (a) and Accuracy of Offered Help (b) as a Function of Previous Experience

a			b		
C 11.47a	E 7.27b	I 10.93a	C 6.13a	E 6.67a	I 7.04a

Note: C = control group; E = extrinsically rewarded group; I = intrinsically rewarded group. The cells with different letters are differing on .05 level or lower (see footnote 9).

It can be seen that the externally rewarded subjects performed worse than the intrinsically rewarded on both measures (but only on the measure of interest did the difference reach a statistical significance).

Kochanska suggests that her "chocolate rewarded" group behaved prosocially on the basis of an ipsocentric mechanism—children learned that a prosocial act can be a useful technqiue for obtaining gratification for oneself. When such learning takes place, there should be some link between concentration upon one's needs and readiness for prosocial acts. But this concentration might, very easily, prevent the individual from seeing the real needs of another person. In other words, interest in the second person, as well as adequacy of prosocial action, will be impaired.

In the case of the group informed about the consequences of its action, the needs of another were made salient. This procedure, apparently, had some impact upon motivation to satisfy those needs. It did not change, however, the cognitive motivation (curiosity) that originally was rather high. We are inclined to think that this procedure enhances cognitive growth in the representation of social objects, and, as a consequence, produces an increment in its regulatory potential.

The growth mentioned above is the growth of a generalized representation of a social object rather than representation of a specific object. This conclusion is implicated by the fact that subjects in the intrinsically rewarded group were more inclined than the children in the other group to share stickers with children from the hospital, even though they were originally dealing with children from the orphanage. The hypothesis that growth of a cognitive representation of a social object is the result of exposure to another person's needs and reactions can be supported by Zajonc's (1968b) findings concerning the so-called "mere exposure" effect. He has shown that repeated contact with some originally neutral object produces increased liking of an object; in other words, interaction with a neutral object produces a positive emotion. But positive emotion, as was argued by Hebb (1949), can be regarded as evidence of cognitive growth. It seems justified, therefore, to conjecture that pupils who were exposed to other children's needs and reactions had, as a result of this exposure, a better opportunity of developing cognitive representations of social objects.

In conclusion, it can be said that both procedures that have been used by Kochanska seem to be more or less effective as means of promoting the specific behavioral pattern—sharing—but the effects were mediated by two different motivational mechanisms. In the case where external material rewards were used, the ipsocentric mechanism apparently was involved; in the case when children were informed about the social effects of their action, intrinsic prosocial motivation was likely to have been activated.

Both mechanisms can account for sharing behavior but, at the same time, they have some "antagonistic" characteristics. Ipsocentric motivation seems to inhibit the behavior that intrinsic motivation facilitates[10] (namely, processing information about state and needs of another person).

It should be noted that the two mechanisms differ with respect to the conditions of their development. The ipsocentric mechanism is fostered by external rewards, whereas rewarding procedures seem to depress the intrinsic one (Kochanska, 1980).

The same antagonistic relationship between conditions of development of different mechanisms of prosocial behavior also was observed in another study conducted in our laboratory under the direction of Karylowski (1982). From about 240 high school female pupils (ages 16-19), three groups of subjects were selected (by means of a specially developed technique[11]): subjects with predominantly endocentric motivation of prosocial behavior (En-group), with predominantly egzocentric motivation (Eg-group), and subjects who showed very rare instances of prosocial behavior in natural settings (NP-group). A specially designed interview was conducted with mothers of the selected subjects. The interview consisted of presenting 24 stories describing typical situations from children's lives that required some form of reaction from their mother—the mothers were supposed to say how they reacted when their child behaved in the way described in the stories. The stories were divided into three parts (eight stories each) concerning three age levels in childhood (preschool age, early school age, recent age).

The socializing techniques that were identified in the interviews differed with respect to the degree they involved the child's self. There were quite a few that apparently were directed toward the self; for example, there is good reason to believe that when a mother evaluates a child as good or bad, if she points out the consequences of the child's behavior for the child's well-being, if she punishes the child by love withdrawal, and if she demands

---

10. The antagonistic relationship between different motivational mechanisms of the same form of behavior has been found in other studies, too. See, for example, Deci (1980).

11. The technique has been described in detail elsewhere (Karylowski, 1982).

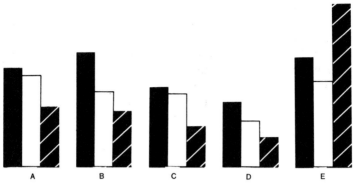

FREQUENCY OF THE GIVEN PROCEDURE

Figure 15.1. **Child-rearing procedures and prosocial motivation. Child-rearing procedures used by mothers of three groups of subjects: Those with dominant endocentric, egzocentric, and nonprosocial attitudes were compared. Solid bars denote endocentric; open bars denote nonprosocial; ruled bars denote egzocentric. The figure presents frequencies with which mothers reported using each procedure: (A) evaluation of a child as good or bad; (B) pointing out to the child the consequences of his or her behavior for him- or herself; (C) punishment by love withdrawal; (D) demand for apology; and (E) pointing out the consequences of the child's behavior for others (induction). It is believed that procedures A, B, C, and D are orienting a child toward the self, whereas procedure E, toward another person.**

from the child an apology—in all those cases, the child's self is made salient since some "manipulations upon a self" are being performed. On the other side, when the mother points out the consequences that the child's behavior might have for the other party's well-being, a representation of another social object in a child's mind is involved. A scoring system that captured these differences was then prepared. Interjudge agreement on most of the scales was no lower than 80%.

The data that were obtained in the study support the notion that if the socializing procedures concentrate the child's attention upon the self, endocentric mechanisms are likely to be formed (see Figure 15.1). However, the procedure that requires concentration of a child's attention on the state of the partner (induction) seems to foster the development of egzocentric mechanisms.

It should be added that in most cases the differences between groups were largest for measures based upon the descriptions of mothers' socializing procedures being used when their children were preschool age. The same mothers differed from one another much less in their descriptions of their reactions toward older children (Wojdan & Szuster, 1979).[12]

12. The results presented here do not give full account of findings of the study; only those are mentioned that were confirmed when reanalysis of the data was performed by J. Karylowski.

We can see that the data clearly support Hoffman's contention concerning the role of induction in moral development (Hoffman, 1970, 1975). The data here demonstrate differences in rearing conditions of children differing in moral orientations; egzocentric children (flexible humanistic in Hoffman's terminology) are reared under different conditions than endocentric ones (Hoffman's conventional rigid). But what should be stressed here is the striking regularity concerning the position of the nonprosocial group; in all scales discussed here, subjects from this group received scores placing them between the prosocial groups. Whereas the low intensity of a given socializing factor fostered development of one mechanism and high intensity of a given factor fostered a development of another, the middle intensity did not "produce" anything that could be a mixture of both, but seemed to suppress each of them.

This conclusion should be regarded with caution since the data at hand are too scanty for any far-reaching conclusions. What seems probable, however, is the proposition that there are some conditions that have a favorable impact upon a development of a given mechanism of prosocial behavior but may, at the same time, hinder the development of another mechanism. It is very likely, therefore, that if such conditions are present simultaneously, their effects are neutralized. In other words, there should be *less* instead of more prosocial behavior.

CONCLUSION

On the basis of the above reasoning, we suggest that a search for conditions promoting prosocial behavior in general might be a rather futile task. There are different possible ways in which this development can take place, and we must be prepared to acknowledge that by pursuing different ways we can obtain products that are phenomenologically similar but that have different internal mechanisms. Prosocial behavior is a heterogeneous phenomenon, and there is heterogeneity in its formative processes.

But this phenomenon of heterogeneity is not limited to only prosocial behavior. It is quite probable that the same state of affairs exists in other domains of behavior as well. And from this point of view, the task of the educator becomes much more complicated than it is commonly believed. It is not so that a parent or teacher can obtain a set of recommendations consisting of a few basic procedures that should be followed if some required educational goal is going to be reached. Reaching one goal may mean that others of equal importance are in jeopardy. It means, therefore, that the educator is confronted with various dilemmas that should be creatively solved. It is rather unrealistic to expect that psychology can ever offer any ready-made technology in the area of socialization. It can elucidate complicated interrelations of various important socializing factors and hidden traps that can be encountered while we are actively intervening in the process of personality development. But the child-rearing task remains an art of dealing with an enormously complex process dialectic in nature requiring not only knowledge but a lot of creativity.

REFERENCES

Abelson, R. P., & Rosenberg, M. J. Symbolic psycho-logic: A model of attitudinal cognition. *Behavioral Science,* 1958, *3,* 1-13.

Cohen, R. Altruism: Human, cultural or what? In L. Wispé, *Positive forms of social behavior. Journal of Social Issues,* 1972, *28,* 39-59.

Deci, E. L. Intrinsic motivation and personality. In E. Staub (Ed.), *Personality: Basic aspects and current research.* Englewood Cliffs, N.J.: Prentice-Hall, 1980.

Festinger, L. The motivating effect cognitive dissonance. In G. Lindzey (Ed.), *Assessment of human motives.* New York: Rinehart, 1958.

Hebb, D. O. *The organization of behavior.* New York: Wiley, 1949.

Heider, F. Attitudes and cognitive organization. *Journal of Psychology,* 1946, *21,* 107-112.

Hoffman, M. L. Moral development. In P. H. Mussen (Ed.), *Carmichael's manual of child psychology* (Vol. II). New York: Wiley, 1970.

Hoffman, M. L. Developmental synthesis of affect and cognition and its implications for altruistic motivation. *Developmental Psychology,* 1975, *11,* 607-622.

Hunt, J. McV. Motivation inherent in information processing and action. In O. J. Harvey (Ed.), *Motivation and social interaction: Cognitive determinants.* New York: Ronald, 1963.

Karylowski, J. Explaining altruistic behavior: A review. *Polish Psychological Bulletin,* 1977, *8,* 27-34.

Karylowski, J. On the two types of altruistic behavior: Doing good to feel good versus to make the other feel good. In V. Derlega & J. Grzelak (Eds.), *Cooperation and helping behavior.* New York: Academic Press, 1982.

Kochanska, G. Experimental formation of cognitive and helping social motivation in children. *Polish Psychological Bulletin,* 1980, *11,* 75-87.

Lewin, K. *A dynamic theory of personality.* New York: McGraw-Hill, 1938.

Lukaszewski, W. *Osobowosc, struktura i funkcje regulacyjne.* Warszawa: PWN, 1974.

Maccoby, E. *Social development.* New York: Harcourt Brace Jovanovich, 1980.

Melewska, H., & Muszynski, H. *Klamstwo dzieci.* Warszawa: PZWS, 1962.

Mussen, P., Harris, S., Rutherford, E., & Keasey, C. M. Honesty and altruism among preadolescents. *Developmental Psychology,* 1970, *3,* 169-194.

Paspalanowa, H. *Niektore czynniki osobowosciowe warunkujace wplyw norm moralnych grupy na zachowania prospoleczne.* Unpublished doctoral dissertation, University of Warsaw, 1979.

Piaget, J. *Six psychological studies.* New York: Vintage, 1967.

Reykowski, J. Motivation of prosocial behavior. In V. Derlega & J. Grzelak (Eds.), *Cooperation and helping behavior.* New York: Academic Press, 1982.

Schaffer, D. R. *Social and personality development.* Monterey, Calif.: Brooks/Cole, 1979.

Staub, E. *The development of prosocial behavior in children.* Morriston, N.J.: General Learning Press, 1975.

Szustrowa, T. Zdolnosc do dzialania na rzecz celow pozaosobistych a niektore wlasciwosci rodzinnego treningu wychowawczego. *Zeszyty Naukowe Uniwersytetu Warszawskiego,* Nr 1, 1972.

Vygotsky, L. S. Development of higher mental functions. In *Psychological research in the USSR* (Vol. 1). Moscow: Progress Publishers, 1966.

Wojdan, A., & Szuster, A. *Oddzialywania wychowawcze a rozwoj endocentryczynch i egzocentrycznych zachowan prospoleczynch.* Unpublished dissertation, Uniwersytet Warszawski, 1979.

Zajonc, R. B. Cognitive theories in social psychology. In G. Lindzey & E. Aronson (Eds.), *The handbood of social psychology* (Vol. I). Reading, Mass.: Addison-Wesley, 1968. (a)

Zajonc, R. B. Attitudinal effect of mere exposure. *Journal of Personality and Social Psychology,* 1968, *9*, 1–27. (b)

Zajonc, R. B. Feeling and thinking: Preferences need no inferences. *American Psychologist,* 1980, *35*, 151–175.

Ziegler, E., & Child, I. L. *Socialization and personality development.* London: Addison-Wesley, 1973.

Subject Index

DEVELOPMENTAL PSYCHOLOGY SERIES

SERIES EDITOR
Harry Beilin

Developmental Psychology Program
City University of New York Graduate School
New York, New York

WILLIAM J. FRIEDMAN. (Editor). *The Developmental Psychology of Time*

NANCY EISENBERG. (Editor). *The Development of Prosocial Behavior*

In Preparation

MICHAEL POTEGAL. (Editor). *Spatial Abilities: Development and Physiological Foundations*